Islands, Forests and Gardens in the Caribbean

Conservation and Conflict in
Environmental History

Edited by

Robert S. Anderson, Richard Grove and Karis Hiebert

With a Foreword by
Sir James F. Mitchell

MACMILLAN
CARIBBEAN

Macmillan Education
Between Towns Road, Oxford OX4 3PP
A division of Macmillan Publishers Limited
Companies and representatives throughout the world

www.macmillan-caribbean.com

ISBN-13: 978-1405012-71-3
ISBN-10: 1-4050-1271-4

First published 2006

Typeset by EXPO Holdings, Malaysia
Illustrated by Tek Art
Cover design by Gary Fielder, AC Design

The authors and publishers would like to thank
the following for permission to reproduce the
following photographic material in the plate
section of this book:
Hulton Archive/Getty Images pp 2, 4

Dr Earle Kirby 1921–2005

Printed and bound in Thailand

2010   2009   2008   2007   2006
10   9   8   7   6   5   4   3   2   1

Series preface

The Centre for Caribbean Studies at the University of Warwick was founded in 1984 in order to stimulate interest and research in a region that is now receiving academic recognition in its own right.

In conjunction with the University of Warwick, Macmillan Caribbean has published a comprehensive list of titles that study the complexity and variety of a remarkable region and reflect the pan-Caribbean, interdisciplinary approach of the Warwick University Centre for Caribbean Studies.

The Series features new titles in the fields of history, sociology, economics and development, literature, anthropology and politics as well as the reissue of major works. Some are contributed by individual authors while others are collected papers from symposia held at Warwick or elsewhere.

Warwick University Caribbean Studies

Series Editors: Alistair Hennessy and Gad Heuman

vi *Warwick University Caribbean Studies*

Paradise Overseas
The Dutch Caribbean: Colonialism and its Transatlantic Legacies
Gert Oostindie   1-4050-5713-0

Prospero's Isles
The Presence of the Caribbean in the American Imaginary
Editors: Rodolfo Popelnik & Diane Accaria-Zavala   0-333-97455-7

Roots to Popular Culture
Barbadian Aesthetics: Kamau Brathwaite to Hardcore Styles
Curwen Best   0-333-79210-6

Sunset over the Islands
The Caribbean in an Age of Global and Regional Challenges
Andrés Serbin   0-333-72596-4

Trinidad Carnival
A Quest for National Identity
Peter van Koningsbruggen   0-333-65172-3

Trinidad Ethnicity
Editor: Kevin A. Yelvington   0-333-56601-7

The United States and the Caribbean
Synergies of a complex interdependence
Anthony P. Maingot   0-333-57231-9

Writing West Indian Histories
Barry Higman   0-333-73296-0

Contents

List of illustrations and credits

COVER

Painting by John Tyley of a West Indian avocado fruit (*Persea Americana* Mill *var. Americana*). A freed slave working in the Botanical Garden on St Vincent, Tyley was commissioned in 1784 by Alexander Anderson to paint over 180 plants on the island. The avocado was carried to St Vincent in the pre-Colombian period from a South American mainland origin. This painting was probably completed in 1791. Permission of the Linnean Society of London to reproduce this painting from the magnificent Tyley Collection is gratefully acknowledged.

MAPS

The three maps in the text other than the two attributed to contributors in this book are the copyright of Macmillan Caribbean.

INSERT

Acknowledgements

The inspiration for this book lies in the anniversary celebrations of the Botanical Gardens and the Kings Hill Forest in St. Vincent and the Grenadines in 1991. Planning of the celebrations always included a book, and our intentions have finally taken form. Through the good will of the members of the National Trust in Kingstown, the Governor, the Prime Minister's Office and government officials, private businesses and interested individuals, an International Conference on Environmental Institutions was held in 1991. Funds for this conference and the public celebrations were generously given, including those by the Forestry Development Project and the Canadian International Development Agency. There was a memorable swirl of stimulating conversations and receptions at Government House and Young Island, and vigorous discussions of environmental history at the conference. This is where and how the authors of this book met and debated questions about gardens and forests in island environments.

We record our debt to Mrs. Norma Keizer, who guided the work behind the scenes with firm and steady hand to ensure the conference was a successful event, and also to Lavinia Gunn of the National Trust, who always kept faith with us, knowing that we would complete the documentation of this unique part of Caribbean history. Karis Hiebert's involvement was made possible by the Forestry Development Project's manager, John Latham. And of course our debt is to Earle Kirby, an extraordinary man with a mind both whimsical and rigorous, who has been the source of so much encouragement to others. We thank him for a lifetime of work to conserve and protect St. Vincent and the Grenadines' environment and educate others. We also thank Jacqueline Mosdell, a Masters student in the School of Communication at Simon Fraser University. Her fine work editing the text is equaled by her professionalism and spirit. We also thank Colette Sauro for her elegant translations. The support and facilities of Simon Fraser University, Burnaby BC, Canada may seem far from the eastern Caribbean, but this book's emergence there in the north is, we think, one of the classic Caribbean traditions, in which we all are learning to transcend separation.

The editors acknowledge the care with which Chester Krone guided the book through its final stages. They are also grateful for the patience shown to them and the book by their families over the years.

The Editors
Robert S. Anderson, Richard Grove and Karis Hiebert

About the contributors

Robert S. Anderson is Professor of Communication at Simon Fraser University. He was project sociologist in the St. Vincent and the Grenadines Forestry Project, 1988–1991. He received degrees from the University of British Columbia and University of Chicago and has also worked in Jamaica, India, Bangladesh and Thailand. Publications include *Rice Science and Development Politics* (Oxford University Press, 1991).
E-mail: randerso@sfu.ca

Adrian Fraser is Resident Tutor and Head of the University of the West Indies School of Continuing Studies in St. Vincent and the Grenadines. He is an historian whose research interests include the Caribbean peasantry and working-class and post-colonial Caribbean politics, culture and society. He writes about these issues in his weekly newspaper column in the *Searchlight* newspaper, Kingstown. He received degrees from the University of the West Indies and the University of Western Ontario, Canada. He is chairperson of the Board of Projects Promotion Ltd. and also of the country's Education Advisory Board.
E-mail: andron@caribsurf.com

Amos Glasgow is a senior forestry officer with the Forestry Division, Government of St. Vincent and the Grenadines.

Richard Grove has received degrees from Cambridge University and was the editor of the *Journal of Environment and History*. Publications include *Green imperialism: Colonial expansion, tropical island Edens and the origins of environmentalism 1600–1860* (Cambridge University Press, 1995).
E-mail: richardhgrove@hotmail.com

Karis Hiebert is a city planner specializing in sustainable urban development Vancouver, B.C. She worked as the assistant coordinator for the Conference on Environmental Institutions held in St. Vincent in 1991. She holds degrees from Simon Fraser University in Communication and from the Massachusetts Institute of Technology in Urban Planning.
E-mail: khiebert@alum.mit.edu

Lennox Honychurch is curator of the Dominica Museum in Roseau, the island's capital. He has a masters and a doctorate degree in anthropology from the University of Oxford. His forthcoming book, *Carib to Creole: A History of Contact and Culture Exchange* was published by the University Press of Florida in 2003. Other works include *The Caribbean People* (Thomas Nelson, U.K. 1995) and *The Dominica Story* (Macmillan, U.K. 1995).
E-mail: lennoxh@cwdom.dm

Richard A. Howard was Professor Emeritus at Harvard University. He held degrees from Miami University and Harvard University. He was Director of the Arnold Arboretum (1954–1977), and Professor of Dendrology. His *Flora of the Lesser Antilles* in six volumes is now completed. He held many honours from professional societies as well as horticultural and scientific organizations and had published 13 books and over 300 scientific papers. Howard encouraged this book from its beginning in the 1991 conference.

Michael Kidston is a Canadian surveyor with extensive international experience.

Clarissa Kimber is Professor Emeritus of Geography at Texas A&M University, College Station. She received her degrees from the University of California-Riverside and University of Wisconsin. She is the author of many publications, among which is *Martinique Revisited: the Historical Plant Geography of a West Indian island* (Texas A&M University Press, 1988).
E-mail: c_kimber@tamu.edu

I. A. Earle 'Doc' Kirby was a resource to Vincentian people on matters ranging from agriculture, veterinary medicine, horticulture, forestry, history and archaeology. He received degrees from the Imperial College of Tropical Agriculture and Guelph University, Ontario, Canada. He founded the Archaeological and Historical Society and later the St. Vincent National Trust.

Madelaine Ly-Tio-Fane is an expert in natural history; her specialties include sixteenth- and seventeenth-century plant transfers and tropical botany. She received her doctorate degree from the University of London and has been a research fellow at the Arnold Arboretum at Harvard, The Research School of Pacific Studies, and A.N.U. Canberra. Address: 28 Shand Street, Beau Bassin, Mauritius.

James E. McClellan III is professor of history of science at Stevens Institute of Technology in Hoboken, New Jersey. Prof. McClellan's research centres on the social and institutional history of French science in the Enlightenment. He is the author of *Colonialism and Science: Saints Domingue in the Old Regime* (1992) and he is presently collaborating with François Regourd of the Université de Nanterre (Paris X) on a comprehensive survey of French science and colonialism in the seventeenth and eighteenth centuries.

Sir James F. Mitchell is the former Prime Minister of St. Vincent and the Grenadines. He received degrees from the Imperial College of Tropical Agriculture and the University of British Columbia in soil science and botany.

Kenneth Rodney is a forester who worked with the St. Vincent and the Grenadines Forestry Project as inventory specialist, 1989–1992.

Hymie Rubenstein is Professor of Anthropology at the University of Manitoba. He received his doctorate degree from the University of Toronto. The results of his long-term field research in St. Vincent were published in *Coping with Poverty: Adaptive Strategies in a Caribbean Village* (Boulder, Westview Press 1987).
E-mail: rubenst@cc.umanitoba.ca

Jorge Trevin is a forester and was siliviculture specialist for the St. Vincent and the Grenadines Forestry Project between 1990–1994. He received his degree from John Simon Fraser University. He resides in Argentina.

David Watts was Professor of Geography at the University of Hull, U.K. He received degrees from the University of London, University of California and McGill University. He was the author of *The West Indies: Patterns of Development, Culture, and Environmental Change Since 1492* (Cambridge University Press 1987) and *Man's Influence on the Vegetation of Barbados* (University of Hull 1996). He encouraged this book enthusiastically from its beginning to his recent death.

Nigel Weekes, formerly the director of the Forestry Division, Government of St. Vincent and the Grenadines, has recently been appointed to manage the National Parks and Beaches Authority.

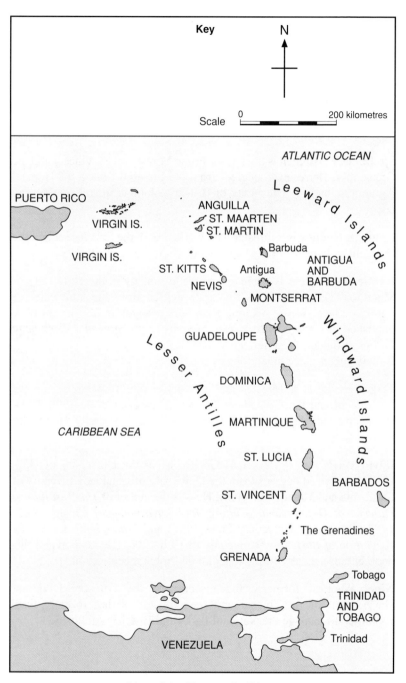

Map of the Eastern Caribbean

Foreword

From 1791 to Our Decade of the Environment

Sir James F. Mitchell

The Kings Hill Enclosure Ordinance (No. 5 of 1791) was assented to by his Majesty King George the Third on April 2, 1791 '…to appropriate for the benefit of the Neighbourhood the Hill called the Kings Hill, in the Parish of St. George and for enclosing the same and preserving the timber and other trees growing thereon, in order to attract rain…'

As we commemorate this enactment which was promulgated more than two hundred years ago, and which sought to preserve a portion of St. Vincent in its pristine state for ever and ever, we cannot but be amazed at the level of wisdom and vision of the people who conceived and executed such a brilliant idea. It must give us cause to reflect, to reflect on what must have been the ethos, the thinking of these people who lived here and made their homes here some two hundred years ago.

It is also interesting to note this sensitivity not only on St. Vincent but in the isles of the Grenadines also where old French deeds two hundred years ago emphasized that trees may be cut only for building vessels and warehouses or works defined by His Majesty.

As we see the tens of thousands of children streaming out of the schools each day, it is hard for us to imagine that there was a time when this island had a population of less than 30,000 people on it. The first official census taken in 1844 recorded a population of 27,248 persons; therefore, about two hundred years ago there were less than 25,000 people on the island. The population pressure on the land with its limited resources was not therefore as intense as it is today, with our 120,000 people and with projections of doubling. The declaration of the Kings Hill Forest Reserve cannot thus be perceived as an act of survival, as our environmental legislation today has become. It was not motivated by health-related urgency. Today we are trying to ensure that pesticides do not seep into our water catchment areas. It is absolutely amazing to recognize that in that dim and distant past among those small numbers, there actually were people who understood more about the preservation of this country than so many of us do today.

We are lucky to have had a series of thinkers and naturalists who came to this country over the centuries and who left an indelible mark on our ecological system. It is fitting that that I pay tribute to them. Pre-eminent among these individuals is Captain Bligh, who after the tragic venture on the *Bounty*, arrived here safely with his breadfruit on the Providence. For those who take both his heroism and the presence of the breadfruit in the Caribbean for granted, I suggest you try keeping a couple breadfruit slips in your home alive for three months, and imagine what it was like fighting the salinity of the atmosphere at sea on a rolling ship, with only a limited supply of fresh water in barrels with which to keep a collection of plants alive. What kind of man would keep himself and his crew thirsty and instead give water to plants? Perhaps as we continue to relish our roast breadfruit, we will one day be mature enough to honour Captain Bligh with more than a label on a tree in the Botanical Gardens, with which he is so eminently identified.

Then there was another Englishman, the Reverend Lansdown Guilding, who first identified the distinctiveness of our parrot and left his name on it – *Amazona guildingii*. Guilding's classic account of the Botanical Gardens is republished at the end of the book.

These men laid the foundations on which the linkage between St. Vincent's Botanical Gardens and Kew Gardens in England were established. Professor Harland, with whose name students of genetics are very familiar, tested his theory in this country.

I want to say that this noble tradition has been emulated by our own Earle Kirby who paid lifelong attention to our pre-history, our flora and fauna, and is today a legend in this field. I want to pay particular tribute to him for his unswerving dedication to this cause. Such dedication is responsible for the Conference on Environmental Institutions in 1991 under the authority of the National Trust and the appearance of this book not authorized by the National Trust.

When I was Minister of Trade and Tourism, I was pleased to formulate and pilot through the Parliament the legislation establishing the National Trust in 1969. Quite fittingly, it was the last piece of legislation enacted under our Colonial status, and I was also pleased to have it assented to by the last British Administrator, Hywel George, who encouraged me to produce it.

Now, with all these noble traditions, where do we go from here? These traditions, beginning with the Botanical Gardens and the Kings Hill Enactment, show that in St. Vincent and the Grenadines we are not newcomers to the idea of environment consciousness. Few in the Caribbean have given as much thought to the idea as we have done with our Decade of the Environment. But we have some tall problems. God has given us, as guardians or stewards, an exquisite area of this earth's surface. However, very few of us are its guardians or stewards. The majority of us are indifferent or careless reapers, insensitive to the incalculable value of our extraordinary inheritance. Some go further and they insist they have a God-given right to use modern technology to rob future generations of this heritage.

The truth of the matter is that we have imported foreign technology and deployed it in the exploration of our island's resources. This has been done without ever attempting to evaluate the impact of that technology and in turn focusing on a strategy that may provide a balance between our needs and the capacity of our resources.

Can a book of this nature show us how to deal with some of these horrendous problems of pillage? How are we to educate and find alternatives for the farmers who attack the watershed areas to make a living? How are we to educate the fishermen to stop using the spear gun, or at least to stop using it in the breeding grounds of the fish? Yes, a book that shows how wise people long ago anticipated the tall problems we face is a book that has value for future generations.

I have been at pains to explain to groups of fisherman in my Constituency of the Grenadines how lobsters are fast becoming depleted only in the short period after 1960. Hitherto, lobsters had been abundant in our waters for million and millions of years. We harvest sea eggs and remove sand from the beaches. We have done more to ruin the marine resources in the last forty years than was done by our forefathers in three hundred million years! Yet we can, with the simple and sensible element of care, ensure that lobster diving will still be a business for future generations.

Environmental inquiries highlight that poverty in the Third World is an enemy of the environment. I will go further and put it this way, that poverty is the greatest catalyst to more poverty. Nature lectures loudly to these exploitive habits of mankind with the age-old message – that reaping is a reward for sowing, and if you reap what you have not sown, if you destroy what you did not create, one day you will have no more to reap and poverty will be your inheritance in the wasteland you created. The environmentalists put it beautifully and simply when they define our goal to be sustainable development. We have no God-given right to rob the next generation.

Surely if all this is so, we have no right to remove any species from this environment which was here before we were. This 'right' to abuse and overexploit is a flagrant contradiction of our easily-mouthed sentiment – that our greatest love is of our children. If this is going to be true, we each must individually have a policy or an attitude to life that shows it.

I miss the sand on the beaches on which I have played in front of my home in Bequia when I was a small boy. I miss the white sand crabs. I miss the birds that scampered along the water line as I chased them. I miss the pelicans diving that entertained me with their ferocious grace. Why should I have savoured these things in my youth and why should my children be ignorant of them? I know I speak for many kindred souls who mourn the transfiguration of our landscape over the years. Although we have transgressed against Nature in our exploitive habits in the past, surely we now have the knowledge at our disposal not only to arrest this deterioration but also to invest in the recovery of our landscape and reefs.

The intensity of inquiries from the tourism trade about our environmental policies shows that people in Europe are fed up with the pollution in the Adriatic. What this tells us is that Germany, which constitutes our greatest area of growth in our foreign exchange income, is exceedingly sensitive to environmental sanity. But they will not come to visit our reefs if they are overgrown with the same kind of algae that has ruined the Mediterranean. I will not tire of explaining to our fishermen how they can make fifty dollars per hour taking a diver to see a parrotfish rather than selling the same fish or eating it once. Why catch and kill the fish that left swimming can earn you a thousand dollars? The parrotfish on our reefs is like the proverbial goose, which lays the golden egg; but for all its united colours on the reef, the parrotfish does not taste good. I hope this book and the conference preceding it celebrating the bicentenery of the Kings Hill Forest and the Botanic Garden will enhance the initiatives that we have already targeted.

I identified the closing decade of the twentieth century as the Decade of the Environment because I was painfully aware of how long it would take us to understand that a plastic cup thrown from the window of a van by one citizen has to be picked up by another. I hope that in this decade we will stop stealing sand from the beaches in the night. I pray that as we begin this century our people have learnt these lessons so that the ambience, sounds and appearance of this country will earn some truth in the tourist brochures as 'unspoiled'. Right now, the Caribbean lies when these countries are described as unspoiled.

I studied botany and soil science professionally, but my greatest insight into the relationship between mankind and the earth came from my great-uncle, Uncle Donald, who saw the doors of no university. At ninety-five he was still planting trees. One day a visitor said to him, 'Why do you plant these trees; surely you will never reap anything from them!' 'Young man,' Uncle Donald advised, 'when I came into this world, there were trees.'

It is not too late for us to correct the sins of the last three decades of aggressive exploitation. The knowledge is at hand. With the international sensitivity on these issues, we can gain access to all the latest research, and all the newly-tested methods that point the way to sustainable development, and in doing so lead ourselves out of poverty. I am confident that we can find the way to ensure that this planet is better for our passing through.

Preface

Earle Kirby

All living things depend on the soil, water and air for their well-being. Whenever there is a change in the normality of any of these, life suffers. Primitive people made a conscious effort to retain the status quo of their environment. All agriculturalists and fishermen do all in their power to retain this condition in their surroundings, whether they live as free people or as serfs.

St. Vincent is lucky in this regard. Firstly, there were the Arawaks and Caribs, then came the Garfuna (the so-called Black Caribs), then the Negroid people from Africa as slaves with their British colonists. It seems that we were particularly fortunate that some of our British were not the 'get rich quick' types but serious agriculturalists out to make money from sustainable planting practices. With their Administration intent on making sure that these practices were adhered to, they did not trust others to be of the same philosophy. As a consequence, they made sure that there was good and strong legislation in place to achieve this. I am speaking of Kings Hill, Crown Forests, and the Botanical Gardens.

When the South East of the island appeared to be getting less rain than normal, they passed into law 'The King Enclosure Ordinance' 1791 to ensure that the highest hill 'Kings Hill' would remain with its cover of trees in perpetuity. The growing awareness of the need for further restraining legislation to prevent the disappearance of the national forests led to the prevention of cutting trees above the 1000-ft. contour line in a Proclamation by Administrator Gideon Murray in August, 1912.

Another of the important pieces of our heritage legislation is that which brought the Botanic Gardens into being and to allow it to have survived the vicissitudes of the last 239 years. It was already established when a spot was needed to plant the breadfuit trees to allow Captain Bligh in 1793 to breathe a sigh of relief on having attained his objective. I just hope that he enjoyed a good meal of beef from the bullock that was presented, to each ship, as a 'thank you' from our island's Council.

With these pieces of legislation, and with people obeying them, we are being paid dividends today even with a doubling of our population. We can still get as much fresh pure potable water as we want. In addition, one spin-off that our progenitors could not have foreseen is that part of our supply of electricity is from waterpower. They should surely be complimented and thanked by us.

By the 1960s there was recognition of the need for more wide-reaching conservation legislation and so legislation was passed in October, 1969 to establish the St. Vincent National Trust. Its mandate included: the location, restoration, and conservation of buildings and objects of archaeological, architectural, artistic, historical, scientific, or traditional interest; and the restoration and conservation of areas of beauty, including marine zones and the protection and conservation of the natural life within.

The Botanical Gardens is under the National Trust's protection. Over the years it has been a place of relaxation for both young and old, and is still used to good effect by teachers to introduce their pupils to the outdoors and to learn to take notice of plants. It is proposed to refurbish the Botanical Gardens and to upgrade it to a botanic station so that it would also be educational to technical persons, as well as to youngsters. I hope that our present and future legislators would take a page out of the books of their predecessors so that in another 239 years our progeny could be as proud of them as we are of our progenitors. This book is a welcome step in that direction.

Earle Kirby's biography

Dr. I. A. Earle Kirby's unselfish service to St. Vincent and the Grenadines in agriculture, veterinary medicine and surgery, livestock development, horticulture, forestry, history, and archaeology is so far unparalleled.

Earle Kirby, or 'Doc' as he was referred to by all, was born on St. Vincent in December, 1921 and had his secondary education at the Boy's Grammar School in Kingstown, from which he graduated having won the prestigious Agricultural Scholarship. He proceeded to the Imperial College of Tropical Agriculture (I.C.T.A.) and continued to display excellence in his academic work. He graduated from I.C.T.A. in 1945, and after a short stint in Agricultural Research in St. Vincent, proceeded to one of the top veterinary colleges in the world at the time – Ontario Veterinary College at Guelph University in Canada. Earle Kirby graduated at the top of the honour roll at Guelph University with distinctions in every subject area. Despite several lucrative offers to remain in Canada, Dr. Kirby returned to his native St. Vincent to accept the post of Chief Veterinary Officer in 1952.

His wide knowledge and interests in St. Vincent made him an invaluable reference in subject areas from mechanical engineering to archaeology. Quietly, and behind the scenes, he involved himself in agriculture and in forestry, in toxonomy, and botany. He fought alone, and later with foreign help, to protect the St. Vincent Parrot, and put a damper on the trade of this now endangered bird. In recognition of his efforts, the Houston Zoo named the first *Amazonia guildingii* to be bred in captivity 'Kirby'.

His labours have extended far beyond agriculture. He became the local and regional authority on the fauna, birds, fish, reptiles and other creatures of St. Vincent. He founded the Archaeological and Historical Society and later the St. Vincent National Trust. His accomplishments in protecting the national identity and ecology of St. Vincent were recognized with two prestigious awards in 1986: the National Garifuna Council of Belize Citation (Development of Garifuna) and the Caribbean Conservation Award. He went on to serve as a Caribbean Conservation executive member for several years.

Dr. Kirby's role in educating St. Vincent's youth has also been honoured with many awards, including: the Duke of Edinburgh Award (1986), National Youth Council Chatoyer Award (1989), Award Service to Education (1993), the Rotarian Paul Harris Fellow Award (1998), and Role Model Award, St. Vincent Ex-Teachers Association, Brooklyn, New York (1999).

On the wider Caribbean scene, he presided over the Congress of Pre-Columbia Studies in the Lesser Antilles in 1977 and 1978. He also served as a Justice of the Peace from 1960, Chairman of the Public Service Board of Appeal, Chairman of the Boundaries Commission of 1989, and Chairman of the St. Vincent National Trust (1986–1996). Still, he found time to be a good husband and father of two, a fine friend and confidante to many, and a grandfather.

1 | Gardens and Forests on Caribbean Islands: Two Hundred Years of Enviromental Institutions

Robert S. Anderson

Small islands inspire the imagination of those who do not live on them. Growing up on a large and beautiful island did not deter me from wanting to explore the smaller ones; the big island just could not satisfy this excitement. In the histories of island peoples from the ancient Greeks onwards, they have a character that is unlike anything 'on the mainland'. The difference between one island and another, set in the same sea, fascinates us. Their separation and distinction, surrounded yet open on all sides, disconnected yet whole – onwards hold our attention and draw us to them again and again. I do not speak here of Madagascar, Java and Vancouver Island – although they are impressive in other ways, they are too large to qualify for this excitement. Corsica and Hawaii might be the largest of the small islands, and from them we glide down the scale to the coral atolls of Bikini and the Grenadines. The Caribbean islands discussed in this book fill the imagination perfectly.

The prodigious richness of the ecology of small islands is essential to our fascination. These islands are imagined to be true microcosms. Like the Galapagos, they provide a laboratory for observation and study. In our imaginations, island ecology includes homes for dragons and elves and enchanting spirits; islands are wild and dangerous, or homey and safe, depending on our definitions. They are usually the imagined home of extraordinary and noble indigenous people.[1] But we also keep dangerous or important prisoners on islands, like Napoleon or Nelson Mandela, explode our most dangerous bombs, store our dangerous wastes, send off those with leprosy. Diseases like rabies, or pests like termites, don't exist on some islands. On other small islands, diseases are intensified and occur in rare forms. On the other hand, each winter, northern peoples spend a small fortune flying and fleeing the cold weather to reach small islands in the sun.

Above all, these islands are imagined to support life in greater abundance than elsewhere, though in practice this support is more delicate than most visitors recognize. Small islands also sometimes

1

frustrate the ambitions of their inhabitants. The tension and risks posed to this delicate support and abundance are the themes in these chapters about gardens and forests, and they draw on the geographic and imaginative traditions just outlined. But it is crucial to remember that the issues discussed in this book are not at all restricted to Caribbean islands. They are replicated on small islands everywhere, not just on tropical islands. Moreover, wherever space is restricted, as in mountainous regions, the tension seen here repeats itself.

Contributions to this book

The strength of the contributions in this book is that they allow to us understand the interplay of very local conditions and individual initiatives with larger regional global dynamics and structures. This interplay shows the importance of legislation, rules and informal practices in building environmental institutions. Our attention is on small islands where there is very little social room to manoeuver, and among small populations where almost everybody knows everybody's business. But the longer view, offered in the chapter by Lennox Honychurch, is essential: that the settlement and cultivation of these islands of the eastern Caribbean are very old, and that tensions around access to space and land are deeply structured. Honychurch shows that a garden at the edge of the forest is also very old, and a well-established cultural model, organized by local rules, with continuing meaning for twenty-first century inhabitants of Dominica, whether Carib, Creole or newcomer. Their staple manioc (*manihot utilissima*) and other tubers, roots, vines, greens and fruits have been cultivated and eaten on Dominica and other islands since 250 AD. The boundary of the forest with the garden and with plantation agriculture has taken on a deep continuing meaning on all the Caribbean islands, as many of the chapters here show.

The environmental consequences of the rapid introduction of sugar in Barbados, examined by David Watts, sets the stage for a series of economic and ecological cycles seen in other islands: sugar moves to each of them at separate moments, and this affects their fortune in the economics of boom and bust. Other commercial crops followed in succession. The institutions of European settlers, Watts shows, were seldom up to the task of environmental protection until crisis appeared, right up to the almost total deforestation of Barbados. An island like St. Vincent, by geography and history, experienced a delay of the arrival of the Barbados sugar syndrome, and so the syndrome was not worked out in the same fashion, including perhaps some lesson drawn from Barbados. Geography elsewhere ensured this difference: had the other islands lacked mountains they too might have been deforested. One of the obvious approaches to approaching environmental crisis was to protect forests.

Madelaine Ly-Tio-Fane describes how botanical gardens were essential to the rapid and successful transfer of plants around the world, promoted by great European crown corporations engaged in the establishment of permanent tropical-based economic and military empires. Botanical gardens were variously managed by states and corporations, supported by a low-cost global scientific network of cosmopolitan botanists and gardeners which sprang up, exchanging plants in all directions (including across 'enemy lines'). But the simple establishment of a botanical garden on St. Vincent in 1765 did eventually permit its involvement in local conservation and economic measures.

Pre-revolutionary Saint Domingue, or what became Haiti, was the most populus of the eastern Caribbean islands, and James McClellan III describes the complexity of scientific, botanical and farming-plantation life there. Probably the most developed in terms of scientists and other expertise, Saint Domingue had three botanical gardens, and very significant forests (none of which were particularly protected). Conflicts between English and French interests did not long inhibit communication between Saint Domingue and English islands in the Caribbean, and what emerged was perhaps the most autonomous of the region's colonial societies in the eighteenth century, according to McClellan.

Clarissa Kimber provides a detailed history of the botanical garden in Martinique, profoundly influenced by directives from Paris (particularly in time of war and crisis) yet attentive to the possibilities of the local economy and exchange even with British gardens in Jamaica and St. Vincent. It was commonly after massive crisis that botanical gardens began to play an effective local role, although the Jardin des Plantes in Martinique was not as fortunate; its destruction by the 1902 volcano was decisive, and it never recovered. The Jardin also depended (as did other gardens) on the quality of its management and staff, which varied dramatically as Kimber shows. Although their earliest role was to support the experiments of big plantation farmers, botanical gardens eventually had an impact on the economy of the poor peasant farmers.

The next five chapters are largely about St. Vincent and its relations with the rest of the world.[2] Building on Guilding's 1825 history of the St. Vincent Botanic Garden (reproduced in 1848, see Appendix), the late Richard Howard examined in detail the changes in the cultivating and research practices of Alexander Anderson and subsequent botanists in Kingstown, as well as their relations with other botanical gardens and their directors. Although their intellectual context is large and ambitious, the gardens have from their beginning a local and practical concern with medicinal and locally useful plants. In fact Howard knew personally the origin of most of the exotic plants and trees in the garden. Grove's chapter on the Kings Hill protected forest on St. Vincent and forest conservation generally shows that French and British ideas about climate change and environmentalism were discussed on St. Vincent and other islands in direct response to larger strategic interests of empire, and that news about experiments moved quickly around the world. For example, reports of the success of the St. Vincent Botanic Garden were influential in obtaining commitment for the botanical garden at Calcutta at the same time. This information moved rapidly among interacting scientific and political networks described by Ly-Tio-Fane, Kimber, Howard and Grove. Carib resistance and response to plantations on St. Vincent and other islands, discussed by Grove extensively, show that Caribs fully grasped the implications for them of new European practices.

Adrian Fraser discusses the struggle over resources like land, soil and water, conditioned by cycles of boom and bust in new crop plantations: he shows how this struggle over gardens in the forest, and over the use of land in general, was routinized by legislation and somewhat contained by special programmes, but even today remains unresolved. The chapter by Kidston et al. focuses entirely on Kings Hill, and provides a surveyor's and forester's perspective on this remarkable 213-year-old protected forest, including a re-examination of part of Beard's 1947–50 classic work in Caribbean forestry. It shows that the intent of protecting this forest has been largely met, though there has been loss along the boundaries and some areas need to be better managed.

Finally, Hymie Rubenstein's careful chronicle of nearly 300 years of settlement on the western coast of St. Vincent yields insight into the ways that marginal small farmers have adapted to economic and ecological stress, how they organize their gardens in the forest with an eye to both subsistence and the market, and how the small farm has evolved in parallel to the decline of the once-powerful plantation estate. This chapter is an ethnographic account of the present; it allows us to think back in time in order to understand (approximately) the eighteenth- and nineteenth-century conditions that are described in other chapters in this book. The paradox of unused and under-utilized land emerges here, on an island where cultivable land is known to be scarce. He also shows how the new crop marijuana constitutes another perhaps temporary solution in a long line of temporary solutions to the small farmer's socio-economic dilemmas, many of which have less to do with agronomy or forestry practices than they do with class, education, life-chances, health, household composition, and access to markets.

Gardens in the forest

Gardens everywhere, like islands, are bounded and defended. Though purposefully set apart from the surrounding ecosystem, they are in practice quite open to it. Gardens are the epitome of cultivated control, and gardeners of all philosophies are very oriented to results. They (usually) remember what is planted, where, and when; they have protected the growth and await the satisfaction of results. There is too much work involved to do otherwise. Even a distinguished Chinese gardener of my acquaintance in Hawaii, cultivating his garden on the Taoist principle he called 'benign neglect', was very particular about the results. The hallmark of the garden is its intent and its separation from its surrounding.

The meaning of a Caribbean garden has evolved considerably since the eighteenth century: slaves were generally forbidden to cultivate a garden, thus keeping them dependent on 'the big house' and its kitchens, and fully available for work. It was reasoned that if the slaves were gardening, they were probably beyond surveillance. Forbidden gardens were cultivated in the forest, nevertheless, to provide autonomy from the plantation as well as unrecorded income for slaves. Gradually the rule against gardens changed as the slave-work economy changed, and subsistence gardens became inevitable and accepted, a marginal zone where slaves supported themselves. Most gardens were in or at the edge of the forest. Mimi Sheller says about garden explanations of slavery's abolition' in her study of nineteenth-century Caribbean movements and radicalism that 'the economic and social space of the garden was crucial to the making of a "culture of resistance" even during slavery, and it became the seed-corn from which post-emancipation freedom could be cultivated'.[3]

In fact no one could live without a garden, and in the nineteenth century commercial gardening began in earnest near ports and towns in the Caribbean. As wage labour expanded within the agrarian economy, the garden filled a need for self-sufficiency. Gardens were the life-line of small farmers, inserted at the margins of big estates with grounds for yam cultivation further up the slope, small banana gardens established as holes cut into the forest, and the wood of the trees used for dozens of purposes. The islands of the eastern Caribbean have been the home of a very complex (and perhaps sustainable) kind of agroforestry, the garden in the forest, for centuries. Growing dependence on imported food has scarcely diminished the value of the forest or the energy put into the garden. Gardens filled a balance of subsistence, medicinal and commercial needs. And for people with land and/or leisure, gardens have filled deep aesthetic needs as well as nutritional ones. A visit to any weekly market in the Caribbean today will show people bringing excellent produce to sell; this is simply not an activity of the past. There are high standards in these gardens and innovations are regularly discussed at the market.

Onto this background I ask you to project the idea of a botanical garden. Changing from the royal pleasure garden and apothecary's herbal nursery garden of the seventeenth century (like the Jardin du Roi in Paris), it became an experimental garden set apart by its larger size and hired labour guided by scientific experts. Cultivation remained in the hands of learned gardeners, but when botanical gardens were established abroad by Europeans a new higher-status kind of gardener emerged, one usually locally born and bred, and necessarily knowledgeable about local plants. At the same time these gardeners were required to learn new classification schemes and names, and to nurture very exotic plants which they had not seen before. There was a commensurate rise in status of botanists, the discipline of botany, and with them their gardeners. Botany became a 'classy' subject. A height was reached in 1770 when James Cook named a well- known site in Australia as Botany Bay (it was finally renamed in 1998): this name was specifically given due to the large number of new and exotic plants observed there. There was gradual movement from the botanical garden as a somewhat controlled and contrived place, a shrine for systematics, to a place of more and more experimentation. The botanical garden in the Caribbean, like so much in the New World, became open to the unknown, to the entrepreneurial 'what if?' impulse. This led to new plants being moved rapidly from garden to garden, country to country, and botanical gardens became the place where one could tie up and lay down the results of a long voyage.[4]

This impulse opened botanical gardens to calculated risks, and started what came to be called bio-technology transfer in the twentieth century. Although the entire history of cultivation is one of experimentation and transfer, in the nineteenth century there was an unprecedented increase in 'economic botany' and then 'plant industry'.

By 1900 the botanical garden was the combination of a public pleasure garden, 'a re-construction of paradise', a valuable piece of real estate in cities, and a symbol and substance of natural science. No state with modern ambitions in the nineteenth century was insensitive to this movement, and botanical gardens appeared in or just outside all major Caribbean cities, from Havana to Kingston. By 1900 modern cities everywhere had established botanical gardens, a new kind of public place that combined weekday science with Sunday afternoon outings. I think of Bandung, Yangon, Istanbul, Montreal, Moscow, and on and on. Few Caribbean cities were far behind.[5]

When our story begins in the eighteenth century, island forests were already fulfilling a number of purposes. For shipbuilders and navies the forest was the source of essential repairs and construction materials. Wood could be stored and traded by merchants. For the Maroons, the escaped slaves resisting recapture, for criminals on the run, and for the original natives of the islands (Caribs and others), the forest was a zone of safety and sustenance. The paths within it were usually along or up and down steep slopes which, when known, were the entry point to gardens and gardeners. The forest was also the place where they were hunted down, unless they escaped to other islands. For slaves at work and planters, as well as the growing force of subsistence farmers, the forest was to be removed, and would return if not continuously pruned or cut back. This process of 'encroachment' is so constant that two hundred years after the establishment of Kings Hill, people were cutting the forest on the highest slopes of some of the steepest least accessible watersheds of St. Vincent for banana and marijuana gardens. Though Kings Hill Forest remained more or less intact, most of the land around it changed, making the original idea of protecting this forest the more prescient and important. The same holds for protected forests on Tobago, Grenada, St. Lucia, Dominica, and elsewhere.

From the point of view of the Forest Department, furniture and coffin makers, house builders, charcoal-producers, flower and herb collectors – the forest was a renewable source of unending benefit, if the forest could be conserved without destruction. For a hydro-electric or drinking water authority, the forest retained and cycled the very water on which their sustainable business depended. For the tourist industry and Tourism Department, the forest was a compelling attraction, a home of parrots and enchantment. The contradictory impulses and projects emerging from this situation can easily be imagined. In the words of the distinguished Caribbean historian Alan Cobley:

> As a microcosm not only of the Americas, but also of Planet Earth, the Caribbean is a laboratory for all the tensions (creative and disintegrative) of the human condition as we have come to know them in these past 500 years, and as they shall continue to show themselves in the next century.[6]

Eighteenth-century conditions

The purpose of this book is to persuade you that there is a direct lineage between us and the eighteenth-century people who founded environmental institutions like the Botanical Gardens and Kings Hill Forest of St. Vincent and the Grenadines. The dozens of subsistence gardens established in the eighteenth and nineteenth centuries are also connected to us. Across the Caribbean and on islands around the world the story is repeated, again and again. This lineage is not simple, but winds around like a creeping vine in the rain forest. We wish to persuade you that the eighteenth-century idea of attracting clouds and rain at Kings Hill, and of conserving and experimenting with plants in the Botanical Gardens, are the same ideas that inform our book and the international gathering which preceded it. Our path of reasoning may be a little different, but these same precious environmental institutions created by those people remain vital to us. We agree with them that there is a relation between forests, rainfall, climate, and our welfare. It gradually matters less and less where our origins in Caribbean islands lie, whether in Guyana, Africa, or Scotland, Spain, Lebanon or China, or in any of the dozen other places from which people came to the Caribbean. We are now all subject to the same ecological discipline.

But first consider the rather different circumstances in which people in the eastern Caribbean built a botanical garden and protected the forest. It is not obvious that these institutions would have survived in these early difficulties. The seventeenth century created an economic context in which some plantations were very successful and profitable, though by the second half of the eighteenth century the absent owner was a common fixture. The high life in Britain of these successful people was the stuff of legends, and their capacity to lobby Parliament for favourable treatment was notorious. But the probability of a British (or French) male dying young in the Caribbean was high, so there was a large turnover in the population and employment opportunities were always good for newcomers.[7] Estates were operated by managers, lawyers, engineers, overseers, 'free coloureds' and slaves. There was a lot of communicating and travelling back and forth to Britain, and some members of the local elite had established professional reputations (Royal Society, Royal College of Physicians, etc.) in London. Alexander Anderson of Kingstown is a good example, even though he had no university degree. Local 'parliamentary' assemblies articulated local interests, sometimes in contradiction to the views or interests of the Governors. There were smaller and middle-sized planters, and their number was high in places like Barbados, but they seldom successfully challenged the elite. The botanical gardens and the protected forests were supported by some educated men from this class (and, I would expect, a number of women), because such environmental institutions not only did not contradict their interests, they furthered them. Ironically we simply do not have their reasons in their own words, but it was surely to do with building a strong island economy, ruling in the Caribbean, and applying scientific ideas to practical problems. What is curious is that these institutions were established in such turbulent times.

The American War of Independence accelerated a fall in Caribbean plantation profits because a large market was withdrawn, and colonial sugar duties and stamp taxes were onerous. There was transience in this population in the late eighteenth century. White settler populations were in a minority everywhere (twenty-seven per cent in Barbados where the proportion was higher than other islands), and many were apprehensive about slave rebellions, which is why local planters and merchants were prepared to bear the British troops' subsistence costs. These troops competed with settlers for food and supplies and British troops stationed in America sought provisions as far south as the Windward Islands. There were numerous slave revolts in the Windward Islands, four in Tobago in the 1770s, three in St. Vincent. The geography of the volcanic islands favoured the emergence of Maroon communities of escaped slaves, and in St. Vincent there was occasional common cause made between these escaped Maroons and the Carib inhabitants against settler attempts to usurp Carib land for cultivation. In 1775 Maroons on St. Vincent, encouraged by Caribs, killed the symbol and instrument of those land usurpations, a land surveyor.

In 1777, a conspiracy to overthrow the British was foiled, but in 1778 the French troops arrived on St. Vincent and with the help of Caribs and Maroons took control (for the next five years) without a shot being fired. Botanical gardener Alexander Anderson's sentiments against the American and French revolutions were quite widely shared among his class, though this was not simply because they were impressed by the quality of British governance and policies imposed on them. When French possessions in the Caribbean were again turned into British possessions, the insecurity of public institutions like gardens and protected forests looked, if anything, greater. Anderson found a very overgrown botanical garden in 1784; though it had been maintained carefully by the French until their final chaotic and uncertain year on St. Vincent. Despite some achievements, rapacious governors, feeble financing and inconsistent administration marked colonial government. Governor Robert Melville helped Dr. David Young in 1765 to establish a garden at Kingstown, St. Vincent (and asked him to develop medicinal plants by consulting with 'practitioners of the country, natives of experience, and even old Caribs and slaves who have dealt in cures'). Melville was succeeded by two Governors who had not the slightest interest and did not help with the garden at all. Encroachment on the garden and misuse of the stream were signs in 1784 that it was indeed vulnerable.

Had Alexander Anderson known more about science on Saint Domingue (modern Haiti), particularly Port-au-Prince, he might not have minded French control for a while. There, in that city, there were at least three public (state-funded) botanical gardens – one located in the

Governor's residence (called the Jardin du Roi), one at the hospital, and a third founded by the scientific group Cercle des Philadelphes. Here was an active dialectic between pure and applied research, linked by voyages to botanists everywhere.[8] This small city was truly cosmopolitan in the scientific sense, according to McClellan, and was the site of a break-through in 1785 when someone discovered an indigenous form of Peruvian cinchona tree growing there. This alternate source of cinchona (for which both the French and British were paying huge prices annually to Spain at the time) was called '*quinquina indigene*', and scientific tests were done and articles published in scientific journals in Paris about it. This was a result of the convergence of botanists' curiosity (many of them missionaries) and the growing field of economic botany. Saint Domingue remained a vital centre of scientific interest. As Richard Howard's chapter shows, Alexander Anderson also identified and used an alternate local source of cinchona bark – on St. Lucia.

Why are those eighteenth-century people important to us now? Because they embodied their reasoning about the environment in an institution, protected it with the discipline of law, and trusted successive generations to honour that law. They nurtured an extremely valuable twenty-year-old botanical garden from a feeble neglected state at the end of the war with France in 1784. We are the beneficiaries of their trust. The assumption that lies beneath the surface of environmental institutions is they must embody trust and discipline if they are to be sustainable. They must inspire both trust and discipline if they are going to help us to live together, and it must be an affectionate trust and a binding discipline.

Environmental institutions

Environmental insitutions are innovations, human cultural inventions to conserve our inter-dependence with biological systems. They also exhibit some of the characteristics of biological systems, which have a tendency to move toward diversification, toward complexity of struc-ture, toward dynamic stability and resilience, and toward adaptability. These tendencies seem to produce (and then require) an enriched flow of information in biological systems. Botanical gardens and protected forests are culturally-constructed environmental institutions; they exhibit, even imitate, these tendencies to diversification, complexity and resilience. Environmental institutions have multiple functions, cutting across single-factor interest groups in their membership, enriching the flow of information and creating more complex networks of communication. Just as there is an important tendency toward bio-diversity on small islands, so there is a tendency toward socio-diversity. This diversity offers a certain stability.

Although I don't wish to draw this analogy too far, what is striking about the resemblance between biological systems and cultural systems is the richness of information, the abundance of signals. This abundance reveals a high level of redundancy. There is a complex interplay on islands between directional selection and random genetic drift, and the biogeography of islands is fascinating for the process of speciation and hybridization.[9] Both the biological and cultural systems are over-determined in this sense: redundancy is everywhere, and too much of it is a good thing.

This book is not about an isolated, self-contained biological system, not on any Caribbean island. As in all other small islands, there are disturbance and disruption, tropical storms and volcanoes, and fires in the forest. The eruption on Martinique that destroyed the Jardin des Plantes in 1902 occurred three days later on St. Vincent: these islands are deeply connected. A swarm of locusts blew in from Africa on the wind and appeared on the beaches in 1990. The ecosystem of all small islands has a turbulent history, the same turbulence to which environmental institutions help us adapt. As a result of these disruptions, the biological and the social-cultural system become more inter-twined. Understanding the effects of one upon the other is crucial, and central to this book.

A good part of this book is about the Kings Hill Forest and the botanic gardens, about the scientific ideas that informed their creators, and about the political and economic strategies that supported their establishment. Those ideas and strategies reach back, as you will see, far beyond the seventeenth century. We do not know how conscious these people were of earlier innovations by Caribs, earlier gardens and protected forests, but they were certainly aware of the preceding hundred years of botanic experimentation. This was the age of expert publicists like James Cook and Joseph Banks, who were very conscious of developing the public's appreciation of their role in history.[10]

You will see how these environmental treasures have evolved over the 200 years to our present, nurtured (or neglected) by the nineteenth-century colonial administrations, but gradually incorporated into the twentieth-century life of the independent community as well as into the government system. So we have those old trees now, attracting clouds and rain to Kings Hill Forest as planned in 1791, and we have the old botanical lands attracting tourists and weddings to the Botanical Gardens as founders never imagined in 1765.

These institutions are part of a nucleus in Caribbean countries for a strategy to re-claim and manage the environment carefully, to cultivate skillfully and extract the valuables that are necessary, and to renew and sustain it. The strategy is also to build greater loyalties between communities and their natural surroundings, loyalties that can survive the pressures of economic recession and changes in world markets. For this purpose, of course, communities must be offered more influence over their surroundings, and must be prepared to accept more responsibility for them. These environmental institutions embody a potential that lies far beyond the original intentions of the eighteenth century people who established them. It is we who can take them beyond these original intentions. And, as shown in chapters here by James Mitchell, Adrian Fraser and Hymie Rubenstein, the pressures to make this progress are inescapable.

Environmental institutions at the turn of the twentieth century

As evidence that environmental institutions adapt and change with their circumstances, let us examine just five years on St. Vincent, namely 1898–1903: this part of the story starts 135 years after the founding of the Botanical Gardens, and a hundred years after the establishment of Kings Hill. I call this a middle period between those foundations and our present. In September, 1898 a ferocious hurricane hit the island, even more destructive than the 1831 hurricane. In 1902 and 1903 there were three eruptions of the Soufrière volcano, greater than the eruption of 1812. The response of the botanical services of the Agriculture Department is impressive and instructive. By the beginning of the twentieth century there was an established colonial agricultural staff and botanical service in all the islands, and (although no mention is made in reports of the Kings Hill) the role of the Botanical Gardens and botanical stations, and the staff was remarkable after the hurricane and eruptions. By this time the Botanical Gardens were dedicated to conservation and experimentation in an international scientific network, joined by its smaller offspring, the Botanic Station 'devoted to raising and distributing economic plants and assisting in the development of local industries'. Botanical gardens were directed at the time by Superintendents, botanical stations by Curators.

The 1898 hurricane was devastating. Wind velocity was so high it could not be measured, and 13 inches of rain fell in 24 hours. People flocked into Kingstown needing shelter and food, their houses and gardens destroyed. Five days later Governor Alfred Moloney (previously appointed in Lagos) arrived from Grenada, preceded by a large quantity of sweet-potato vines. These vines were planted immediately in a one-acre garden for propagation and distribution through the botanic station. Within one month there was sufficient production from this acre to supply small nurseries in other parishes. These were followed by black-eyed peas and French and red beans from St. Lucia, Indian corn from Tobago, cassava stems and yam heads from Jamaica, and even carrot, turnip and cabbage seed from a New York seed wholesaler! Remember that yam plants were first brought to the West Indies by Captain Bligh 'of the *Bounty*', through the Botanic Gardens in St. Vincent. Curator Henry Powell traveled to every parish to encourage restoration of gardens and plantations, and used disaster relief regulations to do so. 'A considerable sum was expended' on clearing the debris in the Botanical Gardens and Government House and neighbourhood. He had to work hard on subsistence nutrients, but also restore cash crops like cacao; 8,900 plants were given free and 2,500 plants were sold. In addition there were 12,000 Liberian coffee berries and 6,400 plants brought from Dominica, and 5,000 Arabian coffee plants from Grenada. A year later cacao was being successfully produced again, and subsistence farmers were recouping their losses. This hurricane established the communication network between botanical stations and cultivators in a way that no amount of policy programming had done in the preceding years, coming at a time of an expanding and demanding small farm and subsistence community.[11]

Thus it was that the volcanic eruptions four years later, starting in 1902, forced the re-starting of these networks. Exploding three days after Mount Pelee erupted in Martinique in May 1902, Soufrière poured molten lava onto the western and eastern coasts of the northern end of St. Vincent, burning or covering about 50 square miles, one-third of the island. Several villages, and all plant life on the surface were destroyed, leaving drifts of lava and dust 20 metres thick in some places, three to five metres in most places, and a few inches only on steep slopes. Again the use of seed and seedlings from less damaged parts of the island, and from other countries, brought small farmers gradually back to subsistence levels, and restarted large estates. Other plants like grasses and ferns pioneered and colonized the burned areas. Adaptation was much quicker on the windward than the leeward side. The Imperial Department of Agriculture opened a botanic station in the heart of the affected area among sugar estates on the windward side and studied the fertility of this volcanic deposit. Using several studies and reports beginning in 1904, the Agricultural Superintendent of St. Vincent (W. N. Sands) concluded in 1911 that there was a temporary increase in fertility in the volcanic debris, then a decline until old soils and new organic wastes are introduced or combined to improve it. Eleven years later, the fields were successfully re-established and growing sugar cane, cotton, arrowroot (major cash crops) and all subsistence food crops – although yields were highly variable and food production remained insufficient.

Just before the 1902 eruption, the distinguished author of the widely used text 'Tropical Agriculture', H.A. Alfred Nichols, had urged an increased use of botanic stations in further settlement and agricultural intensification throughout the West Indies. He urged the pursuit of knowledge from failure as well as success, leading to viable new industries beyond the dependence on sugar, testing new machinery, and creating museums of economic products with agricultural libraries attached. He also proposed new higher altitude mountain botanic stations because there 'were the natural advantages, the pleasant climate, and the healthiness of the mountain lands made generally known, European settlers would doubtless be attracted to the islands...They form an extensive, undeveloped estate of the Crown'.[12] What he says of the climate, availability of heavily-forested Crown land, and agricultural potential is quite true, but most of the lands Nichols described were going to be devastated a few months later by the volcanic eruption. This was the era of concerted efforts to settle colonies with British migrants who would stay.

Perhaps realizing the effect of the loss of habitat due to forest destruction by the hurricanes, and probably due to other pressures on wildlife, there was promulgation of the St. Vincent Ordinance Number 11 (1901), The Bird and Fish Protection Ordinance. It increased the penalties for illegal capture or commerce in specific species, including turtles and turtle eggs, and oysters. Of interest is the listing of the Vincentian parrot, the rare bird found only on St. Vincent that became the national symbol in the late twentieth century. The Botanical Gardens in Kingstown became the home in the 1990s for parrots found or confiscated, and for their young offspring, until they were fed to be strong enough to attempt life in the wild. Although the Botanical Gardens have always been the home of a great variety of birds, tourists frequented the Gardens to see parrots in large protective cages. This is how the protective custody of the Gardens as a sanctuary (note the spiritual origin of the term) was being naturally extended in the public imagination to the parrots, thus reconfirming the value of the Gardens, and recalling 'the re-construction of paradise'. The recent penalties for illegal possession of parrots are severe. The 1901 ordinance, however, imposed a fine of five pounds, 'half to go to the informer'; this would be equivalent to 50 UK pounds today or 250 EC dollars. In 1905 Austin Clarke of Harvard University published his survey of the birds of St. Vincent, and about the risk to the parrot he said 'notwithstanding reports to the contrary, this bird is not at all abundant, being at the present time restricted to a comparatively small area in the centre of the island, and even there it is not to be found in any numbers...Its extermination would not only mean the loss of a valuable game bird to St. Vincent but it would deprive the West Indies of one of their greatest ornithological curiosities, and America of one of its finest birds'. The Curator of the Botanical Station, Henry Powell, reported at the same time that there was a solitary St. Vincent parrot at the London Zoo, and that 'recently five specimens of this rare parrot were killed for a collector'. Clarke pointed out that parrots on Martinique and Guadeloupe, and macaws on Cuba and Jamaica were now extinct, and concluded that the Vincentian parrot should be afforded strict protection using fines that are 'especially heavy'.[13]

By the beginning of the twentieth century, realizing the speed and risks of deforestation, the colonial authorities had instituted Arbor Day through the schools and churches, supplying from the botanic stations hundreds of seedlings for planting of mahogany, palms and white wood – all noted for their shade and beauty. This gesture of restoration has never faded, despite the continuing deforestation. Trees planted in this program can be seen in public spaces all over the islands, as Arbor Day was a common celebration. A hundred years later one of the functions of the Forestry Project was to supply schools and communities with small trees to plant and hold slopes and watersheds intact. This is the same popular nexus of ideas which was in circulation a hundred years earlier – more trees, more parrots, more water – though now this nexus is (partially) to ensure the island's attraction to tourists as well as reassure local inhabitants that the eco-system remains healthy. Unlike settlers, tourists were not part of the calculation a hundred years ago.

In the post-eruption phase after 1903, the Botanic Station played the crucial role in regenerating small-scale gardens and cash crop cultivation. The disruption was used to introduce an improved variety of cacao by propagating it from the Botanical Gardens and the gardens of Government House to the botanic station, and then to farmers. The Curator and Superintendent also bought extra seeds at one of the largest private estates for distribution.[14] To small farmers there were distributed 5,000 plants in 1903–4, 15,000 in 1904–5, and 12,000 in 1905–6 – and then there were, in the same years 8,000 then 10,000 and 5,000 plants distributed to large farmers and estates. It appears some farmers used the loss of fields and plants to change their minds about old crops and shift to new ones – such as cotton and coffee – under new pressures. The dialectical relation of large estates and small gardens plots had become a fundamental fact in the economy, and politics required that the government address both needs. The demand for cultivable land by small farmers was insatiable, and their productivity was often spectacular considering their disadvantages.

Conclusions for the present

The founders of the Botanical Gardens and Kings Hill Forest were far-sighted. They knew there would be deforestation, and wanted to protect climate, albeit on a small scale. They knew there was a potential too for plants that were exotic and potentially beneficial to the economy of an empire. Far-sighted they were, but hardly able to contemplate the role of their institutions in the future. A hundred years later, at the turn of the twentieth century, the island's rehabilitation after the trauma of hurricanes and volcanic eruptions was administered through these very institutions. This was not envisioned a hundred years before, but was accomplished using the same environmental institutions established for other purposes in the eighteenth century. The possibility of further settlement, the need for reforestation and habitat protection, the need to rehabilitate subsistence gardens as well as industrial-scale plantations – these were all the need of the hour for government at the beginning of the twentieth century. A hundred years later, reforestation is being continued, parrots are housed in the Botanical Gardens and enshrined in the popular culture of the Caribbean as 'our bird'. Yet turtles did virtually disappear and lobsters are at great risk, despite the foresight of the 1901 Ordinance. Volcanoes and hurricanes can appear at any time, as the wise people know; when they do arrive environmental institutions will be crucial to survival after the trauma is over, just as they were in 1898–1903. What is needed, therefore, is an institution with a unique form of common responsibility, distinct from or more inclusive than the government apparatus, engaging people in action and thought about the environment for the long term.

Environmental institutions are circles of trust and networks of discipline. They build upon a sense of place and local affection. The trust we are talking about has a unique property: it does not deteriorate but actually improves with use. Because trust is given voluntarily and carefully, bit by bit, it cannot be taken back. It takes years to build and minutes to break. Trust is a circle in which each of us benefits mutually. Trust also comes with its own discipline, a discipline as strict as natural law or juridical law. In many Caribbean countries a National Trust has long been established, an important environmental institution that is building just such a circle of trust and network of discipline. It can thus act as a counter-balance to short-term interests and to shorter-term strategies.

Can we rely only on the discipline of market forces to secure bio-diversity? I think not. Can we rely only on the authority of government agencies to secure bio-diversity? Might the two together be sufficient? I think not. The evidence in this book points in a third direction. We now have enough experience to know that a much stronger combination is necessary. A National Trust can contribute to socio-diversity as well as biodiversity. Its potential lies far beyond the letter of its founding Act, in the same way that the potential of Kings Hill Forest and the Botanical Gardens lies far beyond the letter of their foundation. In this book we are acknowledging the letter and the context of the foundation of these environmental institutions, measuring the time and space we have traveled with them and, at the same time, envisioning a world in which we can live together forever.

Notes

1 For a review of this subject see Samuel M. Willson. *The Indigenous People of the Caribbean.* University of Florida Press, 1997.
2 The nearby Grenadine islands do not figure in these chapters, but they certainly have (or had) small woods on them, and there are gardens in those woods, or where those woods once stood. Measures are now being taken to regrow those woods on the Grenadines.
3 On the contrivance of the modern garden, and its political and cultural implications, see Joachim Wolshke-Bulmahn, (ed.). *Nature and Ideology: Natural Garden Design in the Twentieth Century.* Washington D.C., Dumbarton Oaks Research Library, 1997. See also Mark Francis & R. T. Hester (eds.). *The Meaning of Gardens.* Cambridge, MIT Press, 1995. Gardeners are subjects of historical-fiction, for example Frederic Richaud. *Monsieur le jardinière.* 1999 (translated by Barbara Bray as *Gardener to the King.* London, Haverill Press, 2000).
Mimi Sheller. *Democracy After Slavery: black publics and peasant radicalism in Haiti and Jamaica.* London, Macmillan, 2000, p. 24. See also Chapter 1 'The decline of planter control in Haiti and Jamaica'.
4 The social complexity of this transition in Britain alone can be seen in the composition of an 1804 meeting in a London bookshop that led to the establishment of the Royal Horticultural Society. A wealthy industrialist, the President of the Royal Society, and two 'royal gardeners' met with three 'nurserymen, amateur botanists and gardeners'. See Brent Elliot. *Treasures of the Royal Horticultural Society.* London, The Herbert Press, 1994. Gardens and plants cut through an established hierarchical system. In these networks were women active in botany, gardening, and botanical illustration, and there was constant exchange of plants across social boundaries.
5 See Donald McCracken. *Gardens of Empire: botanical institutions in the Victorian British empire.* London, Leicester University Press, 1997; also John Prest. *The Botanic Garden and the re-construction of paradise.* New Haven, Yale University Press, 1981.
6 Alan Cobley, (ed.). *Cross-roads of Empire: The European-Caribbean Connection, 1492–1992.* Bridgetown, University of the West Indies, 1994.
7 This paragraph relies on the sweeping review of primary and secondary evidence in Andrew O'Shaughnessy. *An Empire Divided: the American Revolution and the British Caribbean.* Philadelphia, University of Pennsylvania Press, 2000. Cf Chapter 1 'British Sojouners'. See also Alison Games. *Migration and the Origins of the English Atlantic World.* Cambridge Mass, Harvard University Press, 1999; Kenneth

Morgan. *Slavery, Atlantic Trade and the British Economy, 1660–1800.* Cambridge University Press, 2000.

8   James E. McClellan III. *Colonialism and Science: Saint Domingue in the Old Regime.* Baltimore, Johns Hopkins University Press, 1992. pp. 117–180.

9   For example, see Tod Stuessy and Mikio Ono. *Evolution and Speciation of Island Plants.* Cambridge University Press, 1998.

10 About the adventurers known as the 'Banksian empire' see David P. Miller and Peter H. Reill. *Visions of Empire: voyages, botany, and representations of nature.* Cambridge University Press, 1996. For a detailed account of Banks himself see. J. P. D. Gascoigne. *Science in the Service of Empire: Joseph Banks, the British State, and the Uses of Science in the Age of Revolution.* Cambridge University Press, 1998. The best recent comparison of botanical gardens across the world in the 17th, 18th and 19th centuries is Richard Drayton *Nature's Government: Science, Imperial Britain, and the 'Improvement' of the World* New Haven, Yale University Press, 2000.

11 Henry Powell. Distribution of economic plants in the island of St. Vincent after the hurricane of September 1898. *West Indies Bulletin,* Vol III, 1902. pp. 285–289.

12 W. N. Sands. An account of the return of vegetation and the revival of agriculture, in the area devastated by the Soufrière of St. Vincent in 1902–3. *West Indies Bulletin,* Vol XII. pp. 22–33.

13 Austin H. Clarke. The Birds of St. Vincent. *West Indies Bulletin,* 1905 Vol V. pp. 81–82.

14 W. R. Ruttenshaw. Distribution of economic plants by the Botanic Stations in the West Indies. *West Indies Bulletin,* Vol VII. pp. 374–386. I am grateful to Richard Grove for guiding me to the Bulletin's location in the Library at the University of Cambridge.

2 'To have a Garden is to be a Man': Caribs and the Transformation of Landscape

Lennox Honychurch

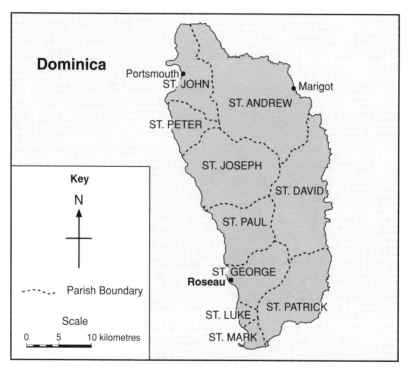

Map of Dominica

As European colonization of the Lesser Antilles advanced during the seventeenth century, the last of the indigenous people of the Caribbean retreated to the rugged volcanic islands of Dominica and St. Vincent. The Caribs of these two islands held on to marginal lands on the rugged northeast coasts and, especially in the case of the Dominica Caribs, maintained a fund of ecological knowledge handed down from past generations. Like the Caribs of these islands, the native peoples of tropical America have utilized rain forest 'webs' of relationship for several millennia and the culture of the people is deeply interwoven with the land. Groups inhabiting the rain forest utilize this most complex of ecosystems in slightly different ways.

When the precursors and ancestors of the Caribs departed the flat coastal fringe of the Guianas and delta region of the Orinoco, and entered the volcanic island chain of the Lesser Antilles, they reconfigured their web of relationships with the land to exploit and explain the new oceanic and volcanic landscape of islands. In comparison to the mainland, the island rain forests sheltered a much smaller variety of floral and faunal species, while there was an increased diversity of marine life associated with the coral reefs and volcanic shores of this chain of islands. This stimulated new associations with the land and what it provided. It demanded new patterns of settlement, new ways of explaining their place in the world. Every web may be conceptualized as a specific mode of production situated in historical and evolutionary space. It is through this web operating in this given space that humans socially interact in order to produce, circulate and consume things or images accorded with value.

Further adaptations to this web were made by the indigenous peoples of Dominica and St. Vincent after contact with Africans and Europeans. The process by which these cultures encountered each other and engaged in a process of exchange is called creolization. It comes from the Portuguese word *crioulo* and Spanish *criollo*, 'to domesticate, to be brought up, to create'. A Creole person or thing was born on, or was a product of, the islands. The word 'Creole' is now variously applied to the people, language and general way of life which emerged on these islands as a result of this contact and culture exchange. It was born of an uneasy, and usually unequal, relationship between different ethnic groups.

Among the small settlements on the rugged east coasts of the Windward Islands, things were somewhat different. The Caribs who remained on these islands had retreated to the periphery of the emergent plantation communities, isolating themselves in the most inaccessible corners of the islands. From Guadeloupe northwards, the high islands of the volcanic Caribbean give way to the flatter, dryer, well worn, Leeward Islands. The less mountainous topography of this group made total plantation development by European colonisers possible. No isolated zones had existed to act as places of refuge for indigenous people. Those indigenes who had reinhabited the Leeward Islands after the Spanish slaving raids retreated south once more into the mountainous Windwards in the earliest years of European colonisation. On Martinique, the Caribs moved to the northeast coast when the French arrived in 1635. On St. Lucia they retreated to the isolated southwest coast in the shadow of the towering cones of the Piton Mountains. Across the sea channel, they converged on the rugged the north coast of St.Vincent where the mixed descendants of the Caribs still live today. The pattern that emerges is one of a population which withdrew to the most isolated corners of the most isolated islands. Here they engaged in a cultural reconsolidation and the transference of skills to a new contact group.

Following initial colonization the topographical features of these volcanic islands came to provide boundaries of ethnicity and clearly defined zones of cultural and ethnic existence. The sheltered west coasts were quickly occupied by colonists and the central backbone of volcanic peaks provided a physical separation between the indigenous people on the East Coast and the colonial society on the West Coast. As colonization advanced, however, these topographical divisions were increasingly nibbled away by colonial encroachment. By analyzing the close links between the volcanic island landscape, the historical developments and the human ecology of the remnants of indigenous communities, it can be understood how these unique settlements emerged and survived.

A man and his 'garden'

Gabriel Valmond is standing on the main road in the village of Sineku at the southern end of the Carib Territory in Dominica and he is looking across the Madjini Valley. It is the end of the twentieth century. Five hundred years have elapsed since Christopher Columbus first sighted the island on November 3, 1493. In front of Gabriel are the intensely cultivated fields that belong to his extended family. His cousins, uncles, aunts, nieces and nephews all share this land and have built their two and three-roomed houses here and there upon it, each one surrounded by a 'yard' of cleared and swept red clay. Every yard is bordered by a variety of low bushes, each with its specific culinary and medicinal uses: 'bush teas' for refreshment or for various ailments, plants with leaves for seasoning food, others for washing hair or for taking baths which will either provide relief or will protect one from misfortune. Among the bushes are a few flowering plants, mainly crotons and canna lilies.

Beyond the yard is the family's agricultural land, planted according to the economic or subsistence requirements of nuclear groups within the extended Valmond family. An acre or two may be planted in bananas with the uniform precision which the Dominica Banana Marketing Corporation in Roseau demands: regulated spacing of 'mats' of banana plants each composed of not more than three 'suckers', limited intercropping, earth cleared of ground cover, plants kept upright with pegged string and young bunches of bananas shielded in blue plastic as they mature. Banana farming has enmeshed the Caribs into the tentacles of the world economy by involving them in an industry that at every stage of cultivation is controlled by a distant centre. This begins with the chemicals required for washing the first banana sucker before planting, the herbicides and insecticides sprayed in the field, the fertilizers used, the string and plastic which ensure an undamaged fruit and the plastic trays, cardboard cartons, stickers and staples required for packaging before shipment. Procurement of all of these 'inputs', and the cash income which is the overall objective of the exercise have, during the last thirty years, drawn the Carib farmer more closely into the world economy. Truillot has examined this in detail in a community elsewhere on Dominica and concludes that 'even though Dominican peasants control the labour process with which they are engaged, that process itself is embedded in a process of production that is controlled by transnational capital'.[1]

Although large areas of the Carib Reserve have been given over to bananas, cultivation of this cash crop operates in conjunction with other earlier forms of agriculture. Adjacent to the Valmond's banana fields are the intermixed subsistence plots interplanted in a manner completely opposite to the methods required for participation in the banana industry. The *jardin caräibe* is a closely planted combination of root crops, tubers, vines, greens and tree crops that was first observed in Dominica by European visitors in the sixteenth century. As colonization proceeded, introduced cultivars from the Pacific, Africa and Asia were appropriated from the plantation gardens and introduced into the *jardin caräibe*. Ober, visiting the Caribs in 1877, made a list of the main crops: 'These are, the Yam *(Dioscorea sativa and D. alata)*; the Sweet Potato *(Batatas edulis)*; the Cassava *(Jatropha manihot and J. janipha)*; Banana *(Musa paradisiaca)*; Plantain *(Musa sapientum)*, and Tannier *(Caladium sagittoefolium)*.'[2]

Manioc *(Manihot utilissma)* has been cultivated and processed in Dominica from the time of the earliest ceramic period, the Saladoid, c. 250 AD. The archaeological data collected on the mainland indicates a variety of adaptations related to the cultivation of manioc spreading throughout the Amazon Basin and Orinoco region from the end of the second millennium BC onward.[3] As for most of the indigenous people of the tropical forests and savannahs of South America, it was the main subsistence crop for the islanders. In Dominica today, three types of foodstuff are still processed from the manioc tubers: a coarse flour known locally as *farine*; a flat, round, firm bread called *kassav*; and, on festive occasions such as Christmas and religious feast days, a sweet, doughy delicacy called *canqui* is produced which is wrapped in little packets of heleconia leaves.

The British Administrator Hesketh Bell was critical of what he saw as the Caribs backwardness in growing 'no produce save the commonest vegetables and foodstuffs, and whenever I have impressed upon them the advisability of planting cocoa, limes and other profitable products, I have always been assured that the land in the Reserve was too arid to grow anything of the kind'.[4] Although intensively cultivated, the Reserve is by no means in an arid region, and it was probably the Caribs' reluctance to become sucked into the plantation economy by way of the 'profitable products' which Bell favoured, which was behind their rejection of his suggestion. Today, more than ever, the subsistence agriculture of the *jardin caräibe* provides an assurance of food supply and nutritional stability that the fluctuating cash income of the neo-plantation economy of the banana industry cannot.

There was a third 'back up' strategy in the agricultural system of the Caribs which has its origins in the earliest years of their occupation of the island and which Ober had observed during the nineteenth century:

> Though each family has a little garden adjacent to the dwelling, any individual can select an unoccupied piece of ground on the neighbouring hills, or mountainsides, for cultivation. All the provision grounds (as are called the mountain gardens where the staple fruits and vegetables are grown) at are a distance from the house, some even two miles away, solitary openings made in the depths of the high woods. As the soil in general is very thin, and does not support a crop for many successive years, these gardens are being constantly made afresh.[5]

Slash and burn agriculture is still practised in the forested hills which rise behind the Madjini Valley and Gabriel Valmond has a garden there, over an hour's walk from his house in Sineku. This is his own personal plot as opposed to that which is worked by himself and his family.

'When I was getting older, I could not just stay working with my father,' he said. 'I had to show that I was a man and that I could make my own garden.' This 'garden' is distinct from the family land, which is at a lower elevation surrounding the settlements. On these lower lands, one has a right to plant on any unoccupied plot within the zone of one's family land. The food crops which are produced from that plot are the property of the cultivator, but a previously planted, mature, permanent crop, such as a mango or breadfruit tree, situated on that same plot, can be harvested by a previous occupier and shared among the family. The '*jardin en bwa*', the garden in the bush, is more personal. As Gabriel explains, it does not come to you through being part of a family or a member of the Reserve. It is something that you have to work for from the beginning and maintaining it requires great stamina. 'You also have to know the land,' he says, 'the soil, the bush, the climate. You have to know it like you know your own body.' A garden is a personal creation, which one, literally, has to carve out of the forest, and in that way it gives you more status than your *'jardin en famille'*. In the first major clearing of the forest for the garden, the cultivator's status is tested by his ability to attract the cooperation of fellow villagers in participating in a *'coup de main'*, or the cooperative clearing of the land. To have a successful garden is a mark of both physical and social achievement as well as being proof of ecological knowledge. As Gabriel puts it, 'Everything about having a garden shows that you are a man.'

To be a member of the Carib Reserve gives one a distinct identity in relation to the people of the rest of Dominica, and to have a garden within that Reserve further defines status in relation to other members of the community, in the same way that being a canoe builder, basket weaver or cassava processor gives one distinction. This positioning in relation to others, whether through the occupation of land or the production of materials, is based on the acquisition and creative reproduction of natural resources which are tested against one's knowledge of, and affinity to, the land on which these activities take place and from which the resources are obtained. All modes of subsistence, no less than separate technical practices or tool-using behaviours, are necessarily embedded in particular webs of social and ecological relations that the process of colonialism has extended into novel configurations. The method of farming and the crops cultivated at Sineku indicate some of these appropriating strategies which have been active during the colonial era, determining ways in which land has been occupied and used from pre-columbian times. The making of charcoal, for instance, had never been a Carib practice. Surrounded by the forest, dry wood was simply collected when needed. It was the Creoles, the French yoeman farmers and African peasantry, who introduced this practice to Caribs that transformed wood fuel into something more easily stored and transported. In the Carib to Creole exchange, it was the Caribs who provided the Creoles with their baskets and dugout canoes.

Like many other Carib men whose lives and systems of production operate entirely within the physical and cultural confines of the Reserve, Gabriel Valmond engages in several other activities besides farming. He is one of the three leading canoe builders in Sineku, he is a canoe sailor and fisherman, he gathers shellfish along the precipitous coastline and he hunts *agouti* and *manicou* in the forest. His wife makes baskets from long strips of Larouman (*Ischnosiphon arouma*). The first reference of the plant in association with baskets was made by Breton.[6] He says that the

Carib name for it was *áticonê*, but that the French 'like the Carib women' called it *oüalloman* which is close to the present day word for the plant.

All of these activities take place in a variety of eco-niches ranging from waters just offshore to as far as the neighbouring French islands, and from the coastal zone to the mountain tops. Optimum achievement in all these areas is dependent upon a detailed knowledge of each environment and their relationship to one another. The farmer-fishermen-hunter-foragers such as Gabriel have, since childhood, acquired both the skills and tactics of procurement required in each zone based on a particular mental construct of the total environment. The Caribs are not alone in this, for the geographic location of the Carib/French Creole communities which developed between the large plantations along the east coast have also created specific linkages to the natural resources in the forested interior of the island and along its coastline. The local knowledge of the land from which their resources are obtained, and the ways in which these resources are used, is contained in a perception of their island habitat. This has come about as a result of earlier Carib knowledge of the landscape which has contributed to the Creolized world view.

This view extends to other islands. From the shores of Dominica one can look north and south to other volcanic peaks rising out of the Caribbean Sea along the arc of the Lesser Antilles. Since the earliest days of Amerindian settlement of the islands, different tribal groups travelled back and forth along the chain exploiting the many varied ecological niches on each island. Some were known as good sources of flint, others for crabs, manatees, conch, iguanas or particular types of ethnobotanical resources. To the north of precipitous Dominica there is reef-bound Marie Galante, then Guadeloupe where the chain of islands forks. One branch (the inner arc) extends onwards to Montserrat, Nevis, St. Kitts, St. Eustatius and Saba. The other branch, (the geologically older, outer arc), curves to Antigua, Barbuda, St. Barts, St. Martin and Anguilla. From Dominica, looking south one sees the volcanically active Windward Islands, first the dome of Mont Pélé on Martinique, followed by St. Lucia, St.Vincent and the Grenadines and then Grenada, the Amerindian cultural gateway that leads to the mainland and ecologically, to another world.

The carib/creole island view

The national motto emblazoned on the coat of arms of Dominica which replaced the colonial crest when the island obtained self-government from Britain in 1967 declares in Creole: '*Apres Bondie C'est La Ter*' (*Apwé bondyay se la té*): After God it is the Land. These words symbolize what remains for most Dominicans, the essential pattern of their lives, tied as they are to the strong Christian beliefs which underpin the popular philosophy of the entire population as well as to their dependence on the natural resources of the island. Despite a rise in business sector commerce and public service employment in the urban areas of the west coast during the latter half of the twentieth century, every islander is ultimately reliant on the viability of agricultural production, both for basic subsistence of their families and for cash income with which to purchase imported food and consumer goods. In turn, due to the activities of these largely small-holder cultivators, agricultural exports provide eighty percent of Dominica's foreign exchange for the national economy. But the associations of the word *la té* are not linked solely to agriculture and the tilling and harvesting of the produce of the soil. It extends to a holistic representation of the island itself and all it provides including the water of the rivers and the bounty of the coastal zone and the surrounding sea.

The Creole words, used to describe *la té* and its component parts, reflect associations with the island in terms of the main activities of the population and the zones of cultivation, hunting, gathering and fishing. *La té* varies in meaning from the word 'land' to a range of other connotations when used in specific contexts and conveys meanings indicating: this island, my property, soil, the planet earth, and natural resources.

The island, *la té nou*, from open sea to mountain top, is divided into several zones. The coastal zone is *bord la mé* and this extends to rocks, islets and reefs where line fishing and shellfish gathering are associated with activities not requiring a boat or raft. The open sea, from *bord la mé* to beyond the horizon is known as *en canal*. The word applies not only to the sea channels which separate Dominica from the French islands of Guadeloupe in the north and Martinique in the south, but also refers to the ocean extending for hundreds of miles to the east and west. *La canal* is what extends their islanded zone to neighbours on islands within sight of their own settlements and to the horizon as far as the eye can see. Beyond that is the wider world.

Social bonds had existed from Pre-columbian times between the Amerindian societies across these channels. Their mariners had plied the sea routes between settlements in their dugout canoes for over two thousand years. The people on the north coast of St. Vincent, for instance, were in closer contact with their cross-channel neighbours in the south of St. Lucia than they were with people in the south of St. Vincent. In those days, the sea united and the land divided. The survival of both the craft and the routes of interaction were maintained after the European encounter in the face of colonial intervention. In the face of this historically and geographically determined configuration of space, the Creole-speaking peasantries within these villages have followed earlier Carib patterns of cross-channel relationships. In more than a century and a half since emancipation, they have been negotiating their own tactics of survival, independent of the successive governments which purported to administer their affairs.

That these arbitrary partitions should be unofficially ignored, confirms Mintz' view of Caribbean peasantries and the cultural patterns they recreated, developed or renewed over time as 'one of the most vibrant signs of resistance on the part of Caribbean peoples against a system imposed from outside and dominated by the capitalist plantation'.[7] Since Mintz' first assessment in the 1950s, 'the capitalist plantation' has been reconstituted in the form of transnational market forces and trading blocks with these fishermen-farmers on the lowest rung. With Creole as a mutually intelligible trading language, the cross-channel bonds are maintained by Carib and Creole fishermen-traders who convey hucksters, drug pushers and job seekers in their open boats across 'official' national boundaries which are percieved as being within their Creole world.

This has been one of the major influences which Carib seafaring has had on the Creole 'sea view'. As with the Caribs, the intervening sea channels became continuous territory that still transcends the physical and legislative confines of land form and nation state. It is the all-encompassing geocultural space of their wider Creole world. By keeping their options open and devising an alternative order to that imposed by the official lines of boundary and language, they have been able to circumvent the system to their economic benefit. Here, the forces of physical geography and cultural ecology have proved to be more powerful than the imposition of political boundaries so that wherever the formal survey points may lie along the watery boundary between France and Dominica, the continuous movement of these people along this well-worn maritime route will probably continue to survive and serve their changing needs as it has done for the last seven millennia. Such a 'sea view' provides evidence of cultural, social, and economic strategies among the Amerindians which in various and reconstituted ways have been maintained to the present day.

From sea to mountain

All the main fifty-four settlements on Dominica are located along the *bord la mer* or within a kilometre of the sea. Behind these coastal villages, in a band of cultivated land which runs roughly around the island four to five kilometres from the coast, is the area referred to by villagers as *au jardin*. Here are their 'gardens' and small farms. Every morning and evening these cultivators leave their coastal communities and travel to and from their gardens, either on foot or by pick-up truck, along tracks or the feeder roads built during the banana boom years of the 1960s and 1970s. The ten small inland villages which exist in the interior are located in this zone and were established along the three main roads, once tracks, which cut across the island.

Beyond *au jardins*, along the head waters of the ravines and river valleys and along the higher ridges which span out from the central peaks, is the *bwa* and the *grand bwa*. The *bwa* is 'the bush', the lower level forest, some of which may be secondary growth. The *grand bwa* are the high woods, the tropical rain forest zone. The mountainous volcanic massif which forms a ridge along the backbone of the island and lies beyond and above the rain forests of the *bwa* and *grand bwa*, is *au morne*, a word Creolized from both the Spanish *morro* and the French *mont*. The Creole division of the island landscape therefore extends from the horizon to the mountain top in six zones each of which are progressively at higher altitude than the other: *en canal, bord la mer, au jardins, bwa, grand bwa* and *au morne*. It follows therefore that in the Creole language, anything or anyone who is inland of where the speaker is standing, is described as being 'en haut' or 'above' as in: 'ou e kai mouché John?' (Where is Mr. John's house?). ' E en haut la' (It is above there). Alternatively it could be towards the sea, in which case it would be 'En ba la' (below there).

Each zone is recognized for the particular natural resources which it provides and the activities which take place within them, be it fishing, gathering, farming or hunting. The range of resources gathered is wide: wild fruit (or the fruit of domesticated plants which have been abandoned by their owners such as mangoes or breadfruit), medicinal plants, particular species of timber, roots and reeds for basket making, grasses and leaves for thatching and weaving, and gum such as that of the gommier *dacreyodes excelsa,* for canoe making or to be used as incense during religious festivals. Particular fish, crustacea and game are also associated with each zone, so that the geographical, botanical and zoological components of the island world are all carefully defined in association with each other and in relation to the human activities within that natural world.

The Creole names given for particular resource areas, which are in official use as place names today, indicate ecological niches important to the first islanders, the knowledge of which was transmitted by them to the later arrivals. Some plant resources associated with place names are:

Fruit and tubers: Ziquac, Fond Calabass, Pointe Coco, Cassada Garden, D'leau Manioc.
Timber: Bwa Diable, Bwa Cotlette, Bwa Blanc, Mahaut, Savanne Mahaut, Morne Acouma, Bwa Serpe, Big Cedar, Grand Bambou, Balata, Gommier, Chatagnier D'Leau.
Thatch and fibre: Crete Balizier, Savanne Paille, Palmiste, Cocoyer.

These places associated with botanical resources are interspersed with those related to zoological niches where wildlife is or was hunted or collected, and where eggs were gathered:

> Pointe Jacko, Morne au Fregates, Riviere Cyrique, L'Anse Tortue, L'Anse Soldat, Trou Cochon, Pointe Crab, Riviere Manicou, Fond Agouti.

These names are applied to headlands, mountains, rivers and beaches where there were, or still are, a preponderance of parrots, frigate bird rookeries, freshwater crabs, sea turtle nesting areas, soldier crabs (used for bait), wild pigs (introduced after European contact), land crabs, the *manicou* opossum and *agouti*. The place names noted above are officially registered by virtue of being included on the published maps of the island, but several more are utilized in the oral tradition of settlements all over the island so that zones around each community possess a detailed oral geography related to micro-niches of natural resources commonly used by the people of that particular village and used only by them.

The scientific view

This Carib/Creole view of the natural environment was only augmented by the Western geobotanical classification in 1937 when the first scientific fieldwork was begun by Hodge. The eventual publication of his *Flora of Dominica* (1954) along with John Beard's regional perspective, *The Natural Vegetation of the Windward and Leeward Islands* (1949) set forth a systematic description of five types of plant community around the island: swamp forest, dry evergreen, seasonal, rain forest and montane. Hodge and Beard established a diagrammatical concept of the five main altitudinal variations of vegetation zones which reflected, and in scientific terms confirmed, the local knowledge. Botanists have subdivided the island's coastal zone into two, accounted for by the distinct micro-climates on the windward as opposed to the leeward coasts:

Windward littoral woodland: Along the east coast of the island there runs a belt of thick shrubby vegetation swept back by the wind and made up of plants which can thrive in the salt-laden sea blast.

The dry scrub woodland: The western coastal zone is the driest part of the island because the rain-laden clouds which blow across the island from the east have lost most of their moisture by the time they reach this coast which is therefore in what is called a rain shadow area. The plants here are hardy scrub, often with prickles and in some areas interspersed with cacti.

The swamp forest: Because Dominica rises so sharply from the ocean, the island has no extensive areas of mangrove swamp as in

Guadeloupe or Martinique, but it does have areas of swamp forest along the estuaries of some streams on the northwest and northeast coast. It was this lack of mangroves as well as reefs which, erroneously I believe, led the archaeologist Clifford Evans (1968) to conclude that Dominica was not an ecologicaly favourable place for Pre-columbian populations.

The deciduous forest: Moving from the coastline we enter the semi-evergreen deciduous forest. This level is also the most heavily cultivated and is the area generally referred to by Creoles as Au Jardin because this is where most of the farms or 'gardens' are located.

The tropical rain forest: the most luxuriant and extensive of all the forest formations on Dominica is the tall broad-leafed evergreen rain forest generally found at altitudes between 300 and 900 metres. Because of the rate of deforestation elsewhere it remains one of the last oceanic or island-based rain forests in the Americas. This zone was the main ethnobotanical emporium of the Carib, the traditional location of plant products used for food, drink, shelter, adornment, medicines and charms. The central forest reserve still maintains stands of forest such as was described in 1493 on neighbouring Guadeloupe by Columbus' crew where 'the trees were so thick they could not see the sky'.[8] In the middle of this century, W. Hodge could still write:

> Of her vegetation and flora Dominica can truly boast, for of all the Caribbees hers is one of the richest, the least despoiled, and perhaps the closest to its original natural state. This tiny island of perhaps 300 square miles has more forested land than any other island of the Lesser Antilles, Trinidad excepted.[9]

The cloud forest: Llying beyond the rain forest, it comprises the montane forest and the elfin woodland. Here the tall rain forest trees give way to shorter, thinner vegetation. It is a misty, windy, dripping world where tree trunks and branches are draped in moss and ferns cover the forest floor. In the elfin woodland at the tops of the highest mountain peaks, vegetation is very stunted and consists mostly of hardy twisted trees, mosses and bromeliads.

Compartmentalized as Hodges' and Beard's particular sciences was in the specific discipline of botany, their studies did not represent or incorporate the more holistic ecological perspective of the island which was present in the Carib and Creole view of their natural world as seen in relation to the activities and material needs. This was knowledge which had been acquired over generations from the island's earliest inhabitants. For the Dominican villager, the knowledge of, and interaction with, the landscape was an integral part of the culture as a whole.

However, in his communication with people throughout the island during his years of fieldwork, and his dependence on them for the local classification of plants, Hodge became aware of this ethnobotanic rupture between western scientific botany and the island culture. His growing awareness of the cultural links contained in his informants' constant references to the relative values, capabilities, and associations of thousands of species, either individually or in conjunction with each other, or in relation to certain animals, or in regard to the particular needs or practices of human beings, made him realize that there was a need to incorporate this culturally-inclusive perspective of the vegetation with the purely botanical.

To achieve this, he teamed up in 1945 with the British linguist and anthropologist Douglas Taylor, who had by then been resident on the island for some fifteen years. This was a most fruitful collaboration between two authorities in their respective fields who combined the skills of their two disciplines with the aim 'to provide accurate botanical and ethnological information about species gathered or cultivated by the Caribs of Dominica not only today but also (as far as possible) in the past'.[10] Historical notes, forty illustrations, indexes to scientific, Creole, and Island Carib names of plants, complete a full description of the plants' uses. Here, after over four centuries of colonization was an attempt to sympathetically interpret the Carib perspective of their island world.

'A place without history'

The European interpretation of the green volcanic mass, which confronted them on first sighting it in 1493, varied considerably in relation to the changing circumstances of exploration, colonization, economic exploitation, and security considerations which motivated their objectification of the island over the centuries.

> For although we are accustomed to separate nature and human perception into two realms, they are in fact, indivisible. Before it can ever be a repose for the senses, landscape is the work of the mind. [11]

Its scenery is built up as much from strata of acculturated memory as from layers of rock or vegetational zones. The same enduring physical elements of Dominica's topography and vegetation received a wide range of interpretations over time and these were often linked to prevailing attitudes towards those 'others' who, at one time or another, lived within that forested wilderness. The place that was perceived as wild was consequentially occupied by 'wild' people, be they 'savage Caribs' resisting the advance of European settlement, 'wretched maroons' escaping plantation slavery, or

Rastafarian 'Dreads' rejecting the post-independence neo-colonialism of the new black elite. The wild forest was for wild people. At the same time the existence of human culture within that forest has been largely denied or at least disregarded. Even in a major recent study of the island by a Caribbean academic, which describes itself as 'the first scholarly study to deal with the entire Dominican nation, past and present', the forested interior is a place without history.[12]

> Historical Dominica is but a narrow belt, at times scarcely a mile wide, which almost encircles the island, but is broken at points, especially on the eastern side, by the steepness of the mountains...Probably fewer than 50 square miles of Dominican territory had ever been systematically used by humans for agriculture, habitation, or transport before the 1910s .[13]

For the non-agricultural, urban people of the west coast, the forest is to their back, or at least 'behind God's back': *derrier doe bondyay* is the Creole phrase. Anyone who inhabited the *grand bwa* or simply made their living there was, and today still is, considered to be *jen bwa*, bush people. Similarly, if the forest is a place without history simply because marks of human activity are not readily apparent, then the people who inhabited it and interacted with it are likewise cast as 'a people without history'. This is because they, and the biodegradable material culture which they produced from the forest resources and which they utilized for their existence, have been recycled within the tropical rain forest ecosystem and are indiscernible.

Although history may depend on material evidence, either textual or three dimensional, for its academic validity, it is obvious that when these clues are not present, or are not 'in evidence', this does not mean that history has not taken place. It is rather the rules or parametres of the *discipline* of history which determines whether it is possible to accept or deny that history has happened in such natural areas. The coast then, from this perspective, was where things happened. The shore looked outward to the world and it received the world that existed beyond Dominica. Taken on these terms, the coast had culture and history, but the interior did not. The texts, matching humans to their states in nature, made little or no mention of 'bush people'. This was another reason why the Caribs in the mountains and on the 'wild' east coast of Dominica, have eluded the historian.

Similarly, it seems, this is also the case in archaeology where, in the dispute over the Carib identification with Suazoid series as opposed to Cayo pottery, the prehistoric Carib remains somewhat of an enigma. Only when the Caribs interacted with the people who recorded history, who in every case have been Europeans, did they become characters in history. But even those literate and adventurous sailors who did chronicle their visits to the island, usually got no further than the coast, and thus provide us with literature which is essentially a record of the custom of the coast. Except for Fr. Raymond Breton, Fr. Jean Baptiste Labat, and an anonymous 'Filibustre Francaise' who recorded his sojourn among the Caribs of Guadeloupe, our historical informants only ever made contact with the Caribs either on the shoreline of the island or out on the open sea.[14] One English visitor to Dominica in 1598 was at least perceptive enough to conceive of the possibility of life beyond the coastal fringe, in a zone to which he had been denied access:

> So Mountainous (certaine in the places where we came neere the Sea-coasts) that the Vallies may better be called Pits then Plaines, and withall so unpassably woodie, that it is marvailous how those naked souls can be able to pull themselves through them, without renting their naturall cloathes. Some speak of some more easy passages in the Inland of the Iland, which make it probable that they leave those skirts and edges of their Countrie thus of purpose for a wall of defence. [15]

But even in those times, Dominica was not the wilderness that the early European colonizers had made it out to be. The Amerindian immigrants into the Caribbean had transported numerous continental plants into the islands, most significantly cassava (*Manihot esculenta*), which were important for their subsistence. Game animals such as the agouti (*Dasyprocta aguti*) were also introduced in this manner.[16] As Riviére has pointed out on the mainland, 'The evidence increasingly indicates that far from being pawns of an intractable environment, native peoples have, or at least had, sophisticated techniques, of which social organization is one, for managing floral and faunal resources'.[17] During historic times, the Antillian landscape was even more radically transformed by the introduction of new species of flora and fauna, the origins of which matched the diversity of its human immigrants. The impact of such a transformation precipitated significant changes in social activity and technological innovation among the indigenous population. Within a generation they had to come to terms with an environment to which access had suddenly become restricted or which in many areas had become unfamiliar to them. Alfred Crosby's concept of ecological imperialism is applicable in this zone where the Iberian conquest and all that followed it created enormous areas of disturbed ground:

> Forests were raised for timber and fuel and to make way for new enterprises; burgeoning herds of Old World animals grazed and overgrazed the grasslands and invaded the woodlands; and the cultivated fields of the declining Amerindian

populations reverted to nature, a nature whose most aggressive plants were now exotic immigrants. [18]

After the arrival of Europeans, and in the course of social contact with the enslaved population imported from West Africa, a transfer of ecological knowledge took place between the remaining Caribs and the newly emergent Creoles. While Pere Labat was visiting Dominica in 1700 he met a Frenchman living among the Caribs 'who knew their language and customs as intimately as a Carib would himself'. Labat did what he could to make him give up 'this savage way of living', but without success.[19] It was in Carib/French liaisons such as these that the exchange was most profound. The French in these islands appeared to be more accommodating to the culture of others. In terms of food, medicinal herbs, the allocation of place names, the knowledge of the respective values of forest woods and in the loan of words from the Carib language, the exchange between the French and the Caribs seems to have been more congenial. This exchange of cultural patterns ultimately led to a new cultural form on the islands. This new culture, created on the islands during the process of colonization, is what we call 'Creole'.

Wherever the Carib cultural presence lingers among their racially mixed descendants today, the villagers of those regions are regarded as the inheritors of traditional Carib skills. They are considered to be island experts in the Carib aspects of 'folk culture'. Here survive the greatest fund of ethnobotanical knowledge, the growers and processors of cassava manioc, the basket-makers and the builders of dugout canoes. Knowledge of the island environment, both terrestrial and maritime is strongest in these localities. Historical geography has had as much to do with the concentration of specific cultural traits in these peripheral areas, as did the social history of ethnic contact. Here the Island Caribs engaged in cultural reconsolidation and transference of skills to a new contact group. Carib place names still appear on the maps of Dominica and St. Vincent and less so on St. Lucia and Martinique. These words provide linguistic proof of the strength and location of the Carib presence at the time of the European and African arrival and their role in introducing these immigrants to the natural phenomena of a new environment. Their centres of settlement became the nuclei for this transfer, and the districts where these influences were strongest maintained links both with the forests behind them and with the districts which mirrored them across the sea channels.

The division of land: the 'legal' view

The Treaty of Paris, agreed to by Britain and France in 1763 at the end of the Seven Years' War, ceded to Britain the formerly French island of Grenada as well as the 'Neutral Islands' of Dominica, St. Vincent and

Tobago. Dominica and St.Vincent were considered to be the last Carib islands, and had been described as 'neutral' by virtue of the terms of the Treaty of Aix-La-Chapelle of 1748. But, even while that treaty was being signed, the islands had already been significantly settled by Europeans of various nationalities. In Dominica these were mostly French small holders who were willing to take their chances among the Caribs, as well as to risk the loss of property rights amidst the fluctuating claims and counter claims being made by the home governments of the emergent powers of France and Britain on the islands of the Lesser Antilles. The British conquest of Dominica introduced methods of landholding rooted in British law which established a 'legal' framework of property rights on Dominica as existed in eighteenth-century Britain.

At that time land settlement on Dominica had been clearly divided by the central range of mountains. The French 'petit blanc' settlers, cultivating small farms of tobacco, cassava, and provisions for sale to the plantations on Martinique and Guadeloupe, were spread out along the sheltered Leeward Coast. The Caribs had retreated to the east, along the Windward Coast. I have defined the position of the French settlements just prior to British occupation in 1763, by documenting the lands leased by the British to the French and referring these lists to the lots on the British map of land sales.[20]

When Britain took over the islands of Dominica and St. Vincent, one of the main tasks which occupied attention was the redistribution, sale, and setting aside of land. As in St. Vincent, a team of commissioners and surveyors was raised to organise the division of Dominica into lots and administer the sale of these lands in the name of the Crown. They were directed to sell the land by public auction to British subjects; an individual could not buy more than 40.5 hectares (100 acres) if the land had been cleared or 121 hectares (300 acres) if the land was forested. The initial task that occupied them was the surveying, sale, distribution and allocation of land on the island. The Chief Surveyor was John Byres and the map which he and team produced laid the guidelines, coastal demarcation and boundaries of all properties on the island until the aerial photographs of 1956 and the first accurate British DOS map was published two hundred years later in 1964.

The large 'Byres Map' measuring four feet by six feet and produced on three sheets, divided the island into ten parishes and subdivided each parish into numerous lots no larger than 121 hectares (300 acres) in size. This large master-map gives the numbers of lots and the areas that were divided. These sections covered most of Dominica except for the extremely mountainous areas in the centre of the island. Even so, very little regard was given to the lay of the land and many of the lots were on the sides of precipitous slopes and deep valleys. Most were almost impossible to get to on foot, let alone establish estates and transport goods and the majority of these lots are still inaccessible today. To accompany his map of the island published in 1776, Chief surveyor John Byres compiled a list of all the properties on the island. The list, complete with alphabetical index, shows the acreage of each lot with its original or present purchaser or lessee for each parish.[21]

The frantic sales were fueled by the high market values of sugar and coffee at that period of the eighteenth century. A new mercantile elite was emerging in Britain, and together with the old monied British landholding class, they were swept up in a buying spree which coincided with the climax period for West Indian sugar fortunes in the eighteenth century. The treaty had added 1,828 square km (706 square miles) to the British Empire. It was the first sale of new British lands in over a hundred years. 'Since our conquest of Jamaica from the Spaniards, in the days of Oliver Cromwell, down to present times, there has been no such opportunity of improving private fortunes,' rejoiced the commissioner of lands.[22] The earlier plantations had created what Pares calls the 'golden age' of West Indian sugar. The British settlement of Dominica was a major part of the second wave of British colonization in the Caribbean during the 'silver age'.[23]

Auctions were held in the ceded islands, but agents were bidding for land of which their absentee proprietors in Britain knew nothing. To achieve optimum sales, the lots covered most of the island. Only the most impossibly precipitous parts of the mountainous volcanic massifs in the centre of the island had been excluded from subdivision. Although it was relatively accurate in outline, the map sketched in only five or six taller peaks and gave no clue of what the rest of the island was like. The layout shows that after an initial attempt at surveying the French-held lands on the coastal zone as accurately as was then possible, the team resigned themselves to cutting the interior into squares and oblongs. This was terrain that they had never traversed, much of which was quite obviously totally unsuitable for settlement and much of what was sold was never cultivated.

The French settlers already on the island had to pay an annual rent on every acre they owned and were not allowed to sell or dispose of the leases on these lands without the permission of the Governor. The commissioners were also empowered to make grants of land of up to 12 hectares (30 acres) to certain British subjects classed as 'poor settlers'. The surveyors also outlined a strip of land three chains wide along the entire coast of the island. This was known as the 'Kings Three Chains' or 'Kings Fifty Paces' because it was set aside for the government to construct any necessary building or fortifications. In all this activity the Caribs were virtually ignored and only a 54-hectare (134-acre) plot was set aside for them in the centre of what is now the Carib Territory. The sale of Dominica raised a total of £313,666, which went to the British Crown.

Plantations and peasantries

There are a number of geological and historical reasons why the Carib Reserve is where it is today, but the final determining factor which entrenched the Caribs in that location was the conquest and formal colonization of Dominica by the British and the sale of lands after 1763. When British land purchasers began to take physical possession of their newly acquired properties, the unforeseen discrepancies between the topography and Byre's survey immediately became patently obvious to many of them. As a result, the land use pattern of the new colony quickly fell into four categories: The first category was composed of the prime plantation lands which had been quickly grabbed and occupied by survey officials and members of the governing elite already on the island. These estates occupied the larger river valleys where water for powering the mills was abundant. The land was not steep along the valley floors, and there were bays providing access to shipping. This was the easiest land to cultivate and the most efficient for sugar production.

The second category of plantation property lay further inland on steeper slopes adjacent to the large river valley plantations and was more difficult to access. These estates in the rain-drenched hills usually grew coffee.[24] The third category was found to be totally unsuitable for profitable large-scale production of either sugar or coffee. Such lands were in the inaccessible interior and in many cases have lain uncultivated up to the present day. The fourth category was situated in the coastal zone, on precipitous cliff-bound terrain between the river valley plantations. These lands alternated with the large river valleys all along the east coast. The few Europeans who occupied such properties were reduced to being yeoman farmers conducting small-scale operations and only able to afford a few slaves. Official accounts of property holding during the slavery period reveal a marked contrast between small holders with two or five slaves and the large valley properties with an average of 200 enslaved labourers.

The 'petit blanc' French settlers who were being edged out by the consolidation of British proprietors on the west coast, moved east to take up lands abandoned or available for sale by disillusioned British purchasers. They were joined by a constant trickle of small holders from northern Martinique during the latter half of the eighteenth century. In some cases the Caribs had 'sold' their land to those Frenchmen who had arrived prior to British conquest.[25] Informants in some of these villages indicated to me parts of their district where Caribs are known to have lived in the past and there is a tradition in all of these villages that their French ancestors mixed with the Caribs who they found living there.

The demographic map that emerged along the east coast during this period, therefore, is one clearly defined on racial lines demarcated by landscape. The large valley plantations contained hundreds of black slaves who vastly outnumbered the small core of white managers and overseers. Because of their concern about this racial imbalance, the land commissioners had stipulated that plantations must maintain one white man, or two white women, on every hundred acres of cleared land under threat of being fined. But it was a regulation never effectively policed despite the governor's defence of it on the grounds that 'the want of (white) people in our West India islands, arises in a great measure from the paucity of women'.[26]

In contrast, the rugged intervening holdings were populated by a largely white French yeomanry and their increasingly mulatto offspring. Today, these villages in the east and the extreme north are still recognized and referred to as the 'light skinned villages' of Dominica. Their inhabitants will tend to make primary reference to their French ancestry, although at the same time recognizing their Carib and African antecedents as well. Landholding for the black peasantry developed much later, but even during slavery they had begun to establish themselves as a proto-peasantry upon marginal land on the edge of the plantation which they were allowed to cultivate on certain days a week. As this black peasantry strengthened, their infiltration into the Carib/French Creole zone became more marked and began to take on its increasingly mixed late twentieth-century form.

Family land

Another feature which is dominant in the older peasant zones is the communal possession of land by entire families; a system known locally as 'family land'. Family landholding is the second largest form of land tenure on Dominica. The main land tenures according to the 1995 agricultural census were freehold ownership with 13,760 hectares (34,000 acres or 65 percent) and family land with 2,307 hectares (5,700 acres or 11 percent) of the total land under farms.[27] What the census lists as 'communal land' is in fact the Carib Reserve, which has 1,174 hectares (2,900 acres) under farms or approximately 6 percent of the island's total. With the total Reserve area estimated at 1,497 hectares (3,700 acres), this shows how intensively cultivated this land has become. When one adds the Creole family lands to the Carib family lands encompassed by the Reserve, the total amount family land accounted for on the island as a whole is 3,480 hectares (8,600 acres or 16.5 percent).

Family landholding developed in response to a number of economic, social, and ecological factors. It exists mainly in those old peasant communities hemmed in by the sea on one side, the mountains on the other and with large estates to the north and south. These physical constraints limited the means by which succeeding generations could expand their areas of landholding during the colonial period even if it had been economically feasable for them to do so. Large estates resisted selling off portions of land until the late twentieth century, and even if they had been prepared to sell, smallholder incomes from marketable cash crops were too low to achieve this. Any large capital investment into land procurement by the peasantry only began with the advent of the banana industry. Family land ensured food security for all family members who, for the most part, were entirely dependent on subsistence agriculture. It also gave security of tenure to family members who emigrated from the island or sought work elsewhere, who departed confident in the knowledge that their rights to land remained on their return. Those who stayed worked their plots communally. This was due both to the absence of capital with which to employ labour, and a pool of manpower from which to obtain it. The maintenance of undivided parcels of land for use by members of the whole extended family was therefore of particular advantage in those closely knit communities where everyone was dependent on each other's labour, and opportunities for the physical expansion of independent landholding was restricted. According to most accounts I came across in the villages, this land had been left by a long dead patriarch 'pour mes enfants, et ses enfants, pour tout les generations'. Lowenthal sees one of the main values of such inheritance as being social or psychic, according descendants a feeling of rightful place in the family lineage. '"Family Land" in the West Indies today,' he says, 'as in medieval England, seldom sustains a livelihood; it is a locus of communal comfort whose fruits all kinsfolk are entitled to harvest, a potential refuge for any descendant.'[28]

For the Caribs, such a system was an evolution of the communal patterns of cultivation and food production that had been witnessed and recorded by the French ethnographers during the two centuries following the first encounter.[29] The emphasis in these earlier times, however, had been on the communality of use of land, rather than permanent possession or even occupation of it, for sites of cultivation and even habitation were frequently shifted. Davies describes Caribs moving their entire settlements: 'as soon as they take the least disgust of their habitation, they immediately transplant themselves to another place, and this is done of a sudden'.[30] Breton gives an account of the chief, Henri Comte, and his community of some forty persons transferring their 'carbet' or village, from *Oyouhao* (Indian River) to *Coulihao* (Colihaut) in 1646.[31] With the restriction imposed by the division of land and colonial landholding, such

freedom to move was completely restricted. Consequently a more seden-
tary form of settlement emerged, influenced as well by the European
concept of land ownership through the physical possession of territory
substantiated by legislation. This was a novel concept introduced by colonialism which had been alien to the Carib cosmology.

Most of the small rugged niches along the east coast to which the
Caribs retreated were so small that they were eventually occupied by, and
shared with, French settlers. But the zone which now forms the Carib
Reserve occupies the largest section of land on the east coast which is not
traversed by a large river valley. This allowed the area a degree of isolation
during the plantation period that enabled the Caribs to maintain certain elements of their culture and ethnicity in a more marked manner than their
fellow Caribs who had remained elsewhere on the island. It was this isolation, and the ethnic and cultural 'survivals' which had been maintained
because of it, which attracted a protective anthropological interest among
ethnologists and administrators at the end of the nineteenth century and led
to the creation of the Carib Reserve.

The actions of the colonial administrator Hesketh Bell in establishing the Carib Reserve in 1903, had its genesis in the late Victorian
anthropological concept of 'survivals' and 'remnants' which itself was
founded on seventeenth-century ideas. Bell's dream of creating this
special community was based on his interpretation of historical and
anthropological texts which he combined with his position of political
authority. The Caribs, for their part, had appropriated the land for
themselves centuries before. Heavily outnumbered, increasingly mixed,
and still recovering from the paranoia of being a stigmatized ethnic
minority, the Caribs now use their material culture of basket work and
canoes as symbols of their distinctive identity. This is done in the face
of the disappearance of visible physical identifiers of their ethnicity.
This distinction is further marked by their place in the landscape, centred on the Carib Reserve, which gives them a unique association to the
island and a particular place within its history and human ecology.

Notes

1   Michel-Rolph Trouillot. *Peasants and Capital: Dominica and The World Economy.*
    John Hopkins Studies in Atlantic History and Culture. John Hopkins University
    Press, Baltimore, 1988. p. 287.
2   Frederick Ober. *Camps in the Caribbees: The adventures of a naturalist in the Lesser
    Antilles*, Lee & Shepard, Boston (also David Douglas, Edinburgh), 1880. p. 79.
3   Adélia Engrácia de Oliveira. The Evidence for the Nature of the Process of
    Indigenous Deculturation and Destabilization in the Brazilian Amazon in the Last
    Three Hundred Years, Preliminary Data. In A. Roosevelt (ed.). *Amazonian Indians
    from Prehistory to the present Anthropological Perspectives*, University of Arizona
    Press, Tuscon, 1994. pp. 95–122.

4 Sir Henry Hesketh Bell. *Report on the Caribs of Dominica*. HMSO. London. No. 35. 1902.

5 Frederick, Ober, **op**. cit., p. 79.

6 Raymond Breton. *La Dictionaire Caraibe-Francaise*. Gilles Bouquet, Auxerre, France, 1665. p. 244.

7 Michel-Rolph Trouillot. *The Caribbean Region: An Open Frontier in Anthropological Theory.* Annual Review of Anthropology, vol. 21, 1992. pp. 19–42.

8 Dr. Chanca. The Letter Written to the City of Seville [1494]. In *Christopher Columbus-The Four Voyages*, (Cohen J. M. ed.) Penguin, 1969. p. 136.

9 W. Hodge & D. Taylor. *The Ethnobotany of the Island Caribs of Dominica.* Webbia Instituto Botanico Dell' Universita, Firenze, Italia, 1957. p. 514.

10 Ibid., p. 518.

11 Simon Sharma. *Landscape and Memory,* Fontana Press, and imprint of Harper Collins, London, 1996. p. 6.

12 Michel-Rolph Trouillot. *Peasants and Capital: Dominca and the World Economy.* John Hopkins Studies in Atlantic History and Culture. John Hopkins University Press, Balitmore, 1988. p. xiii.

13 Ibid., p. 28.

14 Jean-Claire Moreau. *Un filibustre francais dans la mer des Antilles en 1618–1620.* Edition Jean Claire Mareau, Clamart, France, 1987.

15 Samuel Purchas. *Purchase his Pilgrims.* vol. XVI. James Maclehose, Glasgow, 1625.

16 David Watts. *The West Indies, Patterns of Development, Culture, and Environmental Cause since 1492.* Cambridge University Press, Cambridge, 1987. p. 77.

17 Peter Riviére. *The Amerindianization of Descent and Affinity.* L'Homme 126–128 Avr.-Dec. XXXIII (2–4),1993. pp. 507–516.

18 Alfred Crosby. *Ecological Imperialism.* Canto, Cambridge University Press, 1986. p. 151.

19 Jean-Baptiste Labat. *Memoirs of Pere Labat.* Frank Cass & Co. London, 1931. p. 95.

20 Public Records Office, London, CO:76/9 .

21 Public Records Office, London, CO:76/9.

22 Sir William Young. *Considerations which may tend to promote our new West Indian Colonies.* New Bond Street, London, 1764. p. 26.

23 Richard Pares. *War and Trade in the West Indies,* Oxford University Press, Oxford, 1936.

24 John Lowndes. *The Coffee Planter.* London, 1802.

25 Joseph Borome. *Spain and Dominica.* Government Printery Roseau, 1972.
    Richard Pares. *War and Trade in the West Indies.* Oxford University Press, Oxford, 1936. p. 196.

26 Sir William Young. *Considerations which may tend to promote our new West Indian Colonies.* New Bond Street, London, 1764. p. 3.

27 Ministry of Agriculture. *Report on the Agriculture of Domina.* Government Headquarters, Roseau, 1995. p. 41.

28 David Lowenthal. *Heritage Crusade and the Spoils of History.* Viking, London, 1996. p. 32.

29 Raymond Breton. *La Disctionaire Caraibe – Francause.* Gilles Bouquet, Auxerre, France, 1665. p. 282.
    John Davies. *The History of the Charriby Islands.* London, 1666. p. 295.

30 John Davies, *The History of the Charriby Islands.* London, 1666. p. 294.

31 Raymond Breton, *La Disctionaire Caraibe – Francause.* Gilles Bouquet, Auxerre, France, 1665. p. 346.

3 Environmental Institutions, Legislation and Environmental Change in Early Eastern Caribbean Settlements

David Watts

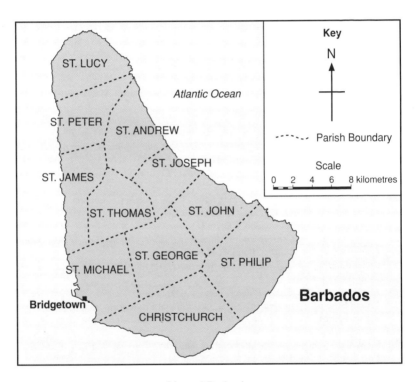

Map of Barbados

The pattern of environmental change in the earliest settlements of the eastern Caribbean islands was an extremely rapid one. Unlike the Hispanic ventures that had proceeded them elsewhere in the Caribbean, these settlements had no grand design other than the basic notion of founding economically self-sufficient, tropical crop-growing colonies, a concept which was almost entirely original at the time. They had virtually no official governmental backing for the most part, other than minimal lip service expressing support, at least until strong monarchs in the home countries (Charles II in England, Louis XIV in France) came to the throne in the 1660s. Most of the early funding for their development came from individual traders and merchants. The vast majority of the settlers had no previous experience of agriculture or even of sustained land clearance, and certainly not in tropical environments. Institutions of settlement – the system of land grants, indenture and indeed slavery – sometimes appear to have played a more dominant role in the islands' development than individuals. Yet often it was the latter – for example James Drax, William Hillard, and James Holdip, in the early days of Barbados; and Philippe de Poincy in St. Kitts – who set them off on new, rewarding tacks by introducing new capital, new crops, (e.g. cotton, sugar) and new techniques of cultivation and crop processing, thus establishing a trend which was to be repeated many times in years to come.

All these colonies were inherently exploitative of the environment, which was indirectly part of their role in the economic scheme of things, and scant attention, if any, was paid to preserving the quality of the land, except for brief periods and certain locations. Yet it was in these circumstances that the earliest legislation for environmental protection was conceived and brought to fruition, albeit only on a small scale to begin with. A continued struggle ensued between the need to preserve the quality of the environment, and the 'market-forces' exploitation of the day; and a subsidiary debate was one to determine what environmental legislation would be introduced, if any, and what measures for environmental protection and the maintenance of environmental quality might usefully be left to the conscience and good sense of individual entrepreneurs. The evolution of such environmental arguments, and the legislation engendered during the seventeenth and eighteenth centuries, is best displayed in Barbados, and it is evidence from this island that I wish to concentrate upon. However, there are traces of it in other Caribbean island settlements, both French and English, which are also worthy of mention.

The initial seeds of environmental legislation in Barbados date back to the period 1646–1665 when, effectively, the island changed from a fledgling economy of some commercial experimentation to one which became a full sugar monoculture, which set massive environmental changes in motion. Prior to 1645, most settlers struggled to make sense of their new locational situation, for almost nothing previously learnt in Europe was directly applicable to it. In the long term, all were forced for a while to use Indian techniques of agriculture (in the case of Barbados, from Indians imported from the South American mainland) and Indian lifestyles in order to survive, even though the Indians themselves were a group of people who were largely disdained. Indian land clearance methods such as ring-barking, were used to remove forest, and the adoption of Indian digging sticks as an agricultural method was accepted without question; neither disturbed the environment to any great extent to begin with. Indian foods became staples, and Indian alcoholic drinks, e.g. mobbie (from the sweet potato) often came to be preferred to those of settlers' homelands, which frequently in any case were unavailable, or spoilt upon arrival. Indian crops such as tobacco and cotton became the first export commodities. Slowly, however, the agricultural systems that evolved changed from simple methods of production to ones of greater sophistication. Thus, while tobacco cultivation needed little more than a small patch of new land, continued hoeing to keep down weeds, and subsequent harvesting; cotton, and later indigo, demanded much more in the way of careful preparation and processing. As the latter two crops began to be grown more widely in the 1630s and 1640s in response to European market wishes, and fetched high prices, so did the financial success of this main settlement become increasingly assured.

From 1645 to 1665, two politically uncertain decades, both in Britain (the Civil War) and in the island, the whole nature of the commercial enterprise in Barbados began to further change and evolve. Under the initiative of individual entrepreneurs such as James Drax and James Holdip and Dutch merchants based in Bridgetown, and with very little help from the home government in England, the transfer of an entire sugar-producing complex from Brazil was envisaged and effected. This transfer subsequently involved immense cultural, economic and social changes to the island, all of which were to have lasting repercussions not only in Barbados, but also eventually throughout most of the other West Indies. Some of the socio-cultural changes are important to our theme. The English in Barbados were always more capitalist and less paternalistic in their approach to cane cultivation and manufacture than were the Portuguese in Brazil. The English estate owner in Barbados, further, was much more likely to be a 'self-raised' man of considerable personal and entrepreneurial resources than his Brazilian equivalent, and much less concerned with the past precedent. As a result, his role in Barbadian society came to be rather different, and much more multi-structured than that of his equivalent in Brazil. He usually presided over a smaller estate, which was much less self-sufficient than most of those in Brazil, so a good deal of timber, equipment, food and clothing were being brought in from outside (adjacent islands, Britain, North America). In the event, a new type of Barbadian sugar-estate system emerged, more capital-intensive and perhaps more efficient than that of Pernambuco, but one which nevertheless retained the classical tropical plantation attributes of raising an alien export crop for sale in temperate lands, through the use of imported labour. But in order to be efficient, economies of scale in agricultural practice had to be set in train: more and more land had to be divested of its forest and put under sugar cane without reference to environmental quality and characteristics. This, unfortunately, was a practice that was to be replicated many times elsewhere in West Indian history.

The story of the first phase of environmental decline in the region, in Barbados, is by now a well-known one. Forest clearance was limited largely to coastlands in 1647, but by 1660, almost all of the forest had gone. As it went, an ecological maelstrom was unleashed: the English in Barbados destroyed virtually entirely a complete, natural island ecosystem. Animals as well as plants disappeared, and were rapidly replaced by a limited range of open-land introduced species, including of course the sugar cane itself, and many weeds, which intermingled with those few native plants and animals that struggled to maintain themselves. Once the forest, and its inherent homeostatic, self-balancing mechanisms had gone, the Barbadians were left with an agriculturally attractive, but ecologically and environmentally unstable landscape. This growing instability manifested itself more clearly first, after a year or two of cultivation, by a liberal loss of soil nutrients, subsequently by increased soil loss, and eventually by major soil erosion, the latter being already evident in places by the mid 1650s.

The individual and official response to this environmental change is revealing. To begin with individual planters were, by and large, not particularly worried about such changes. They had other matters to consider such as establishing the boundaries to their estates (which in many cases were not legally determined until after the post Civil War Restoration in 1660), financing the huge cost of setting up a sugar estate with its labour requirements, and ensuring that profits accrued from it. The acquisition of sufficient labour for the estates was a particular and ever-present concern. In any case, even in the home countries, knowledge of differences in environmental, particularly soil properties, were at this time only just beginning to emerge. It was not until the last quarter of the seventeenth century that men like John Evelyn had described for the first time the details of the main soil types in England, and prescribed appropriate treatments for each.[1] Knowledge of tropical soil environments was even scantier, and for all practical purposes did not exist. These features were reflected in the earliest legislation of the period, most of which was concerned with the dangers to crops created by marauding animals, fire, and boundary abuse, rather than environmental change and decline *per se*. Thus, on October 7, 1652, an 'Act concerning trespasses done by hogs' was enacted by the Barbadian legislature, stating that 'it shall be lawful for any inhabitant of this island to kill...any hog or hogs that shall come into his provision-ground, or canes, cotton, ginger, or tobacco; and the so killed, to weigh and appraise, and to dispose of the same as he pleaseth.'[2] With a financial reduction for any damage to the crops, reimbursement was furnished to the owners of the hogs, and estimates of the damage were considered legally binding when supported by the evidence of two freeholders. Additional clauses in the same act attempted to force the control of other animals: 'cattle, horses, assingoes (donkeys), goats and sheep may be impounded until the amount of damage is determined...the party idemnified is to be allowed two pounds of sugar per day, for every head, during the time he lawfully keeps the same'.

Concern in the early 1650s over the number of cane fires, some of which had been deliberately set either by white settlers with a grievance over land, or indentured servants, was addressed by an 'Act for the prevention of firing sugar canes', passed on April 14, 1655, which sentenced any person who deliberately set fire to a cane field to receive 40 lashes, to become a servant to the owner of the burnt field for seven years, and to be branded on the head with the letter 'R'. The act also established a fine of 500 pounds of sugar, or 20 lashes, for any person found carrying a fire, or smoking tobacco, on a path in which canes were growing on either side. There is no evidence that this legislation was particularly successful. At roughly the same time, draconian measures were put in place, at a time of rapid forest removal, to prevent what one might term 'tree rustling' – the illegal removal of trees from other people's properties, arising in part from the poor definition of property boundaries. Thus in 1656, an 'Act prohibiting all persons to encroach upon their neighbour's line' indicated in its preamble that 'many persons upon pretence that they wanted their proportions of land, have encroached upon their neighbours' lines, and made great parcels of their lands, and fallen and cut down many of their marked and timber trees of good value'. The designated penalty for cutting each timber tree, or a tree that marked a boundary line was the forfeiture of 500 pounds of sugar; for every other tree, a fine of 100 pounds of sugar was imposed.[3] This is the first legislation relating to tree preservation that I know of in Barbados, and probably therefore also in the West Indies generally. It is earlier than the Kings Hill Ordinance in St. Vincent.

In addition to the island's Legislative Council, other environmental matters were controlled by Ordinances issued by parish councils. In Barbados, 11 parish councils were created in 1645, as a basis for within-island government on a local scale. In terms of island infrastructure, the most immediate and intractable problem was the need to improve communications and transport, most existing trackways being in poor condition. An act of the island legislature in 1653 required representatives of parishes to mend highways, and appointed influential parish commissioners, including James Drax, Thomas Modyford and Christopher Codrington to ensure that this was done. There is some evidence to suggest that the absence of good roads in the early 1650s had delayed the clearance of virgin timber to some extent in the middle of the island. However, as trees began to become increasingly scarce after 1655, some parish ordinances also were directed towards slowing down the speed of timber removal. Thus, one of April 29, 1658 in St. Michael parish permitted a Mr. Lumbard to live on three acres of glebe land for six years on condition that 'he shall not waste, sell or otherwise dispose of any wood without ye consent of ye churchwardens for ye time being, unless it be for ye building thereon, and firewood'. Four years later, specific permissions for removing timber from the same parish were obtained by two parishioners: 'Ordered, that Mr Nico Trusteene pay unto William Labon, three thousand pounds of sugar for 500 feete of square mastick for ye use of ye church, and that Mr Nico Trusteene pay to Captain Robert Cullimore four thousand pounds of sugar for mastick timber, to be supplied by himself'.[4] (Both 1662 St. Michael ordinances.) Though such procedures may indeed have slowed the removal of timber to some extent, they certainly did not prevent it. The survival of small patches of what may have been virgin forest, such as that at Turner's Hall Wood, seems to owe more to chance, coupled with its presence on a poor underlying soil stratum which was not really suited to agriculture, than to any particular legislation for conservation.

Overall, it was the speed of removal of forest in Barbados, which I have described elsewhere as being without parallel in an agricultural area, at least until the late twentieth century, coupled with the political mores of the time (pro-development and exploitation), which precluded the further development of legislation for conservation. To some extent also, it was a matter of a more general lack of scientific information about what was happening to the environment. Most contemporary planters considered that all environments exposed from beneath species-rich tropical rain forest or seasonal forest would be fertile, and would stay that way, for the whole landscape looked fertile, particularly when compared with the relative sparseness of the plant cover on agricultural land in their homelands. Moreover, this idea was encouraged by the exceptionally high yields of cane that had been obtained from freshly-cleared land, aided and abetted as these were by the nutrient-rich ash inputs derived from forest burning. Whistler's 1645 view of Barbados, that it had 'a most rich soil always grene (growing) and baring frut' held sway until well into the eighteenth century, when alternative, more rational views of environmental quality began to prevail. And yet, evidence for land deterioration was there for all to see, from the 1660s onwards. Between 1650 and 1700, a severe decline in yields from sugar land was recorded in both Barbados and Northern Leewards. At times, this was expressed in terms of there being a need over time for more slaves to work the same patch of land in order to maintain yields: however, there is an early, explicit reference in Barbados that yields had reduced by one-half in a few years.[5] Much of the most severely depleted land in this island (around one third of the total) had been taken out of cultivation by 1700, and by 1710 some notable gully erosion had been superimposed upon the more general sheet loss.[6] Most of the eroded material ended up in Bridgetown harbour, or eventually out to sea.

The response to this potentially catastrophic decline in yields, and the comprehensive erosion patterns of the late seventeenth and early eighteenth centuries is interesting in that it came largely from individual enterprising planters rather than governmental legislators, even though the latter were almost wholly planters themselves. It is the case that all attempts to improve land quality, and prevent further deterioration, came from planter experimentation, many of the ideas being unique to the island. Such experimentation involved the creation of terrace walls on steep slopes, the carrying back of soil in baskets from the foot of slopes to higher grounds, the greater use of manure, a search for new manure materials (seaweeds, etc.), and eventually the instigation of a total change in planting method. After 1700 canes came to be no longer set in trenches, arranged downslope (so encouraging soil movement after heavy rains) but instead in square 'cane holes' bounded by ridges, which prevent such movement. The origin of the cane hole system for planting is still obscure, though it seems to have been the brainchild of one of this island's planters. Once introduced, it proved to be the single most important aid to the reduction of soil loss in this island, and a system that later was transferred widely elsewhere. In contrast to all this, references to legislative activity relating to the control of soil loss in Barbados at this time are slight, despite the severity of the problem. On October 21, 1670, the island's Legislative Council passed an act 'to prevent the taking away of sand and stones from the shore', which in its preamble drew attention to the accumulation of sand in Bridgetown harbour: 'the sand which blocks up the harbour of this town…is sufficient to supply all uses', for this came from eroded material originating not very far away upslope. A somewhat later act (1733) designed to prevent the export of clay from Barbados mainly to the northern Leewards, makes reference to 'great quantities of it having been from time to time sent off from hence, which tends greatly to the disadvantage of this place, and damage to the inhabitants', and also to the increased impoverishment of soil generally, 'which occasions that the planter and inhabitants are put to abundantly more labour, trouble and expense, and require a good many more hands in making dung and other services, to supply in good measure that defect'.[7] But no specific national legislation to reduce soil loss and conserve fertility was ever enacted, not even during the remainder of the eighteenth century, when severe soil erosion continued to recur periodically (e.g. in the 1730s and 1780s). This is a curious deficiency in West Indian legislative history. Again, methods for the prevention of soil loss, or for soil improvement, were left to be worked out by individuals, such as Samuel Martin, who established a School of Plantership in the 1750s or through the establishment of horticultural societies in several islands, at the end of the eighteenth century.[8]

Most of the remaining environmental legislation of Barbados during the seventeenth and eighteenth centuries continued to address particular points of difficulty rather than the general state of environmental decline. From 1662, several ordinances of parish councils gave permission for the sinking of wells, as population increased, and pressure on existing water resources grew greater.[9] Further acts relating to water extraction were passed in 1713, 1752 and 1754, emphazising one of the major preoccupations of Barbadians, and the need constantly to maintain their scarce water supplies. In 1713, this concern served to restrict monopoly of use on the stream flowing from Three Houses spring, in St. Philip parish, preventing any person from damming the stream for a longer period than 48 hours – with the exception of the Braithwaite's estate, which was permitted to extract water for periods of 72 consecutive hours. Further, a footpath was approved for construction at the stream bank to provide common access for this water. Ordinances of 1752 and 1754 served to encourage the rate of extraction of water from deep aquifers, the first by mechanical means, and the second through the use of a machine working through 'the power of one or more man, or a horse or horses'.[10] Further acts in the 1750s sought to improve the quality of windmill vanes, and to develop a windmill for grinding corn.

Elsewhere in the eastern Caribbean, only St. Kitts was settled earlier than Barbados, jointly by the English and the French in 1624. Early on some misgivings were forthcoming about the clear-felling methods of the French (and by implication, the English as well): one correspondent in 1625 wrote that 'unlike the Caribs, who wisely left shady groves standing in the midst of their fields, the French cut and slashed right and left, intent only on clearing the ground as rapidly as possible, and without a thought of future protection against the sun…(they) tore up the earth, which loosened for the first time, gave forth an unhealthy exhalation, which was often fatal to the labourers in their weakened condition'.[11] Early indications of soil deterioration from excessive tobacco cultivation by 1666, and a consequential switch from the production of that crop to indigo, are also recorded.[12] Yet nothing seems to have been done to legislate against the sometimes excessive patterns of forest removal and soil deterioration until beyond the end of the eighteenth century. Perhaps the reasons for this are linked, because until the late 1660s, difficulties over land tenure were particularly severe on St. Kitts, given the early Anglo-French occupancy. Thereafter, the island was beset by war between the English, the French, the Dutch and the Spanish, all of which perhaps acted against settled legislation, unlike Barbados, which was relatively free of these conflicts.

All other islands in the eastern Caribbean chain were settled later: Nevis in 1628, Antigua and Montserrat in 1632, Guadeloupe in 1635, Martinique in 1639 and Dominica, St. Lucia, St. Vincent and Grenada, all nominally also in the latter year, although in point of fact much later since they were, for a while, largely left to the remaining resident Carib Indians. Although it is known that prior to European settlement, all these islands, along with others (St. Eustatius, Saba, Anguilla) were covered in wood, little is understood about the legislative methods used, if any, to control excessive environmental use and deterioration, except in Antigua and Martinique.[13] In Antigua, parish measures were set in place in 1671 to control the practice of setting fire to fields to clear land of unwanted bushes, for these frequently spread fiercely and widely and potentially could damage top-soil layers.[14] But little else is recorded, perhaps again because of the negative influence of warfare on legislation during the late seventeenth and eighteenth centuries, which was almost as severe here as in St. Kitts.

On Martinique, it is clear that development until 1660 was slow, because of the lack of adequate financing and labour to cultivate sugar. But gradually, and especially from the 1670s, inroads began to be made into the forest, to extend the number of estates, and for other activities such as timber extraction and charcoal burning.[15] Perhaps the French were more aware than the British at this time of the potential dangers to land sustainability of excessive clearance and soil deterioration, and certainly in mainland France concerns with the maintenance of a good water supply and adequate forest resources had been established in Colbert's Ordinance of 1669, which included provisions for the planting of forests for the encouragement of both.[16] Similar pressure for timber retention and replanting for water conservation and forest renewal are seen in Martinique from 1763 and in them may be detected the broader philosophies which were to give rise subsequently to the conservation of the Kings Hill Forest in St. Vincent in 1791.[17]

Perhaps one should not be too surprised at the lack of legislation directed towards preserving environmental quality, both in Barbados and both the Leeward and Windward Islands at this time. After all, similar environmental changes involving deforestation, soil loss and the silting of particular river estuaries (e.g. the Dee, the Torridge) were also taking place in England and France at this time. It was an uncertain political period, with a good deal of warfare and competition for control of territory everywhere in the 'western' world; a time of changing economics, as countries emerged from feudal to mercantilist systems; a time for entrepreneurs (following on from the Elizabethan age), especially in the exploitation of new territory overseas; a time not for subtleties of environmental appreciation, but rather a time to build up empires from the resources of the new territories. Yet by the same token, the environmental difficulties, present after only a few years of West Indian settlement, were real enough. The institutions of settlement and especially the legislative systems, proved to be unable to handle adequately these environmental difficulties, but this could also be said of the economic and financial systems as well. So many planters had run so quickly into such immense problems of debt by the time that environmental difficulties started to show, that they would rather risk financial ruin to take crops off the land, than otherwise modify their activities. Yet, over the years, it was always the individual settler, rather than government, who proved to have the will, the drive, and the expertise to overcome such environmental difficulties. By the time of the Kings Hill Forest legislation, that individuality of response had changed to some extent into one of much greater collectivity. This perhaps reflected more widespread social areas of concern both in the region and beyond, and a greater appreciation of the fragility of the tropical environment – even though forests were still being widely felled in the region, and fauna and flora continued to be depleted. That balance between environmental protection and forest destruction still is tenuous today, where forests are being rapidly clear-felled both in the Dominican Republic and in Cuba at the present time. It is probably true to say that, even now, more environments are being destroyed than protected by legislation, despite the recent proliferation of environmental impact assessment schemes in many countries. Now is the time, forcibly, to change that balance, if our own futures are to be secured both in the region and worldwide.

Notes

1   J. Evelyn. Terra: *a philosophical discourse of earth*. London, 1675.
2   R. Hall. *Acts passed in the island of Barbados*. London, 1675.
3   Both of whose means of livelihood had been curtailed by the amalgamation of smaller estates into larger ones dominated by sugar cane.
4   *Records of the Vestry of St. Michael*. Barbados, Bridgetown Library, 1947.

5   Deputy-Governor Stede. *The groans of the plantations*. London, 1689.

6   Anon. *A state of the present condition of the island of Barbados*. London, 1710.

7   R. Hall. op. cit., 1764.

8   S. Martin. *An essay upon plantership*. (5th. ed.) London, 1773.

9   *Records of the Vestry of St. Michael*. Barbados, Bridgetown Library, 1662.

10 R. Hall. op. cit., 1764.

11 N.M. Crouse. *French pioneers in the West Indies*, 1624–1644. Columbia, New York, 1940.

12 W. Dampier. *Voyages and descriptions*. London, 1699.
    C. De Rochefort. *Histoire naturelle et morale des Isles Antilles de l'Amérique*. Paris, 1658.

13 S. Clark. *A mirrour or looking-glass*. London, 1671.
    N. Gent. *America: or, an exact description of the West Indies*. London, 1653.
    D. R. Harris. *Plants, animals and man in the outer Leeward Islands*. University of California Publications in Geography, 18, 1965. pp 1–184.

14 D. R. Harris. op. cit. *Publications in Geography*, 18, 1965. pp 1–184.

15 C. .M. Kimber. *Martinique Revisited*. Texas A&M University Press, 1988.

16 A. J. Bourde. *The influence of England on the French agronomes*. Cambridge University Press, Cambridge, 1933.

17 Phelipeaux cited in A. J. Reennard. *Tricentenaire des Antilles, Guadeloupe – Martinique 1635–1935*. Martinique, 1933.

4 Botanical Gardens: Connecting Links in Plant Transfer Between the Indo-Pacific and Caribbean Regions

Madeleine Ly-Tio-Fane

By the latter half of the eighteenth century, England and France, relying on the able management of their gardens at Kew and Paris, were able to define ambitious policies of plant introduction and naturalization for the development of their colonies. At the same time, Emperor Joseph II of Austria sent his naturalists and gardeners across the tropical world to collect for the Schönbrunn Gardens. The Garden of Pamplemousses at Isle de France in the Indian Ocean achieved international fame as the tropical base of experiment for the Paris Garden, whilst every encouragement was given to the rapid expansion of the Calcutta Gardens to provide plant material to the St. Vincent nurseries. Joseph Banks recommended the setting up, at strategic points such as at St. Helena, of botanic gardens on the line of communication between Kew and Sydney on the Pacific front and the Caribbean. The creation and development of botanical gardens, in close relationship with the medical sciences, involved the observation and evaluation of indigenous practice, beginning with the geographical and intellectual context of Renaissance discoveries. European exploration and expansion stimulated interest in the study of tropical floras, culminating in the preparation of reference texts such as van Reede's *Hortus Indicus Malabaricus* or Rumpf's *Herbarium Amboinense*. Meanwhile the gardens of Leiden and Amsterdam, supported by the garden situated at the Cape of Good Hope, achieved a position of preeminence in the seventeenth and first half of the eighteenth centuries. The interplay of distant and European botanic gardens was thus well established.

The Caribbean landfall of the fleet of Columbus in October, 1492 was perhaps the most determinant in a chain of events which left their impress on Western man's perception of the natural world. Some years earlier, in January, 1488, Bartolomeu Dias and his crew had gazed on a South African landscape after rounding the southern tip of the Continent, opening the way for Vasco da Gama's fleet to

Calicut (May, 1498). In January, 1500, the Spaniard Pinzón had explored the northern coast of Brazil, and in April, the Portuguese Pedro Cabral and his party landed at Pôrto Seguro, taking official possession of the country. Within thirty years, following the estab-lishment of the Portuguese Eastern Empire with its metropolis at Goa, Magellan's ship on a mission for the Spanish crown (1519–22) had crossed the Pacific and circumnavigated the globe, linking East and West by oceanic communications, an exploit repeated some fifty years later by the Englishman Francis Drake. The enlarged horizons and contact with diverse civilizations and societies put in motion unprecedented movements of population and acculturation processes.

Such a phenomenon, perhaps not the least engendered by the explosion of energy which characterized the Renaissance, had a coun-terpart: an intellectual voyage into time, causing a revaluation of Graeco-Roman thought and its emphasis on the study of Nature. In 1476, a translation of the *Natural History* of Pliny the Elder (AD 23–AD 79) was published in Venice. This encyclopaedic compila-tion of the writings of authors of antiquity contained an important sec-tion on plants and led to a re-appraisal of the work of a student of Plato, the naturalist Theophrastus (*c.* 370 BC–*c.* 285 BC). His *Enquiry into Plants* had proposed the basic principles of botanical study. There was also a revival of interest in the therapeutic treatise of the army physician Dioscorides (fl. A.D 60–AD 77), *De Materia Medica* , which included information on exotic plants he had studied while stationed with the Roman armies in Asia. Dioscorides had paid special attention in his treatise to the description of the plant and its place of origin or habitat, while discussing the preparation of the drug and its use in medicine, thus ensuring the continuity of its influence well into the seventeenth century. The most famous, and perhaps the most influential of the copies of *De Materia Medica* is the *Juliana Anicia Codex*, illustrated with striking naturalistic plant drawings, made at Constantinople *c.* AD 512 for the Imperial Princess, Juliana Anicia, and now preserved in the Austrian National Library, Vienna.[1] Through the Nestorian Christians, the work of Dioscorides was introduced in Iraq and to the Muslim world and transmitted through Persia to India where indigenous plant painting techniques emerged in the Company style of the eighteenth century.[2]

The excitement generated in Europe by the observation and intro-duction of exotic floras and faunas, the curiosity about new food plants, and the search for new drugs stimulated the establishment of ornamen-tal gardens for delight and of botanic gardens for study. It is character-istic of this trend that such great artists as the Italian Leonardo da Vinci (1452–1519) or the German Albrecht Dürer (1471–1528) produced between 1503 and 1508 the first truly botanical studies, initiating a style which was to culminate in the glories of Dutch flower painting of the seventeenth century.[3]

As was to be expected, the first botanical gardens were established in the historic cities in Italy: Professor Luca Ghini set up the University Botanic Garden at Pisa in 1543, Padua and Florence followed suit in 1545 and Bologna in 1567. Since the prime objective was the cultivation and study of plants for their curative properties, a close association was maintained with the medical schools and apothecaries. This relationship remained a guiding principle in the management of later botanic gardens created in various parts of Europe. Charles de l'Ecluse (Carolus Clusius, 1526–1609) was invited by Emperor Maximilian II to Vienna in 1573 to develop his *Hortus Medicus* and to supervise the Imperial Gardens as Prefect. Richer de Belleval (1564–1632) established at Montpellier his *Jardin des Plantes* in 1593, the year Charles de l'Ecluse went to Leiden to direct the University Botanic Garden.[4] From 1626, Guy de la Brosse (*c.* 1586–1641), physician to Louis XIII, planned the setting up and development of the *Jardin Royal des Plantes Médicinales* in Paris, an establishment which was to become famous in the eighteenth century as *Le Jardin du Roi*.

Travellers were instructed to observe indigenous practice and collect material susceptible of extending the *Materia Medica*. Plant lore trickling from the New World increased knowledge from the more traditional East. Following the establishment of a French base in Madagascar in 1642, Etienne de Flacourt (1607–1660), Director of the Compagnie française de l'Orient and Commandant drew attention to the vegetal resources and their indigenous usage in his chapter on plants in the *Histoire de la Grande Isle de Madagascar* (1658).

On the establishment of the St. Vincent Botanic Gardens in 1765, General Melville advised Dr. Young to collect as much information as possible relative to indigenous medicines.[5] Alexander Anderson had, before emigrating to America, a working connection with the Chelsea Physic Garden, which had been generously endowed by Hans Sloane. Anderson searched like many of his contemporaries, especially the French, for the Caribbean varieties of the Peruvian bark, the cure for the dreaded tropical fevers.[6] It is a well-known fact that the final establishment in Asia of the *Cinchona* (observed in 1739 near Loja by Joseph de Jussieu and La Condamine, who sent specimens to Linnaeus) owed much to a long collaboration between the Paris and Kew Gardens.

The search for medicinal plants evolved into the study of tropical floras, as observed in the work of Father Plumier (1646–1706) in the Antilles, or in that of the administrators and the physicians of the Dutch East India Company (V.O.C.) in the course of the seventeenth century, the golden age of Dutch expansion.[7] The Portuguese had done admirable work before them, naturalizing important plants in India such as the cashew nut, pineapple, sweet potato, and cassava derived from Brazil as well as the custard apple, averrhoa, groundnut and chili peppers from the West Indies. In his garden at Goa, established almost at the same time as the Italian botanic gardens, the physician Garcia da Orta cultivated and studied medicinal plants while he enlarged his knowledge by consulting native physicians, yogis and traders of the region, innovating the practice of inviting native collaboration in the study of Malabar flora. He had gone to India in 1534 in the retinue of Martin Affonso de Sousa, later governor of Portuguese India. Da Orta's two volume *Coloquios dos Simples e Drogas e Cousas Medicinais da India*, printed in Goa in 1563 by Johannes de Endem, attracted attention in Europe through the translations of Charles de l'Ecluse.[8] Published between 1567 and 1605, these translations included text by the Seville physician Nicolas Monardes on the medicinal plants of the New World.

Through his widespread international contacts, Charles de l'Ecluse gave the Leiden Botanic Garden a position of preeminence. Bulbs of tulips, narcissi, and hyacinths imported from Turkey and the Levant were grown in the Leiden garden along with American plants including the potato, obtained from the entourage of Philip Sidney and Francis Drake with whom he was acquainted. He also advised the V.O.C. directors to encourage captains to collect plants on their Far Eastern journeys.

Between 1658 and 1663, the Dutch were wresting control of the Malabar coast and surrounding regions from the Portuguese. It is in this context that the Cape was settled by Jan van Riebeeck in April, 1652 and the Company Garden was subsequently created. Developed through the care of Governor Simon van der Stel (1639–1712) and his son Willem Adriaan (1664–1733), the establishment grew into a fine botanic garden where indigenous plants as well as those naturalized from the Far East and East Indies flourished. The expansion of their administration from 1679 to 1706 employed gifted gardeners. Shipments of South African and other exotics thus reached the gardens of Leiden and Amsterdam and other European gardens. In the middle of the eighteenth century the Cape Garden was able to provide naturalists of many nations hospitality and resources for study, thanks to the support of Governor Rijk Tulbagh (1699–1771) and the scientific pursuits of the Commandant Robert Jacob Gordon (1743–1795). During this period, the enterprise of men like Hendrik Adriaan van Reede (1636–1691) in Malabar, Paul Hermann (1646–1695) in Ceylon and South Africa, and George Everhard Rumpf (*c.* 1628–1702) in the Moluccas was brought to fruition.

Commander of Malabar van Reede's enthusiasm and determination succeeded in pooling the expertise of native and European specialists to produce the *Hortus Indicus Malabaricus*; an admirable synthesis of Eastern and Western botanical knowledge, published in Amsterdam between 1678 and 1693 in 12 volumes.[9] It appears that van Reede intended to follow this up with the preparation of a *Hortus Africus*, for during his tour of inspection of Dutch possessions in 1685, he collected dried specimens and paintings of South African plants by Heinrich Claudius (*c.* 1655–*c.* 1697).[10] However, his death in Surat in 1691 did not allow the project to mature.

The apothecary Jan Commelin (1629–92), botanist and commissioner of the *Hortus Medicus* of Amsterdam, which he helped create in 1682, was an editor and commentator of van Reede's *Hortus* and greatly developed the exotic collections of the garden through the shipments sent by V.O.C. captains. The first volume of his catalogue of plants growing in the garden, printed in Amsterdam in 1697 after his death, was devoted to the plants introduced from the East and West Indies. Commelin not only carefully preserved the original drawings of van Reede's *Hortus Malabaricus*, but also engaged two artists, Johannes and Maria Moninckz, to make drawings of the exotic plants growing in the Garden.

Meanwhile, Paul Hermann, who had been appointed Director of the Leiden Garden, increased the collections from the Indies, the Cape and America. He arranged an exchange with the Chelsea Physic Garden and strengthened his English contacts through the friendship of William Sherard (*c.* 1658–1728), who arranged for the posthumous publication of his work. The great medical teacher, Hermann Boerhaave (1668–1738), succeeded Paul Hermann as director of the Leiden Garden in 1709, and attracted students from all over Europe. He was responsible for renewing the ties with Vienna when some of his most famous pupils were invited by Maria Theresa to strengthen the Medical Faculty and assist in the development of the Schönbrunn Gardens. In the middle of the eighteenth entury, Holland had become the centre of tropical botany and Carl Linnaeus arrived there to complete his studies. He was the guest of Johannes Burman (1707–1779), who continued the work of the Commelins as Director of the Amsterdam Garden and also promoted the creation of a botanic garden in Batavia, Java.[11] He was very influential through his own publications, or editions of earlier basic works, especially that of the *Herbarium Amboinense* of Rumph published between 1741 and 1755.

These achievements provided the indispensable background for the naturalization experiments of two great colonial powers of the eighteenth century, England and France, their gardens in Paris and at Kew being under the direction of the towering personalities of the Comte de Buffon (1707–1788) and Sir Joseph Banks (1743–1820).[12]

France's possessions in the Indian Ocean, the Mascarene Islands (Mauritius and Reunion, then known as Isle de France and Bourbon), provided natural laboratories for such experiments. They were ideally situated between Asia and Africa and had suitable climatic ranges. In 1714, Antoine de Jussieu had communicated to the Académie des Sciences the first scientific description of the coffee plant, derived from observations of a specimen presented to Louis XIV by the burgomaster of Amsterdam who had obtained it from the collection of the Botanic Garden. Soon after, coffee plants obtained from Mocha upon orders from the Directors of the Compagnie des Indes were cultivated on Bourbon Island; by 1723 the coffee plants had reached the Antilles.

It was however Pierre Poivre's (1719–86) search in the East Indies between 1748 and 1755 for seedlings of the fine spices, the clove and nutmeg (precious commodities which had contributed to Dutch affluence), which attracted most attention.[13] The quest, successfully resumed in the 1770s during Poivre's period of office as Intendant at Isle de France, and conducted in the neighbourhood of New Guinea, yielded even further information on the vegetal products of the region, in particular of the Philippines and Sulu Archipelago. Fruit seedlings, including the rima and even the cocoa plant naturalized in the Philippines (figured in Pierre Sonnerat's account of the journey, *Voyage à la Nouvelle Guinée*, 1776), were brought back together with the spice seedlings to enrich the nurseries of the Pamplemousses Gardens.[14] These Gardens were already stocked with introductions from China, the Malabar and Coromandel Coasts, and the Cape of Good Hope, (the last received as gifts of Governor Tulbagh), collections which the Director of the Garden Jean Nicolas Céré (1737–1810) could proudly describe as representative of the four continents. One of Céré's predecessors at Pamplemousses was the apothecary Jean-Baptiste Christophe Fusée Aublet (1720–78), who had been sent in 1753 by the *Compagnie des Indes* to establish a medicinal garden, and during his stay in the island had crossed with Poivre on the subject of the introduction of the spice plants. Aublet later explored in Guiana and St. Domingue and was among the earliest of the promoters of plant transfer to link the Indian Ocean with the Caribbean. He embodied his experience and expressed his views in his *Histoire des Plantes de la Guiane Françoise*, 1775, in which was included a *Notice des Plantes de l'Isle de France*.

After the peace of 1763 which deprived France of her mainland possessions in North America and some Caribbean islands, including St. Vincent, plans were made to restore the French balance by strengthening the settlement in French Guiana and enriching it through the introduction of economic crops. In response to advice sought by Minister Choiseul, the naturalist Adanson, a specialist of Senegal, recommended a series of voyages conducted from the French island of Gorée to survey tropical vegetal resources and to introduce them from Africa, the Canaries and Cape Verde.

Such considerations no doubt had their influence on the planning of the great French voyages of the century, from that of Bougainville, d'Entrecasteaux, to those of Nicolas Baudin. During the circumnavigations of Bougainville and Cook, the notes recorded by the naturalist Commerson (1727–73) were offset by those taken down by Banks and his staff: the unforgettable stay in Tahiti, where Banks scrupulously noted down the food habits of the people, and the landfall at Botany Bay.[15] Both of these events had far-reaching consequences.

The conclusion of the War of American Independence brought about a resumption of exploration for the collection of natural history specimens. Joseph II of Austria entrusted a world-encompassing mission to Professor Franz Joseph Märter (1753–1827) across the tropical world to embellish the Schönbrunn Park and Gardens.[16] Meanwhile in an effort to allay the scarcity of food in the colonies and to revive the economy, both England and France elaborated programmes of plant introduction.

The most ambitious was put forward by the Comte de la Luzerne, Minister of Marine from 1787 to 1790, a nephew of Malesherbes (1721–94), the influential Director de la Librairie (that is, of Information). La Luzerne had been a former governor of St. Domingue and had struck a friendship with Matthew Wallen of Jamaica, from whom he had had early news of the planning of the breadfruit expedition. The project was entrusted for development to the Chief Gardener of the Paris Jardin du Roi, André Thouin (1747–1824). Thouin recommended an inventory of plants growing in each colony, followed by a reciprocal exchange of useful plants, and the systematic pursuit of a universal programme of acquisition and dissemination controlled in an absolute manner from the Jardin du Roi. The practicability of this global project rested in a large measure on the success which had attended the naturalization experiments of Céré in the Garden of Pamplemousses.

In 1776, Céré had discovered that the nutmeg plant was dioecious (having the male or female reproductive organs in separate plants); between 1779 and 1782 large distributions of clove seedlings had been made in the Mascarenes.[17] By 1783, Céré innovated in the publication of an *Avis* advertising the plants available for distribution to the colonists. Among the plants offered were seedlings of the acacia (*Albizzia lebbek*), known in the island as '*bois noir*', a plant which Joseph François Charpentier de Cossigny (1736–1809) had introduced from Bengal in 1767. The acclimatization of this plant had been encouraged by Poivre as a substitute for the native trees which were being cut down for economic purposes. In 1781, Céré and Cossigny contracted a large reforestation scheme with the government for the north-western coastline of the island, but the scheme fell through, the only areas actually planted being in Pamplemousses and the arid regions of Port Louis.[18] Seeds of this plant were sent to St. Domingue and Martinique, and from thence eventually reached the St. Vincent Garden.

In their research on Alexander Anderson's work for the St. Vincent Garden, Richard and Elizabeth Howard have drawn attention to the personality of the militiaman Charles Aquart (fl. 1785–92), of St. Pierre, Martinique, who enriched the Garden with plants obtained from Cayenne, Guadeloupe and Guiana, through his French or Danish connections. Evidence of his contacts with international naturalists appears in a letter of July 4, 1785, addressed to the Privy Councillor Philipp Cobenzl offering his services to the Emperor.[19] The opportunity is provided by the arrival in Martinique of the Gardener Franz Bredemeyer (1758–1839) in the expectation of Märter's visit. Aquart mentions that a brother of his had helped Nicolas Jacquin during his stay in 1754. It is intriguing to think that relations between Aquart and Nicolas Céré may have improved because of the Austrian connection. The records of the Pamplemousses Gardens preserve a letter from Aquart, dated July 7, 1787, in which he lists desirable introductions of Asian plants into Martinique.[20]

This is precisely the time of the stay of the Schönbrunn Head Gardener Frans Boos (1753–1832) at Pamplemousses. At the conclusion of his work with Märter's party in North America, Boos was sent with his assistant Georg Scholl to collect in South Africa and to pursue the exploration in the Mascarenes and Madagascar. The collaboration was mutually enriching as Céré benefited from the experience of one who had been trained by Dutch masters. However the visit was fraught with future consequence as Boos travelled from the Cape to Isle de France, and from Isle de France to Trieste conveying the collections for Schönbrunn on *La Pepita*, a ship commanded by Nicolas Thomas Baudin (1754–1803), a man familiar with the Caribbean Seas. Thus began the training of Baudin in the conveyance of live plants and animals during long sea journeys and his service for the Emperor. In the course of further collecting journeys for Schönbrunn, he deposited in Trinidad a collection of plants including several varieties of pepper and vegetables from Malabar and South East Asia.[21]

After the departure of Boos, Céré hosted from July, 1788 to March, 1789 a promising gardener from the Paris *Jardin du Roi*, Joseph Martin, who had been sent on the first mission of importance under Thouin's scheme.[22] He came to collect the spice and other useful plants for acclimatization in the Paris, Cayenne and Antilles gardens, and had an opportunity during his journey to botanize at Madagascar and the Cape. On the successful conclusion of his journey, he was installed as Director of the acclimatization gardens in Cayenne in 1790. As a consequence of the dissemination of plants in the French colonies, the English planters received the plants they fancied from their correspondents; the clove reaching Dominica from Cayenne in 1789 and from Martinique in 1791. Its successful establishment owed much to the efforts of William Urban Buée. Clove was already growing in the Garden of St. Vincent, which also received from Cayenne plants of the nutmeg during the Peace of Amiens.

Always watchful of innovations in the French colonies, Joseph Banks had prevailed on the metropolitan authorities to step up the development of the St. Vincent gardens which would enlarge the nurseries for the introductions from Asia through the agency of the Calcutta Gardens.[23] These had been created in 1786 by Robert Kyd (1746–1793), and were soon to be admirably managed by William Roxburgh (1751–1815). The establishment of the St. Helena Botanic Garden on the line of communication between the Indo-Pacific and the Caribbean to serve as midway base was also undertaken.[24] There the breadfruit plants recovered before reaching St. Vincent and Jamaica, and the fruit seedlings and other delicate plants sent from England to either India or the Caribbean had time to accustom themselves to a warmer climate.[25]

But this was only a beginning. Large areas had still to be explored for their plant and animal resources. Alexander Anderson was desolate that the Spanish territories in America would not be easily visited, and he, like Baudin, had unsuccessfully tried to effect an entry from Trinidad. Although Baudin, on his collecting voyage of 1796–1797, failed to explore the banks of the Orinoco, plants were collected on the Danish Islands of St. Thomas and St. Croix and also on Puerto Rico to be naturalized in the Paris garden. Baudin's last dream, spurred by Antoine-Laurent de Jussieu, the Director of Paris Museum after the Revolution, was to increase the collection in the Paris Gardens by undertaking the exploration of the coasts of South America, of Africa, and of the Pacific islands, a journey which would take him to the Australian region. Alexander von Humboldt had been invited to join this expedition, but the many difficulties which beset the preparation of this journey, which included many delays, induced him to travel independently in the company of Aimé Bonpland (1773–1858). Lack of funds restricted the exploration to the Australian shores, where the famous encounter with Flinders, who was bent on a similar mission, occurred. The collections and illustrations of plant and animal life realized by the scientific staff during both expeditions are a precious record of the nat-

ural history of Australia. Many Australian plants went to adorn
Josephine's magnificent garden at La Malmaison, to be naturalized in
the warm Southern regions.[26]

Baudin and Flinders were to end their careers at Mauritius, the first
to die of his exertions, and the other to languish in long imprisonment.
Valuable plant material was deposited in the Pamplemousses Garden
which could then boast of being the nursery for plants of five continents.
As it had sent material to the gardens of Calcutta and St. Helena in their
early years, Pamplemousses, a recently acquired jewel of the British
Empire, was to enrich with its famed exotics the infant garden of
Sydney created by Charles Fraser for the naturalization of Pacific
plants.[27] Thus we have the establishment of a functioning network of
individual experts and gardens exchanging, studying, and reporting on
plants in new environments. These networks broke across boundaries,
some of them hostile boundaries. A picture of mutual benefit emerges.

Notes

1   W. Blunt. *The Art of Botanical Illustration.* London, 1950. pp. 10–15.
2   S. C. Welch. A confluence of East and West, of art and science. Company botanical
painting: its background and character. In *Indian Botanical Painting.* Hunt Institute
for Botanical Documentation, Pittsburgh, 1980. pp. 9–19.
3   D. O. Wijnands. In the wake of Columbus: American plants in Dutch still life. In *The
Exploration and Opening up of America as Mirrored in Natural History.* Vienna,
Natural History Museum, November 1994.
4   See the section entitled: The world of Clusius: gardens and botanic gardens in
Europe in the 16th Century in *The Authentic Garden; a Symposium on Gardens.*
Edited by Tjon Sie Fat, L. and De Jong, E. Leiden, 1991. The Symposium held in
1990 was one of the events celebrating the 400th anniversary of the foundation of
the Leiden *Hortus medicus.*
5   Correspondence between General Robert Melville and Dr. George Young, 23rd
September 1766 in *Alexander Anderson's The St. Vincent Botanic Garden.* Edited by
R. A. and E. S. Howard. Harvard, 1983. pp. 11–12.
6   A memoir on the subject entitled *Description d'un Quinquina Indigène à Saint-
Domingue (Cinchona cariboea) par Joseph Gauché, Habitant, Concessionnaire
et Administrateur des Eaux Thermales de Boynes* had been read at the Académie
des Sciences on 24 July, 1787. Bibliothèque du Muséum d'histoire naturelle,
Paris, ms. 1275. See also Chapter 5 in this book.
7   Davy de Virville, Ad. *Histoire de la Botanique en France.* Paris, 1954. pp. 59–60.
8   (a) I. H. Burkill. Chapters on the History in India. Calcutta, 1965. pp. 4–5.
    (b) R. N. Kapil and A. K. Bhatnagar. Portuguese contributions to Indian Botany. *Isis*
67: 1976. pp. 449–452.
9   M. Fournier. Enterprise in botany: Van Reede and his Hortus Malabaricus. *Archives
of Natural History* 14: 1987. pp. 123–158; pp. 297–338.
10 M. Gunn. and L .E. Codd. *Botanical Exploration of Southern Africa.* Cape Town,
1981. pp. 32–33.
11 F. A. Stafleu. *Linnaeus and the Linnaeans; the Spreading of their Ideas in Systematic
Botany, 1735–1789.* Utrecht, 1971. pp. 165–169.

12 (a) Laissus, Y. Le Jardin du Roi. In *Buffon, 1788–1988*. Paris, 1988. pp. 49–71.
(b) Desmond, R. The transformation of the Royal Gardens at Kew. In *Sir Joseph Banks, a Global Perspective*. Kew, 1994. pp. 105–115.

13 M. Ly-Tio-Fane. Pierre Poivre en son temps. In *Pierre Poivre (1719–1786) Intendant du Roi pour les Iles de France de Bourbon*. Sommet des Pays Francophones, Octobre 1993, Amicale Ile-Maurice-France. Port Louis, Maurice, 1994. pp. 20–29.

14 M. Ly-Tio-Fane. *Pierre Sonnerat, 1748–1814; an account of his life and work*. Mauritius, chap. 3, 1976. pp. 71–96.

15 J. Banks. ed. by J. Hooker. *Journal of the Rt. Hon. Sir Joseph Banks during Captain Cook's First Voyage on H.M.S. Endeavour in 1768–71*. London, 1896. Breadfruit mentioned pp. 137–138.

16 H. Hühnel. Botanische Sammelreisen nach Amerika im 18. Jahrhundert. In *Die neue Welt: Österreich und die Erforschung Amerikas*, Wien, Nationalbibliothek, 1992. pp. 61–77.

17 M. Ly-Tio-Fane. *Mauritius and the Spice Trade*, volume 2. *The Triumph of Jean-Nicolas Céré and his Isle Bourbon Collaborators*. Paris and the Hague, 1970.

18 J. F. Charpentier de Cossigny. *Moyens d'Amélioration et de Restauration Proposés au Governement et aux Habitants des Colonies*. Paris 1: 1803. pp. 189–190.

19 Österreichische Nationalbibliothek, Ms. Dept., Cod. Ser. n. 3517: pp. 125–126.

20 Correspondence of Nicolas Céré, known as *Lettres du Jardin de l'Isle de France*, kept in the Royal Society of Arts and Sciences of Mauritius, *Réduit* 5: 231 (323).

21 M. Ly-Tio-Fane. Contacts between Schönbrunn and the Jardin du Roi at Isle de France (Mauritius) in the eighteenth century: An episode in the career of Nicolas Thomas Baudin. *Mitteilungen des Österreichischen Staatsarchivs*, 35: 1982. pp. 85–109.

22 M. Ly-Tio-Fane. A reconnaissance of tropical resources during Revolutionary years; the role of the Paris Musèum d'Histoire naturelle. *Archives of Natural History* 18(3): 1991. pp. 333–362.

23 R. A. Howard and D. A. Powel. The Indian Botanic Garden, Calcutta and the Gardens of the West Indies. *Bulletin of the Botanical Survey of India* 7(1–4): 1965. pp. 1–7.

24 Correspondence from Sir George Young, War Office, to Alexander Anderson, Feb. 6. 1785, March 1787, transmitted by Robert Adair. Cited in transcription of R. A. and E. S. Howard, 1983, p. 28–29. See note 4.

25 D. A. Powell. The voyage of the plant nursery, H.M.S. *Providence*, 1791–1793. *The Institute of Jamaica, Science Series* No. 15(2): 1973. pp. 18–22.

26 F. Horner. *The French Reconnaissance: Baudin in Australia, 1801–1803*. Melbourne, 1987. pp. 363.

27 W. G. McMinn. *Allan Cunningham, Botanist and Explorer*. Melbourne, 1970. p. 102–103. A collection of 59 contemporary documents recently edited by Alan Frost under the title *Sir Joseph Banks and the Transfer of Plants to and from the South Pacific, 1786–1798* (The Colony Press, Malvern, Victoria, 1994) throws light on this particular aspect.

Table 1.   *Botanic gardens of relevance to the text and the names of those who either promoted, established, or significantly developed these gardens.*

1543	Pisa	Luca Ghini
1545	Padua, Florence,	
	Goa	Garcia da Orta
1567	Bologna	
1573	Vienna	
1590	Leiden	Charles de L'Ecluse
1593	Montpellier	Richer de Belleval
1626	Paris (1st Edict)	Guy de la Brosse
1635	(2nd Edict)	
1640	Oxford	Jacob Bobart the Elder*
1652	Cape of Good Hope	Jan van Riebeeck
1673	Chelsea Physic Garden	Philip Miller*(Gardener at C.P.G. 1722–70)
1682	Amsterdam	Jan Commelin
1750	Schönbrunn	Gerard van Swieten, Adriaan [van] Stekhoven
1750	Batavia, Java	Johannes Burman, Chr. Kleinhof
1753	Pamplemousses	Fusée Aublet
1759	Kew	William Aiton* (Gardener at Kew 1759–93)
1765	St. Vincent	George Young
		Alexander Anderson (Superintendent 1785–1811)
1767	Pamplemousses	Pierre Poivre
1774	Liguanea, Jamaica	Hinton East*
1781	Samalkot	William Roxburgh
1784	Port-au-Prince	César-Henri, Comte de La Luzerne
1786	Calcutta	Robert Kyd
1787	St. Helena	Sir Joseph Banks
1790	Cayenne	Joseph Martin
1791	Manila (Malate)	Juan de Cuéllar
1803	St. Pierre, Martinique	Bélanger
1810	Ceylon	William Kerr* on Slave Island & at King's House, Colombo
1817	Peradeniya	Alexander Moon* at Peradeniya
1817	Buitenzorg (Bogor) Java	Casper Georg Carl Reinwardt
1819	Sydney*	Charles Fraser

Information derived from Desmond, R., 1994 Dictionary of British and Irish Botanists and Horticulturists.

5 | Gardens and Forests in Colonial Saint Domingue[1]

James E. McClellan III

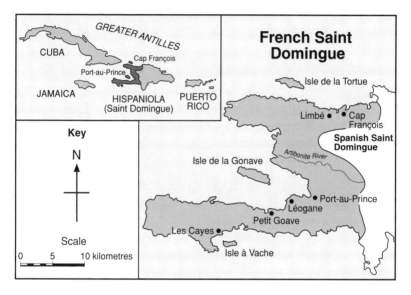

Map of 'French Saint Domingue' (by permission of the author)

From 10,000 feet in the air the border between Haiti and the Dominican Republic is starkly apparent to even the most casual observer flying into Port-au-Prince from the north across the island of Hispaniola. To the left is a verdant Dominican Republic. To the right is brown-tinged Haiti. On the ground, of course, Haiti is (for the most part) green and lush and every bit a piece of the Caribbean, but the line is there to see. It attests to different population densities, different patterns of land use, and different ecological pressures. That observation should not imply that the Dominican Republic is somehow pristine or that modern Haiti is simply degraded. Rather, the border demarcating the two countries so vividly is to be understood as an historical artifact, the latest testimony to Hispaniola's six thousand years of human occupation.

Paleo-indians first arrived on Hispaniola from Central America as early as 5000 B.C.E.[2] The forests and ecology they encountered were

65

truly pristine, but from that point forward various Indian groups and their European and African successors consciously and unconsciously shaped their island habitat. Many chapters would make up the book about Hispaniola's forests and gardens. This one concentrates on one extended episode, the period of French colonial rule over Western Hispaniola in the seventeenth and eighteenth centuries. Much of fundamental importance happened in the region subsequent to the French Revolution and the creation of the Republic of Haiti in 1804, but the French colonial period left an indelible imprint on the people, culture and ecology of the country. You can see that imprint from the air in the line that separates francophone Haiti from its Spanish neighbor.

Arawaks, Spaniards, and pirates

Migrating up the Lesser Antilles from South America, groups of Arawak Indians began to settle on Hispaniola from about 250 C.E.[3] Although the numbers are still debated, by 1492 the indigenous population may well have reached three to four million people on the 'mother island' of the Arawak.[4] In his authoritative treatment, David Watts documents the environmental effects of such large numbers, notably the establishment of a Neolithic pattern of settled villages and subsistence swidden horticulture in the form of Arawak gardens known as *conucos*, complemented by hunting and gathering.[5] Villages of 1,000–2,000 people arose in forest clearings, and the Arawaks felled timber for building houses and canoes. In addition to *conucos* the Arawaks cultivated kitchen gardens in villages. Although the creation and maintenance of *conucos* also made inroads into the forests, Watts and others emphasize the ecological balance achieved by the Arawaks.[6] Apparently, before the arrival of the Spanish, aboriginal population densities and natural resource availability were not so much in conflict as to undermine a (temporary) harmony between these pacific people and their environment.

Columbus landed on the north coast of Hispaniola in 1492, and within two decades the Arawaks and their culture essentially had been eliminated from the island, forced labor and smallpox being the primary instruments of destruction.[7] The collapse of the Arawak population and their *conucos* meant the return of wild growth to vast stretches of the island, disturbed only by growing numbers of feral pigs and cattle. In the sixteenth century, after an initial period of intense exploitation of limited gold deposits and after Cortez' conquest of Mexico, Hispaniola became a backwater for the Spanish. The center of the Spanish empire in the Americas shifted to the mainland in Mexico and South America. In the Caribbean Cuba became the primary Spanish outpost and transit point to Spain. And, in 1605 the Spanish 'foolishly' withdrew from western Hispaniola in an effort to cut off contraband, thereby creating a no-man's-land and allowing the land to return to the wild.[8] As a result, the ecology of western Hispaniola, while not pristine, was actually more wild in the seventeenth and eighteenth centuries than it had been in the heyday of the Arawaks and before the discovery of America. Into this lush and uninhabited niche slipped the next people to make their way to Hispaniola: the pirates.

Tortue Island off the northwest coast of Hispaniola formed the centre of French piracy in the Caribbean in the seventeenth century.[9] (See map above.) A diverse group of brigands, many with Protestant backgrounds, established the first pirate enclave there in the early 1630s. Tortue, like Port Royal in Jamaica, was a place of contact with the outside world where pirates could revel and be fleeced in peace. By 1650 the population of Tortue grew to 1,150, and because pirates seem not to have enjoyed large groups, offshoots from Tortue soon moved over to Hispaniola proper. Settlers founded Petit-Goave on Hispaniola's southwestern arm in 1659. The town of Léogane followed there in 1663. In 1670 twelve colonists, led by a former pirate with the evocative name of Pierre le Long, established an agricultural and fishing settlement on the north coast, Cap François.

These minor enclaves had little impact on the great forests that surrounded them. Buccaneers hunted feral cattle in the forests, with a resulting small trade in hides and smoked meats cooked on *boucans*. Like their Arawak predecessors, these residues of pirate culture planted their kitchen gardens, but they also grew tobacco. These cultivations were trivial, of course, but the latter – the production of a commodity product for consumption in Europe – represented a potent novelty that in time would transform the ecology and the economy of the entire region.

French Saint Domingue

Formal French colonization of western Hispaniola began in 1665 when the French trading company, the Compagnie des Indes Occidentales, sent a governor to oversee its interests and the development of the nascent colony.[10] In his eleven years of rule Bertrand d'Ogeron became the founding father of the French colony of Saint Domingue. He successfully asserted French claims in the area and unequivocally established French authority over the western third of Hispaniola. He and succeeding governors encouraged immigration, conceded lands, and generally promoted agricultural settlement. In Europe, the Treaty of Ryswick of 1697 formally acknowledged French sovereignty over western Hispaniola, but the agreement did not insure stability. Finally, after the

1713 Treaty of Utrecht and the death of Louis XIV in 1715, pacific conditions established themselves in Europe and in the Caribbean, and with them began the golden age of the Saint Domingue colony.

At its peak in the 1780s French Saint Domingue was the single richest and most productive colony in the world.[11] The French West Indian possession was then the world's leading producer of both sugar and coffee. Already by 1776 the single colony of Saint Domingue produced more exportable wealth than the whole of the Spanish empire in the Americas.[12] Contemporary Saint Domingue meant a great deal to France, where one French person in eight is said to have lived off colonial trade in one way or another. Eighteenth-century Saint Domingue has rightly been called a pivot in the world economy of the day and a key link in the evolving global system of contemporary European colonialism.[13]

The sheer size and density of the colony's eighteenth-century population put Saint Domingue at this cutting edge. In 1790 approximately 560,000 people lived in the colony. That figure about equals the combined populations of contemporary New York and Pennsylvania, then the two most populous states in the new United States. However, more than half million people in French Saint Domingue were tightly packed into a mountainous area about the size of the state of Maryland, making Saint Domingue one of the most densely populated spots in the New World at the time.[14] There were thirty-two thousand free whites in the colony, a tiny minority, overwhelmingly immigrants from France. Twenty-eight thousand inhabitants were mixed-race free people of color, virtually all born in the colony. The overwhelming majority, slaves constituted nearly 90 percent of the colony's population (500,000), most born in Africa. In dramatic contrast, the most heavily slave state in the United States, South Carolina, was only 60 percent slave at the time. French Saint Domingue thus stood at the unhappy vanguard of contemporary race relations and the forging of multiracial towns and societies in the Americas.[15] The fact that in 1791 its slaves rose up in history's largest and most successful slave revolt exemplifies the extraordinary character of Saint Domingue as a slave society. That revolt culminated in the establishment of the Republic of Haiti in 1804, the second independent country in the Western Hemisphere after the United States.

The urban centers that arose in Saint Domingue added to the colony's contemporary fame. Situated on the Atlantic coast, the main town in the colony, Cap François, had a population of 18,850 in 1789, making it roughly the same size as Boston in North America or Dijon in France. Cap François was vibrant and lively, much more so than its sleepy Caribbean and South American counterparts. The quality and diversity of life in Cap François, for a privileged white minority at least, largely matched anything offered in Havana, Philadelphia, New York, or Charleston. Its busy port, its government and military presence, its theater, its scientific and intellectual life, its decadence – all conspired to make Cap François and the social order that flourished in Saint Domingue at the end of the eighteenth century an advanced center of civilization in the Americas.

Urban civilization represented one pole of a continuum, the wilderness another. Only eight percent of the population lived in real towns with populations of over a thousand. Three communities stood in the first rank as veritable cities: Cap François, Port-au-Prince on the central coast, and Les Cayes on the southern coast.[16] Eight towns, fifty villages, and a dozen or so hamlets and docking sites complemented these three urban centers. The overwhelming majority of the population lived deep in colonial isolation on rural plantations. No one in the towns or the countryside was ever very far from the bush.

Mountains and forests

Beyond the plantations and enclaves of civilization so laboriously carved out by the French and their slaves, the natural setting and wilderness of Saint Domingue provided defining features of the colony and its history. French colonization proceeded along an inhospitable frontier, and development faced imposing stretches of wilderness and a wall of raw nature. French Saint Domingue bordered on the bush, and the itchy natural world intruded unavoidably.

Heavily forested wherever climatic conditions permitted, the land was colonized in the first instance by human conquest and exploitation of the forest. Unlike Haiti today, which has become wholly deforested, deep woods persisted across huge areas of Saint Domingue late into the eighteenth century. Humans interacted with the forest in various ways, first by clearing the forest for settlement. Around towns especially, colonists cut down entire forests. Sugar plantations and field agriculture seem to have been established in more open areas, but the coming of coffee cultivation in the 1730s growing marked another onslaught against native forests. A number of hardwood forests in Saint Domingue supplied good wood for construction, for naval timber, and for the mahogany furniture industry back in France. Mangroves were cut back for firewood. Goats were also a factor in diminishing woodlands. The availability of wood, or rather its opposite, became a problem as the eighteenth century unfolded, and in all areas around human habitation forests soon became scarce. In 1745 authorities ordered the end of uncontrolled cutting of trees for free firewood.[17] As forests receded, the costs of transporting felled trees from the interior to the coasts rose prohibitively, to the point where it actually became cheaper to import lumber from the United States than to log it in Saint Domingue.[18]

The land's natural division into mountains and plains represents a fundamental fact of the topography and history of Saint Domingue. The colony was about 60 percent mountain and 40 percent plain. Three mountain chains effectively broke the colony up into its primary administrative districts, the northern, western, and southern departments.[19] The mountains of Saint Domingue and Haiti today range upward of 8,000 feet, and many peaks in the eighteenth century had not yet been climbed by Europeans.

Mountains imposed formidable barriers to intracolony communication and transportation, barriers never completely overcome and not even adequately overcome until the last years of the Old Regime. The northern chain of mountains in particular proved a major obstacle to the creation of a system of royal roads. The first land connection between Port-au-Prince and Cap François was effected only in 1751. An improved link cut into the mountains in 1781 was serviceable only on horseback or on foot. Travel by carriage between Port-au-Prince and Cap François became possible only in 1785. By 1789 the principal settlements of the colony were connected by roads, but still many areas remained isolated and cut off, and in Cap François one spoke of the Caribbean coast of Saint Domingue as one might speak of the Andes.

The combination of mountains and considerable rain meant that Saint Domingue possessed many, mostly short rivers carrying runoff from the mountains to bottomlands and the sea. At least thirty-two named rivers flowed in Saint Domingue.[20] The little Dalmarie extended just over one mile long; the Artibonite was the longest river in Saint Domingue, stretching nearly 60 miles in French territory. Flooding often became a dangerous problem, when swollen and powerful courses would seasonally burst their banks. For example, two hundred people drowned when the Grande Rivière of Gorge Ste. Rose flooded in 1722; the Limbé River took out the town of Limbé in 1744.[21] Engineers undertook river control and hydraulic projects not only to irrigate plantations, but also as a matter of public safety.

Saint Domingue possessed eight major plains, structuring the colony in much the same way that mountains divide plains and valleys in Greece. Four of these plains assumed a major importance in the development of the colony. The largest, called the northern plain, the Plaine du Nord or the Plaine du Cap, amounted to a thin strip of land along the north coast; it covered an area of about 1,000 square miles, of which perhaps 500 were level and arable. The northern plain became highly developed agriculturally, and Cap François became its urban center and commercial outlet. In the western department the Artibonite

Plain of 250 square miles flanked the Artibonite River that flowed from the interior of Spanish Saint Domingue. Saint Marc served as the main port center for this plain. The third largest plain, the Cul-de-Sac around Port-au-Prince, blanketed 132 square miles and was very flat. The Cul-de-Sac ended up surpassing all other areas in agricultural development, and after 1787, when political power shifted entirely to Port-au-Prince, it became the decided center of the colony. Several other smaller plains, including that of Léogane, dotted the northern side of the south arm. The fourth largest plain and the major one on the south coast was the plain of Les Cayes, the Plaine des Cayes, 110 square miles. While not as developed as the other regions, the area around Les Cayes was growing rapidly in the 1780s and represented the most promising part of the colony.

French Saint Domingue possessed an extraordinarily long coastline of over 800 miles, counting bays and coves. That distance exceeded by over 100 miles the length of the coast of Spanish Saint Domingue, a colony twice as large in area.[22] Such a long, extended coast gave Saint Domingue even more of an orientation toward the sea. All was littoral, and the sea represented another natural expanse and frontier faced by colonists as they looked one way, complementing the mountains and forests they faced on the other. Colonization proceeded inward from the coast, and all activity flowed to and from the coast and its ports. The interior became less developed as one proceeded inland, and some mountain fastnesses stood as far from contemporary French civilization as one can imagine.

Obstacles and resistance

Nature offered some riches but mostly presented obstacles to overcome. Pests of various sorts, for example, tormented the everyday lives of the people of Saint Domingue. Depending on the locale, giant mosquitoes swarmed, and flies produced severe bites, subject to infection. Moreau de Saint-Méry, the famous creole chronicler of Saint Domingue, recommended mosquito netting to all who could afford it. Insect attacks on crops posed an especial danger, and ants in particular threatened sugar cane fields. Colonists completely abandoned agriculture in the Côtes-de-Fer region, for example, on account of drought and the blistering 'sticky worm.' A plague of ants, caterpillars, aphids, and rats combined to assault agriculture around Les Cayes in 1750. Rats and mice infested Saint Domingue, and on occasion populations of these creatures swelled.

Crabs were major pests. Large land crabs made holes everywhere, and ate the roots of sugar cane. For its inhabitants, the annual crab migration through the town of Jérémie proved a great and trying confrontation with nature. Every year literally millions of breeding crabs formed a rolling wall and invaded Jérémie on their way to the sea and back. Moreau de Saint-Méry reported that they got in everywhere – even one's bed. They could not be stopped. Their creeping, chitinous noise was infernal. The stench of dead crab was horrendous. Conditions became so bad in 1774 and for three years running that authorities formally ordered all Jérémie residents to dispose of their dead crabs twice a day during the invasion.[23]

The mobilization of resources to fight pests is a noteworthy feature of the colonizing process in the Caribbean. A group of patriotic citizens founded a learned society in Cap François in 1784, the Cercle des Philadelphes, and one of their first acts was to establish a generous prize of 1650 colonial pounds (*livres*) for the best means of preserving paper from the ravages of insects.[24] Insect depredations on paper was a non-trivial problem that affected colonial administration, record keeping, and the long-term stability of the colony. Unfortunately, the one effective solution received by the Cercle des Philadelphes involved treating paper with arsenic and was deemed too dangerous for use. In a related episode, with the approval of colonial and royal authorities, the planters of Martinique joined together to offer a truly extraordinary prize of one million pounds for a means of preserving cane fields from ant attacks. The prize for an effective ant repellent was never awarded, but its existence testifies to what the colonial war with nature involved and what was at stake.[25]

On the positive side, the sea provided an important source of food, and local fishing was active. Shellfish (including oysters, conch, sea urchins, and crabs) was plentiful, but the palates of Europeans spurned these foods (excepting oysters), fearing poison. Shellfish did, however, form a notable part of the diets of slaves. But sea life in the form of the teredo posed a particular threat, for these wood-boring sea worms voraciously attacked ships' hulls and made all pilings and piers transitory.

On land, crocodiles were common but seemingly not a danger to man. A large gray lizard upward of 3.5 feet was also common, and apparently quite tasty. Sea turtles and tortoises abounded, and were hunted and eaten by humans, crocodiles, and wild pigs. Saint Domingue did not have poisonous snakes, but grass snakes sometimes proved to be a nuisance.

Saint Domingue harbored plentiful game. Sea birds and forest birds provided a variety of fowl. Colonists trapped parakeets and other exotic birds as pets, and they sometimes took rodent piloris and agoutis for food. Feral cattle and pigs roamed the bush, survivors from the early days of the Spanish. Hunting feral cattle proved important in the early days of the colony, and humans still hunted feral cattle and pigs in the eighteenth century, sometimes using dogs, and packs of wild dogs hunted on their own. Slaves in the Tiburon region hunted pet monkeys that had returned to the wild. Wild (and domestic) cats acted as a check on rat and bird populations.

Not to be neglected among the fauna of Saint Domingue were tribes of 'feral men' living beyond the pale in forest enclaves in the mountains. Slaves escaped constantly, and some groups of maroons managed to establish permanent or semi-permanent encampments, the most famous being the maroon colony in the Bahoruco mountains on the Caribbean in the south. From the first years of the eighteenth century, maroons found a safe haven in these isolated mountains straddling French and Spainish Saint Domingue. An independent enclave emerged that was composed of runaway slaves, military deserters, and true 'forest people' actually born into the Bahoruco colony. In principle and in practice Bahoruco maroons represented such a threat to French colonization and the slave system that colonial authorities mounted at least a dozen military campaigns against them over the course of the eighteenth century. In 1785 French and Spanish authorities concluded a treaty with the Bahoruco enclave, whereby the maroons of the Bahoruco gained freedom and resettlement in return for their services in hunting other maroons.

Plantations

If the colonization of Saint Domingue proceeded against a formidable natural frontier, the ecological impact of colonial development was also extensive.[26] In the long run in Saint Domingue, as elsewhere, nature could not withstand the power of the human onslaught.

The most important 'gardens' in French Saint Domingue were the thousands of plantations that dotted its plains. The tobacco era and the era of the small farmer ended early in the eighteenth century, and an entirely different and much more imposing set of agricultural industries emerged, centered on the production of sugar, coffee, indigo, and cotton. By 1789 colonists cultivated as many as 2.5 million acres in French Saint Domingue with at least 1.5 million acres under 'high cultivation.' Over 7,800 plantations churned out commodity products for export back to France.

Extensive hydraulic-engineering works were installed in the colony for irrigating fields and for processing crops, especially indigo and sugar, and irrigation utterly transformed large areas of Saint Domingue. The combined effect of the sun's tropical heat and water from irrigation created intense and ideal growing conditions for the commodity crops raised in Saint Domingue. The Cul-de-Sac region around Port-au-Prince led the colony in the extent of its irrigation. In all, on the eve of the French Revolution, hydraulic systems there irrigated fifty-eight plantations and some 36,000 acres, nearly half of the Cul-de-Sac plain. That flat and well-watered expanse, with its lush and regularly laid-out fields and its straight and well-maintained roads, must have been a remarkable sight in 1789.

Sugar was the leading colonial product, and in 1791 nearly 800 plantations produced 192 million pounds of raw sugar for export. Coffee was the colony's second great commodity product. Coffee began to be grown in Saint Domingue in the 1720s, but the takeoff in coffee production occurred only after 1765, when authorities imported 100,000 trees into the colony. The mountains and climate of Saint Domingue proved ideal for growing coffee beans. Saint-Domingue's coffee rivaled the world's best, and by the end of the 1780s, Saint Domingue had become the world's largest producer of coffee. Ironically, coffee came to Saint Domingue as the result of a scientific exchange that backfired. Coffee tree seeds reached the Amsterdam Botanic Garden in 1706, and in seeming innocence the Dutch sent some on to the Jardin du Roi in Paris. The French then turned around and launched coffee production in the Caribbean, introducing the tree into Martinique in 1723 and thence to Saint Domingue in 1726. Coffee provided a potent example of the possibilities of applied botany, an example not lost on colonial planners who would make systematic attempts to replicate the accomplishment.

Gardens

Colonists brought with them an ark of plants and animals that also transformed local ecologies. Many small-scale, private, and accidental introductions occurred as part of the colonizing process. Colonists seemingly cultivated the entire range of European fruits and vegetables in their gardens and orchards: potatoes, cabbages, onions, leeks, carrots, artichokes, strawberries, grapes, and various kinds of trees (fig, apple, mulberry, and cherry). Another range of plants, now thought typical of the Antilles, were likewise brought to Saint Domingue from Africa and elsewhere, including bananas, cassavas, the citrus fruits, mangos, pineapples, and avocados.

Colonists also introduced animals into the colony. Moreau de Saint-Méry counted 40,000 horses, 50,000 mules, and 250,000 cattle, sheep, goats, and pigs in the colony in 1789.[27] Elsewhere Moreau mentions chickens and both the European and African duck, and a strange buffalo-cow hybrid existed in the colony, at least in limited numbers. In addition to the previously mentioned monkeys, camels from North Africa added to the colony's fauna in the 1750s, but the camels scared the horses and would not reproduce. Animals had to be fed, even if ultimately to be eaten, and pens and barns and stock areas had to be set aside. Among the more interesting and useful animals introduced into Saint Domingue were bees. Apiculture began with bees from the Spanish side of Saint Domingue originally brought from Cuba; another introduction brought bees from Martinique. Beeswax and honey were obviously useful and both reported to be of good quality in Saint Domingue.

The ecological impact of bees was no doubt benevolent, but the same cannot be said of a last example: the introduction of French snails into the colony. Presumably for delectation, the Séguineau brothers imported escargot from their native La Rochelle and released them on their coffee plantation in the Arcahaye region. The European snail succeeded all too well in the local struggle for existence, and populations skyrocketed. Snails quickly infested an area of several square miles, and they proved a threat to coffee trees. Concerted action was called for, and the Séguineau brothers went so far as to *pay* their slaves to collect snails, and they gave them salt with which to season and eat snails.[28] The ultimate outcome of the effort to eradicate snails in Arcahaye remains unknown, and the escargot example is wholly minor, but it illustrates well the principles involved in considering the ecological impact of colonialism or, more particularly in this case, French colonialism.

Botanical gardens

By the end of the colonial period a number of true botanical gardens could be found in Saint Domingue. Louis XVI lent his name to the Jardin Royal, established in Port-au-Prince in 1777. A succeeding Jardin du Roi arose in the latter 1780s, and a third garden existed in Port-au-Prince at the headquarters of the colonial administrators. In the north, on the outskirts of Cap François the Brothers of Charity maintained a substantial botanical garden on the grounds of the Hôpital de la Charité. Likewise in the Cap-François area, the Cercle des Philadelphes, the colony's scientific society, established the first of its two botanical gardens with government support in 1785. A.-J. Brulley, a colonist, maintained a sizable private garden and nursery on his property in the Marmelade district in the northern mountains, as did another colonist, Paul Belin de Villeneuve in Limbé on the north coast.

The botanical gardens in Saint Domingue in large measure grew out of efforts to establish cochineal dye production in the colony. The cochineal insect (*Dactylopius coccus*) is a parasite of cactus plants, and its dried residue makes an intense red dye. Through the 1770s the Spanish guarded their monopoly on the production of cochineal, for which the French paid dearly to supply the Gobelins dye works in Paris. One J.-N. Thierry de Menonville had studied with the great Parisian botanist, Bernard de Jussieu, and in early 1777 with permission from the highest levels of government and with a substantial government purse, he traveled from Saint Domingue to Mexico to steal samples of cochineal for husbandry in Saint Domingue. In an adventure fraught with dangers, Thierry de Menonville succeeded in his mission, returning to Saint Domingue with his precious cargo of so-called *fina* cochineal in September of 1777.

The Jardin du Roi in Port-au-Prince was established especially to receive Thierry de Menonville's treasure, and experimental cochineal husbandry proceeded satisfactorily under his guidance as a very well-paid *botaniste du roi*.[29] P.-J. Macquer, professor of chemistry at the Jardin du Roi in Paris and *pensionnaire* of the Academy of Sciences there, performed the first tests of Saint Domingue cochineal as a dyeing agent. But Thierry de Menonville died in 1780, the Jardin du Roi languished, and its *fina* cochineal perished. Fortunately for them, colonists discovered a wild, *sylvestre* form of the cochineal insect in Saint Domingue and proceeded with further efforts at applied botany.

Brulley seeded his own nopalry or cactus plantation with four thousand cacti and succeeded with several harvests. In 1787 he sent samples of his cochineal product to France, where the Paris Academy of Sciences conducted tests that showed the samples very nearly equal to that of Mexican *fina* cochineal. Brulley also supplied the starter stock for the garden of the Cercle des Philadelphes in Cap François, and by November of 1785 the Cercle des Philadelphes had produced three cochineal harvests of its own. The Cercle sent samples of the dyestuff back to Paris for testing. Swatches from these tests survive, still brilliantly scarlet after more than two hundred years. As part of this effort, the Cercle also undertook publication of Thierry de Menonville's opus, *Traité de la Culture du Nopal et ...de la Cochenille*, which appeared in 1787 in a handsome two-volume octavo set of 436 pages with four colored plates. The second volume, especially, was a practical manual of cochineal husbandry destined to instruct potential growers. In his review of this book, Charles Mozard, the editor of the colonial newspaper, the *Affiches Américaines*, suggested that cochineal production might someday rival coffee in economic importance to Saint Domingue. While far from challenging coffee, the nascent cochineal industry followed the established model of applied botany provided by coffee cultivation, and it did hold great promise for the long-term economic development of the colony. Colonial authorities had taken the necessary first steps, and in the process the institutions and infrastructures of applied botany arrived in Saint Domingue.

A major discovery with great potential for French economic botany occurred when someone found an indigenous form of Peruvian cinchona in Saint Domingue in 1785. The famous 'Peruvian bark,' taken from the cinchona bush served as a specific against malaria. Botanists transferred the newly discovered cinchona plants to the Jardin du Roi in Port-au-Prince, where they prospered. Samples were sent to France for clinical trials, and medical authorities passed the ambivalent word back that Saint Domingue quinine could replace genuine Peruvian bark in certain respects but that it proved inferior in others.

Botanical activity continued to mount in Saint Domingue as the 1780s progressed. In 1785 the Cercle des Philadelphes gave a public course on botany in its garden on Tuesdays and Saturdays from 2:00 to 4:00 p.m. One could find mango, the Senegal date, Chinese mulberry, the Cape of Good Hope palm, and 'the precious breadfruit,' all in the gardens of the Charité Hospital in Cap François.[30] A 1788 inventory of the Jardin du Roi in Port-au-Prince depicts an even more vibrant establishment. Its nopalry numbered four to five hundred cacti covered with cochineal provided by Brulley. Seventy-two different types of exotic trees and plants graced the botanical garden, including clove, cinnamon, ipecac, aloe, fig trees from various parts of the world, various types of palm tree, jasmine from the Cape of Good Hope, Madagascar indigo, Surinam mustard, green tea plants, litchi trees, Chinese rose bushes, chestnut trees from Virginia, wax bushes from Louisiana, Cuban cedar trees, genuine sago, and other trees and plants from Egypt and India. Bamboo grew well in the nearby government garden, and it probably grew in the Jardin du Roi as well. Pecan trees from Mississippi were likely to be found there, too, as the government had distributed seedlings for propagation trials in 1787.[31] All of this activity contributed to the effort to establish a fourth botanical garden in the capital.

The French and Haitian revolutions cut off possibilities for further efforts at applied botany in the colony. Still, in France, a plan backed by the Société Royale d'Agriculture before the National Assembly in 1791 called for the creation of a set of commercial gardens in Saint Domingue to raise spices and exotic plants. And in Saint Domingue itself, in the midst of a civil war and a raging slave revolt, as late as January of 1792, a colonial Provincial Assembly was calling for a new botanical garden for Port-au-Prince. These stillborn efforts testify to just how deeply economic botany was felt to be necessary for colonial development.

Saint Domingue's gardens in international context

The 'precious breadfruit' and list of foreign trees and plants mentioned above raise a fundamental point that needs to be highlighted in considering the history of botanical gardens in Saint Domingue. That is, the gardens of Saint Domingue cannot be thought of in splendid colonial isolation. Rather, they formed an integral part of a larger network of French botanical gardens that spanned the metropolis and other contemporary French colonies.[32] Indeed, the French colonial gardens on Hispaniola were the last pieces to fall into place of an intercontinental system designed to secure, nurture, and bring valuable plant commodities into large-scale production. Here again, coffee provided the model.

The magnificent Jardin du Roi in Paris stood as the centerpiece of this system.[33] The Jardin du Roi originated in the 1620s and 1630s as a royal garden for medicinal plants. In the later decades of the seventeenth century it became transformed into a 'scientific' garden devoted to the study of botany and the cultivation of plant specimens, and by the end of the eighteenth century it flourished as a world center, if not *the* world center for botanical research. It was a well-endowed state institution with a large, paid staff of professors, demonstrators, curators, and gardeners. Six thousand different species of plant could be found on its grounds, many in hothouses especially intended for foreign and tropical plants.

The royal gardens at the Trianon and Rambouillet on the outskirts of Paris complemented the Jardin du Roi as further elements in the burgeoning system of gardens in the metropolis.[34] The Queen's garden at the Trianon at Versailles is notable, not just as a major botanical installation, but also for nurturing gardeners and botanists who later filled positions in other gardens elsewhere.[35] Louis XVI acquired the property at Rambouillet in 1784 with the particular aim of turning it into a station for experimental horticulture for native American species. The royal botanist, André Michaux, on assignment in the new United States from 1785 to 1796, sent many tree specimens back to Rambouillet. The Abbé H.-A.Tessier managed the Rambouillet gardens. Tessier collaborated with André Thouin at the Jardin du Roi, and he is well known as an instigator of colonial exchanges.[36]

Elsewhere in France, botanical gardens dotted the provinces, in part as an outgrowth of the 1707 edict of Louis XIV that each medical faculty was to have a professor of botany and an associated botanical garden. Provincial academies were likewise great promoters of botanical gardens, and for a while under Louis XV there were official state nurseries in every province.[37] The garden of Compagnie des Indes in Lorient in Brittany deserves separate mention as an entrepôt for plants from China destined for the Jardin du Roi and the Trianon.[38] Similarly, at the outlet of the Loire the botanical garden in the port city of Nantes occupied a special place among contemporary botanical gardens in France. Beginning in the 1720s, it became a government garden and a formal subsidiary of the Jardin du Roi in Paris with the particular mission of acclimatizing plants from overseas. Its royal Letters Patent dictated that captains putting into port at Nantes had to deposit a certain number of seeds and plants or face a fine. Before the loss of Canada in 1763 the Nantes garden received many plants from that region. Officials in Martinique also were especially effective in delivering specimens from the Caribbean to Nantes and thence to Paris.[39] Royal gardens in Marseille, La Rochelle, Brest, and elsewhere were likewise involved in the transshipments of colonial plants to the metropolis and the Jardin du Roi.[40]

In the Indian Ocean the French East Indian Company established the first garden, known as Pamplemousses, on the Île de France (Mauritius) in 1735. After 1750 colonial administrators upgraded and enlarged the Pamplemousses garden, which then functioned as an experimental horticultural station. Two more government gardens arose on Île de France, one (Le Réduit) in 1748 and another (Palma) in 1775. A sister garden was planted at Saint-Denis on nearby Île Bourbon (Reunion) in the Indian Ocean in 1769, and other botanical stations and transplant gardens may have existed there. In another chapter in this book Madeleine Ly-Tio-Fane provides details of the Indian-Ocean gardens, and she retells the wonderful story of Pierre Poivre and his dramatic raids on Dutch and Spanish possessions in Southeast Asia in the 1750s to obtain pepper, cinnamon, nutmeg, clove, and other valuable spices. The goal was to inaugurate French spice production in the colonies and to establish a new and profitable branch of the economy for France. Poivre returned to the Mascarienes to direct two more successful expeditions, one in 1769 and another in 1771–1772. Officials distributed clove, nutmeg, and other spices to private and public gardens on Île de France and Île Bourbon for propagation.[41] The next step was to transport plants and establish spice cultivations in the Americas.

A notable element of these developments and the success of French economic botany in this period was the creation of the post of royal botanist (*botaniste du roi*). These were botanical specialists paid by the crown, most of them trained by the botanists and gardeners at the Jardin du Roi. They represent a new, more professional generation of experts concerned with botany in colonial contexts. They succeeded royal doctors who dabbled in matters botanical while on colonial duty and, before the doctors, independent travelers, many with connections to religious orders. The existence and activities of French royal botanists testify to the seriousness with which economic botany was being pursued by French authorities at the end of the eighteenth century.

In the Americas one Pierre Barrère served as royal botanist in Cayenne in South America from 1722 to 1725, an early date. J.-F. Autur who was trained at the Jardin du Roi in Paris succeeded Barrère from 1735 to 1770. J.-B.-C. Fusée-Aublet was posted to the Île de France in 1753, later transferring to become royal botanist in Cayenne from 1762 to 1764. Other royal botanists and physicians served in the equatorial jungles of French Guyana and Cayenne in the eighteenth century.[42] In this context the agricultural station arose on the La Gabrielle plantation in 1778 specifically to receive and multiply spice plants from the Indian Ocean.

In the Caribbean a significant effort began in 1710s to create a botanical garden on Guadeloupe. The Paris Academy of Sciences was involved, and Caribbean specimens were sent back to the Jardin du Roi. The effort seems to have faltered, however, and the royal gardens in Guadeloupe were upgraded only in 1775, with J.-A. Barbotteau becoming superintending botanist for the Windward Islands. On Martinique the Intendant, J.-F. de Foulquier, was instrumental in vivifying botanical activity on that island, and he and several royal physicians were elected as correspondents of the Paris Academy of Sciences. Then, with the appearance of royal gardens in the Saint-Domingue colony in the later 1770s, the infrastructure of French applied botany was completed, and it is in this larger global context that botanical gardens in Saint Domingue need to be evaluated.

The functioning of this intercontinental system of botanical gardens began in the 1770s. The first shipment of exotic plants from the Indian Ocean arrived in Saint Domingue in 1773 with plants brought aboard the *Artibonite* distributed to colonists and doubtless producing some local impact. The American War of Independence interrupted further efforts until 1786. In that year and again in 1786 the *Sincère* made two trips from Saint Domingue to Cayenne to pick up clove, cinnamon, nutmeg, and other spice plants that had been sent from Île de France to South America. These were distributed to the Cercle des Philadelphes and to private individuals for propagation. In July of 1788, another botanical shipment, this one directly from the Indian Ocean, arrived in Saint Domingue aboard the slave ship *Alexandre*. Sent by the government botanist, J.-N. Céré, from the Île de France gardens and accompanied by another government botanist, Darras, the shipment included pepper plants, cinnamon trees, mango trees, mangosteen fruit, and a few breadfruit trees from Tahiti. Kept in the ship's hold, nearly all the plants died before arriving in Saint Domingue. But seventeen different types of tree and plant and sixteen different types of seed did survive, including the 'precious breadfruit'.

Curiously, at the same time that the *Alexandre* winded its way to Saint Domingue in 1787 and 1788, Captain William Bligh was transporting the breadfruit tree to the Caribbean for the English aboard the *HMS Bounty*. The mutiny aboard the *Bounty* incidentally secured a victory for the

French in the race to be the first to get breadfruit to their respective West-Indian colonies. Colonial authorities recognized the value of the breadfruit as especially suitable for the climate of their Caribbean possessions and for the hundreds of thousands of captive mouths that had to be fed there. The royal botanist in Saint Domingue, Hippolyte Nectoux, distributed bread-fruit to twelve private and public stations around Saint Domingue, includ-ing the garden in the government compound, the second garden of the Cercle des Philadelphes, and the gardens of the Charity hospital in Cap François.[43] The full effect of the breadfruit project remains unknown, but the instance illustrates again the mounting efforts to promote economic botany in Saint Domingue in the 1780s.

Rather than becoming discouraged by the high mortality associ-ated with intercolonial plant transfers, the government redoubled its efforts, and in June of 1789 another shipment from Île de France arrived in Saint Domingue aboard the *Stanislas*. Although many plants again did not survive the long crossing, enough clove trees in particular did to make the voyage worthwhile. No further opportuni-ty for exchanges between Saint Domingue and the Indian Ocean occurred after 1789.

While shipments from the Indian Ocean to the Americas proceeded on the periphery of the French colonial system, a feedback loop operated between Saint Domingue and Paris, notably between Nectoux and André Thouin, chief royal gardener at the Jardin du Roi. This facet of the system's functioning can be seen in the list of six hundred different seeds sown at the Jardin du Roi in Paris in the spring of 1790. They came from Saint Domingue, Martinique, Cayenne, Île de France, Île Bourbon, Madagascar, Senegal, the Cape of Good Hope, Florida, Louisiana, China, India, Manilla, the Dutch East Indes, and Botany Bay (Australia).[44]

France was not the only colonial power to create colonial botanical gardens or to undertake the transport of valuable plants from one part of the world to another. The history of colonial botanical gardens in the eighteenth century represents another dimension of the geo-politics raging at the time between and among European colonial powers, notably the British, French, and Dutch. By the same token, nationalism did not always prevail, and interludes of peace brought moments of botanical cooperation. Following the American War, plant specimens from Saint Domingue and Martinique were sent to the English gardens on Saint Vincent, and Nectoux twice traveled to Jamaica (in 1788 and 1789) to confer with his English counterpart, Dr. Thomas Clarke, and to exchange rare and valuable specimens, including tea.

The apprentice royal botanist, Joseph Martin, provides a wonder-ful concluding vignette that captures something of the state of colonial botany among the great powers at the end of the eighteenth century, and it frames the larger scene for considering the botanical gardens back in Saint Domingue. In 1788 Martin was sailing from France to the Indian Ocean to pick up plants for transshipment to the Caribbean. On his way to Île de France his vessel put in for provisioning at the Cape of Good Hope. In a letter dated July 2, 1788, Martin wrote back to Thouin in Paris from False Bay at the southern tip of Africa:

> A merchant vessel is here bound for Cayenne that took on a cargo of spice trees at the Île de France at a cost of 52,000 francs. [This is the shipment aboard the *Alexandre* mentioned above.] It put in at the Cape of Good Hope. There was also an English packboat in port at False Bay that was going to the Tahitian islands to get breadfruit. Their ship was sent for this express purpose. The ship is carrying hothouses, a botanist, two astronomers, and a geographer.[45]

This antipodean intersection of two French botanical expeditions to and from the Indian Ocean and the *HMS Bounty* on its way to Tahiti in 1788 epitomizes the forces and factors at play in the history of contemporary European colonialism, the story of economic botany, and this account of the gardens of Saint Domingue.

Postscript

This overview of the gardens and forests of old Saint Domingue ends with the French and Haitian revolutions that began in 1789 and swept across Hispaniola through 1804. New themes emerged to shape the ecology of western Hispaniola in the nineteenth century, notably the collapse of the plantation system, population growth, and the division of the land into smaller and smaller parcels. That story is for another historian to tell. Although the French chapter ultimately left much of an imprint on the land and the people of Haiti, old Saint Domingue itself has long since disappeared.

Notes

1 This chapter is based in large part on the author's 1992 volume, *Colonialism and Science: Saint Domingue in the Old Regime*. In the absence of other citations, readers are directed to this work as the reference source for points discussed here.
2 Watts, *The West Indies*, p. 45.
3 Watts, *The West Indies*, p. 51.
4 McClellan, *Colonialism and Science*, p. 35 and note. See also extended discussion of the issue of aboriginal population numbers in Watts, *The West Indies*, pp. 71–75.
5 Watts, *The West Indies*, pp. 53–71. Manioc and sweet potato were the major cultivars. Hunting and gathering was primarily of sea life.
6 Watts, *The West Indies*, p. 60.7

7 McClellan, *Colonialism and Science*, pp. 35 and 308n.6; Watts, *The West Indies*, pp. 71–74, 103.

8 Devèze, *Antilles*, p. 144.

9 On the pirates, see Butel, *Les Caraïbes*, and Ritchie, *Captain Kidd*, passim. See also Lewis, *Main Currents*, pp. 78–83, the pioneering study by Burg, *Sodomy*.

10 For background on the general history of French colonization in the seventeenth and eighteenth century, including Saint Domingue, consult Meyer et al., *Histoire*, esp. Part III, and Pluchon, *Histoire*, esp. Part II.

11 See sources cited in McClellan, *Colonialism and Science*, pp. 2, 63. The ur-source on these matters is Tarrade, *Le Commerce colonial*.

12 Lewis, *Main Currents*, p. 123; Devèze, *Antilles*, p. 267.

13 Maurel, 'La Poste,' makes this point, p. 1.

14 Moreau de Saint-Méry put the population in the French Saint Domingue at six and one-half times that on the Spanish side of Hispaniola; see his *Description...de la Partie Française* (hereafter *DPF*), p. 28.

15 Hoetink, 'Race,' p. 55.

16 McClellan, *Colonialism and Science*, pp. 75–78 and his Map 2.

17 Moreau de Saint-Méry, *DPF*, p. 1270.

18 Moreau de Saint-Méry, *DPF*, p. 856. With so little wood in Haiti today, charcoal is made from cactus.

19 On the topography and climate of Saint Domingue/Haiti, see Anglade, *Atlas Critique*, and Centre d'Études de Géographie Tropicale, *Atlas d'Haïti*.

20 Maurel and Taillemite in *DPF,* pp. 1427, 1430–31.

21 Moreau de Saint-Méry, *DPF,* pp. 226, 683.

22 Moreau de Saint-Méry, *DPF,* pp. 27, 1409.

23 Moreau de Saint-Méry tells this story, *DPF*, pp. 1404–5. Crabs also posed a real danger of poison because they ate and transmitted the poison from the fruit of the manchineel tree, which was rigorously exterminated.

24 On this episode, see McClellan, *Colonialism and Science*, pp. 217–218.

25 See Archives Départementales, Fort-de-France, Martinique, Série B, Registre 13, fol. 152; Durand-Molard, vol. 3, pp. 256–58. Many of the papers submitted for this prize can be found in the dossier, Archives Nationales, Paris, Marine G146, 'Procédés pour détruire des formis, 1775–1778.'

26 Lacroix, *Figures*, makes this point, vol. 3, pp. 138–41; see also Crosby, *Ecological Imperialism*.

27 Moreau de Saint-Méry, *DPF*, p. 111.

28 Moreau de Saint-Méry tells the story in *DPF,* pp. 933–34.

29 Thierry de Menonville was paid 2/1/2 times the salary of the chief government doctor in the colony; see Moreau de Saint-Méry, *DPF*, p. 1020.

30 Moreau de Saint-Méry, *DPF*, pp. 574–76. The mulberry tree was brought by a colonist who got it from Buffon at the Jardin du Roi in Paris.

31 McClellan, *Colonialism and Science*, p. 162, citing an inventory published in the colonial newspaper, the *Affiches Américaines*, on March 8, 1788. See also Moreau de Saint-Méry, *DPF*, p. 1021.

32 These points are taken up in McClellan, *Colonialism and Science*, chapt. 9. See also McClellan and Regourd, 'The Colonial Machine,' pp. 40–44, Regourd, 'Sciences et colonisation,' pp. 469–89, and the Ly-Tio-Fane chapter elsewhere in this volume. The article by Bourguet and Bonneuil, 'De l'inventaire du monde,' is an important recent analysis of the connections between botany and colonialism that needs to be consulted in this connection.

33 On the Jardin du Roi, see the recent volume by Spary, *Utopia's Garden*. See also Letouzey, *Le jardin des Plantes*, and the still-valuable Laissus, 'Le Jardin du roi.' In

emphasizing the colonial and acclimatizing aspects of the Jardin du Roi, the study by Kury, 'André Thouin,' is also to be consulted.

34 Bouchenot-Déchin, *Henry Dupuis*, provides an entry into the royal gardens of the Bourbon kings. See also Velut, *La rose*, for more on the larger social context.

35 The best example is Louis-Claude Richard (1754–1821). His grandfather founded the Trianon gardens, and he was nephew of Antoine Richard, the head gardener at the Trianon. L.-C. Richard in turn became director of the colonial garden in Guyana in 1785. One of a veritable dynasty of royal gardeners, he apparently had a brother who was a botanist on Île de France prior to the Revolution. André Michaux likewise studied at the Trianon.

36 See Tessier, 'Mémoire,' and the informative letter dated 'Paris 10 February 1787,' written by Tessier probably to the Minister of the Navy and the Colonies outlining his views 'sur les avantages qu'il y auroit de favoriser dans nos Colonies la culture des arbres et des plantes, qui peuvent ou servir a la nourriture des Colons et de leurs negres, ou formés des objets de commerce pour la metropole...;' Archives Nationales (Paris), Marine G101, fols., 179–180.

37 Velut, *La rose*, p. 69. On the provincial academies, see Roche, *Le Siècle des lumières en province*. For a case study of an academy garden, see Bret, 'Le Jardin de Dijon.'

38 The garden of the Compagnie des Indes at Lorient has yet to be investigated by historians. See mention of this garden in the minutes of the contemporary Comité d'Agriculture in Foville and Pigeonneau, *L'Administration*, p. 104, and other avenues of inquiry in A. Legrand, *Inventaire*.

39 On the Nantes garden, see McClellan, *Colonialism and Science*, p. 149; Laissus, 'Le Jardin du roi,' p. 293n, and Juhé-Beaulation, 'Du jardin royal,' pp. 271–273.

40 Juhé-Beaulation, 'Du jardin royal,' pp. 273–74

41 See Ly-Tio-Fane, *Mauritius and the Spice Trade: The Odyssey of Pierre Poivre*, and her *Mauritius_and the Spice Trade:The Triumph of Jean Nicolas Céré*.

42 On French botany in Guyana, see sources cited in note 32, Regourd, 'Maîtriser la nature,' and Le Seigneur, 'Un naturaliste français en Guyane.'

43 On these episodes and on Hippolyte Nectoux, see McClellan, *Colonialism and Science*, pp. 157–60, and the informative article by Bret, 'Le réseau.' See also the related article by Bret, 'Des 'Indes'.'

44 See sixteen-page manuscript list, Bibliothèque Centrale du Muséum National d'Histoire Naturelle, Paris, Ms. 47.

45 See letter, Bibliothèque Centrale du Muséum National d'Histoire Naturelle, Paris, Ms. 47: 'Il y a Monsieur un vaisseau marchand qui a frêté pour 52 mille francs a lsle de france d'arbres a Epices pour Cayenne. Il a relaché au cap de Bon Esperence. Il avoit aussi un paquebot anglais en relache a falsebaie qui alloit aux Isles des taitis pour chercher l'arbre a pain leur vaisseau a été expedié pour cet seul chose il y dans de vaisseau des serres chaudes un botaniste et deux observateurs astronome et un geographe.' Before the franc became the official currency of France in 1795 the term was used colloquially for the *livre tournois*. If true, the fifty-two thousand francs/livres spent on this endeavor was an enormous sum, the equivalent of the salary for a top military officer or government minister. The Navy's Inspector General, for example, saw only 12,000 livres a year. Such an expense powerfully underscores the importance government authorities placed on establishing spice cultivations in the New World.

Bibliography

Anglade, Georges. *Atlas Critique d'Haïti*. Montreal: Erce & CRC, 1982.
Bouchenot-Déchin, Patricia. *Henry Dupuis, jardinier de Louis XIV*. Versailles: Perrin, 2001.

Bourget, Marie-Noëlle and Christophe Bonneuil. 'De l'inventaire du monde à la mise en valeur du globe: Botanique et colonisation (fin XVIIIᵉ siècle – début XXᵉ siècle,' *Revue Française d'Histoire d'Outre-mer* 86 (1999), pp. 7–38.

Bret, Patrice. 'Des 'Indes' en Méditerranée? L'utopie tropicale d'un jardinier des Lumières et la maîtrise agricole du territoire.' *Revue française d'Histoire d'Outre-Mer* 86 (1999), pp. 65–89.

____. '"La conservation et l'utilité journalière du jardin botanique": l'apothicaire Jacques Tartelin (1748–1823) et le premier Jardin de Dijon,' in Louis Fischer, ed., *Le jardin*, pp. 91–109.

____. 'Le réseau des jardins coloniaux: Hypolite Nectoux (1759–1836) et la botanique tropicale, de la mer des Caraïbes aux bords du Nil,' in Laissus, ed., *Les naturalistes français*, pp. 185–216.

Burg, B. R. *Sodomy and the Pirate Tradition: English Sea Rovers in the Seventeenth-century Caribbean.* New York: New York University Press, 1984.

Butel, Paul. *Les Caraïbes au temps des flibustiers, XVIᵉ–XVIIᵉ siècles.* Paris: Aubier Montaigne, 1982.

Centre d'Études de Géographie Tropicale. *Atlas d'Haïti.* Bordeaux: C.N.R.S./Université de Bordeaux III, 1985

Crosby, Alfred W. *Ecological Imperialism: The Biological Expansion of Europe, 900–1900.* Cambridge: Cambridge University Press, 1986.

Devèze, Michel. *Antilles, Guyanes, La Mer des Caraïbes de 1492 à 1789.* Paris: S.E.D.E.S., 1977.

Durand-Molard, M. *Code de la Martinique,* nouvelle édition, 3 vols. Saint-Pierre, Martinique: Jean-Baptiste Thounens, 1807–1810

Fischer, Jean-Louis. *Le jardin entre science et représentation.* Paris: Éditions du CTHS, 1999.

Foville, Alfred de and Henri Pigeonneau, eds. *L'Administration de l'Agriculture au Contrôle général des Finances (1785–1787): Procès-verbaux et rapports.* Paris, 1882.

Hoetink, H. '"Race" and Color in the Caribbean,' in Mintz and Price, eds., *Caribbean Contours*, pp. 55–84.

Juhé-Beaulaton, Dominique. 'Du jardin royal des plantes médicinales de Paris aux jardins coloniaux: d'eveloppement de l'agronomie tropicale française,' in Fischer, ed., *Le jardin*, pp. 267–284.

Kury, Lorelai. 'André Thouin et la nature exotique au Jardin des plantes,' in Fischer, ed., *Le jardin*, pp. 255–265.

Lacroix, Alfred. *Figures de Savants,* 4 vols. Paris: Gauthier-Villars, 1932–1938.

Laissus, Yves. 'Le Jardin du Roi,' in René Taton, ed., *Enseignement et diffusion des sciences en France au XVIIIᵉ siècle,* pp. 287–341. Paris: Hermann, 1986. [Original edition 1964.]

Laissus, Yves, ed. *Les naturalistes français en Amérique du Sud XVIᵉ–XIXᵉ siècles.* Paris: Éditions du CTHS, 1995.

Legrand, A. et al. *Inventaire des Archives de la Compagnie des Indes (Sou-Série 1P).* Paris: Imprimerie de la Marine, 1978.

Le Seigneur, Marie Jacques. 'Un naturaliste français en Guyane: Jacques-François Artur, médecin du roi à Cayenne, 1736–1771,' in Laissus, ed., *Les naturalistes français*, pp. 137–156.

Letouzey, Yvonne. *Le jardin des Plantes à la croisée des chemins avec A. Thouin (1747–1824).* Paris: Muséum national d'histoire naturelle, 1989.

Lewis, Gordon K. *Main Currents in Caribbean Thought: The Historical Evolution of Caribbean Society in Its Ideological Aspects, 1492–1900.* Baltimore: Johns Hopkins University Press, 1983.

Ly-Tio-Fane, Madeleine. *Mauritius and the Spice Trade: The Odyssey of Pierre Poivre.* Port-Louis, Mauritius, 1958.

_____. *Mauritius and the Spice Trade, Volume 2: The Triumph of Jean-Nicolas Céré and his Isle Bourbon Collaborators*. Paris and the Hague, 1970.

Maurel, Blanche. 'La Poste entre la France et les Isles de l'Amérique à la fin de l'ancien régime.' *Revue de la Société d'Histoire et de Géographie d'Haïti* 6 (1935), pp. 1–12.

McClellan, James E. III. *Colonialism and Science: Saint Domingue in the Old Regime*. Baltimore and London: Johns Hopkins University Press, 1992.

_____ and François Regourd. 'The Colonial Machine: French Science and Colonization in the Ancien Régime,' in Roy MacLeod, ed., *Nature and Empire: Science and the Colonial Enterprise*. Chicago: The University of Chicago Press, 2001. [*OSIRIS* 15 (2001), 31–50.]

Meyer, Jean, Jean Tarrade and Annie Rey-Goldzeiguer. *Histoire de la France coloniale I: La_conquête*. Paris: Armand Colin, 1991.

Mintz, Sidney W. and Sally Price, eds. *Caribbean Contours*. Baltimore and London: Johns Hopkins University Press, 1985.

Moreau de Saint-Méry, Méderic Louis Élie. *Description Physique, Civile, Politique et Historique de la Partie Française de l'Isle de Saint-Domingue*, presented by Blanche Maurel and Étienne Taillemite. Paris: Société Française d'Histoire d'Outre Mer, 1984. [Original edition, 1797–1798.]

Pluchon, Pierre. *Histoire de la colonisation française*. Paris: Fayard, 1991.

Regourd, François. 'Maîtriser la nature: un enjeu colonial: Botanique et agronomie en Guyane et aux Antilex (xviie – xviiie siècles),' *Revue Française d'Histoire d'Outre-mer* 86 (1999), pp. 39–64.

_____. *Sciences et colonisation sous l'Ancien Régime. Le cas de la Guyane et_des Antilles françaises XVIIe–XVIIIe siècles*. Doctoral thesis, Université Bordeaux III, 2000.

Ritchie, Robert C. *Captain Kidd and the War against the Pirates*. Cambridge, Mass., and London: Harvard University Press, 1986

Roche, Daniel. *Le Siècle des lumières en province: Académies et académiciens provinciaux (1680–1789)*, 2 vols. Paris: Mouton, 1978.

Spary, E. C. *Utopia's Garden: French Natural History from Old Regime to Revolution*. Chicago and London: The University of Chicago Press, 2000.

Tarrade, Jean. *Le Commerce colonial de la France à la fin de l'Ancien Régime: L'évolution du régime de « l'exclusif » de 1763 à 1789*, 2 vols. Paris: Presses Universitaires de France, 1972.

Tessier, Abbé Henri-Alexandre. 'Mémoire sur l'importation et les progrès des arbres à épicerie dans les colonies françaises,' *Mémoires de l'Académie Royale des Sciences* (1789), pp. 585–96.

Velut, Christine. *La rose et l'orchidée: Les usages sociaux et symboliques des fleurs à Paris au XVIIIe siècle*. [Paris:] Découvrir, 1993.

Watts, David. *The West Indies: Patterns of Development, Culture and Environmental Change since 1492*. Cambridge: Cambridge University Press, 1987.

6 Le Jardin Colonial des Plantes of Martinique

Clarissa Kimber

The Jardin Colonial des Plantes de Saint-Pierre, was the first botanical garden in the French Antilles. It was an agro-political response by France to the institutions founded previously by the British in their holdings in the West Indies. Established on Martinique in 1803, its director began receiving plants almost immediately from older botanical gardens in St. Vincent, Jamaica and Cayenne, Surinam, as well as from gardens in Mauritius, Réunion, and Paris.[1] The purposes in establishing this botanical garden, elsewhere called the Jardin du Roi, was to naturalize the plants of the East Indies in Martinique, especially the economic species; to provide the botanical gardens of metropolitan France with plants from the Antilles; to assemble the indigenous plants according to a botanical system; and to form a depot of medicinal plants for the use of the poor. The objective of the crown was to create a model establishment of its kind.[2]

At first administered by persons appointed by the governor as agent of the crown, in 1840 the garden was made the responsibility of the island's Agricultural Society.[3] Later in the mid 1840s it fell under the guidance of administrators sent by the Musèum d'Histoire Naturelle de Paris. Finally in 1882 it was taken over by amateurs and professionals from the local area. Responsibility for the garden was transferred from one governmental agency to another, but each director kept to the original roles. Through the continued introduction and reintroduction of exotic plants, the garden contributed to the accumulation of diversity within the gene pools of the economic species. It also contributed to the island's biodiversity. The rate of introductions was considerably faster than the known rate of loss of species. The garden lasted 99 years and was a critical institution in the collection and redistribution of plants from its inception until its destruction by the eruption of Mont Pelée in 1902.

This chapter focuses on the processes by which the plant introductions and exchanges took place under the auspices of the Jardin des Plantes. The plant migrations are documented in some detail. Some of the consequences for genetic conservation within the garden space and conservation of biodiversity for the island of Martinique are identified. First, however, the layout of the garden space, the development of the garden functions, and the administration of the garden are sketched.

The Creation of an Oasis of Delight[4]
Aucun établissement de ce genre qui fut
comparable au Jardin des Plantes de Saint-Pierre
Charles Bélanger 1853.[5]

To celebrate the return of Martinique to France, the newly established government under *prefet colonial* Bertin and Admiral Villaret Joyeuse decided in 1803 to enhance the ambiance of the two principal towns of the colony, Fort-de-France and Saint-Pierre.[6] Among their projects was the Jardin Colonial des Plantes at St. Pierre. A botanical garden was to be established, 'devoted to the cultivation of all useful plants whether indigenous or exotic and of spices of all species and, if it is possible, the cultivation of the fruits of Europe.'[7]

The garden was located on the land between the Rivière des Pères and its tributary on the south, Rivière Poirier. Just north of the Convent of the Ursulins on what had formerly been convent land, it extended to the end of the first plateau. Less than a mile from St. Pierre, the physical plant was developed on the slopes and in the ravines of Morne Parnasse. Two maps in the Archives Départemental de la Martinique (A.D.M.) in Schoelcher from the 1820s show the lay out of the garden. Both were commissioned by Lieutenant général compte Douzelot, Governor of Martinique. One map was of the town of Saint-Pierre by M. Monnier, a military engineer; the other, by E. Bodin, an equally gifted cartographer.[8] The large, flat areas had been laid out in parterres in the approved eighteenth-century fashion used earlier in other such gardens, but the majority of the garden space had a more natural arrangement.

The garden was carved out of the natural vegetation. The original nine hectares extended from the native seasonal forest at the lower elevations into the rain forest in the upper elevations where rapids and a beautiful waterfall created lovely vistas.[9] Openings were created in the native vegetation to accommodate planting areas and to provide prospects or views. Wide stairs of stone connected the levels of the garden. The relatively steep slopes of the mountain made possible numerous microhabitats within short distances. Adroit modification of slope and construction of stone fences and parterres created entirely new vistas and views that conformed to the current landscape gardening mode. Full advantage was taken of the cascades and waterfalls present on the streams. The canyon-like walls of the Rivière Poirier provided good display places for ferns, aroids, and other native ornamentals, as well as for introduced plantings. Large openings in the native vegetation on the relatively flat areas were made for fountains and pools; and stepped beds were planted in exotic introductions that required sunlit space. Avenues were created for promenades that led to the steeper, winding paths, which accessed the upper parts of the garden. Introductions were thus fitted into the existing natural vegetation as well as planted in newly contrived settings.

Unlike the botanical gardens of the earlier centuries that conformed to the more stylized concept of formal French and Italian gardens, like the botanical garden in Paris, the ideas of a picturesque or landscape garden had become the taste in French gardens.[10] This was despite the strong influence of the antiquarian Antoine-Chrysostom Quatremère.[11] The change in taste had been truly revolutionary from 'garden as architecture' to 'garden as constructed natural landscape'. Whether d'Auros, the first Director of the garden, had read any of these books or the works of other guides of aesthetic taste is unknown, but the 'natural history inclined' island intellegensia was a literate group. In any case, the careful exploitation of the natural environment as the fabric into which new plants were placed in the Jarden des Plants made it different from the origins of others in the West Indies and contributed to its reputation as the most beautiful of the lesser gardens of the tropics.

A few reports tell us how the garden did look toward the end of the period under the control of the Muséum de Paris and at the end of the century. Eduard André visited the garden in the late part of the nineteenth century, described the plantings of the School of Botany as beautiful and reported that rare species were arranged in successive terraces surrounded by a metal fence. He comments favorably that small canals to various parts of the garden carefully distributed irrigation water.[12] The placing of these features may have been anticipated in the garden designs as shown on the map by Bodin. Natural disasters did strike the garden at times. Unfortunately, in September 1875, probably after André's visit, a hurricane destroyed much of the garden, especially the large trees.[13] However, the garden recovered, and with the passage of time it became as luxuriant, although perhaps less well organized.[14] Each director approached the gardening process differently, but an improved, natural landscape remained the dominant aesthetic objective.[15]

Directors and the Administration of the Garden

Pour récolter, dit un vieil adage, il faut seme;
nous ajouterons-nous, que pour semer et pour récolter,
il faut dispose amender et fertiliser le sol que l'on veut cultiver.
Reisser 1847, p. 45[16]

The garden was administered by a number of able and some very distinguished directors (Table 1).

Table 1. *Directors of the Jardin des Plantes at St. Pierre, Martinique*

Castelnau d'Auros	1803–1814
Roland Legrand	1815–1827
M. Artaud	1827
Monfleury de l'Horme	1827–1833
Celestin Desmarinières	1833–1838
Mancet	1838–1840
Victor Segond	1840–1841
M. Artaud	1841–1843
M.Verger	1843–1845
Charles Barillet	1845–1853
Charles Bélanger	1853–1881
Armand-Justin Thierry	1882–1888
Ville de St. Pierre	1888–1890
Eugène Nollet	1890–1902

Compiled from Reisser 1847 Bulletin agricole, and Thésée 1990.

The first Director was Castelnau d'Auros (1803–1814), a *commissaires d'administration de deuxième classe,* who developed the original garden throughout a period of considerable turmoil that included a period of British control.[17] He was responsible for the original design of the garden and for incorporating the natural landscape elements. It was his genius that caused the new species to be inserted into a natural setting. From the beginning in 1803, d'Auros quickly began collecting plants from the older private collections on the island and from botanical and private gardens on the other islands of the Caribbean: St. Vincent, Jamaica, and Cayenne, Suriname, and from gardens in Mauritius, Réunion, and Paris.[18] He obtained many rare and exotic plants for the garden from Alexander Anderson, director of the already famous botanical garden in St. Vincent, with whom Reisser says he had frequent and friendly relations (see Richard A. Howard's chapter in this volume).[19]

An engraving of Chatoyer, the black Carib leader (and his wives), who led the resistance to British annexation of the St Vincent forest lands from 1763–1791.

Admiral William Bligh (1754–1817), sent to Tahiti on *HMS Bounty* to collect specimens of breadfruit (a highly nutritious and easily cultivated plant) for dissemination to slave plantations in the Caribbean. Setting sail for home, his crew mutinied and put Bligh and 18 of his officers aboard an open boat without maps. Eventually, the open boat, after a 1000-mile journey, reached safety.

Kingston, St Vincent, in about 1800. The Kings Hill Forest is to the right of the print and Anderson's Botanic Garden beyond the church tower at the left and centre.

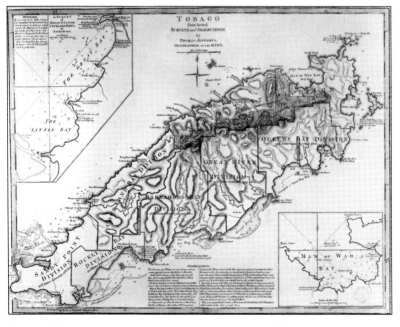

Map of Tobago showing the forest reserves established according to Proclamation of 1764. The reserves run along the main mountain chain in the north-east of the island and are marked 'Reserved in wood for rains'. The map, by Thomas Jefferys (Geographer to the King) is based on the original survey of John Byres, which was published in 1776.

Sir Joseph Banks (1743–1820), British botanist and explorer, who promoted the introduction of economic plants from their native regions to other countries. He was president of the Royal Society from 1778 to his death. Banks was in direct communication with botanists throughout the Caribbean, including Alexander Anderson at the Kingston Botanic Garden.

This 19th-century photograph of the Cascade in the Jardin Des Plantes in St Pierre, Martinique, was reproduced in Lafcadio Hearn's *Two Years in the French West Indies*, published by Harper and Brothers Publishers, New York and London, 1890. The Jardin Des Plantes was designed and evolved to take advantage of the natural vegetation and terrain of the island environment.

The Kingston Botanic Garden in St Vincent and the Grenadines as it is today, some 300 years after its founding. Note in the upper photograph that the breadfruit tree (*artocarpus altilis*) is descended from Bligh's original import in 1793.

An armed marijuana grower somewhere in the hills of St Vincent inspecting his crop.

A grower critically examining the state of his major 'cash crop'.

An abandoned marijuana garden being burned for new plant growing.

While d'Auros was collecting from gardens, he also received plants directly from the naturalist Baudin, who provided him with living plants from India, including leechees (*Litchi chinensis*) and screwpine (*Pandanus odoratissimus*).[20] Towards the end of 1819, a single specimen of the highly prized, medicinal camphor tree (*Camphora officinalis*) was introduced into the garden. With care it finally became established.[21] The specimen was the source of a number of cuttings later distributed throughout the island. This sharing of plant material was characteristic of plant lovers in the islands and the *Jardin* authorities continued the long-standing practice.

Although the British retook Martinique for a time, the fighting did not impede the development of the botanical garden. In fact English Governor Charles Wale asked d'Auros to stay on and encouraged him to collect the rare, indigenous plants and to make available medicinal plants for the poor population.[22] Little is known about d'Auros in Martinique but we do know from Reisser that d'Auros had to return to France in 1814 to tend to family business.[23] During his stay in France, he consulted with M. Thouin, a professor of plant culture at the Musèum d'Histoire Naturelle and had some seeds and living plants sent out from the Musèum that were provided by the Jardin Royal.[24]

M. Roland LeGrand (1815–1827) was an important man in the design of the structure of the garden. M. LeGrand or Legrand as he is more often referred to, had come to Martinique in 1796 after having served in the French army during the Revolution.[25] He had taken on a number of jobs, among them *officier de l'état-civil* and Lieutenant commissaire-commandant of the parish of the Fort in Saint-Pierre. He continued the work of multiplication and distribution of new plant material to the planters and other inhabitants. In 1819 Legrand published a catalog identifying 504 species of plants in the garden and that of 1823 mentioned 646 species.[26]

During Legrand's tenure, in 1816, the French king prescribed that the botanical gardens of Bourbon (Réunion), Guyana, and Martinique should develop and print catalogs to be exchanged frequently so that each should know what it lacked and could ask for the lacking specimens from other gardens.[27] As part of their missions, the governors, officers of the Marine, ambassadors, and consuls had the fostering of plant exchanges and the development of networks of correspondence with museums and other gardens. Precise instructions were given to those involved for improving the quality of the collections and the sending of natural history objects.[28]

Monnfleury de l'Horme (1827–1833) was director from December 3, 1827 to January 6, 1833. During his administration the director's salary was raised and Celestin Desmarinière, a gardener, was employed to conduct the daily, more routine, cultivation activities. Desmarinière took on many of the responsibilities very effectively and was supplied with 12 slaves including three females. Later, eight more slaves were added to the garden staff. This meant that de l'Horme could continue with his extensive acclimatization experiments. These took place at an old sugar estate, which de l'Horme had turned into a naturalization garden for exotic plants. The garden was high enough that apples from Europe could thrive there.[29]

De l'Horme discovered two new small waterfalls and rapids above the larger waterfall developed by d'Auros. He cleared away the vegetation creating vistas and excavated the small pool at the base of the large waterfall, forming a small masonry-lined basin. De l'Horme greatly extended the horticultural activities, and created a nursery for multiplying the introductions for distribution to the people of the colony. He practiced grafting and marcotage to vegetatively reproduce those introductions which did not easily reproduce from seed. He introduced the system of using metal tags for identifying the specimens in the garden; part of his effort was to identify for the interested visitor the garden plants according to a botanical system.[30] This enlarged the garden space by several hectares over the garden officially mapped in the 1820s. When de l'Horme decided to resign as director because of his business interests, he recommended his gardener take over the responsibility of the garden.

Celestin Desmarinières (1833–1838) was locally described as 'practical and intelligent'.[31] During his five years as Director of the garden he continued the horticultural interests of de l'Horme. He is credited with multiplying and distributing many individuals taken from the single rubber tree in the garden. He set to multiplying mulberry plants from trees imported from the Philippines when the colonial officials attempted to implement the silk industry effort ordered by the crown. He was skilled in grafting and greatly facilitated the growth in area of the exotic orchard crops. After a period of illness Desmarinières died in 1838.

The Governor of Martinique now appointed A. M. Mancet (1838–1840) who was given the authority and was empowered to act, but under him the garden was ill tended and many of the plants were neglected. In January, 1840 the garden was turned over to the Société d'agriculture et d'économie rural de la Martinique.[32] The next five years of control by the Société that began under Victor Segond saw some very substantial changes in mission and management objectives. In the preamble to the enabling *arrête de 1 janvier 1840* is an interesting clause, which freely translated, says:

> Since the Botanical Garden of Saint-Pierre is not a public
> promenade but a botanical institution created at great expense

by our predecessors for encouraging the naturalization of plants and trees which could be useful to the colony and contribute riches to her; …[and] since up to this time, it has not attained its mission because neither the care of the central administration nor even the supervision of several amateurs of horticulture could replace a local scientific director, we pronounce that…

The language points up a long-standing controversy among the local botanically-minded about the administration of the garden and its mission. The directive was explicit, and some very important activities resulted from this change in administrative responsibility. 'Conserve, improve, strengthen' was the motto of the Society.

Victor Segond as president of the society, began the administration under the society's care, but he was soon replaced by M. Artaud (1841–1843), who was reassigned control over the garden, to be followed by M. Verger. They undertook many renovations and the restoration of the garden fabric. The famous jets of water played again, the plant nurseries and germination houses were put in order, and the houses and kitchens for the staff rebuilt or renovated. He saw to the renewal of plant imports including the African oil palm from Guyane, and the Saint-Dominique coffee and some new pasture grasses, etc., from Haiti. Segond was responsible for the distribution of some introductions directly to dependable planters who were charged with their multiplication.[33] His bypassing of the botanical garden was a return to the way plant introductions had taken place in the seventeenth and eighteenth century.

The agricultural society made a concerted effort to help in the diversification of agricultural products. After disagreements with some planters and influential commercial interests, the society renounced its work with the botanical garden.[34] The colonial administration now turned to the Muséum de Paris, which sent out Charles Barillet, a gardener-botanist. He arrived January 8, 1845 and remained until 1853.[35] This was a period of attention to the fundamentals of plant culture. Barillet began a scientific study of the climate and turned his attention to the exhausted soils of the garden. He re-ordered the nursery beds and sorted species in them according to taxa. He fenced the garden that controlled access so vandalism was better monitored. He rebuilt the huts of the day laborers. It was during Barillet's tenure that numerous entries appear in the records of the department for substantial credits extended, sometimes 3,000F at a time, for horticultural activity or works in the garden.[36] Other payments for works in the garden followed in 1850 and again in 1851.[37] Barillet requested numerous introductions and he sent plants from the Jardin des Plantes to other gardens in the tropical botanical garden network. But despite his activities, the garden did not flourish in the manner desired by Martinique authorities, and so possibly at their request, the Museum of Paris sent Bélanger to replace Charles Barillet.

Charles Bélanger (1853–1881) was a very different sort of person from those who had preceded him. Member of the Legion of Honor, he had gained considerable experience in botanical gardens through his work in the garden at Pondicherry and as a voyager-naturalist. Sent out to Pondicherry in French India to develop a botanical garden, the twenty-year-old departed France for India traveling overland, collecting as he went. After starting the garden, he then continued east to Java, Pegou, and Rangoon. He returned twenty-three years later by way of the Isle de France (Mauritius), Bourbon (Réunion), the Cape of Good Hope, and Saint Helena, all of which by this time had established botanical gardens and were used as naturalization centers.[38]

When Bélanger arrived, he was able to see past the disorder and appreciate the collection, which had been assembled in the Jardin des Plantes at Saint-Pierre. Some species had been lost but he said the garden at St. Pierre contained riches of the first order.[39] When the planters reminded him that sugarcane was the important crop and asked why they needed any other, Bélanger took the opportunity to argue for the continued role of the garden in importing improved sugarcane varieties to enrich those grown on the island. At the same time, he argued for diversification of the small estate agriculture, called secondary cultures, of coffee, cacao, cotton, and tobacco and urged the improvement of these crops with new genetic material from other locals.

Additionally, Bélanger saw a need to develop market gardens, to improve orchard fruits, and to form a collection in the garden devoted to useful industrial plants such as oil palms and coconuts, while not neglecting flowers 'which give pleasure to the eyes'. He argued for an *in situ* agricultural science to be created on the island. Bélanger saw a need to codify the experience gained so far in the garden for the use of others. In other words, he saw a great public educational role for the garden. He also pointed out that the garden was for the mother country as well – all the riches of Martinique needed to be shared with the rest of the world.[40]

After getting the garden in order, putting the species present into classes according to their uses, and collecting back from older private gardens the plants and trees not then in the garden, Bélanger set about increasing the species richness of the garden. He made exchanges with the other botanical gardens of Algeria, Senegal and Pondicherry, with the intermediary action of the Ministère de la Marine, or directly with Jamaica, Trinidad, Kew, Belgium, and the French departmental gardens of Rochefort, Toulon, and Montpellier. In a catalog listing the plants acquired since 1853, he named 400 species, all newly received from his connections. A large number of these were suited to the temperate zone and could grow in the mid-elevation, temperate zone of the island. He expressed a hope to have 1,850 species by the end of 1856.[41]

Since nothing was left of the nursery, Bélanger cleared a plot on a small plateau next to the school for botany and created a coffee bush area and a coconut grove. He enlarged the area for experimental work and acclimatization. He produced 22,000 individuals of trees and shrubs by grafting, which he distributed free to the people of the island. In thirty months he had distributed over 2,000 plants. He also distributed 400 seed packets of 100 different species.[42] In this respect he was doing what the directors of other gardens in the Caribbean were doing for their populations.

Not only did Bélanger finally get the support of the planters and other islanders; he cultivated the press in France. A long article in a leading magazine rhapsodized about 'a corner of the world where nature in all its primitive state had been given new charm by the effects of art.'[43] On a visit to France in 1857 Bélanger delivered and received credit for donating a large collection of plants from the mountains of Martinique. In August of the following year he sent to the Muséum de Paris 320 species, and each year thereafter, he sent collections to Paris until 1879.[44]

As part of his activities, Bélanger participated in various world expositions to advertise the garden and Martinique. Not only were there reports on the garden at Saint-Pierre in the scientific journal *La Nature* but also in the society magazines. Visiting dignitaries included visits to the garden on their itineraries. Bélanger, with his carefully cultivated local connections, saw to it that any distinguished visitors would be shown the garden.

Because all this activity was straining the garden's resources, Bélanger asked for and got authorization to annex two hectares over the twelve that the administration had reserved from the sale of a piece of property next to the garden. He put the experimental fields in order and arranged with neighbors a realignment of property lines. In 1866 the garden at Tivoly, which had been reattached in 1861, was made into a permanent exposition center to display the products of Martinique. Bélanger added to the library and made the garden available to local scientists as well as to visitors. Amateur and professional botanists visited the now famous garden. In 1863 Bélanger requested from the Muséum de Paris a head gardener who could take on the numerous jobs of a subordinate. They sent him Ludwig Hahn but the two men turned out to be incompatible. Bélanger found Hahn to be inclined to 'peregrinations', wishing more to botanize than to tend to gardening, so he nominated Hahn for a scientific expedition to Mexico. After Hahn returned to Paris, he got himself nominated as director of the garden by arranging for Bélanger's retirement. Only 66 years old at the time, Bélanger fought retirement and won. Bélanger died in 1881 while still in his post at the garden. However, Hahn did return to the island on a collecting expedition for the museum, and, in fact, died on the island as well.

Hahn did not become director but wrote a very interesting short work, *Manuel du bon jardinier aux Antilles*. Thésée includes a long set of excerpts from Hahn as an appendix to her text.[45] Hahn included several lists of plants identifying the length of the period that they were viable for planting and the length of time for germination of seeds or the rooting of vegetative propagules for the species. He also gave a brief summary of the activities concerning medicinal plants at the garden and on the island. He reported the receipt of ipecacuanha (*Cephaelis ipecacuanha*) from Peru and efforts to multiply seeds so that they could be distributed. Through Hahn, connections were made with the botanical garden in Berlin. The German connection with Martinique continued after Hahn died. Urban's *Notae biographicae perigrinatuorum Indiae occidentalis botanicorum* (1904) was made possible by the information furnished him by R. P. Duss, an active botanical investigator befriended by Bélanger.[46] Duss sent herbarium specimens of many plants to Berlin.

Armand-Justin Thierry (1882–1888), a planter and amateur botanist, was appointed as Bélanger's replacement. He had neither the scientific qualifications, nor the time of his predecessor for the garden. However, his expertise was in secondary crops, and the appointment underscores the change of direction in agriculture in Martinique, which in turn affected the garden's concerns with plant introduction. Several professors of the new Lycée of Saint-Pierre assumed roles in the garden, which helped Thierry both in administration and in the educational activities. These were Gaston Landes, teacher of natural history; M. Saussine, responsible for the sciences; M. Fulconis, the drawing and design professor; and Eugène Nollet, an agricultural engineer. They took over when Thierry was absent and generally acted as a friendly consulting committee for him.[47]

The Conseil général de la Martinique reordered priorities and made changes in the way the garden was to be administered.[48] Thierry finally resigned in 1888 because the demands were growing and devolved mostly on the director. The Conseil général decided to eliminate the position of the director and to turn the garden over to the city of Saint-Pierre.

The city was unable to maintain the level of scientific activity or even the appearance of the garden, so in 1890, the Conseil général reentered the picture and proposed the famous botanist Father Duss as director. His superiors in France, however, thought that the position would take Duss' away from his religious duties and he was assigned to Guadeloupe. Gaston Landes, one of the professors at the Lycée and former member of the faculty at Montpellier, volunteered to serve without pay until the end of 1889. At that time, Nollet, already involved in the agricultural laboratory, accepted the position and took up residence in the small house of the director of the botanical garden.

Eugène Nollet (1890–1902) continued the experimental work and field trials, and continued to exhibit in international expositions. Nollet showed products in Chicago at the World's Columbian Exposition of 1893; Thierry showed his indigo from Trinidad, *Indigofera disperma*; and Ledoux of Paris, the different coffees of the Antilles.[49] Considerable discussions arose among the various planter groups as to the proper conduct of the botanical garden. In 1896 the Conseil général again acted, deciding to give the director a Consulting Committee to guide him in the proper management of the garden.[50]

Nollet was able to continue the distribution of plants to other gardens. The work of exchanges continued, correspondence with chambers of agriculture, experimental stations, agronomic societies of the métropole and the colonies continued. Jean Dybowski, director of the botanical garden of Vincennes, wrote on receiving a group of plants from Saint-Pierre in 1902, 'Grâce aux nombreux envois que faisait sans cesse le zéle directeur du jardin, la plupart de nos colonies sont pourvues maintenant en essences rares qui composaient ces magnifiques collections.'[51,52] Gaston Landes presented a report to the governor of Martinique on his visits to the botanical garden at Port-of-Spain, Trinidad, and to Demerara, British Guiana in 1902.[53]

Botanical exchanges of plants and information continued right up to the eruption of Mont Pelée.[54] The Jardin des Plants lay within the zone of complete destruction.[55] The garden was blasted by such hot air that all plants were instantly killed, and many structures were destroyed. Nollet and his family, who lived in the garden, Landes and Saussine, were killed.[56] It is not known whether the latter two were in the garden or in Saint-Pierre but they died at the time of the disaster.

It is clear that the role of this botanical garden was being reinterpreted at the end of the century. Its role as pleasure garden had been reduced, but the work of botanical exchanges had continued, even expanded. It was being pushed in the direction of an agricultural station, just like what was happening to the gardens in Trinidad, Jamaica, and St. Vincent.[57] The agricultural laboratory, which had begun to function as experimental agricultural station with responsibilities in crop improvement, propagation, and experimental culture, was re-established at Desclieux Estate in Fort-de-France.

The Modern Species Sum

Quelques plantes, qui sont l'objet du jardinage
et de l'agriculture depuis les temps les plus reculés,
ont accompagné l'homme d'un bout de globe à l'autre.
von Humboldt and Bonpland 1807.[58]

The first objective of the crown in founding the botanical garden was to introduce new useful species of plants to the island. Alien species are abundant in the modern flora of Martinique. Roughly one-fourth of the contemporary higher plant flora has been introduced from continental America, Africa, Europe, and Asia. This estimate is based upon the assumption of 4,000 species more or less in the modern flora. Fournet lists 2,779 phanerogams for Martinique and Guadeloupe.[59] If one uses his figures, the proportion is more nearly 37 percent. The team at the Galerie Botanique, Fort-de-France, is documenting new species records, but they have not published reports as yet.

A very large proportion of the introductions was intentional which began almost immediately upon the founding of the colony of Martinique in 1635. Planters and amateur gardeners exchanged species among themselves and with fellows on other islands of the Caribbean. The governors and intendents over time requested living plants and seeds to enrich the biotic resources available to the inhabitants and to enrich the colony for the mother country. Weedy species arrived along with the more highly prized species. The botanical garden at Saint-Pierre gave a great boost to the introduction of new species as well as more genetic material of species already on the island. The scientific agronomic and horticultural establishments associated with the garden as it developed greatly accelerated the effectiveness with which these introductions were established, reproduced, and made available to the agriculturists and gardeners of the island.

While the governors had initiated purposeful introductions and intendents and private efforts had already introduced many plants into Martinique, the botanical garden did greatly facilitate the distribution of plants to the farmers and gardeners of the island. It was a valuable environmental institution during the century of its existence.

The Record of Imports and Exports

L'Administration et les habitans de cette colonie verront
dans ces pensées de bienveilance de votre département,
une nouvelle manifestation de l'intérêt que porte la
Métropole au bien' êtres des ses colonies.
Valdailly 1842.[60]

Records for the annual receipt of new species and varieties of plants to the garden are not good, nor is there a good introduction total for the years of its existence. It is known that in 1812, some 486 species (local and exotic) had been put into the garden. Louis XVIII was most eager to establish active interactions of the Muséum in Paris with the colonies that had been left to themselves during the long maritime war.[61] Garden managers were ordered to prepare catalogs of holdings in their gardens, to publish the catalogs, and to exchange them among the circle of gardens in the empire. The exchange of the catalogs would permit each island government to know and to acquire what each lacked and what to provide other islands to enrich their holdings. Governors, offices of the Marine, ambassadors, and consuls were charged with facilitating such exchanges and to create a circle of correspondence of the museums and gardens.[62] Such catalogs were undoubtedly exchanged with their British counterparts, but I have found neither official directives nor any correspondence of such exchanges. Since the local directors initiated these exchanges, copies of such correspondence were unlikely to be sent to Paris and those left in Martinique were destroyed during the eruption. A catalog of the holdings in the garden published in 1819 contained a list of 504 species; and one of 1823 mentions 646 species, so the species numbers within the garden had increased by over a half.[63]

There are a number of catalogs and references in correspondence available which provide evidence as to how the Jardin des Plantes was introducing exotics to the Island of Martinique.[64] In order to put these documents and contemporary accounts into perspective, three summary accounts of what was going on in the garden have proved invaluable. Two were contemporaneous with the garden, the last more recently published. One of the most valuable contemporary, printed sources is the 1847 report on the botanical garden, the *Historique du Jardin des Plantes de Sainte-Pierre,* by M. Reisser, who was Sub-Commissioner of the Marine, and member of the Société d'Agriculture et d'Economie Rural de la Martinique. In this report Reisser presented a summary of activities for the first part of the century. Gaston Landes (1900), a professor at the Lycée in Saint-Pierre and contributor to the garden, provides many details about the plants in the island and the role of the botanical garden during the later half of the century in his report on Martinique for the 1900 World Exposition in Paris. Françoise Thésée (1990) has assembled a great amount of information from the archives in the metropolitan France and in the island, *Le Jardin botanique regional de Saint-Pierre, Martinique (1803–1902)* published by the Conseil régional de la Martinique.

The first of the published reports used in the analysis of introductions is the de l'Horme catalog of the plants being cultivated in the botanical and naturalization garden in 1829, some six years after the date of Bodin's map of the garden, published in the *Annales Maritimes et Coloniales*.[65] The catalog listing has Latin binomials on the left side and common names on the right side. The list uses Linnean binomials and is ordered according to Jussieu's botanical classification scheme including class, order, genus and species. According to Thésée quoting Reisser there were, in the 1829 catalogue some 1,036 plants in the garden in 1829.[66] There were, in fact, a smaller number of species since examination of the list shows that de l'Horme listed some varieties as species, particularly among the cultivated plants. For example, he separated *Saccharum officinarum* from two varieties and again separately listed five cultivars of sugarcane. He divided bananas into the plantains, red and green, and the bananas, which he calls *figure banane*, a name that continues in use to this day. There are four species of *Canna* that he calls 'balisier,' a term used today for *Heliconia* species which he calls 'bihai'. The common names in the catalog generally are consistent with the present usage, but there are enough differences to suggest that some of the vernacular names may have changed over time, but contemporary reports are not always consistent with the catalog usage. Although the reasons for the discrepancies are unknown, it is possible that De l'Horme was not a native of Martinique, since he was sent out from France to oversee the garden. He would not, therefore, have known the common names for the forest plants or might have confused them.

Among the trees in the garden were two cycads, one from India and one from Japan. Also on the list is the domesticated date tree, *Phoenix dactilifera* as well as two 'West Indian almond' species, *Terminalia catappa* and *T. benzoin* from the Indo-Malayan realm, and *Melia azedarach,* now know as lilas-pays but then recorded as azédirach, a French transliteration of its Indian name. Two magnolias are listed: one, *Magnolia grandifolia* is from North America, the other, now known as *Tauluma plumeria*, is native to the islands. The fruits and shade tree mango, *Mangifera indica* is on the list. Three mulberries, *Morus alba*, *M. nigra*, and *M. madagascaria* are on the list, probably left over from an early seventeenth century effort at silk growing, rather than the newer effort. The lumber tree, teak, *Tectona grandis* from Burma, and the beobab (*Adansonia digitata*) from Africa, and the Australian pine, *Casurina equisitifolia*, called filao, illustrate how far and diverse the regions the importations had come from.

Tumeric, *Curcuma longa,* is listed well before East Indians arrived as indentured laborers, as are the East Indian yam, *Dioscorea alata*, and its relatives, *D. sativa*, and *D. bulbifera*. The French pot herb, *Portulaca oleraceae*; called '*pourpier cultivé*' is on the list. The South African ground cover *Mesembryanthemum crystallinum,* called Ficoïde and the medicinal poppy from Mexico, argémone, *Argemone mexicana* had found their way to Martinique by this time.

De l'Horme lists three breadfruits, *Artocarpus integrifolia*, *A. incisa*, and *A. seminifera*, which he called the '*Chataignier de Malabar*.' The jackfruit (now *A. heterophyllus Lam.*) seems to have been first introduced to Martinique and from there to St. Vincent, but the breadfruit proper was introduced in 1793 from the British islands. However, there is a report from the archives in France, dated January 25, 1790 saying, 'and especially the bread fruits brought by Fournier and Martin are fine'.[67] Often it takes more than one introduction to achieve establishment, and any additional introductions enrich the gene pool within the species.[68]

The de l'Horme catalog is an invaluable reference concerning the plants in the garden but should not be taken as a complete list of what had been introduced to the island from abroad. For instance, there is a reference in the correspondence in Mauritius that William Urban Buée of Dominica bought fourteen clove plants in Martinique in November 1791.[69] Many more species had been introduced into the gardens and estate fields than are in this list. Also, there were a number of native species in the region and probably spontaneous within the garden at that time, that do not show up in the catalog, but do find themselves in Duss's catalog.

However, if one examines the list carefully, eliminating any doubtful introductions, we find that at least 310 species are non-natives and therefore additions to the garden flora of Martinique. Some of these already had become widely distributed among the planters of the island, had entered the gardens of the small farmers, and become incorporated into the flora of the spontaneous vegetation, thus contributing to the biodiversity of the island.

According to M. Reisser, a Mr. Werbna, Jr. sent eleven tree and shrub species to the garden from Trinidad, then controlled by the Spanish, about the same time.[70] In 1823 the Naturalization Garden in Cayenne sent a fine gift. Among those sent were *Curatella Americana* (whole leaves are used to polish wood), *Psidium Aromaticum* (which produces attractive fruit), *Maranta Arouma* (used to make baskets that are used to press manioc), and *Myristica Aromatica* (aromatic nutmeg). In the same shipment was *Elais Avoira (guineensis)* whose fruits furnish eating oil, perhaps the first introduction of the African oil palm.

The second document used to establish the pattern of introduction is a reprint in *Le Courrier de la Martinique*, dated November 15, 1842, of a letter from Arch. Bedier, President of the Comité d'Agriculture de Bourbon to M. Artaud, who was then Secretaire-Archivist of the Société d'Agriculture et d'Economie Rural de la Martinique and the third director of the garden. M. Artaud had requested plants for the Jardin Colonial. According to Bédier, M. C. Richard, botanist and Director of the Jardin des Plantes of Bourbon had been charged with filling the order for the plants requested by Director Artaud.[71] These plants were sent in four '*caisses*' (generic term for tubs for shrubs and trees or boxes for smaller plants, but sometimes also used for glass cases) on the *Prévoyante*, going directly from the Indian Ocean to the Antilles. In this way Bédier hoped the plants would arrive in good condition. He especially recommends the two varieties of mango, Augusic [sic] and Charlotte, which he has sent. He expresses regret that the fine plant of *Sapotille de Curaçao* that Artaud had sent him had not survived and he hoped Artaud will send him another when there was an opportunity to do so.

He reported, in answer to Artaud's questions, that the cotton industry, that was so important in Bourbon 30 years ago, had been almost abandoned. The cultivation of mulberries was being expanded and a machine for the spinning of silk had been imported. He closed with expressions of sympathy and support for the society in Martinique and expressed a desire to continue collaboration between the two organizations. The newspaper article goes on to list the contents of three caisses. The names of the plants reproduced as listed in the newspaper text for three caisses (Table 2).

The fact that such an article appeared in the local newspaper indicates that there was keen interest by the general literate public in plant introductions and that the lists and details of such correspondence were of concern to people on the island. Numerous examples can be found in the later editions of the paper in the same century. But by the early twentieth century virtually no mention of such cargo went into the newspaper. This is similar to the situation in Galveston Island in Texas in the nineteenth century when items of the ships' landings were reported in the local paper.[72]

The third document is a report by Governor M. du Valdailly, dated November 11, 1842, to the Ministre, Secrétaire d'Etat de la Marine & des Colonies about some plant introductions being received in Martinique.[73] It supports much of the information

Table 2. *List of Plants Contained in Three Cases for the Société d'Agriculture et d'Economie Rural de la Martinique*

First Case

		left
5. Different species of oranges with sweet fruit from Brazil (5 dead) sent	7	2
6. *Piper nigrum*, Black pepper (in good condition)	3	3
7. *Cycas circinalis*, Plant of Madagascar (in good condition)	2	3
8. *Piper cubebum*, Cubube pepper (in good condition)	1	1
9. *Garcinia Mangostans*, Cultivated mangoustan (2 dead)	3	1
10. *Piper Betel*, Betel pepper	2	2
11. *Garcinia carnea* (not the fruit tree, dead)	1	0
12. *[Garcinia] purpurea* (cultivated in India, in good condition)	1	1
13. *Euphorbia punicea* Leechee (cultivated in China, 3 dead)	4	1
14. *Citrus aurantium nobilis*, Manderine orange of China, (3 dead)	6	3
15. *Id, media*, Bourbon lemon, (living)	2	2
16. *Id .limeta*, Sweet Indian lime (living)	2	2
17. *Euphorbia punicea*, Plants with seeds (3 dead)	4	1
18. *Garcubua purrecta*, Cultivated mangoustane (dead)	2	0

Second Case   All plants destroyed

Third Case

26. *Chammaearops excelsior,* Indian palm, several individuals	0**	42
27. *Sagoustia*, Madagascar Sagoutier (1 dead)	2	1
28. *Ravanela madagascariensis,* Traveller's tree (living)	3	3
29. Arica rubra, Red palm of Bourbon (living)	2	2
30. Grafted mangos called "Charlotte" (dead)	2	0
31. *Croton tyglinm*, Pignons from India (2 dead)	5	3
32. *Thea*, Tea of Assam cultivated in India (dead)	1	0
33. *Rubus rosoefulins*, Bourbon raspberry (dead)	6 [sic]	6
34. *Curcuma zoiada*, zedoary, East Indies (living)	2	2
35. *Curcuma longa*, Indian saffron from bourbon (living)	3	3

Fourth Case

36. *Areca alba*, White palm of bourbon, (7 living)	0*	7
37 *Latania burbonica*, Bourbon lantana (32 living)	0*	32
38. Peaches from Bourbon (all dead)	0	0
39. [Peaches] acclimatized at Bourbon (moribund)	1	0
40. Mangos, grafted called Auguste (dead)	2	0
41. *Thea boc[o]*, Black tea of China (in good condition)	2	2
42. id, *viridis*. Green tea of China (in good condition)	2	2
43. id. *Pyramidalis*, Pyramid tea of China (in good condition)	2	2
44. *Terminalia Benjoin*, Benjoin trees of Bourbon several (in good condition)	0	3

Source: Le Courier de la Martinique 15 Nov. 1842

furnished by the newspaper account above. However, one set of plants, carried by the *Gabane* in the form of twenty cases that had been off-loaded at Fort Royal, was not in the newspaper account. Under the supervision of the Direction de l'Intérieur, Martinique, these plants had been distributed within the two principal cities of the colonies by the Director of the Jardin des Plantes, presumably M. Artaud in his second service, in proportion to the capabilities of the planters. Du Valdailly reported that not all the plants had arrived in good condition. He mentioned that he was sending him a copy of the article in the *Courrier de la Martinique* reporting on the number of young live plants received from nurseries in that shipment.

Du Valdailly reported with glee that five cases containing seeds of Moka coffee collected in the Yemen had arrived in good condition at the end of September (1842). He further reports that the amount of seed distributed to the settlers was proportional to the lands held by each. The letter continued with the news that from the same ship the Société d'Agriculture et d'Economie Rural de la Martinique had received five cases of plants from India, Madagascar and from Bourbon, as well as a caisse of different seeds sent directly by the Comité d'Agriculture du Bourbon. These had been immediately sent to the Jardin des Plantes.

Finally, du Valdailly mentioned the arrival of the *Aube* with 20 cases of sugarcanes from Tahiti, not all of which had arrived safely. A listing of the contents of five cases put together in Tahiti provided by Consul M. Moerenhous shows again how assiduously exchanges of economic plant material was carried out by the staff and aides to the gardens directors. Each one contained cuttings of a different sugarcane variety: *Tuavere, Jei motu, O'Ochi, Vuroc,* and *Rutu.* There is a note appended to du Valdailly's report saying that the French Consul to Tahiti went to a plantation of an Englishman called Johnson to get these samples. It is clear from these records that a nice discrimination among sugarcane varieties had developed, and the directors of botanical gardens were willing to exchange the varieties they held.

The fourth is an 1851 report of plants sent from the Jardin Colonial de St. Pierre in three *serres* to the government's Central Nursery at Algers by way of the Port of Martinique, presumably Fort-de-France Bay, carried by Captain Ferandy of Marseilles.[74] C. Barillet, then director of the botanical garden, with a note that all the plants were six-month old plants in bamboo pots and all in good condition, sent the list. One can almost hear the good bureaucrat insisting that he had done his job well and that any damage found upon arrival in the land of destination was to be chalked up to the captain's negligence. There is no reference to spoilage, and this comment may have been an effort to escape blame if the plants should have arrived in bad condition, which they often did.

There were 52 plant lots, usually a pair, but occasionally only one and rarely three plants constituted a set, sent to the nursery in Algers and some nineteen seeds laid down in bamboo pots but not germinated when they left the garden. Included in the first Wardian case was a *Cieba* called *Bombax guinatum,* the common name of which is listed as 'fromager.' This is much too late to help in illuminating the pan-tropical distribution of the New World *Ceiba pentandra* but it documents that a separate name had been applied to the African individuals by the mid-nineteenth century only later to be repudiated.[75] Also going from the Caribbean were small plants of the sandbox tree, *Hymenea courbaril,* the West Indian cherry, *Malpighia punicifolia*, the olive wood, *Andira racemosa,* and seeds of a selected, 'choice' cacao, *Theobroma sativa,* as well as several individual plants of cacao. Returning Old World plants were included in the shipment. Nutmeg, and source of the mace, *Myristica aromatica* from Molluccas and seeds of Yemen coffee, 'said to be a very good variety, pretty rare,' moka coffee, and breadfruits, *Artocarpus incisa*, and the 'amandier du pays,' *Terminalia catappa.*[76]

Associated with this document is a request from Barillet for some seed or plants desired by the Jardin des Plantes from the government's nursery in Algers. He requested 114 species or varieties of plants, ornamental and economic. Among those requested were *Hibiscus rosa-sinensis*, 'a yellow one,' *Melia sempervirens, Crotalaria spectabilis, Indigofera anil, I. Argentia,* and *Pistacia vera.* It may be that he was responding to a list of holdings in a catalog recently received, such as were required to be made frequently available by each of the gardens as mentioned above.

The fifth set of documents illustrates again the two-way movement of plants out of the Jardin des Plantes in St. Pierre. The report, dated January 11, 1860, begins with the announcement that, as requested, some 24 spice plants and 48 of the best fruit and spice trees of the Antilles were being sent to Gabon via the *Tigre*. There, they were to be installed in the acclimatization garden of the Colony of Gabon. The author requests that the *serres* belonging to the Jardin des Plantes be returned filled with some plants of that colony. The enclosed list, in a different hand, is dated January 8, 1860 and signed by Bélanger. While the majority is West Indian plants he also lists the already introduced *Mangifera indica, Ficus carica, Citrus aurantium, Piper nigrum, and Myristicha moschata.* This suggests that, for spice plants at least, each of the gardens was still attempting to grow the plants and, whenever there was success, the resulting plants were shared among the different botanical gardens.

Included in this shipment were the American mammy apple, *Mammea americana;* pomme cithère, *Spondias dulcis;* hog plum,

S. lutea, and the West Indian cherry, *Malpighia glabra.* But interestingly, the non-native fruit trees, *Achras* from Africa, *Sapota* from Central America, *Musa Sapientium* from Southeast Asia via Africa, and *Mangifera indica* from India. Cinnamon, *Cinnamomum zeylandicum* from Ceylon and Southwest India, and black pepper, *Piper nigrum,* from the Pacific were also in the shipment.

The Director of the Jardin des Plantes in Martinique, who had put together the shipment for Gabon, passed a request through the Governor. This list of requests included plant species or varieties of plants for horticulture, agriculture, and ornamentals. It was forwarded by the administration of Martinique on January 11, 1860 to the Direction of the Colonial Administration and Financial Services of Algeria and the Colonies. The majority of the requests are for West Indian species, but the list includes Old World fruits and spices as well. What this suggests to me is that plants were sent for growing out to other colonies where insect and other pests of the place of origin would not be present and therefore inhibit the early growth of nursery plants. Many plantation crops succeed better away from the countries of origin; e.g. sugarcane in the states of the Western Hemisphere, rubber in the countries of the Eastern Hemisphere.

The last set of materials are a paper on the flora by Le R. P. Duss, perhaps the most important of the botanists who worked in the island during the later part of the nineteenth century. His most significant work was *Flore phanérogamique des Antilles françaises*, which he published in 1897. In the flora are numerous comments to 'abondant dans les champs cultivés'[77] or 'abondant dans les jardins;'[78] or, for *Phyllanthus epiphyllanthus*, 'cultivé au Jardin botanique et dans beaucoup d'autres jardins comme plante d'ornement'.[79,80] Or again, Jatropha *multifida*, 'Se rencontre souvent dans les jardin, les cours, et dans les campagnes autour des maisons'.[81] These are additions to the spontaneous flora that added to the species richness of the island.

Father Duss's earlier paper on the legumes has a phrase that is interesting to us on the same subject.[82] He notes that 11 legumes are 'cultivé au jardin botanique, d'où il s'est répandu dans les environs,' one of the strongest expressions for that time by a botanist of the dispersal – intentional or by chance – concerning introduced plants and their naturalization in the landscape. Father Duss lists six *Crotalaria* species. *C. quinquefolia* is listed as 'cultivated in the botanical garden from which it has spread locally'. Jacque Fournet (1967), author of the most recent flora of Martinique and Guadeloupe, lists 21 species of *Crotalaria* in the islands for 1975.[83] While there was a concerted effort to introduce the leguminous crotalarias in the 1920s for fodder and amending the soil, it is probable that more had entered by the end of the last century, some by the efforts of planters. Duss says *Desmodium latifolium* was also cultivated in the garden and had become spontaneous and widely distributed. Of the flowering small trees he mentions the butterfly tree, *Bauhinia megalandra,* as being in the botanical garden and that it had dispersed into the countryside. The botanical garden at Saint-Pierre was functioning in the late nineteenth century as a plant introduction center for the island's inhabitants and it is evident that some of the plants had been 'jumping the fence' and become naturalized and part of the spontaneous flora.

The spontaneous dispersal of intentionally introduced plants from the Jardin Botanique parallels the experience of places elsewhere. Mediterranean plants escaped from the gardens at Kew into the roadsides of southern England; the introduction of the mesquite tree to Hawaiian gardens led to an explosive colonization of coastal scrublands or, the introduction of 30 species of cacti from the New World led to the pestiferous migrations of nine species over much of southeastern Queensland and northern New South Wales.[84] In Martinique there seem to have been no real catastrophes associated with a plant introduction, although the introduction of European and African weeds have resulted in a pan-tropical, subtropical weedy flora along highway verges. Bermuda grass is the dominant grass of the coastal areas of the Saint-Anne region of southeastern Martinique. There is one plant that was introduced in the twentieth century, which drastically transformed the landscapes of the dry ecosystems in the south. This is a legume species of the woody *Gliricidia* brought in to provide fodder during the dry season. This small tree has replaced other living fence material, which has transformed the highway landscapes much to the dismay of at least one local resident, Emil Hayot.[85]

The Demise, The Oasis in Decline

Devant l'immensité du désastre qui
engloutit en quelques instants une ville
anéantissant d'un seul coup
toute une population active et laborieuse,
c'est à peine si l'on ose parler des pertes matérielles.
Jean Dybowski 1902.[86]

Le Jardin des Plantes grew beautiful during the early years of its installation. However, after the fall of the Empire, the cutting down of introduced trees grown large reduced much of the charm of the garden. The preparation of the utilitarian working environments for the scientific and agronomic activities of the garden took away from the area in the park. While there was a continued traffic in importations and exports from the garden, the care and attention given to the park seems to have fallen off, reducing some of its charm. Nonetheless, in 1861 during the time of Bélanger, Prince Alfred of England, while on a state visit, was shown the garden by daylight at his particular request.[87] The visit was reported as a great social event in *Les Colonies* and *Le Moniteur* and the general description of the garden included descriptions of waterfalls, lakes, ponds, and grottos.[88] About twenty years later in 1880, France's famous engineer, Ferdinand de Lesseps, on his way to build the canal in Panama, was entertained in the garden.[89]

But, by the late 1880s, a passing traveler would write, 'The beautiful garden is now little more than a wreck of what it once was... Some agronomist sent out to take charge of it by the Republic began its destruction by cutting down acres of enormous and magnificent trees, including a superb alley of palms for the purpose of experimenting with roses.... Subsequently the garden was greatly damaged by storms and torrential rains; the mountain rivers overflowed, carrying bridges away and demolishing stone work.'[90] (Why acres were cut down, we do not know, perhaps a defiant gesture for his unwished-for stationing in the alien tropics. However, there was much interest paid to roses by European horticulturists in the mid-nineteenth century). But in contrast, Louis Garaud wrote in 1892, 'The garden of Saint-Pierre is one of the marvels of the world, but a marvel unknown to the world.'[91] It is possible that the romance of a place in decay appealed to the melancholy of Garaud and contrasted with the more conventional attitudes toward gardening of Lacfadio Hearn. According to him, no attempt was made to repair the storm's destruction rampant in the garden.[92]

However much the public park declined in importance, the botanical work proceeded regularly in the last years of the century. Under Bélanger's long reign it became one of the truly important gardens of the great tropical garden network. Its exhibit was one of the jewels at the 1900 Paris exposition. In 1902 the explosion of Mont Pelée caused its complete destruction. Jean Dybowski, writing an obituary for the garden in *La Nature 1902,* said that the vast program undertaken by the several directors had continued right up to the end.[93] The last shipment of seeds and young plants from the Jardin Colonial, sent two days before the eruption of Mont Pelée, arrived in France in good condition. When the glass cases were opened, all the plants were covered with fine dust from the pre-eruption ash venting of the volcano.

With the eruption of May 8, 1902, St. Pierre and its environs were destroyed in a few seconds. Heilprin writing from his observations in the late May, reported, 'The beautiful Jardin des Plantes...lay buried with its palms, its ravenalas, rubber trees, and mangos, its giant cactuses and red hibiscus, beneath a cap of gray and white.'[94] Apparently, no attempt was made to restore the garden. Botanist Richard Howard, Director of the Arnold Arboretum, visited the garden in the 1960s and, together with a colleague from Geneva, wrote a short article on the formation of the garden and its decline.[95] M. Jack Lang, Ministre de Culture of France, visited Saint-Pierre in the early 1990s and declared the town a *Cité Historique*. With this designation there should now be funds for restoration. It remains to be seen whether funds will ever be spent on restoring the nineteenth-century Jardin des Plantes.

Other environmental institutions in Martinique

On saisisra l'immense perte que fut pur
la science la disparition du jardin de Saint-Pierre,
(mais le travail doit continuer).
Thésée 1990:59.[96]

Because the Jardin Colonial de Saint-Pierre was a late-nineteenth century creation, some of the functions of other botanical gardens in the Caribbean fell earlier to other institutions and organizations in Martinique and later were created not in competition but in concert with it.

Legislation to preserve certain habitats was slow to develop, but the land adjacent and on the coast was protected after 1670 and known as the *Cinquante Pas du Roi*.[97] This protected zone was intended to hinder movement of enemy personnel. It also made possible access to the sea for all inhabitants and land communication between settlements possible. Later known as the *Cinquante pas géometriques* the zone measured inland about 80 meters from the high-tide mark. The zone was sufficiently large to provide land for coastal defenses and wood for captains of visiting ships to repair their vessels. Merchants were allowed to build small entrepôts, but always the land and the buildings had to be relinquished if there was a need.[98] By the 1730s, the zone was difficult to cross in the dry areas, because the coastal woodlands had been reduced to savanna with numerous cactus plants.[99] However, when the land was privatized in the 1980s, much of the coastal areas were in spontaneous vegetation much like the native vegetation of earlier centuries. Exploitation of the lands near the sea by the tourist industry has put considerable stress on the coastal zone vegetation.

While there was talk of protecting the timber and water resources by preserving the inland forests on steep slopes, little was discussed officially and virtually nothing was implemented. Even as late as 1901, a forest consultant reported 'but clearing in the present period is being pursued in a blind rage. At all points of the forest, in the interior as on the perimetre, one finds clearing, small, large, in all dimensions and something extraordinary, which one cannot see without being profoundly saddened, it seems the preference is for the steepest slopes where all remunerative agriculture is impossible (my translation)'.[100]

Although members of the Agricultural and Waters and Forests Services continued to call for protection of forest, especially interior forests, the government proposed to the Agricultural Service that land be found for small farmers, particularly during the resettlement of farmers after earthquakes, the volcanic eruptions, and hurricanes. Despite the activities of Fathers Duss in the nineteenth century and Delaward in the twentieth century, and the botanists Landes and natural historians Lucienne Maurice in the lycées, and historians such as Jacques Petitjean-Roget and Emile Hayot, conservation thinking and activities were not foremost in governmental objectives. It was not until the movement of appreciation of nature as part of the national patrimony came to Martinique that serious and effective measures were taken to reserve certain areas of ecological importance. This movement came directly from metropolitan France rather than from nearby islands, although after the initiatives were begun, some interchange between British and French islands developed.[101]

In 1974 lobbying by citizens groups of the government began to be effective and in 1976, two political decisions rewarded the conservation-minded. These were the Délibération du Conseil Régional de la Martinique of September, 1976, and the Arrêté Ministériel of August, 1976. They provided for an organizational charter for the Parc Naturel and charged the local authorities, the Director of the Rural and Urban Mission, and *préfet* of Martinique Region, to carry out the order.[102] In 1982 members of a syndicate including Regional and Departmental personnel, the City of Fort-de-France, tourism's institutions, labor organizations, the Chamber of Commerce and Industry, the Chamber of Agriculture, and two regional organizations: Le Syndicat intercommunal d'aménagement touristique du nord (SIATNO) and Le Syndicat intercommunal Vocation Multiples du Sud (SIVOM), set up the park and developed the mission for the park. A number of functions and uses were identified. Five objectives were considered of prime importance:

1. Identifying and protecting the natural environments, the historical items and architectural patrimony;
2. promoting rural development and local products;
3. stimulating outdoor activities;
4. improving access and rest lodges according to local abilities; and

5.   undertaking an information program and developing public sensitivity to the problems of the environment.

A coastal mangrove-dominated park was the first park established. The idea was to have the distinctive ecosystems set aside for the benefit of tourism as well as for the conservation of nature. A projected park in the seasonal woodland near Marin in the Sainte-Anne Peninsula, and a rainforest and high mountain park in the interior Forêt Demaniale have been under discussion. Conservation education, public opinion and enabling legislation changed the conservation movement into an active force for monitoring the environment. In the early 1990s, the Gallerie Botanique and the Gallerie Géoloque were set up by the Conseil Régional to collect information concerning the physical and environmental patrimony of the island populations. Physically located in the Parc Floral of Fort-de-France, their research and public information responsibilities are foremost. Increasingly staffed by professionals, the role of the amateur has declined.[103]

The Chambre d'Agriculture et du Commerce set up laboratories in the nineteenth century for the improvement of the economic plant dominants and for those enterprises inspired by innovations of the crown. Chambers of Agriculture and Commerce during the ninteenth and early twentieth centuries were important international forces for the improvement of commerce, industry and agriculture. By holding international conferences in the developed world these organizations, quasi-governmental in some cases, became spokespersons for the colonial territories of different metropolitan governments.

The Chamber of Commerce and Industry has been actively supporting the growth of agro-industries such as developments of copra and manufactures from that resource. They are strong supporters of the draining of the marshes surrounding Fort-de-France Bay and the creation of artificial landscapes near the principal city of the island. The Waters and Forests Service has been actively replacing systematically as much of the spontaneous forest as possible with economically useful timber plantings. The first attention was on Caribbean pine and the Mahoganies. Later experiments with Blue Maho and Teak were made as well as efforts with a native species *Simaruba amara*.

The destroyed plant improvement gardens of Tivoli were replaced by some gardens nearer to Fort-de-France, at Desclieux under the direction of the Agricultural Service. As in all islands of the Caribbean, some of the planter class, which in Martinique invariably lived on their plantations, and some of the merchants of the towns were keen observers of nature and were scientifically literate in natural history. As they exchanged information with planters on other islands – one even corresponded with Thomas Jefferson in Virginia about soil conservation methods, such as contour plowing – the pool of information in the Caribbean became general and even at odds with imperial aspirations.[104] Local concerns overbore the more distant metropolitan concerns.

Other environmental institutions have taken on the role of the botanical garden in Martinique. Le Jardin de Balata, a botanical garden located a few miles north of Fort-de-France, is a garden where the natural rain forest has been underplanted with exotics from around the world. Les Ombrages is a naturalized botanical garden in the mid elevations north of Ajoupa-Bouillon, developed in the grounds of an old rum distillery. Private gardens continue to serve as plant introduction centers, as fine collections are both hobbies and status symbols of the elite. A strong environmental ethic introduced from metropolitan France is furthered by voluntary organizations of informed citizens, while public institutions have taken over the roles of conservation education, plant improvements, and even suppliers of health services to the local population.

Conclusions

C'était là une précieuse ressource pour
tous les jardins d'essai de nos nouvelles colonies.
Jean Dybowski 1902.[105]

France had been sending plant materials to Martinique long before the garden was established. But the establishment of the garden and the appointment of a director gave better coordination to the effort of building living plant collections. Documents such as those presented for discussion demonstrate the important role the Jardin des Plantes had in the exchange of genetic materials among the great floristic realms and provinces of the world.[106] There were four stated purposes for the establishment of the gardens: 1) to introduce and naturalize the exotic plants and to serve as a place to tend, multiply and improve the cultivation of all the useful plants and the attractive ornamentals – the indigenous as well as the exotics and to enrich the local agriculture with a collection of food plants for people and animals; 2) to furnish the gardens of metropolitan France with the plants of Martinique and the other Antilles; 3) to assemble, according to a botanical system, the indigenous plants; 4) to form a depository for medicinal plants for the use by the poor.

Of the four stated purposes for which the garden was established, most has been said about the importations to the colony. A lively exchange with Martinique was carried out by Paris and by other botanical gardens. The importance of these exchanges was great. The great traffic in plants that supported the agricultural economies of the colonies of exploitation in the Indian Ocean and the West Indies were supplied and supplied again by botanical gardens and introduction gardens.

These plants were acclimatized, sometimes with great difficulty and after many attempts before real success. The next step was establishing a stock for disseminating plants that could be useful to the islanders. All the directors in Martinique engaged in such activities with the possible exception of Mancet. Some like Artaud, Barillett, Desmarinières, and Thierry made it their primary concern. Exchanges between botanical gardens delivered the more vigorous stocks of different species and the island colonies were enriched.

The second objective was certainly realized. Heilprin, doubtless repeating common knowledge, pointed out, 'Many of the plants of tropical cultivation in the famous Jardin des Plantes of Paris had been obtained from this garden.'[107] Many different Martiniquan plants were sent not only to Paris but to other plant introduction gardens to be distributed throughout the rest of the French Empire and to be exchanged with other islands of the Caribbean. In this way the objectives of empire could be satisfied. Government-sponsored nurseries that gave away the plants grown in the gardens helped the colonial powers to compete with one another. During wartime, the taking of an enemy ship with a cargo of living plant material was an achievement of high order.[108] The botanical garden was indeed a political pawn, as well as an instrument to increase biodiversity.

The introductions to and from the Pacific, Indian Ocean, and Africa from the Antilles were numerous and repeated. New genetic material was being introduced and reintroduced into the cultivated plant populations of the plantation-based colonies. Similarly, the genetic information base was being enlarged in the new West Indian plant populations. While the introduced populations always contained a subset of the genetic information of the parent populations, the genetic resource loss from the original population was not so great as it might have been. The multiple introductions carried on over time by the directors of botanical gardens provided for new genetic material to be added to that which was already in the garden. While much is now being made over the role of botanical gardens in maintaining gene pools and seed banks, it seems clear that this function was important from the time they began playing a role in supporting the empires of the mother countries.[109]

If the documents are examined for the amount of reintroduction of sugarcane genetic information, we can see that throughout its 99 years the garden repeatedly received new material to use in the experimental work of the garden from many different sources. After the discovery that sugarcane did flower, it was possible to conduct breeding experiments with the material already in the garden. Thierry brought back a set from Jamaica. Sugarcane appeared in five of the documents examined above. The most important plantation crop of the last half of this century in Martinique, the banana, had many introductions to the island. It was listed in the 1830 and 1860 documents. The secondary crops, coffee (1830, 1851), cacao (1830 and 1851), and indigo (1830, 1842 and 1860) show up collectively in all the documents except the legumes paper. Ornamental plants were constantly being exchanged according to these documents. As the introductions were many, over a long time, and had become selected for different properties, there was always a need to keep abreast of innovations. So the motive for exchange continued.

Additionally, we have seen the exchange of Old World and New World plants going in both directions. Acclimatization of Old World plants in West Indian gardens were sometimes more successful for the Indian Ocean and African plantations than the plants that were acclimatized in their own introduction gardens, and vice versa. The French and the English gardeners were in regular communication and even in the seventeenth century, John Evelyn, who had traveled extensively throughout the Netherlands, France and Italy, spoke of the desire to enfranchise plants from all over the world and thought that 'without some tincture in Medicine, gardening was a voluptuous and empty speculation.'[110] There is also no doubt that this garden and others like it was part of the strong tradition of the botanical garden as a depository for 'the recovery of knowledge and power over nature'.[111] Scientific knowledge of this type was power.

Whether the third objective, of putting the garden into a class such as an arboretum with plants of the same families and orders grouped in close proximity, was realized is unknown. Certainly de l'Horme was aware of the botanical classification system of his day as his catalog attests. Bélanger was reported to have arranged the garden beds in this way. More study of the scattered garden's records should yield useful information to this end. The landscape architectural aesthetic of the early establishment may have contributed against this achievement. Certainly, it was that a large number of amateur and professional botanists passed through the gates with its blue-glazed ceramic guards.

That the fourth objective was being considered is evidenced in the catalog of M. V. de l'Horme of 1824, in which he mentions in the descriptions of some plants their uses as medicine. Father Duss makes reference to the medicinal uses, if any, of plants in the garden during his time. Whether the garden acted as a botanical pharmacy for the poor has not been determined. A medical doctor had a house on Morne Mirail overlooking the Jardin when the garden was destroyed in the volcanic eruption of 1902. Perhaps, the garden had been his apothecary shop.

The active work in the introduction of quinine, and other medicinal plants that might be commercially grown in Martinique, was supported by the governmental administrations of Paris and Martinique. There was some interest in investigating the local flora for plants that could be used for medicine as well, especially in the earlier years as is indicated by Admiral Wade's injunctions to d'Auros.

Many persons were involved in developing the garden, and strong support from the island and métropole governments was an aid in getting plants from abroad. The main responsibility of development was that of the director of the garden. The first director was a M. d'Auros, who started the garden in 1803. He was a good choice because he had been acquiring plants from other islands for his own garden. His principal objective seems to have been exchanges for the advancement of agricultural production. Artaud seems to have been a very active director, collecting plants from scientific institutions as well as utilizing his connections with planters. But it was Bélanger who really put the garden into the first rank of tropical botanical gardens of his time. Not only was he qualified to supervise the accumulation of rich materials from abroad, but also to begin an extensive set of locally initiated scientific investigations.

The initiative for the support of the garden came originally from the crown and the local political administration, and then, the local planters became intimately involved. Finally, the great Muséum de Paris took over the leadership role. When management returned to local control, the pattern had been set. All reflected the concerns of the social and intellectual milieu in which the garden was functioning. The garden was a place of beauty, an experimental farm, a repository of exotic plants, and a great conservator of genetic information from abroad. Because of it, the flora of Martinique was greatly enriched. It was one of the pre-eminent environmental institutions of the nineteenth century.

Not only was the garden contributing to the accumulation of diversity within the gene pools of the economic species, it was contributing to the islands's biodiversity. The rate of introductions was considerably faster than the rate of loss of species. In fact it would be difficult to maintain that there was any species lost during this period of the nineteenth century. The consequence of these introductions was that the biodiversity, certainly the species richness, of the island increased through the Colonial Period until the 1830s.

In the twentieth century the National Parks movement began to argue for the protection of soils and water supply by conserving the Rainforest and Upper Montane forests. The influence for the protection of nature seems to have really diffused from the metropolis rather than from other islands of the Caribbean; however, once begun, Martiniqais turned to their fellow Caribbean dwellers.

The garden with its vicissitudes exemplifies nicely the courses of both fashion and science in gardens in the Caribbean. We know that the directors and managers of the garden carried on correspondence with the British gardens in St. Vincent, and Jamaica, but also with the Dominican Republic. The botanical garden in Cuba was established after the Peléan destruction, but correspondence between botanically inclined Cubans and Martiniquans took place. Pride of place goes to the Garden in St. Vincent; it was the first and, despite destruction by storms and volcano, it continued as the most important environmental institution in that island. The Jardin botanique came later, and always shared with other environmental institutions the role of plant introduction and scientific amelioration of economic plants. Its mission was similar to that of other gardens, but it had a tragic history, which kept it from the important role it might have played in the natural history of the Caribbean. However, for the nineteenth century, none outshone it in the hearts of the Martiniquais and in scientific circles.

Notes

I wish to thank Mme. Lilian Chauleau, Directeur des services d'Archives de la Martinique, for kindly putting the resources of Archives départemental de la Martinique at my disposal, giving me permission to copy documents and publications, and especially for bringing to my attention the maps by Monnier and Bodin. I thank the staff of Bibliothèque Schoelcher for permitting me to copy large portions of books held in that collection. I thank both Dr. Richard A. Howard, who generously sent materials when he came across useful items and Madeleine Ly-Tio-Fane who has kept up an intermittent stream of correspondence on tropical botanical gardens.

1   Service Agricole. *Bulletin Agricole de la Martinique*. Fort-de-France, Martinique, 1918. pp. 14–16.
2   M. Reisser. *Historique du Jardin-des-Plantes de Saint-Pierre, Martinique*. Fort Royal, Martinique, E. Ruelle & Ch. Arnaud, Imprimeurs du Gouvernement, 20 juin, 1847. p. 10.
3   *Bulletin Agricole.* 1919. pp. 14–18.
4   With apologies to Phillada Ballard.
5   There is no establishment that could be compared to the Jardin des Plantes of St. Pierre.
6   Occupied by the British since 1794, Martinique was returned to the French after the Peace of Amiens on 25 March, 1802.
7   Archives Nationales [A.N.] C8Afo 158–Article 8 of an arrêté du pluviose an XII [19 Feb. 1803].
8   Plan de la Rade et de la ville de Saint-Pierre (Ile de la Martinique) levé en 1825 par M. Monnier 1827 au Dépôt-général de la Marine, cited in Thésée 1990. p. 12.
    Plan topographique du jardin des plantes de Saint-Pierre by Esprit Bodin, Ingénieur Géographe Militaire, by order of his Excellency the lieutenant general,

Comte Donzelot, 1823. Located in the Archives Nationales d'Outre-Mer (A.N.O.M.), Aix-en-Provence. Photocopy in the Archives Départementales de la Martinique, Fort-de-France, Martinique.

9   See map of reconstructed native vegetation in Clarissa T. Kimber. *Martinique Revisited: The Changing Plant Geographies of a West Indian Island.* Texas A&M University Press, College Station, TX. p. 46.

'La vue est soudainement frappée par le grandiose de cette végétation fougèreuse, cadre si bien approprié au tableau qu'elle décore. L'eau tombant avec fracas, par flocons écumeux, de soixante-dix pied (22m, 70) de hauteur, dans un basin semicirculaire, forme une nappe en globules d'argent, tandis que les reflets de la lumière qui se projettent perpendiculairement; se jouent et chatoient sur sa surface comme les rayons de la lune sur les vagues fouettées de la brise.'

'One is suddenly struck by the grandiose fernlike vegetation, framing the scene with precision. The water crashing down in foamy flakes, seventy-feet high, into a semicircular basin forms a sheet of silver globules while the light reflections that are cast perpendicularly play and glisten on its surface like the rays of the moon on the wind whipped waves.'

Moreau de Jonès's 1893 description of a sight in 1802 when he was conducting a military survey for Villaret-Joyeuse, cited in Thésée, 1900. p. 13.

10   Christopher Thacker. *The History of Gardens.* University of California Press, Berkeley and Los Angeles, 1985.

R. G. Saisselin. The French garden in the 18th Century from Belle Nature to the landscapes of time. *Journal of Garden History,* July-September 1985. p. 289.

11   T. H. D. Turner. Loudon's stylistic development. *Journal of Garden History,* April-June 1982. p. 180.

12   Eduard André. Le jardin botanique de St Pierre, Martinique. In *Revue Horticule.* 1902. p. 256.

13   Thésée. 1990.

14   L. Garaud. Trois ans à la Martithe lieutenant general, Comte Donzelot, 1823. In *Martinique: Etudes de moeurs, paysages, profiles et portraits.* 2nd ed. Editions Alcide Picard et Kaan, Paris, 1895. Reprinted in 1978. p. 203.

15   Andre. 1902. p. 256.

16   To harvest one has to sow, as the old saying goes, but we may add that to sow and harvest, one has to enrich and fertilize the land that one wants to farm.

17   Andre. 1902. p. 253

J. H. Parry and P. M Sherlock. *A Short History of the West Indies.* 2nd ed. St. Martin's Press. 1965. pp. 170–172.

18   *Bulletin Agricole.* 1918. pp. 14–16.

19   Reisser. 1847. p. 23

20   Thésée. 1990. p. 17.

21   Reisser. 1847. p. 28.

22   *Bulletin Agricole.* 1918. p. 15.

23   Reisser. 1847. p. 24.

24   Reisser. 1847. p. 24.

25   Reisser. 1847. p. 31.

26   I have not located these catalogs, but Thésée uses them in her account 1990. p. 25.

27   Thésée. 1990. pp. 17–18.

28   *Instruction pour les voyageurs et pour les employés des colonies sur la manière de recueillir, de conserver et d'envoyer les objets d'histoire naturelle.* Paris 1818. Cited in Thésée, 1990.

29   Reisser. 1847. p. 35.

30   Reisser. 1847. p. 40.

31   Reisser. 1847. pp. 40.
32   Martinique, Directeur de l'Interieur, *Arrêté du 1er janvier.* 1840. Appointed by
     the governor were a number of men from the Conseil Colonial and several nota-
     bles from Saint-Pierre, namely Artaud, Brière de l'Isle, Bouisset, Dariste, du
     Peyrat, Adrien Eyma, Hue, Le Pelletier du Clary, Richard de Lucy, Victor Segond,
     Payraud, Vautor des Roseaux and August Pecoul, the president. According to
     Reisser, all were very interested in innovations and all subjects concerning agri-
     culture. 1847, p. 46.
33   Reisser. 1847. pp. 51–53.
34   Reisser. 1847. p. 58.
35   Thésée. 1990. p. 37.
36   A. D. M. 5k17, 1846 2 mars, n°6 and 5k17, 1846, 2 mars n°°18.
37   A. D. M. 5k22, 1850, 6 mai, n°9, T. p. 88 and 5k24, 1851, 17 octobre, n°9, T. p. 98.
38   Thésée. 1990. pp. 37–38.
39   Le jardin botanique de Sainte-Pierre. In the *Revue coloniale.* Mars 1856. Cited in
     Thésée. 1990. p. 10.
40   Thésée. 1990. pp. 39–41.
41   Thésée. 1990. pp. 40.
42   Thésée. 1990. pp. 43.
43   Eduard Hommaire de Hail. Le jardin botanique de Saint-Pierre, 1856. In
     l'Illustration, 30 Janvier, 1856. p. 1.
44   Thésée. 1990. p. 47.
45   Ludwig Hahn. *Manuel du bon jardinier aux Antilles.* Saint-Pierre, Martinique. n.d.
     Copy of booklet in the Archives de la Guadeloupe. Excerpted in Thésée. 1990.
     pp. 75–95.
46   Thésée. 1990. p. 52.
47   Thésée. 1990. p. 56.
48   Conseil général de la Martinique. *Arrêté du 8 Octobre, 1887.*
49   Geoffroy. *Rapport de mission la Martinique et à la Guyane.* Impriemerie Protat
     Frérs, Macon France. p.13.
50   *Bulletin agricole*, Août, 1898.
51   *La Nature.* 1902.
52   'Thanks to the numerous mailings made constantly by the zealous director of the
     garden, most of our colonies are now equipped in rare essences that were part of
     these magnificent collections.'
53   *Bulletin agricole.* Août 1898.
54   André and Jean Dybowski. Le jardin de la Martinique. In *La Nature.* 1902 II.
     Angelo Heilprin. *Mt. Pelée and the Tragedy of Martinique.* J. B. Lippencott Co.
     Philadelphia and London, 1903.
55   Heilprin. 1903. pp. 65 and 232. See as well A. Lacroix. *La Montagne Pelée et ses
     Eruptions*, Masson et Cie. Paris, Frontispiece.
56   Dybowski. 1902 II.
57   Howard. 1953. p.120.
58   Some plants that have been cultivated in gardens and agricultural land since the most
     ancient times have been man's traveling companion all over the world.
59   Jacques Fournet. *Flore illustrée des phanérogames de Guadeloupe et de Martinique.*
     Institut National de la Recherche Agronomique, Paris. pp. 11–16.
60   The administration and the inhabitants of this region will see through these thoughts
     of kindness of your department the new interest shown by Metropolitan France for
     the wellness of its colonies.
61   Thésée. 1990. p. 17.
62   Instructions. 1818.

63 Thésée. 1990. p. 25. Such documentation for individual species is not so easily discovered; however, some very interesting archival documents provide information about the process of acquisition and redistribution of species in the botanical gardens. In an effort to illustrate how such information can be used, selected documents and materials from the Bibliothèque Scholecher in Fort-de-France, Martinique, Archives départemental de la Martinique in Tarteson, Fort-de-France in Martinique, and the Archives Nationales de France have been examined. Many were used in the study, but some have been specifically referenced as illustrative of their kind. Photo copies made available from the Archives Nationales, Paris, and from the Archives of the Ministre de France d'Outre Mer (FOM), formerly Ministry of the Colonies, especially from those of the Administrative correspondence, Series D, contain a collection of reports and letters, concerning the introduction of vegetables, spices, cacao, citrus plants, forage plants, grains and other plants to the island. Some old newspapers were examined and articles were copied from the archives in Martinique and Guadeloupe.

64 1. Catalogue des plants cultivees au jardin botanique et de naturalisation de la Martinique, année 1829 in Catalogue General des Plantes Cultivées aux Colonies. Annals Maritimes et Coloniales 1830, Part 2, Vol. 1.;
2. Letter from Ach. Bedier, president of the Cmite d'Agriculture de Bourbon to M. Dupuy, Corresponding Member of the Société d'Agriculture de la Martinique published in the *Courrier de la Martinique,* 15 Nov. 1842;
3. Letter from M. du Valdailly to the Ministre Secretaire d'Etat de la Marine et des Colonies in which he reports on the cargo of plants brought by the *Aube* from Tahiti;
4. List of plants sent to the Jardin Colonial de Saint-Pierre in three conservatories from the government's central nursery at Alger carried by Cap. Ferandy of Marseilles. The director of the botanical garden (the nursery) sent this list;
5. Request from the Jardin des Plants in Martinique for some plants from Gabon. It was forwarded by the Administration of the Directeur de l'Interior of the Gouvernement de la Martinique 11 January 1860 to the Direction of the Administration Coloniale et des Services Financiers de l'Algerie et des Colonies;
6. R. P. Duss. Les Legumineuses de la Martinique. In *Compte Rendu du Congres.* ed 1891. *Scientifique International des Catholiques.* Paris, Alphonse Picard. And R.P. Duss. *Flore phanèrogamiqiue des Antilles françaises (Martinique et Guadeloupe).* 2 vols. Protat Frères, Impremeurs, Macon, France. New edition Société de Distribution et de Culture, Fort-de-France, Martinique. 1972.

65 Montfleury V. De l'Horme. Catalogue des plantes cultivées au jardin botanique et de naturalisation de la Martinique, année 1829. In *Annales Maritimes et Coloniales*, Part 2, Vol. 1. 1830. pp. 118–148.

66 According to the *Catalogue Général de 1829* printed in 1830, the first part was printed in 1828 and nothing was printed in 1829. De l'Horme. 1830. p. 118.

67 A.N.O.M., Fonds Martinique-Généralités. F3, 89.

68 Montfleury V. De l'Horme. Catalogue des plantes cultivées au jardin botanique et de naturalisation de la Martinique, année 1829. In *Annales Maritimes et Coloniales*, Part 2, Vol. 1. 1830. pp. 118–148.

69 Buée 1797, cited in Madelaine Ly-Tio-Fane. *The Triumph of Jean Nicolas Céré and his Isle Bourbon collaborators.* Mouton & Co., Paris and The Hague. p. 64.

70 Reisser. 1847. p. 29.

71 Claude Richard became Director of the Jardin du Roy at Saint-Denis, Réunion, in 1831 and remained there for 36 years. Previous to his appointment to the post, he had spent time in various posts in France and in the New World tropics including Guyane.

72 Darrel McDonald. *The Historical Cultural Plant Geography of Urbanized Galveston: Implications of Gardening on a Sub-tropical Barrier Island.* Ph.D. dissertation. Texas A&M University, 1990. p. 270.
73 F. O. M. C21.
74 Glasshouses called 'Wardian cases' in English literature.
75 See the monograph by H. G. Baker. The evolution of the cultivated kapok tree: a probable West African product. In *Ecology and Economic Development in Tropical Africa* edited by David Prokensha. University of California Press, Berkeley.
76 Latin names are given as in the documents while the common names are either translations of the French name or, when missing, furnished by the author for the convenience of the readers.
77 'abundant in cultivated fields'
78 'abundant in the gardens'
79 'cultivated in the Botanical Garden and in many more gardens cultivated as an ornament plant.'
80 Le R. P. Duss. *Flore phanérogamique des Antilles Françaises.* Protat Frères, Imprimeurs, *réédité* par la Société de Distribution et de Culture, Fort-de-France, Martinique, 1972. Vol.1, p. 25– 26.
81 'can be found in the gardens, in the courtyards and in the countryside outside the houses.'
82 Les Legumineuses de la Martinique. In *Compte Rendu du Congrès scientifique international des catholiques tenu à Paris 1–6 avril 1891*, Alphonse Picard, Paris. pp. 235–245
83 Jacques Fournet. *Flore illustrée des phanérogames de Guadeloupe et de Martinique.* Institut National de la Recherche Agronomique, Paris.
84 Jonathan D. Sauer. *Plant Migration: The Dynamics of Geographic Patterning in Seed Plant Species.* University of California Press, Berkeley, Los Angeles, and London. p. 121–124.
85 Emil Hayot, businessman and historian, Personal Communication, 1985. More serious is the effect of the introduced mongoose, which effectively eliminated the ground nesting birds and some ground nesting spiders.
86 Faced with the enormous disaster that in moments swallowed a city and destroyed at once the whole working population, it is very difficult to talk of material damages.
87 Richard A. Howard and Claude Weber. The botanical garden of Saint-Pierre 1803–1902. In *The American Horticultural Magazine.* 1966. p. 399.
88 *l'Illustration* 25 mai 1861.
89 M. Salvina. *Saint-Pierre, la Venise Tropicale.* Saint-Pierre, Martinique. p. 281.
90 Hearn. 1890. p. 62–63.
91 Garaud. 1895. p. 203.
92 Hearn. 1890. p. 63.
93 Jean Dybowski. Le jardin de la Martinique. In *La Nature* 1902 II.
94 Heilprin. 1905. p. 65.
95 Howard and Weber. 1966.
96 One will comprehend that the loss of the garden of St. Pierre was a great loss for science, [but work must go on].
97 M. de Bass. Rapport de M. de Baas, gouverneur des Iles d'Amerique a son ministre, 8 fev. 1674. In *Annales des Antilles* Vol. 8. p. 8.
98 L.P. May. *Histoire Economique de la Martinique (1635–1763).* Marcel Rivière, Les Presses Modernes, Paris. p. 72.
99 E. Durand-Molard. *Code de la Martinique, 1807–1811.* 4 vol. Impremerie de gouvernement, Fort-de-France, Martinique. Vol. 1. p. 375.

100 M. Lasaulce. *Rapport de mission sur l'étude et l'organisation des bases d'un régime forestier à la Martinique*. Ministre des Colonies, Fort-de-France, 1901. p. 30.

101 Henrie Petitjean-Roget, Director of Museums for Guadeloupe, Personal communication 1985.

102 France, Ministre de la Qualité de Vie 1977.

103 Jean-Pierre Fiard, Personal communication.

104 T. de Chanvalon. *Voyage à la Martinique*. P. Angrand, Paris, 1763. p. 28.

105 This was a very precious resource for all the gardens that were tested in our new colonies.

106 Ronald Good. *The Geography of the Flowering Plants*. Longman, London, 1974. facing p. 62.

107 Heilprin. 1903. p. 19.

108 Howard. 1954. p. 384.

109 See Heywood, in *Botanic Gardens and the World Conservation Strategy* edited by D. Bramwell, Orlando. Published for IUCN by Academic, 1987.

110 Cited in John Claudius Loudon. *An encyclopdedaea of gardening*. A new edition. Longman, Res, Orme, Braown, Green and Longman, London, circa 1830. p. 74.

111 John Prest. *The Garden of Eden: the Botanic Garden and the Re-creation of Paradise*. Yale University Press. New Haven and London, 1984. p. 54. See Heywood. In *Botanic Gardens and the World Conservation Strategy*. Edited by D. Bramwell, Orlando. Published for IUCN by Academic, 1987.

The St. Vincent Botanic Garden – The Early Years

Richard A. Howard

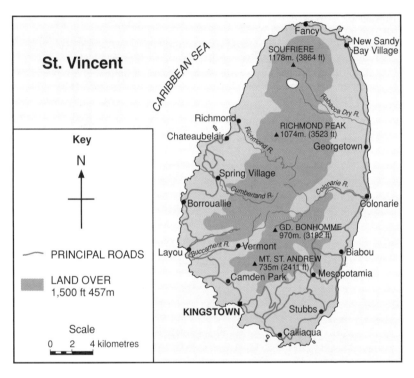

Map of St. Vincent (by permission of Hymie Rubenstein)

The Peace Treaty signed in Paris in 1763 ended, for a brief period, the fighting between Britain and France in the Caribbean. British General Robert Melville (1723–1809) was appointed governor of the southern British Caribees: Tobago, Grenada, St. Vincent and the Grenadines, and Dominica. He made Grenada his headquarters. In June, 1765 he visited St. Vincent and in conversation with Dr. George Young, surgeon of the military hospital, discussed the role of a botanical garden in helping the hospital to obtain medicines and in improving the life and economy of the colony. Melville suggested that Dr. Young write a letter to him requesting permission to create a garden and to suggest a site for it. Later, Melville ordered that a portion of the barracks land designated for military purposes be used, and that Dr. Young be the superintendent. Thus, the first allotment of six acres marked the beginning of the St. Vincent Botanic Garden, although twenty acres were finally put aside for it. The garden was to be a repository for all useful plants that could be introduced but, in contrast to the European botanical gardens of the time, it was also to be a nursery to increase the numbers of plants to be distributed on the island and to other islands. Melville wrote to Young in 1766:

> I need not repeat to you how desirous I am that my foundation of a botanical plan entrusted to your skill and perseverance should prove successful, nor do I suppose it necessary that I give you fresh assurances how much my attentions and support may be relied on, for already you know my assistance shall be as great as my situation and multiplicity of public affairs will possibly permit.... The articles of plants and seeds commissioned from the Main near Honduras I shall soon hope to receive, and seeds of the best cinnamon from Guadeloupe. If you have once made tolerable progress in raising useful and curious plants, I should not despair of obtaining from Home encouragement in books, machines, instruments, etc., but till then I find I must hazard what expenses are unavoidable (as I have already done).[1]

Trying out some immediate objectives, Melville also said to Young:

> Pray get as much information as possibly you can from all quarters relative to the indigenous medicines. It is against your craft but would be highly beneficial to the public and do yourself honour. And I should think for this purpose physical practitioners of the country, natives of experience, and even old Caribs and slaves who have dealt in cures might be worth taking notice of, and if at any time you should think that a secret may be got at or even an improvement for small expense, I shall readily pay for it.

Melville was, however, unable to obtain government money to support the garden. He recognized that Young's salary as a surgeon in itself did not meet his expenses as director of the garden. So he suggested and permitted Young to sell plants and garden produce to help meet expenses. This procedure was criticized. Neither of Melville's two successors as governor, Leybourne and Morris, found it expedient to assist in maintaining the garden, and Young had only Melville's continued verbal support from England.

Although little is known of Young's actual administration of the garden, he did instigate the first program of plant introduction in the British West Indies.[2] The War Department and the East India Company were instructed by Sir Joseph Banks to obtain seeds and plants for the Garden. These were sent to Banks or to Melville and then forwarded to Dr. Young. In the papers of John Hope of Edinburgh there is a note dated 1784 recording the books he sent to Dr. Young in exchange for seeds.[3] Young did have some contact with the French horticulturists in the area.

Young was aware of the premium offered by the Society for the Encouragement of Arts, Manufacture and Commerce.[4] He tried to get safflower seeds and seeds of logwood to qualify for one of the premiums, but before he succeeded, the time limits had expired. Young later complained, 'Now I have thousands of plants of logwood, nay, the very hedges with which the botanic garden is fenced in and divided consist of logwood.' As for cinnamon, Young had received only two plants from Guadeloupe by 1768, so in 1770 he traveled to Guadeloupe himself to obtain ten more plants. In 1771 he obtained 1200 seeds from a tree in Grenada and raised 130 plants, then having a total of 140 trees in the garden.

In a rare publication, *Some Additional Observations on the Method of Preserving Seeds from Foreign Parts, for the Benefit of our American Colonies, with an Account of the Garden at St. Vincent, under the Care of Dr. George Young* (1773), John Ellis stated, 'Dr. Young has favored me with a catalogue of what plants are now growing in this garden, and of the plants he has lately collected here to carry out with him; which I take the liberty to insert, for the satisfaction of the public.' The plants in the Garden were: cinnamon, logwood, safflower, turmeric, East India mango, paper mulberry, (*Convolvulus*) scammony, (*Citrullus*) colocynth, rhubarb, Tobago nutmeg, simarouba, spigela, citron, bergament orange, bamboo cane, Italian senna, aloes, coriander, vanelloes, morus papyrifera, nopal, balsam capivi, sesamum, *Cassia fistula*, dates, annatto, guaiacum, China root, gum galbanum (*Ferula galbaniflora*), China tallow tree. 'Besides these articles, there are several without names that have been raised from Chinese and other seeds.'[5] A second list indicated those plants Young would be able to get from the Royal and other botanical gardens in and about London.[6]

In 1773, the Society for the Encouragement of Arts, Manufacture and Commerce published a list of the premiums bestowed on trade with the colonies by the Society. The Gold Medal was awarded to Mr. George Young, 'Surgeon on that island, for the Botanic Garden, in the Island of St. Vincent, for superintending its cultivation, and for relating the event of some trials and proposing further attempts.'

Early in 1778 hostilities were renewed in the Caribbean and Dr. Young was ordered by the Commander-in-Chief to head the military hospital in St. Lucia. Young left the Botanic Garden in charge of a Mr. Swartz (or Zwartz), who later obtained a position as secretary to the commanding officer of the French forces occupying St. Vincent. Swartz later claimed that the French officer had given him title and ownership of the Garden. The French occupied the island from June, 1778, for five years. In 1780 a destructive hurricane hit St. Vincent and damaged the garden. However, the French did maintain the garden until they learned that St. Vincent was to be returned to the British. Then for a year the garden was abandoned and grew up in weeds. When the war ended in 1784, Dr. Young returned to St. Vincent, but he was no longer interested in resuming the directorship of the Botanic Garden.[7]

Clearly, the condition of the garden had deteriorated. It had been reduced in size, for portions had been given over to the cultivation of cotton and tobacco by local people. Swartz pressed his dubious claim to the land, which led to legal wrangles. The military also wished to resume full control of the land, and the financial operations were no more secure than before the war.

Young recommended the appointment of Alexander Anderson as his successor, and Anderson's appointment as the second director was approved by Sir Joseph Banks in 1785. It was under Anderson's administration, as the 'King's Gardener' between 1785 and 1811, that the Garden flourished and increased its significant contribution to tropical American horticulture.

Alexander Anderson's early years were not recorded, for he is cited in most biographies as: 'fl. 1785–1811'. We have now determined that he was born in Aberdeen, Scotland, and for a period was a student at the University in Edinburgh but did not complete the work for a degree. He knew Professors William Cullen[8] and John Hope.[9] He was employed briefly at the Chelsea Physic Garden by William Forsyth, Philip Miller's successor as director.[10] In 1774 Anderson traveled to New York to seek employment as a gardener and lived with his brother John, a printer and a rebel favouring independence from England.[11] Alexander, a loyalist who supported the King, wrote to Forsyth of the developing rebellion.[12] He collected botanical specimens and seeds on Long Island and York Island (now Manhattan), which he returned to Forsyth. He also listed other plants he could send to England and asked for plants he wished to receive in exchange. When the American revolution proceeded and he was pressed into military service, Anderson eventually sailed for Suriname as the only safe haven for loyalists in the New World. En route the ship was captured by an American privateer and Anderson was imprisoned in St. Pierre, Martinique. It is not known how he reached St. Lucia, but by

1783 he was employed as an orderly in the military hospital at Castries and had established contact with Dr. Young. Anderson was given the opportunity or the assignment of searching for medicinal native plants to be used in the hospital. In particular, he was to locate a local source of quinine to treat malaria. A plant he found in St. Lucia, called quina or china, was tested in the military hospital in St. Lucia and then sent to London for further tests. It was finally described and named as *Cinchona santae-luciae*, a relative of the true source of quinine.[13] Anderson traveled to other islands of the Lesser Antilles, both with Dr. Young and alone, at his direction. In 1784, when Dr. Young revisited the Botanic Garden of St. Vincent, Anderson became the first person known to climb the Soufrière of St. Vincent. He described the three-day ascent and the appearance of the crater in an illustrated letter to Forsyth.[14] Dr. Young saw Anderson as a naturalist and an active field man and recommended that he succeed him as director/superintendent of the garden.

Among the instructions Anderson received with his appointment by Banks and the War Department was the order to submit a list of the plants then growing in the botanical garden and, at quarterly intervals, to report the new introductions or other developments in the garden. In *A Catalogue of Plants in His Majesty's Garden on the Island of St. Vincent,* dated June 1, 1785, Anderson listed at least 348 different kinds of plants in the Botanic Garden, his heritage from Young. The manuscript is preserved in the British Museum (Natural History) but was partially burned during the bombing of London in World War II. The top portions of several pages of the manuscript are charred and missing. It appears the listing was by the categories Anderson was to employ in subsequent reports, viz., commercial, medicinal, esculent, exotic, timber species, etc. This list included the thirty-one plants of economic importance Ellis had indicated were in the Garden in 1773. Near the end of his administration, probably about 1800, Anderson compiled a manuscript entitled *Hortus St. Vincentii,* describing the plants then found in the St. Vincent Botanic Garden. This list of nearly 2,000 taxa was supported with Latin and common names in English, French, Carib, and Negro; descriptions; data on propagation and culture; uses and sources of the plants. The manuscript reveals that Anderson grew many native plants in the Botanic Garden, noting the difficulty of growing plants from high elevations at the lower altitude of the garden. He also sought out the plants cultivated or used by the Caribs and the Negroes, fulfilling General Melville's instructions to Dr. Young.[15]

Anderson had the full support of Sir Joseph Banks, General Robert Melville, Dr. George Young, General Robert Adair, the Inspector-General of the regimental hospitals, members of the War Department, and members of the East India Company. However, he often lacked support from the local administrative officials.[16]

There is evidence that Anderson was a prolific correspondent. Most of the available correspondence was with William Forsyth, who was first at Chelsea Physic Garden and later at the Kensington Palace Gardens.[17] Other correspondents in England were the Dowager Lady de Clifford, Lady Amelia Hume, Thomas Evans, Mr. Greig of Stepney and Richard Salisbury. In the United States Anderson sent plants and seeds to George Inglis of South Carolina and Dr. William Rush of Philadelphia, but his most important contact was William Hamilton of Woodlands, Philadelphia, from whom he obtained many plants of the eastern United States for trial in St. Vincent. Through Hamilton and his contacts with the American Philosophical Society, he also established exchanges with William Roxburgh of Calcutta. Anderson mentioned a few of his contacts in the French Islands, such as Victor Hughes, Mr. Aquart, and the Duc de Choiseul. Thomas Hibbert was Anderson's correspondent in Jamaica, as was William Walker in the Bahamas. In Barbados Anderson had contact with Edward Ellcock, an estate owner; Mrs. Cornelius Cuyler, the wife of a general who was helpful to Anderson; and Mrs. David Parry, wife of the Governor of Barbados (1782–1794). However, his closest contact was with Lord Seaforth, Governor of Barbados (1801–1806). Anderson regularly sent plants to Seaforth, who trans-shipped them more easily to England.[18] There are several plants whose introduction to cultivation in Europe is credited to Lord Seaforth, when the plants were actually obtained in the wild by Anderson. Plants came to Anderson regularly from Kew, from sea captains, and from other gardeners. The Kew Garden Record Book noted shipments from Anderson from 1787 to 1798, the largest being the plants brought by Bligh on his return from the *Providence* expedition with the breadfruit in 1793.[19]

Although Anderson never returned to England or Scotland, he did travel to collect plants in the Lesser Antilles, the Spanish Main, Trinidad and Tobago, and he made one important and successful trip to the Guianas.[20] He had as an associate William Lochhead, an apparently wealthy man from Antigua, who had a schooner that was used for some excursions. Many plants from the Greater Antilles, the Virgin Islands, the northern Lesser Antilles and Trinidad came via Lochhead.

Anderson is best known from his handling of the plants Captain William Bligh introduced on the voyage of the *Providence*, including the breadfruit. Bligh had been a lieutenant on the first of Captain James Cook's expeditions to the Pacific (1768). Sir Joseph Banks had secured a space for himself and his staff as naturalists on the same voyage. Cook reported enthusiastically on the role breadfruit plays in the food supply of the natives. When planters in St. Vincent and Jamaica renewed their appeal for the introduction of the breadfruit, Banks influenced King George III to order such an expedition.[21] It was Banks who knew Bligh and was instrumental in his choice to command the vessel *Bounty* and to make the first attempt to transport living breadfruit plants from Polynesia to the West Indies. Anderson was aware of the goals and the schedule of the voyage of the *Bounty*. The St. Vincent garden was to be the first place for unloading the breadfruit. Anderson had prepared a large shipment of potted plants to be put aboard the *Bounty* before it continued its voyage to Jamaica and back to England. But a mutiny occurred only a few days out of Tahiti, and the *Bounty* never reached St. Vincent.

The second attempt had the *Providence* as the principal vessel, with the armed brig *Assistant* accompanying it, manned with twenty marines to prevent another mutiny.[22] The *Providence* had nearly twice the tonnage of the *Bounty* and was well equipped to carry the plants. Anderson was not aware of the exact schedule of the *Providence* and, in fact, her arrival at St. Vincent was a full month ahead of the schedule Bligh had planned. The *Providence* had on board 1,245 or 1,390 plants (accounts varied) when she arrived in St. Vincent, the majority from Tahiti. A total of 559 plants, including 331 breadfruit, were left at St. Vincent. Anderson noted that many of the plants were sickly or in poor condition. Bligh kept the healthiest for the voyage north to Jamaica, and some of the Polynesian plants were destined for Kew. Anderson hastily potted 350 plants from his botanic garden to send to Kew on the *Providence*. Some of these were his own introductions from the Guianas. A few were destined for gardens in Jamaica. The *Providence* arrived in Jamaica and found the botanical garden at Bath too small for the Jamaican allotment. Hinton East, who was to have grown many of the introductions at his garden in Liguanea, Jamaica, had died the previous year, so additional sites had to be improvised to accommodate the introductions. James Wiles, one of the two botanists who had accompanied Bligh, stayed on in Jamaica to care for the plants. Dr. Broughton of Kingston later complained that many of the plants Anderson had sent were merely cuttings stuck in soil and obviously hastily prepared. As Bligh prepared to sail for England, he received orders to off-load the plants and join a Honduras convoy.[23] It was several months before the *Providence* and the *Assistant* could again set sail for England. A large shipment of plants from Jamaica was placed on board but the list of those delivered to the Royal Gardens at Kew does not distinguish the Anderson plants, and many were mistakenly credited to the horticulturists at Jamaica.[24]

Anderson propagated the breadfruit and other plants he had received from Bligh and shipped them to other areas. Further, he care-fully husbanded the soil in which the breadfruit plants had been shipped and cultured the seedlings that developed. The inadvertent introductions as recorded by Anderson number at least six. Bligh's lists claim that several kinds of breadfruit were transported. In his *Hortus St. Vincentii* Anderson described and discussed eight varieties, including one from Timor. A few of Anderson's letters indicate how widely he distributed the breadfruit plants he had propagated, i.e. from the Bahamas to Trinidad and to the Guianas.

In the last decade of the eighteenth century Anderson had more time to write. He left behind a number of unpublished manuscripts now in the archives of the Linnean Society of London. Two of these have been transcribed by Richard and Elizabeth Howard and were published in 1983, copyrighted by the President and Fellows of Harvard College and the Linnean Society of London.[25] *The St. Vincent Botanic Garden* is the history of the early years of the development of the Garden, and *The Geography and History of St. Vincent* is a firsthand account of his travels around the island and of some turbulent years on St. Vincent. Of great interest to botanists and horticulturists are the manuscripts describing the plants of St. Vincent and the Garden. Anderson may have had two manuscripts or publications in mind: a *Flora Caribbea* and the *Hortus St. Vincentii*. The plants named and described in the *Hortus* have been largely identified and a transcription of these parts organized into families and genera by the author, so as to be useful to botanists. The text gives the origin or source of each plant along with suggested names, of which some are new, and brief descriptions. Anderson's associate, John Tyley, made watercolor illustrations of many of the plants. These are referred to in the text; most are preserved at the Linnean Society, and a few are at the Hunt Institute for Botanical Documentation. The drawings have aided in determining modern names for those of the older manuscript and references.

Some botanical specimens were prepared by Anderson and shipped to Forsyth in Scotland. Many of these are now in the herbaria at the British Museum (Natural History) or the Royal Botanic Gardens, Kew. It is often difficult to associate the specimens with the descriptions. Nevertheless, the text of the *Hortus* represents the earliest records of plants introduced into cultivation in the British Lesser Antilles.

Anderson died in 1811 and was succeeded for a short time by his friend and associate, William Lochhead.[26] Lochhead was appointed superintendent in 1812, suspended for undetermined reasons, and re-appointed within the year. He died unexpectedly in 1815. George Caley was appointed from Australia to succeed Lochhead. His tenure on St. Vincent lasted from August, 1816, until December, 1822, and was marked by his constant dissatisfaction with everything in St. Vincent and the Garden. It was during Caley's administration that the local chaplain, Rev. Lansdown Guilding, compiled the *History of the St. Vincent Botanic Garden*, published in 1825.[27] This publication included letters and lists of plants which may have been the Anderson manuscripts, apparently available to Guilding but not to Caley. With Caley's departure, the Garden was returned to local administration and began a long decline. The last printed inventory of the plants in the Garden was that of 1806, compiled by Anderson and later published by Lansdown Guilding.[28] That wealth of plant material has never again been assembled in the American tropics. Anderson was a master plantsman to be remembered for his active program of introduction, propagation and distribution. He is commemorated with one genus and at least six species named for him. Over 100 plants he collected were new to science, but none was ever published under the name he applied to it. The manuscript Anderson compiled was never published. Examining the manuscript today, one can understand why it was not edited. If it had been, probably seventy-five common plants of the Caribbean vegetation would now have the names proposed by Anderson.

Hopefully, the horticultural information of that manuscript and the records of plant introduction can be salvaged and published in the near future as a tribute to this outstanding man of science from the King's Botanic Garden of St. Vincent, then the horticultural capital of the Western Hemisphere.

Notes

1 Alexander Anderson. Letters. 1852 *Cottage Gardener.* 1853. 8: 59; 9: 417.
   Wm. Forsyth. Correspondence. *Letters from Alexander Anderson, 1775–1789*. Kew Archives.
   Rev. L. Guilding. *An Account of the Botanic Garden in the Island of St. Vincent from its First Establishment to the Present Time.* Richard Griffin & Company, Glasgow, 1825.
   R. A. Howard & E. S. Howard. *Alexander Anderson's The St. Vincent Botanical Garden*. Harvard College, Cambridge, MA. & The Linnean Society, London, 1983.
2 John Ellis. *Some Additional Observations on the Methods of Preserving Seeds from Foreign Parts, for the Benefit of our American Colonies and With an Account of the Garden at St. Vincent Under the Care of Dr. George Young.* London, 1773.
3 A. G. Morton. *John Hope, 1725–1786. Scottish Botanist.* Edinburgh Botanic Garden Trust. 1986. 47 pp.
4 Premiums offered by the Society instituted at London for the encouragement of Arts, Manufacturers and Commerce, London 1775.
5 John Ellis. *Some Additional Observations on the Methods of Preserving Seeds from Foreign Parts, for the Benefit of our American Colonies and With an Account of the Garden at St. Vincent Under the Care of Dr. George Young.* London, 1773.
6 Ibid.
7 R. A. Howard & E. S. Howard. *Alexander Anderson's The St. Vincent Botanical Garden*. Harvard College, Cambridge, MA. & The Linnean Society, London, 1983.
8 R. A. Howard. & K. Clausen. The Soufrière plant of St. Vincent. *J. Arnold Arb.* 1980. 61: 765–770.
9 A. G. Morton. *John Hope, 1725–1786. Scottish Botanist.* Edinburgh Botanic Garden Trust. 1986. 47 pp.

10 Hazel Le Rougetel. *The Chelsea Gardener Philip Miller, 1691–1771.* Sagapress, Inc./Timber Press, Inc. Portland, Oregon, 1990.

11 Gerald Fothergill. *Emigrants from England, 1773–1776.* N.E. Historic Genealogical Society Boston, Reprint, Baltimore, 1977.

12 Alexander Anderson. Letters. 1852 *Cottage Gardener.* 1853. 8: 59; 9: 417.

13 James Britten. An overlooked Cinchona. *J. Bot.* 1915. 53: 137.

Richard Kentish. *Experiments and Observations on a New Species of Bark Shewing its Great in Very Small Doses; also a Comparative View of The Powers of the Red and Quilled Bark; Being an Attempt Towards a General Analysis and Compendious History of the Valuable Genus of Cinchona, or The Peruvian Bark.* London, 1784.

14 Alexander (James incorrectly) Anderson. An account of Morne Garu, a mountain in the island of St. Vincent, with a description of the volcano on its summit. *Philos. Trans. R. Soc. London.* 1785. 15: 16–31.

R. A. Howard. Volcanism and vegetation in the Lesser Antilles. *J. Arnold Arb.* 1962. 43: 279–311.

R. A. Howard. & K. Clausen. The Soufrière plant of St. Vincent. *J. Arnold Arb.* 1980. 61: 765–770.

15 R. A. Howard. Eighteenth Century West Indian Pharmaceuticals. *Harvard Papers in Botany.* 1994. 5: 69–91.

16 R. A. Howard & E. S. Howard. *Alexander Anderson's The St. Vincent Botanical Garden.* Harvard College, Cambridge, MA. & The Linnean Society, London, 1983.

17 Alexander Anderson. Letters. 1852 *Cottage Gardener.* 1853. 8: 59; 9: 417.

18 British Museum. [Add. MS 28610] *Catalogue of Described Plants in the Botanic Garden, Calcutta,* with list of West Indian and other plants sent to England by Lord Seaforth and others 04–06 addressed to Lambert. 1803.

19 D. Powell. 1973. *Kew Record Book.* 1793–1806. Royal Botanic Garden, Kew, 1973. p. 115–123.

20 R. A. Howard & E. S. Howard. *Alexander Anderson's The St. Vincent Botanical Garden.* Harvard College, Cambridge, MA. & The Linnean Society, London, 1983.

21 D. Mackay. Banks, Bligh and the Breadfruit. *N. Zealand J. History.* 1974. 8(1). 61–77.

22 D. Powell. The Botanic Garden, Liguanea. *Bull. Inst. Jamaica Sci.* 1973. ser. 15 (1). 1–94.

D. Powell. The Voyage of the Plant Nursery, H. M. S. Providence, 1791–1793. *Bull. Inst. Jam. Sci.* 1973. ser. 15 (2). 1–70.

23 Ibid.

24 D. Powell. *Kew Record Book.* 1793–1806. Royal Botanic Garden, Kew, 1973. p 115–123.

25 R. A. Howard & E. S. Howard. *Alexander Anderson's The St. Vincent Botanical Garden.* Harvard College, Cambridge, MA. & The Linnean Society, London, 1983.
R. A. Howard & E .S. Howard. *Alexander Anderson's Geography and History of St. Vincent, West Indies.* Harvard College, Cambridge, MA. and The Linnean Society, London, 1983.

26 Rev. L. Guilding. op. cit.
R. A. Howard & E. S. Howard. The Reverend Lansdown Guilding, 1797–1831. *Phytologia.* 1985. 58: 105–164.

27 Rev. L. Guilding op. cit.
R. A. Howard & E. S. Howard. The Reverend Lansdown Guilding, 1797–1831. *Phytologia.* 1985. 58: 105–164.

28 Ibid.

8 The British Empire and the Origins of Forest Conservation in the Eastern Caribbean 1700–1800

Richard Grove

Until recently it was a truism among environmental historians and historical geographers that ideas about conservation, and forest protection in particular, originated in the United States. Not surprisingly this notion has been put forward quite frequently by American scholars, above all by David Lowenthal, the biographer of George Perkins Marsh, an American diplomat often known as the 'father of American conservation'.

Gifford Pinchot and Theodore Roosevelt are often thought of in the same terms. Ironically, despite the precocious institution of the idea of the National Park at Yellowstone, Wyoming in 1872, the United States government was actually a latecomer to the practice of conservation. Even Franklin Benjamin Hough, the almost forgotten founder of the United States Forest Service, depended largely for his inspiration on long-established British and French models of forest protection. But these in turn had been based on precedents established (more than a hundred years before the American national parks), at St. Helena island, the French colony of the Isle de France (Mauritius) and above all, on the forest conservation practices established in the West Indies, especially on St. Vincent and Tobago. This chapter seeks to tell the story of that early phase of environmentalism insofar as it affected the Eastern Caribbean.

It is a story that depends on understanding the historical, biographical and philosophical background of a few enlightened and often contradictory but highly motivated individuals. The importance of the development of pioneer conservation in the Caribbean may seem merely antiquarian, or even inappropriate to societies that were, in the eighteenth century, ravaged by the awful oppressions of slavery. But in fact this account may be seen as very relevant and topical to contemporary worries about global climate change and biodiversity decline. This is because the often eccentric pioneers of Caribbean conservation were obsessed both with the effects of deforestation on rainfall levels, and on the possibility of species extinctions. These kinds of proto-modern concerns are especially poignant and relevant today, when the islands of the

Eastern Caribbean (and especially their forests) are facing unprecedented environmental threats from rapacious and foreign-funded tourist
developments. Tobago and St. Vincent, where modern forest conservation began, and which have some of the oldest forest reserves in the
world, are especially vulnerable in this respect. Indeed they are so old,
and so ecologically and aesthetically valuable, that they deserve special
protection by government from poor planning and the depredations of
multinationals such as the Hilton Hotel chain, which have, sadly,
already caused such serious environmental damage in Tobago. Knowing
the history of forest protection on these islands is an essential step to
safeguarding the natural and cultural heritage of the islands.

Some initial attempts had in fact been made to control deforestation on the Leeward Islands well north of St. Vincent and Tobago,
especially on St. Kitts and on Montserrat. On the latter it had quickly been realized that there was a connection between deforestation
and the clogging-up and flooding of the rivers and 'Guts' that ran
down into Plymouth, the capital of the Montserrat colony. Forest
reserves on the high volcanic peaks of the island were thus established as early as 1702.

It was the Peace of Paris in 1763 that provided the impetus for the
establishment of forest conservation in the southern islands of the Eastern
Caribbean. These islands, annexed by Britain under the treaty, were
heavily wooded, but thought suitable for plantation agriculture. At the
very same time on Mauritius, the French started a system of forest conservation based on the thinking of a few adherents of Physiocratic and
Enlightenment philosophies. In the Caribbean case two figures stand out
as having played a seminal role. These were Soame Jenyns, otherwise
better known as a Tory writer and political commentator, and Alexander
Anderson, a radical Scottish physician, botanist and first curator of the
St. Vincent Botanic Garden. They may seem an unlikely duo. Both men,
for very different reasons, shared a highly critical attitude towards the
whole project of imperialism. Anderson, for example, was especially
uneasy about the treatment meted out to indigenous peoples by the colonial ruler. In this context a climatic and medical environmentalism provided a powerful discourse. The circumstances of colonial rule allowed
Anderson, in particular, to make claims that closely connected an analysis of natural processes with a social critique, and to substantiate these
claims in legislation and in texts which he intended to publish. Overtly
religious reasons for presenting environmental claims and prescriptions
were not prominent in either Jenyns's or Anderson's involvement with
Caribbean forest policy. Nevertheless, we cannot neglect this element
altogether. Soame Jenyns wrote extensively on the theology of evil,
while Anderson was probably much affected by the dissenting science

of Joseph Priestley. Subliminally, at least, environmentalism may have been a vehicle for religious messages.

This chapter explores the development of this environmentalism on Tobago and St. Vincent. It also briefly surveys the cultural confrontation between a land-hungry colonial state and an indigenous culture. In this context the colonial state justified its actions through a codified and manipulated legal ideology which conferred annexation rights explicitly on those who cleared forest and 'cultivated' land. The new professional (and state) scientist, making environmentalist claims, found himself thrust into the uncomfortable and potentially subversive position of arbitrating (or simply articulating) an incompatible and entirely unequal set of competing interests. The climatic-environmentalist discourse thus emerges as a potential field of conflict between scientist and state. Ultimately, whoever controlled the terms of this powerful discourse, in science and in legislation, might also affect or even police the control of people and land. These issues remained largely unresolved in the Eastern Caribbean during the eighteenth century. Nevertheless, the environmentalist legislation of the period was explicit in its intentions and offers a useful starting point to consider the growth and dynamics of colonial conservationism.

As early as 1764 a system of forest reserves and environmental legislation was set up in the 'Ceded Islands' of St. Vincent and Tobago. In later years the forest-conservation model evolved on these islands influenced the course of colonial forest conservation in many other parts of the colonial world. The three relevant legal instruments were the Grenada Governorate Ordinance of March, 1764, the Barbados Land Ordinance of 1765 and the Kings Hill Forest Act passed by the St. Vincent Assembly in 1791. All three instruments were intended quite specifically to prevent local climatic change.

The local political impact of the introduction of forest reservation in the Caribbean was dramatic, as it provoked episodes of determined resistance by the Carib population of the islands. Moreover, the connections between colonial forest control and attempts to control indigenous colonised people became well established on the Caribbean islands. A new framework of consensus in international law tended to encourage, and was used to justify, this kind of oppression. In particular Emmerich de Vattel's *Law of Nations*, first translated into English in 1760, legitimated colonial annexation and the acquisition of 'sovereignty' by reference to the exercise of forest clearance and cultivation. Those who did not cultivate it, Vattel claimed, had no right to retain control of the land.[1]

Local resistance to the new environmental policies in the Caribbean is an important but neglected field; it certainly affected colonial environmental attitudes. However, it has to be somewhat marginal, in this chapter, to our main attempt to understand the developing colonial discourses on nature and environmental control in the region. What we may term the 'desiccationist' origins of early Caribbean forest policy were rooted both in the climatic and arboricultural concerns of the French *agronomes* and their British imitators and in the physiological researches of John Woodward, Stephen Hales and the Comte de Buffon.

British Caribbean forest-protection policies relied almost entirely for their initiation on the institutional role played by the London Society for the Encouragement of Arts, Manufactures and Commerce (generally known as the Society of Arts and later the Royal Society of Arts). Even then the transfer of the new climatic ideas was dependent on close membership connections between the Academie des Sciences, the Society of Arts and the Lords Commissioners for Trade and Plantations.[2] Such connections were, however, relatively likely to be made, as the Society of Arts had, since shortly after its inception, developed a strong interest in stimulating agricultural and arboricultural development in the colonies, especially those in North America and the Caribbean. After the Peace of Paris, the Society suddenly found itself able to exert a very direct influence over colonial land-use policy. Some examination of the antecedents of the Society is therefore appropriate here.

The Society of Arts had been founded in 1754. Its philosophical justifications lay in a line of direct descent from the Baconian notion of a 'Solomon's House', in the activities of the Hartlib circle and in imitating the Royal Society itself. It had other forerunners too. In 1683 a Philosophical Society had been founded in Dublin based on the Royal Society. This had foundered, and in its ashes had arisen the Dublin Society for Improving Husbandry, Manufactures and Other Useful Arts. The Dublin Society, along with a number of other groupings, may have provided William Shipley with the model for his Society of Arts, actually founded in March, 1754, at a meeting in Rawthmells Coffee-house, Henrietta Street, Covent Garden.[3]

Almost from its inception, the Society became associated with tree planting. The first suggestion that the Society should involve itself in such an activity originated in the ideas of Henry Baker, who on March 20, 1755, presented the Society with a quarto pamphlet published by him to 'promote the planting of timber trees in the common and waste grounds of the kingdom for the supply of the Navy, the employment and advantage of the poor as well as the ornamenting the nation'. This led directly to the inclusion of three 'premiums' for tree planting in the Society of Arts prize list for 1758.[4] 'A continuous supply of useful timber', the Society's journal recorded at the time, was 'absolutely necessary as well for the ornament and conveniency as for the security of these kingdoms'.[5] In the same year prizes of £40 were offered for planting and securing the 'greatest number of Logwood trees' in the colonies, not 'less than 500 in any one plantation before the third week in December 1760'.[6] Tree planting and colonial enterprises were therefore combined in the Society's activities at an early date in its history. The Society of Arts took a particular interest in the West Indies, possibly through the influence of Sir Joshua Steele, one of the early members of the Society and later the founder and president of the Barbados Society of Arts, one of the first learned societies to be founded in a British colony.[7]

The Society was especially keen to promote the development of plant transfers between the Pacific, the East Indies and the West Indies. As on Mauritius, this commercial interest encouraged an official concern with environmental matters. In 1760 prizes were offered specifically for the successful introduction of cinnamon trees into the West Indies. In the same year, in one of its premium lists the Society suggested that land should be reserved in the colonies for gardens or nurseries for 'experiments in raising such rare and useful plants as are not the spontaneous growth of the kingdom or of the said colonies'. It added that if the colonial legislatures or 'other incorporate bodies would help establish such gardens', the Society would provide proper premiums for plants raised in them. The first of these gardens was started in 1765 at Kingstown, St. Vincent, by General Robert Melville, the new governor of the Ceded Islands, or 'Southern Caribbees'.[8] As a member of the Society of Arts, Melville appears to have decided to found the garden as a result of the Society's advertisement of 1760.[9] Dr. George Young, an army surgeon on St. Vincent, was appointed curator of the botanical garden. He acted as such until 1774, in which year he sent a full report on the new garden to the Society in London. As the first botanical garden in the Americas, the St. Vincent establishment was to prove significant in the subsequent history of early environmentalism and in providing the institutional basis for the diffusion of desiccationist ideas about deforestation and changes in rainfall.

In 1763 the Society acquired a much more direct political influence over developments in the West Indies as a result of the territorial concessions made by the French at the Peace of Paris at the end of the Seven Years' War. The cession of St. Vincent, Dominica, Grenada and Tobago to Britain as the constituent territories of the 'Grenada Governorate' meant that a whole series of decisions were required to determine land allocation and ownership in the new colonies.[10]

Considerable capital was available at this date for investment in sugar cultivation, and the drive to develop sugar plantations became the main plank of official strategy in the area. Rapid deforestation was an inevitable consequence of this policy, as it had already been in other parts of the Caribbean.[11] Robert Melville was appointed first governor of the Grenada Governorate under a proclamation of August 3, 1763, and his scientific interests began immediately to play their part in events, not least through his interest in climatic theory. Climate and health on Tobago were matters of particular concern to Melville, and he soon told the Lords Commissioners for Trade that epidemics 'were an evil much to be dreaded and carefully to be provided against in the beginning of a West India settlement'.[12] Initial orders by Whitehall for the new civil authorities to take control of the island were made by Lord Egremont on August 13, 1763.[13] It was at this stage that the first formal plans were drawn up for the occupation of the Ceded Islands. Tobago, the first object of these plans, was the only one of these islands that did not have a long-standing British military presence. It was also at this stage that some of the more innovative features of the land-settlement scheme became evident.[14] The plans presented for Tobago are of considerable interest, especially with regard to the proposals for forest reservation. The area of the island was estimated at 100,000 acres. It was proposed to divide Tobago into parishes of 6,000 to 10,000 acres, with 1,000 acres set aside for an island capital. A large part of the island was deliberately to be set aside as forest reserve. Each parish, it was originally proposed, should retain a certain portion of land as uncut forest.

The settlement proposals of the Lords Commissioners for Trade were submitted to the Lords of the Committee for Plantation Affairs on November 18, 1763. In early 1764 they were laid before the Lords of Treasury and the King in Council, Lord Hillsborough representing the Lords Commissioners for Trade on the council. The proposals were issued as a proclamation on March 1, 1764. The proclamation (no. 20 of 1764) stipulated specifically that:

> ...such a number of acres as the Commissioners should from the best of their judgement project should be reserved in woodlands to His Majesty's His Heirs and Successors in one or more different parishes in each part of each island, respectively in order to preserve the seasons so essential to the fertility of the islands and to answer all public services as may require the use and expense of timber.[15]

This order was further elaborated and its semantics and practical implications slightly altered in an ordinance issued 'by the Kings authority' on Barbados on January 19, 1765. This ordinance stated that woodlands should be preserved 'as shall seem necessary for the constitution and repair of fortifications and public buildings and *to prevent that drought which in these climates is the usual consequence of a total removal of the woods'.*[16]

Significantly, the same proclamation laid down that 'the native Caribbees of St. Vincent are to remain undisturbed in the possession of their cottages and goods'.[17] In the event, nearly a year passed before the proclamation, first issued in London in March, 1764, was actually translated into policy on the ground, and the Barbados ordinance was the first effective and local step in this direction. William Young, appointed chief settlement commissioner of the Ceded Islands, soon took the process of executing the ordinance further, beginning with the survey and settlement of Tobago. However, he appears to have treated the intentions of the 1764 proclamation quite liberally, and his instructions to the surveyors on the ground reflected this. 'Settlement reservations of woodlands,' Young announced, 'should be made in the most hilly parts of each parish for the construction and repair of mills, farms and public buildings and for the preservation of the seasons. Likewise,' he added, 'such reservations [shall be made] in proper places along the coast as shall seem expedient for land and shipping and other public purposes ... attention shall be paid to the nature and quality of the soil.'[18] The priority accorded to sugar production and the wish not to use cultivable lowland for forest reserve were clearly factors of importance when Young came to make the local decisions. By shifting the locations of the reserves to the 'hilly areas' he started a process of altering the original plans of the Commissioners for Trade, which ended with the plans being dropped altogether on some islands. The extent of local alterations was strongly affected by the fact that, unlike the Commissioners for Trade, local colonists often took a hostile view of the properties and influences of primeval woodland. In particular the native tropical forest cover was thought by many to promote disease and insanitary winds. Young himself, charged with reserving the forests, was actually a proponent of the view that they should be done away with. 'The rains,' he said, 'are less frequent and the sea air pure and salutary by reason of its not yet being infected in its passage over hot and reeking woods...the heat and moisture of the woods are likely to be the chief obstructions to the [speedy settlement of the colony].'[19]

Such sentiments indicate the extent to which the notion of forest protection 'for the preservation of the seasons' was as yet a relatively controversial concept. Young seems to have accepted the view that the frequency of rains was related to the extent of the forest cover of an island. While having, of course, to follow instructions, he clung to the view that forests and their associated humidity were undesirable. Even so, by this date it was well accepted that high humidity and low wind speed were essential for the successful cultivation of sugar cane. It was this factor which had probably helped to encourage the inclusion of desiccation concepts in the settlement plans espoused by the Commissioners for Trade. However, the story behind the acceptance of desiccationist notions in the Caribbean colonial situation was a good deal more complex than this. In order to understand the background of the new policy, it is necessary to look more closely at the origins and social context of the development of desiccationism in England and in particular at the intellectual influences affecting the Lords Commissioners for Trade.

Soame Jenyns, tree planting and desiccationism

A survey of the membership of the Lords Commissioners for Trade in 1763 helps to give a number of clues to its highly unusual excursions into the implications of contemporary climatic theories. At the time that the Commissioners' representations to the King were made in November, 1763, the members were Lord Hillsborough (an Irish peer who was effectively secretary of state for the colonies), Soame Jenyns, Edmund Bacon, John Yorke (a member of the Hardwicke family) and one Bamber Gascoyne.[20] Among the Commissioners, Soame Jenyns, and Edmund Bacon were also members of the Society of Arts. Of these two, Soame Jenyns appears to have been the key figure responsible for arousing the interest of the Commissioners in the climatic consequences of deforestation and for encouraging his colleagues to incorporate the implications of the new climatic theories into their colonial land settlement and forest policy.[21] The early development of desiccationism was bound up with the close relations between French and British science and in particular with the arboricultural writings of Duhamel du Monceau. These had in turn drawn heavily on the plant physiological insights of Stephen Hales, a fellow of Corpus Christi College, Cambridge, and probably the most distinguished Newtonian scientist in early-eighteenth-century Britain.[22] Hales had been a founder member of the Society of Arts. However, he had died in 1761 and did not himself play a direct part in promoting the practical implications of contemporary thinking about the relationship between trees and climate. The critical question to be established, therefore, is how Soame Jenyns, a friend of Stephen Hales', was persuaded to adopt the treeplanting enthusiasms of the Society and take on current desiccation ideas and lobby to institutionalize them in colonial policy.

Jenyns' interest in tree planting, by no means unusual by the 1760s, would have been reinforced by his close acquaintance with Lord Hardwicke and the Yorke family.[23] Jenyns frequently visited the Hardwicke seat at Wimpole Hall in Cambridgeshire, only 20 miles from his house at Bottisham Hall, near Cambridge, and would have been impressed by the magnificent gardens and recently planted avenues of limes and elms. Indeed, it was not long before similar lines of trees, planted by Jenyns himself, graced the grounds of Bottisham Hall. In 1755 the Hardwicke connection had furnished the Cambridgeshire landowner with a seat among the Lords Commissioners for Trade. In 1761 this social elevation was supplemented by an election to the Society of Arts. Jenyns was also by now the Member of Parliament for Cambridge.[24]

By joining the Society of Arts, Jenyns would soon have come into contact with the physiocratic enthusiasts in the Society and encountered their treeplanting, agronomic, and botanical (including plant transfer) interests. He would also have become open to lobbying by those members of the Society who had financial or land stakes in the colonies, and especially in the West Indies. Chief amongst the latter was Joshua Steele, a liberal West Indies sugar planter and later founder of the Barbados Society of Arts.[25] Jenyns may have been convinced on economic grounds that the forests of the Ceded Islands should be protected in order to enhance potential sugarcane yields. But the agenda of the Society was more complex and long-term. In 1760 the Society had made plain its commitment to the cause of interoceanic plant transfers with its support for colonial botanical gardens and especially the one on St. Vincent. Projects for plant transfer and the cultivation of new crops were, of course, closely tied up with the growing intellectual interest in climate and its effects on culture, vegetation and the development of man. Climate change, it may be argued, represented a major potential threat to colonial economic projects. Moreover, such thinkers as Buffon often raised fears that climate change could bring about degeneration in crops and man. Human interventions might help to counter this threat, it was thought. By transferring crops from one part of the world to another, or preventing rainfall change through forest reservation, man could hope to reassert control over the chain of natural processes and restore his supremacy. For Jenyns, schooled in ideas about the 'Great Chain of Being', the project of reconstructing and 'improving' the colonial landscape in the way he had already done on his estate near Cambridge was attractive and transferable. With the territorial cessions of the Peace of Paris, the West Indies colonies could, it seemed, be improved and controlled in the same way. For a man of Jenyns' upbringing, the idea of saving and controlling land was a familiar one. His father, Sir Roger Jenyns, had made a fortune in fen drainage and had known Cornelius Vermuyden.[26] Moreover, Soame Jenyns himself, alongside his more academic works, had written extensively on the organization of fen drainage.[27]

Why, then, did deforestation become such an apparently urgent political issue in the West Indies during the eighteenth century? The connections between the powerful sugar lobby and the state of the Barbados economy and landscape provide much of the answer and part of the explanation for nascent conservationism in the colonial West Indies, quite apart from the rise to prominence of climatic theories. Quite simply, Barbados was experiencing a severe ecological and resource crisis by the time of the Peace of Paris. As early as 1665 the island had been almost totally deforested.[28] Most of the forest clearance had taken place very rapidly, between 1625 and 1660, as sugar cultivation expanded over the island. A report of 1667 emphasizes the almost complete loss of woodland on the island. In Barbados, it was said, 'all the trees are destroyed, so that wanting wood to boyle their sugar, they are forced to send for wood to England'. Significantly enough, the same report went on to describe the resources of Tobago as wild and untouched in comparison to Barbados.[29] There was some truth in this. Both Tobago and St. Vincent remained fully forested and relatively undisturbed by Europeans until 1764–5.[30] With Barbados deforested, Tobago, in the words of John Poyntz, was still 'covered in a prodigious growth of her massy and prodigious timber trees'.[31] Poyntz's 1683 description of Tobago as a naturalistic island idyll soon attracted the attention of Daniel Defoe, who used the careful descriptions of the uncolonized 'desert island' as the basis for the descriptive setting of *Robinson Crusoe*, first published in 1719. As on Mauritius, where the cultural shadow of the 'robinsonnades' had exercised a great impact on the romanticisation of the island environment, a potential link emerged between a new typology of environmental risk and colonial perceptions of the West Indies in terms of literary constructions of tropical nature and the exotic 'other'. However, the perceptions of the Barbados colonists were at first largely utilitarian.

Since the early seventeenth century, Tobago had been used as a reliable source of supply for hardwood timbers. The Barbados timber cutters visited Tobago principally for cedar (*Cedrus*), lype, locust (*Hymenaea courharil*), mastic (*Mastichum*) and other indigenous woods. A contemporary observer noted that as long as the cutters did not stay too long on the island the Cacciques (Caribs) 'gave them freedom of the axe'.[32] The contrast with Barbados and Tobago would have become more and more obvious, particularly after 1665, when only one woodland was left on the former (at Turner's Hall).[33] Furthermore, over the ensuing century as a result of the stripping of woodland, soil erosion also became a steadily more serious problem on Barbados.[34] These factors, then, must have influenced the approach taken by the Commissioners for Trade to the planning of land use on the Ceded

Islands and on Tobago in particular. The theories diffused through from the Society of Arts would have been an additional and possibly decisive factor. The lessons of Barbados were not going to be ignored, or so it seemed.

Some mention has already been made of Soame Jenyns' connections with the Society of Arts and its effectively environmentalist agenda. But what of Soame Jenyns as an intellectual and a theological writer? Martin J. Rudwick and Stephen Jay Gould have both copiously demonstrated the critical part played by shifting religious convictions in shaping the progress of debates about geology and chronology during the late eighteenth and the early nineteenth century.[35] Similarly, there is little doubt that religious temperament and development continued to exert an influence over the evolution of environmental concerns in the late eighteenth century. This is not surprising, as the growing awareness of 'deep time' was, in fact, closely linked to the development of anxieties about species and climate change. Soame Jenyns was no exception to this pattern. His dual interest in natural theology and the 'Great Chain of Being' are much evidenced in his prolific writings, for which he was well regarded by some of his contemporaries and much denigrated by others. The latter included Samuel Johnson, a particularly savage critic of Jenyns' theological masterpiece, *The Nature and the Origins of Evil*.[36] There is no doubt, too, that Jenyns was acutely conscious of contemporary debates on the connections between climate and culture. While he did not actually visit the West Indies or any other part of the tropics, he was still quite content to pass judgement on the risks involved in living in them. 'If the Southern Climes,' he wrote, 'are gilded with a brighter sunshine...provided with more frequent gales and decorated with a greater profusion of plants and flowers, they are at the same time perpetually exposed to pestilential threats, infested with noxious animals, torn by hurricanes and rocked by earthquakes unknown to the rougher regions of the north.'[37] This construction of the tropical and colonial landscape as an essentially hazardous environment would have been affected by a whole variety of literary and non-literary impressions. Moreover, only a very few years had passed since the devastating Lisbon earthquake of 1755 had registered its dramatic impact on the European psyche.[38] Clearly, the notion of a chaotic and hazardous tropic may have encouraged Jenyns to favour measures which aimed to control and artificially manipulate an unstable climate. However, there is little evidence that he actually favoured the colonization process at all. On the contrary, his writings indicate that he regarded the accumulation of colonies as having contributed dynamically to the severe national debt that had accumulated in Britain by the 1760s. This debt, he believed, amounted to a subtle form of revenge by the colonized territories. 'All these infallible marks of riches,' Jenyns wrote, 'have committed and progressively increased with our debt and are therefore undoubtedly derived from it. No small part indeed of them has flowed in from the West and East Indies but these ought also to be placed to the same account because, without the aid of this fictitious wealth, we could never have so far extended our commerce and our conquests.' The revenge of the colonies, he thought, would take the form of the growth of corruption in the mother country.[39]

The introduction of forest reservation in this political context represented a reaction against the profligacy that had impoverished the Barbados soils and robbed the island of essential timber. By contrast, the control exercised by the Commissioners for Trade over the development of the Ceded Islands seems to represent a remarkably cautious policy. Indeed, the careful survey and subdivision of the island lands into plantation plots and forest reservations was highly reminiscent of the laying out of the East Anglian fenlands after drainage, an activity in which Jenyns and his ancestors had been intimately involved and from which they had made their fortunes. While notions of control and exclusion (of indigenous peoples) were never far from the surface, the highly planned nature of the Grenada Governorate land settlement seems also to have represented a highly innovative and interventionist response to past profligacy in the use of resources.

The innovative tree-planting policies of the Society of Arts require some explanation, as they were clearly instrumental in the new environmental planning developed for the Ceded Islands. It is possible to argue, as Simon Schama does, that the new enthusiasm for tree planting that had developed in Europe during the late sixteenth and the early seventeenth century was principally related to a cult of freedom or of liberty, co-opted, in the English case, by a royalist or statist commitment to stimulating a ready timber supply for a 'liberating' Royal Navy.[40] However, in transferring such arguments for controlled cultivation of trees to the colonial context, it is necessary to avoid explanations that are too facile or naive. In particular, one should not underestimate the novel and growing significance of trees as essential explanatory components in the new climatic theories. Furthermore, far from any associations with liberty, the Commissioners for Trade were planning for a slave-dependent plantation economy which, as parliamentary investigations of the 1790s showed, was to be almost unprecedented in its espousal of deliberate and cruel punishment as a way of increasing the productivity of the sugar estates. A distinction also needs to be drawn between an atavistic interest in preserving the 'natural' or the ancient and primeval and a more manipulative and power-conscious interest in constructing a new landscape by planting trees or, conceivably, marking out reservations. Mindful of the continuing association of forests with lawlessness, tree connoisseurs and landowners were usually careful in England to distinguish areas which were effectively appropriated and managed from those which were not.[41]

As noted, Soame Jenyns himself was, like many Cambridgeshire landowners of the 1760s (especially his friend Lord Hardwicke at Wimpole Hall), an enthusiastic tree planter. He left a series of long avenues of limes at Bottisham Hall that could still be seen more than two hundred years later. However, contemporary British colonial tree planting and forest reservation seems to have concealed a variety of other agendas, some climatic, others clearly not. In New England, colonial forest reservation had been designed, from its beginnings in 1691, largely for the purpose of securing sustainable supplies of white-pine masts and other timber for the navy. As a result, the reservation laws were actively resisted and treated by the European colonists with the contempt which they showed for other arms of an economically oppressive colonial government. During the early nineteenth century, colonial forest reservation, especially in South Africa, India and Java became part of a means of responding to anxieties about climate and the timber supply.[42] However, it also became useful in controlling unruly peoples and 'tribes', claiming territory and organizing economic space. As a result, early colonial forest reservation frequently became associated with forced resettlement. It might also involve an effective biological reconstruction of the forest environment to serve the economic interests of the state. Indigenous food or material needs were rarely a priority in this process of gaining control of the biological landscape so that impoverishment and famine often followed colonial forest reservation.

It seems very likely that this kind of historical development in the relations between colonial forest control and indigenous tropical forest-dwelling peoples found an early expression in the Eastern Caribbean after 1763. This was at a time when similar patterns of control and resistance were appearing in the German states and in colonial Java. However, the parallels should not be exaggerated. The intentions of Jenyns and his colleagues were expressed against the background of what was perceived to be an extremely hazardous tropical environment. By attempting to control atmospheric processes through rational means, a land-use strategy was adopted that was highly innovative and marked a complete break from what had gone before in the Caribbean. (Previously perhaps only the Venetians had attempted the kind of comprehensive control over the landscape that was sought by the Commissioners for Trade in the Grenada Governorate.) And there was a further item of climatic doctrine on the agenda. This was the idea that by managing to control rainfall the processes of degeneration which

Buffon had so feared might be controlled. The Commissioners for Trade were familiar with land degeneration in a very specific form. In 1750 Hughes had vividly described the chaos of landslips, soil erosion, and hurricanes that periodically afflicted Barbados.[43] It was this kind of disorder which the Commissioners sought to control. But, as we shall see, successive governments in the Grenada Governorate (later the Windward Islands) were faced with vigorous and long-lived indigenous opposition to their land-use policies, particularly on St. Vincent.

Desiccation ideas and the scientific and agronomic programmes of the French physiocrats were major components of environmentalism on Mauritius. Similarly, Soame Jenyns and his colleagues in the Society of Arts and among the Commissioners for Trade certainly shared in promoting the elevated status of science and specialized or professionalised knowledge that was advocated by the physiocrats. They were also institutionally linked to the Newtonian thinking of Hales, Buffon and Duhamel Monceau and, indeed, gave such thinking official credibility. However, the Commissioners for Trade do not seem, in general, to have shared in the Romantic or Utopian Edenism that had proved so important on Mauritius at the same period. This was despite the fact that seventeenth-century descriptions of Tobago had been an important inspiration to Defoe in writing *Robinson Crusoe*. However, Tobago certainly provided the raw material for a variety of commercial propaganda on plantation settlement, particularly that written by John Fowler in 1774.[44] In general, the characteristic British perception of the West Indies environment seems to have been somewhat less associated with romantic meanings than was the case in the contemporary French context. However, the critical significance of the botanical garden in acting as a stimulus to a whole set of metaphorical as well as botanical agendas was certainly duplicated after 1765 in the Ceded Islands, specifically in the garden at Kingstown on St. Vincent. Furthermore, from the first foundation of the St. Vincent garden in 1765, close practical links were maintained between it and the garden at Pamplemousses on Mauritius, almost to the point, arguably, where they represented elements of a single institutional construct or network rather than discrete and independent intellectual entities.

In some respects, however, it has to be said that for adherents of that version of a tropical Eden that included the notion of a noble savage, Tobago, St. Vincent and some of their neighbours (especially Dominica) were a field far fuller of indigenous human meaning than the previously uninhabited Mascarene Islands of the Indian Ocean. This was because, at the time of the Peace of Paris, they still sheltered a considerable population of indigenous Carib aboriginal peoples, some sections of which had long since intermixed with the descendants of escaped slaves. In this social setting, the British project of surveying and reserving town, plantation, and forest lands quickly acquired a meaning distinctly different from that on Mauritius. This meant that the language of desiccationism and forest reservation soon became identified, especially on St. Vincent, with an exercise in political domination, population exclusion and relocation, and eventually with open conflict among British colonists, Caribs and insurgent French revolutionaries. Particularly in the case of the latter, the whole discourse of the 'Liberty tree' (insofar as it relates to the emergent eighteenth-century European interest in forest protection) took on an unexpected dimension. This new identification meant, too, that the motivations behind forest reservation on what had been conceived of as island Edens became increasingly ambiguous and confused. The construct of the forest as a desirable component of a programme for climate control and stability starkly confronted a more confused (and more antique and atavistic) image of the forest as the characteristic dwelling place of fearsome rebels and indigenous bandits. In the course of this developing confrontation as it emerged in the thirty years after 1763, the notion of the noble savage died a violent metaphorical death in the Caribbean at the same time as the indigenous social reality of the 'black Caribs' emerged as constituting one of the most effective groups of organized military (and non-military) resisters ever encountered during British colonial rule.[45] The encounter was made the more complex in that the terms of the London proclamation of March, 1764 for the settlement of the Ceded Islands envisaged the creation of a whole society of plantation owners, town dwellers, slaves, and even 'poor white' settlers for whom smallholdings were to be provided in a kind of deliberately transplanted class dispensation. The large amounts of land left over from this project of landscape and social construction were to be declared forest reserve. No provision was made in this projection for land for the indigenous Caribs. In fact, the methodology adopted to plan the land closely resembled the strategy adopted on Mauritius during the 1760s, where there was no indigenous population. The task of map making and surveying acquired a particularly oppressive meaning in such a situation. Cartographically, what was left out of the survey became just as important as what was included in the map. On Tobago the Caribs were left out of the map-making process altogether and within twenty years had disappeared as a separate population. This deliberate and highly symbolic cartographic omission serves to indicate the need to appreciate the historic power of the act of map-making in shaping the nature of the discourse on colonial conservation and desiccationism in the Caribbean.[46]

The process of taking control of the government of Tobago and the process of surveying the island and designating forest reserve were almost synonymous. Ottley tells us that Alexander Brown, the first British governor, 'walked through the forest all the way to the new capital, Georgetown' (later moved to a new site and called Scarborough) to 'take up residence in the gubernatorial hut at Fort Granby'.[47] Cultivation spread quickly as new colonists, mainly from Barbados, arrived. In 1764 four thousand acres were planted out with sugar cane, and by 1767, a further 25,000 acres. A decade later the colony exported 24,000 cwt of sugar, 100,000 gallons of rum, 150,000 lb. of cotton, and 5,000 lb. of indigo.

The forest reserves established by proclamation in 1764 became a permanent feature of the landscape and were little altered during the next two centuries. Even during subsequent phases of French occupation, the forest-protection legislation was recognized, and regulations continued to be enforced.[48]

In 1777 the Commissioners for Trade found it necessary to demand the repeal of a law passed by the Tobago Assembly in April, 1776. This law had effectively attempted to curtail the power of the Crown to alienate land for forest reserve. Its underlying motivation, it seems, had consisted in settler resentment of the original land-use dispensation and a determination to do away with the forest reserves.[49] By this stage some Tobago colonists had clearly felt that the area gazetted for forest reserve was far too extensive and trespassed too far on opportunities for profit at a time when the sugar market was buoyant. Moreover, deforestation on other islands, as well as development on Tobago itself, sharply encouraged efforts to export the valuable timbers of the highland area, especially its fustic (*Chlorophora*), sirmac and gumwood (*Nyssa*). Undoubtedly the forty square miles of the main forest reserve contained an enormous quantity of valuable timber.[50] Despite settler opinion, however (and the interruptions of the periods of French occupation), the boundaries of the original Tobago forest reserves were maintained with few changes.

Resisting survey and fighting from the forest: the black Caribs of St. Vincent and the struggle to define the boundaries of power

The remarkably stable institutional and ecological history of the 'rain reserves' of Tobago contrasts markedly with the history of those envisaged under the same 1764 proclamation on St. Vincent, Grenada and Dominica. The cartographic team superintended by James Simpson of Barbados had found its task to be relatively easy on Tobago. Its experiences on the other islands of the Governorate were far more uncomfortable, particularly on St. Vincent. Here the Caribs contrived to enforce their own alterations to the settlement and survey scheme. They thereby permanently altered and distorted the programme of colonial land allocation, forcing compromises both in the scheme and the meaning of the survey and in the connotations attached by the colonists to different parts of the island environment. In other words, indigenous meanings in the environment survived and even changed the colonial set of meanings, at least for some years. The process of surveying and dividing Tobago up into lots had formalized the allocation of land use and exercised a remarkable influence over later patterns of land use. Above all, no notion of common land was entertained at all, even the forest reserves being considered Crown land. The Tobago Caribs, failing to resist the new designations, were forced to become a labour pool or were ignored and finally disappeared, the victims of random killings, food shortages and imported diseases.

The survey of St. Vincent, by contrast, was much longer in the making. This was principally because the indigenous black Carib population of the island put up a spirited and successful resistance to the process of survey and land allocation as a continuance of a pre-existing tradition of resistance to attempted colonial depredations. As a result, the colonial construction of the landscape, so formally adhered to on Tobago, was temporarily altered and adapted on St. Vincent to suit Carib requirements. Ultimately, Carib resistance on St. Vincent and latent European settler resistance to the provisions of the 1764 proclamation meant that it became a dead letter, at least until the Carib rebellion of 1791.

It is worth looking at part of the background to this pattern of resistance. By the terms of the Treaty of Aix-la-Chapelle in 1748, St. Vincent had been declared a neutral island by the French and English. In fact, the treaty recognized the two highly successful efforts made by the Caribs to repel French and English attempts to invade and settle the island, in 1719 and 1723 respectively. The approach taken by the English to colonization in 1763 was, therefore, rather more hesitant than it had been on traditionally docile Tobago. We find, for example, that the likelihood that the Caribs would vigorously oppose settlement was recognized explicitly by William Young in a pamphlet published in 1764, shortly after he had been appointed chief settlement commissioner.[51] 'When the Black Caribs of St. Vincent,' Young wrote, 'are daily appraised of the humanity and generosity of our gracious sovereign, and *assured of the enjoyment of their lands, freedom, favour and protection,* they be gained over to our cause and even rendered useful.'[52] This degree of caution was soon extended to the plans for surveying the island. Instructions of December 16, 1764 stated that 'no survey should be made of lands occupied or claimed by the Caribs until further instructions are sent out'. By February, 1764, the Caribs had in fact already appointed a missionary, the Abbé Valledares, as their public agent to negotiate with the British invader. The settlement commissioner, Young reports, 'opened an immediate correspondence with Valledares and succeeded in engaging him to cooperate with the views of the British government in settlement of the district inhabited by the Caribs'.[53] This negotiation process ran into an immediate problem, as the Caribs did not accept the concepts of private property implicit in the settlement proposals planned by the British. The areas of Carib settlement, it was reported at the time, were 'occupied mostly in common as by an erratic nation of savage warriors and hunters'. What little cultivation there was, Young went on, 'appeared merely in small disturbed spots of provision ground near to their cabins…worked entirely by women; for the rest of the Caribs drew their sustenance by their guns or from the seas'.[54] Young complained that the Caribs had as little idea of their 'obligation to cultivate the earth' as they had of their 'having no right to appropriate more than they could cultivate'. Furthermore, Young ambivalently observed, they understood 'the abstract reasonings of Wolfus and Vattel no more than they appreciated the grant of St. Vincent to Lords Carlisle and Willoughby by Kings Charles 1st and 2nd'.[55] This was an important statement historically, as it gave a clear indication of the extent to which a highly exclusionist political ideology of land use had become an accepted part of the justification for the expropriation and colonization of native lands. As Young implied, only cultures practising settled agriculture could be considered legally entitled to claim sovereign rights over land. Here, then, it may be possible to locate at least some of the antecedents of the very long-running critique of shifting cultivation and pastoral nomadism.[56]

In fact the Caribs' appreciation of the European legal standpoint on St. Vincent was a great deal more sophisticated than Young appeared to realize. What was more, the black Caribs were quite prepared to legitimate their claims in European terms by reference to the invited intervention of the governor of Martinique in an old land dispute that had surfaced in 1700 between the black (mixed-race) Caribs and the red (pure-blooded) Caribs. A geographic line, the 'Base de l'isle', had been drawn to separate the populations. As Young records, this intervention grew shortly into a sacred prescription in 'the short memories of a savage people and perhaps one not to be cancelled but with the strong arm of conquest and control'.[57] The social memory of this legitimation was, of course, long rather than 'short', as Young mistakenly thought.

All attempts to involve the Caribs in the survey, redistribution and sale of their own long-occupied lands during 1764 and 1765 failed, despite their being offered the carrot of 'full rights as British subjects'. In 'this situation of affairs', Young disingenuously tells us, 'the conduct of the Commissioners was embarrassed and undecided, but in all cases just and even favourable to the Caribs'.[58] The operative word here was 'embarrassed'. The Caribs had provoked a crisis of sovereignty and control and persisted openly in disclaiming allegiance to the British Crown. The Crown, the settlement commissioners thought, 'could not with either honour or advantage, hold a divided sovereignty in an island only twenty-one miles in length'.[59] A major part of this sovereignty dispute concerned the forests of the island and their rightful ownership. The issue emerged prominently in an agonized letter sent by the settlement commissioners to the Lords Commissioners of the Treasury in Whitehall on August 10, 1765. In it the commissioners (William Young [the elder], Robert Stuart and Robert Gwynne) stated that, '...the Caribs live in huts scattered in an *irregular manner* at a great distance from each other, without any established subordination, claiming large tracts of woodland intervening of which they make no use; and are besides possessed of other lands in the cleared part of the country, which interfere much with the large area of plantations for sale'.[60]

To settle this 'problem', the commissioners suggested, alternative land should be offered to the Caribs on the nearby island of Bequia. However, Bequia, it was soon realized, was deficient in water and would not actually support the Caribs at all. But the idea of compulsory resettlement had now been firmly sown in the mind of officialdom, and the Bequia scheme accurately prefigured the forced resettlement of the Caribs which was to take place to that island, in much harsher circumstances, in the 1790s. Moreover, the Bequia scheme effectively exposed the underlying intentions of the commissioners in their attempts to survey and allocate Carib land. Theirs was, of course, an exclusionist programme of which the Carib leadership had, from the outset, been acutely and sensitively aware. Indeed, the 1764 land proclamation, applying to the whole Grenada Governorate, made no provision whatsoever for Carib land interests and their mode of forest and land use. The relatively docile Carib response to the proclamation on Tobago, in a territory where the indigenous population was anyway very low, seems to have encouraged the commissioners to expect a similar response among the very different and much larger population on St. Vincent. As it turned out, the St. Vincent Caribs were, in the medium term, able to find ways of intimidating and manipulating the settlement commissioners so as to adapt the survey project to their own ends. In the course of doing so, they effectively disrupted the forest-reservation schemes so beloved of the Commissioners for Trade, although less beloved of large elements of the settler population.

In doing so, the Caribs managed also to further exacerbate the highly ambiguous situation in which the colonizing power found itself vis-à-vis people who were both 'Indian' and 'Negro' in their ancestry. While Indians had frequently found themselves eligible for easier treatment as noble savages, the black African affinities of the black Caribs invited cultural comparisons with the groups then being imported to other West Indian islands as plantation slaves at a time when the brutality meted out to slaves in the British Windward Islands was almost unparalled in severity. This was further complicated by the fact that the British soon developed a very healthy respect for the experience, organization and guerilla fighting skills of the black Caribs. In February, 1768, after a period of three years in which the Caribs successfully held up the survey and land-allocation programme, new proposals were announced that finally led to a break in the uneasy truce between Caribs and colonists. The apparently contradictory provisions of the new proposals serve to indicate the important change of mood that had taken place in the ranks of the now seriously frustrated colonial power. The new settlement provisions included two significant ideas: (1) That no step shall be taken towards the removal of any Charaib [Carib], till the whole arrangement and design should have been notified and explained to the satisfaction of their chiefs; and that they be made to comprehend the conditions in which settlement was proposed and that the plan be carried into effect with the gentlest hand and in the mildest manner; and (2) Under these terms the spots of cleared land which they now occupy should be sold, and made part of plantation allotments, with the woodlands which surround them; and on the final removal of the Charaibs shall make part of such plantations.[61]

It is quite clear that at this stage the Carib leadership, and above all Chief Chatoyer, realized that, despite the interceding efforts of the Abbé Valledares, the period of a phoney land war had come to an end.[62] The Caribs thus determined to prevent any further road-building or surveying taking place on the island. Matters then came quickly to a head, and from December, 1768, the surveying teams under James Simpson (who had surveyed Tobago without any resistance) were continually harassed and threatened by armed Caribs. On April 29, 1768 Levi Porter, an assistant surveyor, reported that the Caribs had burnt his house and 'stolen my maps and equipment'. They would 'not have the Great Road go any further', Porter told Simpson in his letter. The Caribs did not stop at this symbolic act. After burning Porter's house, three hundred well-armed Carib warriors then proceeded to demolish the new military barracks on the Great Road.[63] On May 1, forty men of the 32nd Infantry Regiment found themselves confronting the same three hundred Carib warriors. The commander, Captain Wilkin, decided to retreat and avoid any decisive engagement, which, in the confines of the forest, he was by no means sure of winning. Instead Wilkin decided to retreat south to Kingstown to consult the governor and council about the strategic situation.[64] On this occasion, on May 1, John Byres, the government cartographer, was forced to hide his new half-made survey maps in a field.[65] However, the Caribs soon found and burnt the hidden maps, and Byres too retreated to the safety of Kingstown. A peace was then declared by the British on the basis that no further attempts would be made 'to interfere in the country or build further roads'.[66]

The situation was then reported by the settlement commissioners to the Commissioners for Trade. The report, dated July, 1769, made the very specific point that the Caribs were able to use the extensive forest cover of the island in a very effective military sense. The Caribs, the commissioners said, would continue to 'be very dangerous and may at some time prove fatal to the [white] inhabitants of the country as their situation, surrounded by wood, makes any access to them impracticable'.[67] The St. Vincent planters themselves, however, now revealed that they disagreed with the commissioners' bellicose stand. In a letter written by a group of settlers directly to Lord Hillsborough in early 1770 it was made clear to Whitehall that the settlers believed that any detachment of soldiers sent to reinforce the island should be used to protect settlers rather than to try to wipe out the Caribs. As the colonists pointed out, the Caribs now had the open backing of the governor of Martinique so that any aggressive action against them might prove counterproductive and seriously affect the security of white settlers. In this connection the settlers again made the point that 'a very small proportion of the island...has yet been cleared of wood so that all efforts should be made to clear the forest'.[68] As the settlers' letter was addressed directly to the Earl of Hillsborough and wholly conflicted with the policy of the Commissioners for Trade, it seems to have received little attention. Indeed, their appeal contained opinions which were radical for the time and which would seem uncomfortably at odds with the attitudes of a slave-using society. 'It is not the wish of your memorialists,' the settlers had added, 'that the Charaibs should be otherwise dealt with than in a manner entirely becoming humanity.'[69] The problem with the forest cover on the island was, as Young explained at length, that 'the large tracts of woodlands, from river to river, were claimed by families or tribes of Charaibs in common, and any sales made by one family would probably be disavowed by every other'.[70]

During 1770 ministers in London were even led to annul land sales already made by individual Caribs. The commissioners, moreover, were led to report on December 15, 1770 that 'His Majesty's Commissioners have found it necessary to desist from the execution of his instructions to report home a State of the Case and wait respectfully the King's further orders'.

By this stage the Commissioners for Trade appear to have decided that the original proposals had been 'contrary to the facts of treaties (i.e. the neutrality provisions of the Treaty of Aix-la-Chapelle) and...omitted acknowledgement of any right in virtue of possession by the inhabitants'.

By determined resistance over a five-year period, the Caribs had thus brought about a fundamental shift in position by the colonial power. For one thing, the British had been forced to accept the legitimacy of the 'base de l'isle' as a European legal form that the Caribs had actively and voluntarily elicited from the French government on Martinique at the beginning of the century. Moreover, the Carib construction and perception of the landscape as common or clan rather than individual property had effectively won the day. This was partly because so much of the island remained under forest cover. So much was admitted by the commissioners in a remarkable statement:

> It may be easy to determine who are best entitled to the possession of cleared and cultivated lands, since it is equitable that those who have toiled should reap the fruits of their labour [this did not, presumably, apply to African slaves!]... yet it will be difficult to *prove any natural right or title to the large tracts of woodlands* in St. Vincent's which certain Charaibs may presume to claim: there is apprehension of endangering the peace of the island from the disputes and contests among the Charaibs themselves. The sellers of these lands, as set forth in the memorial, are only three Charaibs, now it can no way be demonstrated that others of them do not conceive they have an equal claim to the enjoyment of the woods, perhaps esteemed amongst them a common right of nature; if so it is probable that those who have no share of the advantage rising from that sale may be dissatisfied with their comrades and oppose a precedent, which may gradually endanger their other possessions by admitting strangers (colonists) into their neighbourhood without the general consent of the whole.[71]

Thus by 1770 even the settlement commissioners themselves opposed the original land-use plan and the idea of forcibly resettling the

Caribs. As a result, all purchases of Carib land by colonists were officially set aside on December 15, 1770.

Alexander Anderson and the official advocacy of environmentalism on St. Vincent, 1784–1811

Carib resistance to the land-use allocation implied in the 1764 proclamation effectively terminated the original model of forest conservation for the British Caribbean in the form in which it had been developed on Tobago. The realities of military strategy and the economic priorities of the colonies had delivered a further fatal blow to the concept. There was, of course, an underlying weakness in the environmental policy of the governorate during the 1760s. In contrast to Mauritius at the same period, there was no local involvement by professional naturalists and thus no real continuity of ideological commitment to any form of sustainable economic development justified through climatic arguments. William Young, as we have seen, was actively hostile to the notion of forest protection, even though charged with its execution.

After the return of St. Vincent to British control in 1783, a rather more committed kind of official environmentalist consciousness came to the surface. The fact that it was able to do so was due both to the effective institutionalization of natural history on the island as a result of the development of the St. Vincent Botanic Garden and to the increasing official interest in the garden taken by Sir Joseph Banks.[72] This institution in turn facilitated the introduction to the island colony of a whole spectrum of current European scientific debates and discourses in the person of Alexander Anderson, a Scottish physician and botanist who was appointed curator of the garden in 1785. While the introduction of desiccationist forest legislation had been a remarkable feature of the early settlement of Tobago, it had taken place as the remote effect of a distant debate and, indeed, as a conceptual constraint much at odds with the immediacies of colonial perceptions. Any real impetus to innovations in environmental policy had lain in specifically European ideas, whose philosophical inspiration and texts were located mainly in France and then acted upon in England. The 'centre of calculation', to use Latour's terminology, remained firmly set in Paris (in the Académie des Sciences) or in London (in the Society of Arts).

While politically feasible on Tobago, the practical and symbolic rejection of the colonial map of St. Vincent by the Caribs had provoked the loss of the dependent structure of desiccationism in favour of a compromised construct based more on indigenous social reality. As a result, the environmental opinions and policies which developed in government circles on St. Vincent after 1783 were very much more indigenous and locally constrained. In particular, the botanical garden on St. Vincent became the site of a centre of environmental calculation which, while still partially dependent on outside networks and intellectual structures, also incorporated a good deal of autonomous intellectual work. Above all, the coupling of the institutional setting of the botanical garden (and its networks) with the intellectual personality of Alexander Anderson allowed the full impact of Enlightenment science and current environmental thinking to be felt on St. Vincent and on its processes. But the intellectual process went further than this. While resident on St. Vincent, Anderson produced a set of coherent environmentalist writings that were influenced both by the rapidly changing ecology of the island and by contemporary thinking in Europe. Most important among these texts were *A Geography and History of St. Vincent* and a series of drafts of a book called *The Delugia*. All were written between about 1799 and 1805.[73]

The principal piece of environmental legislation with which Anderson was connected was the Kings Hill Forest Act of 1791. While in concept apparently based on the 1764 proclamation for the Grenada Governorate, the Act was also a specifically local development that had been much influenced by the views of Anderson as well as other colonists. In terms of text and legislation, the emergence of a relatively autonomous environmental consciousness on St. Vincent between 1783 and 1800 represents a cross-fertilization between European scientific thought and the more autonomous physiocratic responses to tropical environmental change which had evolved on Mauritius a decade earlier. These two environmentalisms were in fact closely connected. Thus the climatic theories and desiccationist thinking current on Mauritius and in the Eastern Caribbean by the 1780s can be seen as the first isolated indications of what was, within a few decades, to become a more general and global environmental critique.

The 1773 treaty between the British and the Caribs meant that, at least temporarily, survey and forest-reservation plans were abandoned on St. Vincent. Instead, forest clearance and cultivation continued in the southern parts of the island, mainly for sugar production. In much of the zone designated for the Caribs, as well as in the European areas on the leeward side of the island, the forest remained largely untouched. Towards the end of the French occupation, between 1779 and 1785, the process of forest clearance resumed, stimulated by an increasingly buoyant market for cotton. This rise had begun at about the time that Alexander Anderson first visited the island in 1784. In 1785 he returned to St. Vincent as superintendent of the St. Vincent Botanic Garden at Kingstown (in succession to Dr. George Young, whom he had earlier met on St. Lucia) and remained in the post until his death in 1811. It was not long after Anderson's arrival that the notion of forest reservation reappeared on the official post-occupation agenda.

By 1784 cotton cultivation was already known to be damaging to the island soils. Moreover, in many of the West Indian islands, but particularly on St. Kitts, Nevis and Jamaica, some limited soil conservation measures had been adopted in response to the erosion problems caused by prolonged periods of uninterrupted sugar-cane cultivation.[74] Diffusion of awareness of the dangers of soil erosion may well have affected St. Vincent by the 1780s. However, it seems likely that the consequences of the Post-1785 clearance for cotton cultivation (linked to a subsequent rapid appearance of erosion and gullying) soon made an impact on local settler opinion. Detailed discussions took place, for example, in the St. Vincent Assembly in January, 1790 on the subject of soil erosion and the causes of gullying. Particular mention was made by members of the size of the new gullies, which were so wide that even fully harnessed ox teams could not cross them without the aid of specially constructed wooden bridges.[75] However, by this time legislation to gazette a 'climatic' forest reserve at Kings Hill had already been set in train as a result of active lobbying of the St. Vincent government by Alexander Anderson and a member of the Assembly, William Bannatyne. The original bill had been tabled in the Assembly on November 13, 1788. The bill, apparently drafted by Bannatyne with Anderson's advice, was intended to 'appropriate for the benefit of the neighbourhood the hill called 'The Kings Hill'.[76]

Some mention is appropriate here of the precise status and characteristics of the Kings Hill, a small but highly significant site in the history of colonial environmentalism. The hill is in the south-eastern section of the island where the natural vegetation is (in the twentieth century) known as 'dry woodland'.[77] It is an area peculiarly susceptible to drying winds that created particular hazards for sugar-cane cultivation, which was at the time still expanding rapidly in that part of the island and particularly on the land of George Stubbs, adjacent to which the Kings Hill Forest was located and on to which the forest drained.

The Kings Hill Forest Bill experienced considerable delays and opposition in the course of its passage through the St. Vincent Assembly, largely because of the fears of some planters that parts of their estates might become sterilised under other forest reserves gazetted on the model of Kings Hill. A committee on the bill which met on January 2, 1790 served to expose some of these fears. Some members suggested that it was entirely beneficial that 'wild and unfrequented woods' should be turned to cotton and sugar planting. Their real fear, however, appears to have been articulated in the concern that 'the Charaibs should be kept behind the line', that is, the zonal boundary line which had been established in the 1773 treaty with Chief Chatoyer.[78] Forest clearance, it was implied, would help to ensure the integrity of the boundary, whereas forest reservation might merely give the Caribs potential cover for future insurrections. These discussions make it quite apparent that the notion of forest reservation was not seen as offering support to efforts at social control of the Caribs; in fact, quite the contrary. Instead, the preferred colonial construction of the landscape for most European settlers, as it had been on Barbados, consisted in the development of a cleared and thoroughly socialized island.[79]

For these reasons, a second reading of the bill was deferred on February 5, 1790 and again on March 13, 1790. However, the bill was finally read a further time on June 2, 1790. On December 8, 1790, it was agreed to lay the bill before the governor for assent. After this the bill went through fairly smoothly. Even so, the governor, James Seton, insisted on an important final amendment. As it originally stood, the bill had aimed to appropriate the Kings Hill Forest on behalf of the colony rather than on behalf of the King. This reflected the local origins of the scheme, which contrasted with the provisions of the Grenada Governorate proclamation of 1764. Once this political matter was dealt with, the bill finally received the governor's assent on February 9, 1791. The key climatic provision, as it was included in the third reading of the bill, ordained that the law would 'appropriate for the benefit of the neighbourhood the hill called The King's Hill in the Parish of St. George and for enclosing the same, preserving the timber and other trees growing thereon *in order to attract rain*'. When altered by the governor to bring it firmly back into the ambit of Whitehall, the final Act read significantly differently. Thus it was eventually enacted by the authority aforesaid that 'the hill called the King's Hill and the timber and other trees and wood growing, or that may grow thereon, according to the extent and bounding thereof is reserved by His Majesty's said Commissioners [and] shall be and is hereby *reserved and appropriated for the purpose of attracting the clouds and rain*'.[80]

The addition of 'clouds' to the wording of the final Act suggests that some detailed theoretical and meteorological debates had taken place in committee or among Seton's advisers. Unfortunately, if there were any such discussions at this stage, they have not been recorded. Certainly both legislators and governor seem to have been remarkably cautious in allocating land for purposes of the Act in comparison to the generous allocation made in 1764 on Tobago. Indeed, the Kings Hill reserve as eventually gazetted was small almost to the point of being experimental.

The precise site of the reserve was surveyed, as laid down in the 1791 Act, on June 5, 1791, and was subsequently resurveyed in 1808,

1812, 1846, 1912, and 1991.[81] During this period the forest suffered little encroachment, despite considerable local and sustainable use of the
woods for firewood and yam growing.[82] Despite its limited size,
the principle upon which the Kings Hill reserve was established appears
to have exercised a remarkable institutional influence in the ensuing
decades, particularly in the practice of tree planting and forest reservation on St. Helena and, less directly, over wide areas of India. While part
of the provenance of the Kings Hill legislation can be attributed in very
general terms to the Grenada Governorate proclamation of 1764, the
revived form of desiccationism seems directly attributable to
Anderson's influence and his personal agenda. But other lobbies may
also have been at work, particularly amongst the membership of the
Society of Arts. It had been General Melville himself who had sponsored William Bannatyne, the original tabler of the Kings Hill bill, for
election as a corresponding member of the Society of Arts. As such,
Bannatyne would have joined Joshua Steele of Barbados as one of a
small group of influential West Indies planters who were already
Society members.[83]

It seems likely that both Melville and some of his colleagues in
the Society of Arts were keen to renew the climatic measures abandoned during the recent disastrous conflicts with the black Caribs.
However, the part played by Melville and the Society in founding the
St. Vincent Botanic Garden proved ultimately more decisive in promoting environmental ideas, particularly by providing Alexander
Anderson with a base both for supporting the Kings Hill legislation
and for developing his environmentalist theories in a series of specific
writings. The most important and coherent of the latter were included
in his unpublished manuscript entitled *The Geography and History of
St. Vincent*. This text allows one to place Anderson in his true historical context and to define the antecedents and terms of his eloquent and
elaborate environmentalism.

A crisis of conscience and chronology: Alexander Anderson and the characteristics of his environmental critique, 1785–1811

The origins of Anderson's environmentalism emerged initially from his
professional interest in plant transfer, a field of activity which the
Society of Arts had sought to support by its vigorous sponsorship of the
St. Vincent Botanic Garden. For both men the study of the constraints
of soil conditions for plant transfer had stimulated an interest in the
dynamics of the wider environment and its interrelationships. In fact,
Anderson precisely pinpointed the beginnings of his interest in soil
conditions as having been aroused by an acquaintance with the work of

the Dutch botanist Rumphius, and particularly his book *Herbarium Amboinense*.[84] It would be very difficult, however, to place an exact date upon Anderson's espousal of environmental fears and climatic anxieties. His ideas clearly evolved a great deal during his residence on St. Vincent and were affected both by his own gathering of empirical data and by his dual response to the social crises on the island and the crisis taking place in natural science, particularly with regard to geological chronology and awareness of species extinctions. Anderson's wide reading would soon have made him aware of contemporary debates about vegetation, airs and climate. We know, for example, that he had read Edward Long's *History of Jamaica*, a large work that contained a very extensive analysis of theories that had recently been expounded by Joseph Priestley on air and the atmosphere, together with accounts of the work of other pioneers in atmospheric chemistry, including Stephen Hales.[85] Anderson may also have become acquainted with both Hales' and Priestley's theories quite independently of Edward Long's work, because direct evidence of his familiarity with the work of Priestley emerges only after 1800, so it remains difficult to reconstruct the pattern of Anderson's intellectual development with any certainty.

Conceivably, an incipient interest in the physical effects of deforestation may have developed through Anderson's friendship with Dr. George Young, whose botanical correspondence with the Pamplemousses garden on Mauritius may have familiarized him with the first French forest-protection and afforestation programmes on that island. In fact, there is little doubt that both Young and Anderson would have had frequent opportunities to acquire a knowledge of developments on Mauritius, and they may actually have discussed them.

A letter written by Anderson to William Forsyth, the curator of the Chelsea Physic Garden (where Anderson had originally trained in the early 1770s), and later published by Sir George Yonge in *Philosophical Transactions of the Royal Society* indicates that Anderson was by 1784 already deeply interested in geology and meteorology and in the relationship between woodland and cloud cover.[86] The letter, written after an ascent of Soufrière, the main volcano on St. Vincent, mentions that the mountain 'was surrounded by thick wood and during the night the whole of the mountain is covered with thick clouds, from which it frequently rains'.[87] 'I am sorry,' Anderson remarked in the letter, 'that I had no instruments to take the state of the air.'[88] This statement provides us with a small but important key to Anderson's theoretical inclinations and especially to his interest in atmospheric dynamics. In particular, Anderson was interested in measuring the qualities of the air, attributing causes to those qualities and associating them with the character of climate. In connecting air quality, volcanoes and climate, Anderson was in illustrious company, particularly with Benjamin Franklin. Alerted to the possibility of rapid climate change by the very severe winter of 1783–4, Franklin had reached the conclusion that a global cooling in the temperate latitudes could safely be attributed to a rise in volcanic activity. The cooling layer of dust that could be observed in the skies of France and the United States was, he thought, due to 'the vast quantity of smoke, long continuing to issue during the summer from Hecla in Iceland'.[89] While it is difficult to prove, it is likely that Anderson would have become familiar with the theme of this paper, as during the 1780s he became more and more interested in the structure of volcanoes and their geological and climatic consequences. Dominating the island as it did, and with the effects of its frequent eruptions only too plain to see, Soufrière was bound to dominate Anderson's understanding of natural processes.

Initially, however, it was the small and circumscribed nature of the island that alerted Anderson to the rapid pace of tropical environmental change. During his long term as curator of the botanical garden, he came to know the island in great detail. He crossed and recrossed the colony collecting plants, insects, birds and geological specimens. Apart from voluminous notes on plants, his letters also comment on soils, deforestation, the need for forest protection and the desirability of diversifying away from simple sugar-cane cropping. He frequently collected plants adjacent to Carib habitations and described those which he thought had been introduced on the island by the aboriginal people.[90] This information was carefully documented in letters to William Forsyth at the Chelsea Physic Garden and other botanists. Anderson's expertise on the island was distilled in his manuscript *The Geography and History of St. Vincent*, written in about 1800; it is from this text that one can adduce the main strands of his environmental thinking. His justification for writing the work was based on the simple but significant premise that 'Saint Vincent has been pitched upon for the establishment of the garden'. He added that:

> …as the Royal munificence has been the support of the institution [the botanical garden] it appears necessary to give some idea of the situation, structure, climate, seasons and soils of the island. The more so as the island is to be regarded as a nursery for supplying all the other islands with the useful plants that can be obtained from the different climates of the world.[91]

Here, then, was the initial stimulus to a book in which the two main topics of concern emerge as, first, the relations between people and climate and, secondly, the relations between colonist and Carib. There was a strong aesthetic theme to the book too, and Anderson's language is strongly reminiscent of contemporary Romantic literature. Perhaps few islands in the world, Anderson felt, displayed as great a variety of 'pleasing and romantic scenes as St. Vincent'.[92] 'Its size and form,' he informs us later in the text, 'very much resemble that celebrated island of Otaheite in the South Seas, and when Captain Bligh approached it [St. Vincent] in *Providence* two natives of that island on board leaped for joy and called out "Otaheite, Otaheite!" conceiving it to be their native land.'[93] Once again we are dealing here with an exact parallel to the new intellectual stereotypes transferred by Commerson (and to a lesser extent by Poivre) from Tahiti to the Mascarene Islands. Indeed, this throw-away comment in the *Geography* goes a long way towards explaining Anderson's preconceptions with St. Vincent and the role which its visual nature might perform in his personal cosmology. It also helps to account for Anderson's very disturbed and ambivalent response to the brutal treatment of the indigenous Caribs by the British. The image of Tahiti may also shed some light on Anderson's sensitivity towards the destruction of the forests in which the Caribs lived. In other words, the notion of a 'nouvelle Cythère', with all its Utopian social connotations, may be important to understanding Anderson's formulation of an environmentalism in circumstances in which it might have been least expected, at least in terms of the social context, which was one of oppression.

Nevertheless, for Anderson the decisive factor in his growing sensibility was the rapid deforestation that he witnessed even in the immediate environs of the botanical garden at Kingstown. In the course of a wide-ranging description of St. Vincent in his *Geography*, Anderson carefully notes the changes in forest cover which had taken place in the years since he first arrived on the island. He records, for example, the disappearance during the 1790s of 'the thickest and most impenetrable forests in St. Vincent'.[94] The whole account is coloured by the fact that Anderson had lived through the almost complete removal of the indigenous Carib population and through French insurrections against British occupation in 1795. The sense of guilt and insecurity that seems thereby to have been induced in Anderson himself may help to explain his confused and ambivalent attitude towards the Caribs, who had depended for their survival on the forests which Anderson so much valued and who had then been forcibly removed from the island at the end of the rebellion. The St. Vincent government, Anderson believed, had been entirely responsible for provoking rebellion among the Caribs in the first place and had compounded this fault by expelling them from the island in what he considered to be a brutal and unjust fashion.

Indeed, Anderson appears to have directly equated the unfair treatment of the Caribs with the uncontrolled deforestation of the island for sugar planting.

While he left the colonial treatment of the Caribs to the further judgement of others, the intensely religious Anderson was in no doubt about what sort of climatic retribution would be exacted for the deforestation of the windward parts of the island, where the most fertile estates were to be found. The seaside estates, he asserted, 'in some years suffer by drought and it is feared will suffer more as the interior lands are cleared of their native forests…the clouds are naturally attracted by the high and woody summits of the primary chain and then much condensed in passing down their leeward sides'.[95] The planters were, he complained, acting the same inconsiderate and imprudent part as the first settlers of Barbados and Antigua 'by the total extirpation of all the natural woods within their bounds. The loss of crops for many years past in these two islands, owing to the extermination of the native trees and woods', Anderson adds, 'ought to have been a warning to the planters on the windward side of St. Vincent'. These remarks preface a part of the *Geography* manuscript which amounts to a wide-ranging summary or even personal credo of Anderson's conservationist views. It is quoted here at length, since it provides us with a comprehensive account of colonial environmental notions as they had developed in the Caribbean by 1800:

'Turn all into cane' is too much the invariable maxim of the planter, and before it fall indiscriminately all woods, altho' of the greatest value. The noxious weed is eradicated; at the same time is the most useful plant. Not a tree is left to vary the scene. Nor do they consider that one day the expense of mill timber must oblige them to reproduce what they have so inconsiderately destroyed. Much fruitless labour has been bestowed in clearing tops of hills, found afterwards to be too barren for the cane or any cultivated plant. Had they been left in the natural clumps, they would have highly improved the look of the country and given a continued supply of useful wood and trees for shade, which is found to be absolutely necessary in pastures in this climate. The cattle resort to them for shelter against the sun, wind and rain, and against their stems clear themselves of the tick and insect, [which are] very troublesome and renders them lean. A proper proportion of woodland always tends to keep a country cool. How necessary then for man and beast within the tropics. Nor is there any reasonable doubt that trees have a very considerable effect in attracting rain, upon the certainty of which no crop depends so much as that of sugar cane. From the same cause they promote the circulation of the atmosphere and consequently health of the inhabitants. It is well known that [in] the back settlements Europeans from among the woods or in cleared spots among them where great part of the year they are enveloped with clouds, frequent rains, constant dews and damps with a cold atmosphere, the inhabitants are far more healthy, lively and robust than the seaside inhabitants. This in great measure accounts for the health and longevity of savages whose habitations are in the middle of woods and little cultivation around them...Mr. Long in his *History of Jamaica* has the very just observation that all lands on first settling are healthy but after being cleared to a certain extent become unhealthy. This is also probably the case in extra-tropical countries. Had the planters next the sea only reserved the natural trees on the rocks and dry barren ridges, between the canes and the sea, as well as on those uncultivable hills and rocks scattered by beneficent nature on their estates, they would have preserved ornament as well as shelter to the cane from the spray of the sea, than which nothing is more injurious to it. They would have shown greater wisdom and foresight besides studying their own interest more effectually than by their destruction, if no more had been lost than the fruitless labour of clearing the barren hills and rocks of their native productions. It is astonishing the idea of ornament only did not preserve them, for surely to one never so little accustomed to such scenes and natural beauties, even to a savage a well-cultivated country interspersed with clumps of trees and woods is more pleasing to the eye than bare and bleak hills and rugged, ill-shapen rocks staring them in the face. On windward coasts during the dry season, from the strong regular sea breeze the saline particles raised by evaporation and agitation of the waves on the rocks rise like a mist, which affects vegetation for some miles back. To guard against it, it might have been supposed that art would have been called in, if possible, to affect the purpose in planting trees along the headlands, but nature on the windward coast of St. Vincent had done what art never can perform. She had reared a natural and beautiful border of white cedar,[96] a valuable wood for many mechanical purposes and effectively screened the adjoining land, but strange to tell, not even a stump of a tree is to be seen along this bleak and dreary rock. On most of the seaside ridges and hills the mastick was a common tree. It is the most valuable wood for mill timber in the West Indies as well as buildings. So wantonly was it destroyed that not only negroes cut the trees up for fire wood, but they were piled in heaps and burnt on the fields. This will appear the more strange: that those very planters who thus destroyed it are now importing their mill timber from Demerary and Porto Rico at a vast expense and on a precarious footing.... From the variety of situations and temperatures in the atmosphere, St. Vincent produces a great variety of indigenous plants on the summits of the mountains, many rare and beautiful, several of which are nowhere else seen. What is remarkable, some of the identical species, natives of the forests of Guiana, are natives of its woods. This is the more striking when we regard the great distance, vast difference in the soils and face of the two countries. Had these plants, common to both, been all fruit-bearing or medicinal, then introduction into St. Vincent might have readily been by the aborigines, which undoubtedly was the case with all the now common fruits of the island. By them probably have been introduced Carapa and Allamanda, as they are Indian medicines, but for others of no known use we are at a loss to account.[97]

These unedited manuscript remarks made by Anderson give us a very clear indication of his public reasons for pursuing the cause of forest protection so vigorously during the 1780s. An explicit landscape aesthetic is invoked and supplemented by a whole variety of fears about climate change, health, sustainability of timber supply and species extinctions. The notion of an ideal society in an ideal landscape is never far from the surface of this text. It would, I think, be unwise simply to attribute the character of the text to the influence of Rousseau and the French Romantics. In Anderson's case a distinctively empirical and botanical consciousness pervades and informs the idyll. He is sharply aware, for example, of the apparent equilibrium of the Caribs with the pre-colonial environment and is particularly admiring of their efforts at medicinal plant transfer. This is not surprising in view of the fact that he was himself concerned with transfer projects. A realization of the relative harmony between Carib and the 'healthy' forest environment encouraged him to a much stronger critique of European-caused deforestation than he might otherwise have developed. As far as the climatic influence of forests was concerned, Anderson's reading of Edward Long's three-volume *History of Jamaica*, published in 1774, had clearly exercised a powerful influence over him. Through Long, Anderson would have received a thorough grounding in the writings of Halley, Dobson, Pringle and, above all, Hales and Priestley.[98] Priestley's work was still very recent when Long wrote but was frequently quoted in his discussions of the connections among forests, climate and health, much as it was to be forty years later for Edward Balfour and other members of the Indian medical service.[99] Edward Long, unlike Alexander Anderson, was chiefly concerned with the dangers posed by deforestation for the health of Europeans in the tropics. He appears to have utilized the powerful social messages of Priestley's atmospheric theories and his environmental medicine to a very particular regional purpose.[100]

By the second half of the eighteenth century, the Hippocratic epidemiology and meteorology of an earlier period had been elaborated into a much more complex philosophy of the aerial system that directed attention to stagnation, overcrowding and dirt. These changes were related to several wider issues, including the development of cameralism (a largely German offshoot of French physiocracy) and the origins of medical police.[101] It has been suggested that British physicians during the eighteenth century increasingly looked to meteorology, pneumatics and the powers of the atmosphere to demonstrate the whole system of nature and in turn explain health and disease. This medical understanding of circulation in the atmospheric economy created a role for physicians in the policing of health and the management of sickness in society at large. In Europe the explanation of disease directed epidemiogical concerns to the sources of putrefaction, corruption and decay, where pathology resulted from stagnation of the vital circulation. In the West Indies, on the other hand, the explanation of disease directed attention to the status of vegetation and thus potentially to a policing of change in the landscape. For Edward Long (and therefore, one may surmise, for Anderson) the decisive insights of Priestley and Stephen Hales were those which dealt with the power of vegetation to ensure a healthy atmosphere. 'We owe to Dr Priestly', Long wrote:

> ...the suggestion of two grand resources for this salutary end; the first he assigns to the vegetable kingdom, the next to the sea, and other large collections of water; not however excluding Dr. Hales's principle of ventilation from a share in this important office. He finds that the effluvia of vegetables are endued with the power of reviving common air, that has been vitiated, or fouled, by fire or respiration. That the aromatic vapours of plants, are not necessary participants in the office of restoring this purity; for that vegetables that have an offensive smell, or no smell at all, but are of quick growth, prove the very best for this purpose.[102]

By linking human health to the status of the tropical forest and to rainfall frequency, Long touched on very basic European worries about vulnerability to tropical diseases. At another level he also entered the realm of contemporary anxieties about 'degeneration' in tropical climates. All these concerns would legitimate the kinds of interventions to protect forest that were implicitly advocated by Long and explicitly argued by Anderson. But the matter went further than this. Sir John Pringle, in a speech made in 1773 (quoted by Long in his publication of the next year), reinterpreted Priestley to find the preservation of vegetation as being valuable not only in a negative sense but also in a much more intrinsic and universal sense.[103] 'We are assured [implicitly by Priestley] that no vegetable grows in vain,' he wrote, 'but every individual plant is serviceable to mankind; if not always distinguishable by some private virtue, yet making a part of the whole, which cleanses and purifies the atmosphere.' This 'virtue' was worth cultivating as much in remote regions as in those which were more familiar. 'Nor is the herbage', he concluded:

> ...nor the woods, that flourish in the most remote and unpeopled regions, unprofitable to us, nor we to them; considering how constantly the winds convey to them our vitiated air, for our relief and their nourishment; and if ever these salutary gales rise to storms and hurricanes, let us still trace and revere the ways of a Beneficent being, who not fortuitously, but with design; not in wrath but in mercy, thus shakes the waters and the air together, to bury in the deep those putrid and pestilential effluvia, which the vegetables upon the face of the earth has been insufficient to consume.

Long developed this argument still further. These discoveries, he said, were 'noble, and open to us a new source of investigation into the wholesomeness or insalubrity of local situations in different countries, whether in the neighbourhood of large woods...or whether the inhabitants are deprived of some, or all these purifiers'. If it was necessary to preserve 'virtue' in the air for the good of temperate regions, still more was it necessary in the tropics. 'If such is the grand provision made for our globe at large, may we not indulge a thought, that it is dispensed in a more liberal portion to those regions, whose climate seems to require it?' As the processes of corruption were more active in the tropics, Long reasoned, then vegetal growth was 'more powerful and more abundant than in Northern countries'. But it might happen, he feared that 'the leafy cloathing of the woods may be parched, arid and juiceless'.[104] In those circumstances only 'tempests' and hurricanes could save the vegetation and restore the climate. Alexander Anderson, of course, had seen ample evidence of far more permanent vegetation change than Long apparently had on Jamaica. Moreover, the extreme events of hurricane and earthquake mentioned by Long in his *History* were supplemented on St. Vincent by regular volcanic eruptions. In these circumstances any attempt to maintain stability in the landscape, through forest protection or other means, must have seemed desirable to Anderson.

Climatic concerns and a contemporary landscape aesthetic both affected Anderson's desire to control deforestation and construct a stable environment. However, the text of the *Geography* indicates that there was a third and related motive for landscape protection which was linked both to the rarity of the island plant species and to the extinction of the Carib population on St. Vincent. In his desire to protect the forests, climate, plants and landscape of St. Vincent, it seems likely that Anderson was, perhaps at a subconscious level, attempting to expiate the savage colonial repression of the black Carib and Carib population after their successive insurrections. Some clues to this are present towards the end of the manuscript, where Anderson questioned the morality of forced resettlement:

> Altho' factions and rebellion may be the cause of extirpating a people from a government under which they might have ever remained free and happy, yet who can avoid melancholy sensations on a whole race of mankind transported forever from their native land inhabited by them for generations and not conceive that there has been something radically wrong in the principle of government necessitated to that act?[105]

By discussing the policy of forced removal alongside an environmental critique, Anderson highlights the connections between his desire for a reformed ethic of governance and his wish to reform the ethos of land management. Such notions of environmental morality, often linked with discourses on social justice, were soon to become typical of much colonial conservationism. Alexander Anderson emerges simply as the first in a long line of Scottish colonial experts who linked together their biological, religious and social insights. To some extent, his nascent environmentalism may have served to resolve at a psychological level the conflicts that developed in Anderson's mind over the colonial treatment of the Caribs and their forest environment. But this was not the end of the story. His later unpublished writings indicate that Anderson became steadily more enmeshed in contradictions between his observations of natural and social change and his inherited religious and social preconceptions. His geological observations in particular led him to an assessment of geological time scales that conflicted with his religious beliefs. It is in this context that we need to set his concerns about plant extinctions and the extinction of a Carib population. The real threat, one may suggest, was one posed to Anderson's own 'nature'. His original interest in climate had first been expressed in a description of his ascent of Soufrière, the main volcano. The volcano had recently undergone, he emphasized, 'great convulsions of nature' and 'some terrible convulsion' of nature.[106] There are obvious risks involved in deconstructing Anderson's volcano drawing and the language of his *Morne Garou* article. Even so, it seems safe to conclude that the evidence of recent, ongoing and even catastrophic natural changes presented in the environs of Morne Garou, within the confines of a small and intimately known island, clearly made an overwhelming and even appalling impact on Anderson. These emotions are faithfully portrayed in his drawing of the crater of the volcano. Here we see the image of a body torn apart, even of a womb rent asunder, with the lava like blood flowing forth and the adjacent forest trees burnt to black skeletons. In the face of this, Anderson tells us, with the quixotic enthusiasm of the fanatical botanist, there 'was a probability of meeting with plants on it I could find in no other part of the island'.

In fact, besides demonstrating the potential for catastrophic change, the volcano presented Anderson with data incompatible with his own religious beliefs and notions of geological time scales. This confrontation between belief and the evidence of process occupies hundreds of pages of tortuous and unresolved argument in his unpublished *Delugia* manuscript. In questioning geological time scales, an existential crisis of human origins was added to the situational crisis of defining the role of the colonist in a territory once inhabited by an indigenous people. However, in seeking to protect the forests Anderson may in fact have found a successful strategy to protect his own personal integrity in the context of a set of social assumptions about creation which he found himself forced increasingly to question. Climatic environmentalism, at the very least, restored the apparent power of the colonist to act amid a chaos in which old assumptions about chronology, process, origins and belief were all threatened. For Anderson, the tropical-island predicament had focused this crisis. Nevertheless, before long the crisis was one that began to enter a geographically much wider social and scientific consciousness.

Notes

1   E. de Vattel. *The law of nations, or principles of natural law, applied to the conduct and affairs of nations and sovereigns: A work tending to display the true interest of powers.* London, 1760.
2   The last was the predecessor of the Board of Trade.

3 See D. G. C. Allan. *William Shipley, founder of the Royal Society of Arts: A biography with documents.* London, 1979. The eleven founding members were Viscount Folkestone; Lord Romney; Dr. Stephen Hales, F.RS.; Henry Baker, F.R.S. (naturalist and author, married to Daniel Defoe's youngest daughter); Gustavus Brander, F.R.S.; James Short, F.R.S.; John Goodchild; Nicholas Crisp; Charles Lawrence; Husband Messiter; and William Shipley.

4 A gold medal and two silver medals were offered for sowing the greatest quantity of land with acorns at the rate of four bushels to the acre. Similar premiums were offered for planting Spanish chestnuts, elm and Scots pine.

5 Royal Society of Arts. *Premiums by the society, established at London, for the encouragement of arts, manufactures and commerce.* London, 16 June, 1760.

6 Ibid.

7 Tree planting and the cultivation of exotic crops were among Steele's main enthusiasms; see Henry Trueman Wood. *A history of the Royal Society of Arts.* London, 1913. In the *Transactions* of the Society, vol. 4, p. 219, it is recorded that 'Steele sent the Secretary an account of an ancient Mango tree then existing in a plantation in Barbados called 'The Guinea'.' The tree had been imported by Edwin Lascelles in 1742. Wood notes that Portuguese missionaries had in fact introduced the mango to Brazil from the East Indies. Steele, however, was one of the first English colonists to take an interest in plant introductions and seems to have pioneered the idea of the Society of Arts' taking an active role in colonial plant transfers and the development of botanical gardens.

8 Robert Melville, F.R.S., F.R.S.A. (1723–1809), attended grammar school and the universities of Glasgow and Edinburgh. In 1744 he entered the army as an ensign in the 25th Regiment (the King's Own Scottish Borderers) and served in Flanders. He was promoted to captain in 1751 and major in 1756 and then commanded the 38th Regiment (the South Staffordsire Regiment) at Guadeloupe in 1759. In a very full life Melville became a biographer, botanist, antiquarian and ballistician. In many ways he typified the university output of the Scottish Enlightenment, particularly in his alertness to technical and cultural developments in France and its colonies.

9 R. Dossie. *Memoirs of agriculture*, 3 vols. London, 1768. III, p. 400.

10 The background to the cessions of 1763 is recorded in Jean-Claude Lorrain, *La mise en valeur de l'île de Tobago (1763–1783).* Paris, 1969, and in David Watts. *The West Indies.* pp. 240–58. For a basic political history of Tobago, see Douglas Archibald. *Tobago, 'Melancholy Isle', vol. I, 1498–1771.* Port of Spain, Trinidad, 1987. A good contemporary account of the Eastern Caribbean is W. Young. *A tour through the several islands of Barbados, St Vincent, Antigua, Tobago and Grenada in the years 1791 and 1792.* Published as part of Bryan Edwards, ed., *The history, civil and commercial, of the West Indies.* London, 1818.

11 See Chapter I.

12 Public Record Office, London [henceforth cited as PRO], CO 101/9, Letter of 23 Jan. 1764.

13 PRO, CO 101/9, 'Order to commanding officer at Tobago', 13 Aug. 1763.

14 PRO, CO 102/1, Report of 3 Nov. 1763: 'Representations of the Commissioners to His Majesty upon the method of disposing of the lands in the islands of Grenada, Dominica, St. Vincent's and Tobago'.

15 PRO, CO 101/1, no. 26, proclamation of 1764, p. 123: 'Plan for the speedy and effectual settlement of His Majesty's island of Grenada, the Grenadines, Dominica, St. Vincent's and Tobago and for the designated parts of H.M. Lands…to H.M. Order in Council made upon the representation of the Commissioner for Trade and Plantations dated 3rd November, 1763 and the alterations proposed therein by the

reports of the Lords of the Treasury and Commissioners for plantation affairs of 25 Jan. and 4th Feb. 1764'.

16   PRO, CO 106/9, Copy of printed ordinance issued in Barbados 19. Jan. 1765 (my italics).

17   Ibid.

18   PRO, CO 106/9, lcttcr/order of 22 Feb. 1765: 'Resolution of meeting of Board [of Settlement Commissioners] on board Storeship *Melvill*, Barbados Bay, Tobago'.

19   Ibid.

20   PRO, co 102/1, 'Representations of the Commissioners …'

21   For a full biography of Jenyns, see Ronald Rompkey. *Soame Jenyns*. Boston, 1984.

22   D. G. C. Allan and R. E. Schofield. *Stephen Hales: Scientist and philosopher.* London, 1983. p. 139.

23   For a fuller account of treeplanting fashion (but one that takes no account of contemporary climate theory), see Keith Thomas. *Man and the natural world.*

24   Ronald Rompkey. Soame Jenyns, M.P: A curious case of membership. In *Journal of the Royal Society of Arts*, 120 (1972), 532–42. This article documents Jenyns' membership of the Society of Arts and attempts to identify his likeness in the mural *Human Culture*, by James Barry, which was painted at the Society of Arts in the 1770s. See also Rompkey. Some uncollected authors: XLIX, Soame Jenyns, *Book Collector*, 25 (1970), 210–11. Jenyns was M.P. for Cambridge in 1741–54 and 1758–80 and a Lord Commissioner for Trade in 1755–80. He died in 1787.

25   Letter from Joshua Steele to Secretary of the Society of Arts, 24 May 1785, Royal Society of Arts archives, John Adam St., London WI, Letters from West Indies, 1780–90; Wood, *History of the Royal Society of Arts*, p. 97.

26   Vermuyden stayed at the Jenyns seat in Bottisham for much of the time he was employed in fcn drainage, and some of his diaries remain there. See also Darby, *The draining fens* for further details of Vermuyden's life.

27   E.g. Soame Jenyns. *Remarks on a bill presented in the last sessions instituted A Bill for preserving the drainage in the Middle and South Levels.* London, 1777.

28   David Watts. *Man's influence on the vegetation Barbados*, p. 45, and David Watts. *Plant introduction and landscape change in Barbados, 1625–1836*. Ph.D. diss. McGill University, 1963.

29   PRO, COI /21, 'Memorial of the island of Tobago', 1667, P. 171.

30   PRO, CO 101/18, fol. 312: Replies by George Gibbs, captain of militia in Courland (Tobago), to an enquiry by a British minister, 6 Oct. 1773. There had been some very limited phases of deforestation for sugar-cane cultivation during the Dutch occupation of Tobago from 1632 to 1667. According to Rochefort, who visited the island in 1664, there were then six well-equipped sugar factories; see C. Rochefort. *Tableau de l'Isle de Tobago*. Leiden, 1665. There is also a record of a party from Barbados led by a Captain Marshall that settled in Tobago in about 1642 but abandoned plantations of tobacco and indigo to settle in Surinam; see David L. Niddrie. *Land use and population in Tobago*. London, 1961. p. 16.

31   John Poyntz. *The present prospect of the famous and fertile island of Tobago*. London, 1683. This work was subtitled *Proposals for the enclosures of all that are minded to settle there*.

32   C. R. Otticy. *Romantic Tobago*. Port of Spain. Trinidad, 1969.

33   Watts. V*egetation of Barbados*. p. 45.

34   See Hughes. *Natural history of Barbados.*

35   Rudwick. *The great Devonian controversy: The shaping of scientific knowledge among gentlemanly scientists*. Chicago, 1985; Gould. *Time's arrow, time's cycle.*

36   S. Jenyns. *A free enquiry into the nature and origins of evil, in six letters…* London, 1757.

37 C. N. Cole, ed. *The works of Soame Jenyns.* 4 vols. London, 1788–90. A poem included in this collection is entitled 'To a young lady going to the West Indies'.
38 Glacken. *Traces on the Rhodian shore.* pp. 521–2.
39 Cole. *Works of Soame Jenyns,* III. p. 272.
40 'Primaeval forests and the cult of nature'. Lecture at Christ's College, Cambridge, 7 May 1991.
41 K. Thomas. *Man and the natural world.* p. 215; see also S. Daniels. The political iconography of woodland. In D. Cosgrove and S. Daniels. *The iconography of landscape.* Cambridge, 1988.
42 See Grove. Colonial conservation, ecological hegemony and popular resistance; and Nancy L. Peluso. The history of state forest management in colonial Java. In *Forest and Conservation History,* 35 (1991), 63–73.
43 Hughes. *Natural history of Barbados.*
44 John Fowler. *A summary account of the present flourishing state of the respectable colony of Tobago in The British West Indies.* London, 1774.
45 Bernard Marshall. The black Caribs: Native resistance to British penetration on the windward side of St. Vincent, 1763–1773. *Caribbean Quarterly,* 79 (1973).
46 For a comparable approach to the 'discourse of maps', see J. B. Harley. Maps, knowledge and power. In Cosgrove and Daniels, eds., *The iconography of landscape.* pp. 277–312.
47 Ottley. *Romantic Tobago.* PNM
48 Lorrain. *La mise en valeur de l'île de Tabago.*
49 PRO CO 101/6, Report by Mr. Jackson, r8 Jan. 1777; CO 102/2, Report of the Board of Trade, 18 Feb. 1777.
50 Statistics on forest-reserve area are given in L. G. Hay. *A handbook of the colony of Tobago.* Scarborough, Tobago, 1882.
51 The existence of this pamplet is reported by William Young's son (also called William Young) in *An account of the black Caribs of St. Vincent.* London, 1795. pp. 19–29. For a modern account, see Marshall. The black Caribs.
52 Young. Account of the black Caribs, p. 23 (my italics).
53 Ibid., p. 21.
54 Ibid.
55 Ibid., p. 22.
56 Vattel. *The law of nations.* The operative passages in Vattel's text are: 'The cultivation of the earth causes it to produce an infinite increase…it forms the resource and the most solid fund of riches and commerce for the people who enjoy a happy climate…the sovereign ought not to allow either communities or private persons to occupy large tracts of land in order to have it uncultivated. These rights of common, which deprive the proprietor of the free liberty of disposing of his lands, that will not allow him to farm them, and to cause them to be uncultivated in the most advantageous manner, these rights I say are contrary to the welfare of the state and ought to be suppressed or reduced to just bounds…Spain is the most fertile and the worst cultivated country in Europe, (p. 3)]…China is the best cultivated country in the world…those people like the ancient Germans and the modern Tartars, who having fertile countries, disdain to cultivate the earth and choose rather to live by rapine, are wanting to themselves, and *deserve to be exterminated as savage and pernicious beasts*…there are others who, to avoid agriculture, would live only by living on their flocks. This might doubtless be allowed in the first ages of the world, when the earth, without cultivation, produced more than was sufficient to feed its few inhabitants. But at present when the human race is so multiplied it could not subsist, if all nations resolved to live in that manner. Those who retain this life usurp more extensive territories than they would have occasion

for, were they to use honest labour, and have therefore no reason to complain if other nations more laborious and closely confined come to possess a part.' (p. 37: my italics).

57   Young. *Account of the black Caribs*, p. 23.
58   Ibid., p. 24.
59   Ibid.
60   Ibid., p. 27; (my italics).
61   Ibid., pp. 31–7.
62   Ibid., p. 38.
63   PRO, CO 106/11, Assistant Surveyor Levi Porter to James Simpson, Kingstown, 29 April 1769.
64   PRO, CO 106/4, Letter from John Poynes to James Simpson, 3 May 1769.
65   Byres had already by this time draughted the first settlement map of Tobago.
66   Young, *Account of the black Caribs*, p. 47.
67   Ibid.
68   Letter of the St. Vincent colonists to the Earl of Hillsborough, quoted in Young. *Account of the black Caribs.* pp. 56–7.
69   Young adds his own bias here: 'The statement that the large tract of uncultivated land in wood could never be useful to the Charaibs is perfectly true; for a hunter's country can be of no use to the Indian where there is nothing to hunt.' (p. 62).
70   Ibid., p. 63.
71   Quoted in ibid. (my italics).
72   For a full historical account of the garden, see Lansdown Guilding. *An account of the botanic garden in the island of St. Vincent.* Glasgow, 1825 and ch. 7.
73   The four main texts, all MSS in the Archives of the Linnaean Society, are:
      (1) 'The St. Vincent Botanic Garden',
      (2) 'The geography and history of St. Vincent',
      (3) 'The Delugia', and
      (4) 'Hortus St. Vincentii'.
      The first two documents have been produced in typescript editions by the Arnold Arboretum, Harvard College, Cambridge, Mass. Anderson's letters are also preserved in a variety of collections, esp. Kew Gardens Archives, Richmond, Surrey.
74   These soil-conservation methods are extensively described in Watts, *West Indies.* So-called cane holes were the main soil-conservation structure adopted.
75   PRO, CO 263/21, Assembly discussion, 28 Jan. 1790, passage on gullies.
76   PRO, CO 263/21, Assembly Proceedings, 13 Nov. 1788: 'William Bannatyne prays to have read a Bill…being delivered in at the table was read the first time, asked to be read a second time on the next meeting.'
77   J. S. Beard. *Natural vegetation of the Windward and Leeward Islands.* M. Kidston, J. Trevin, K. Rodney, A. Glasgow and N. Weekes. *Recent studies of the King's Hill Forest reserve.* ch. 9 this volume.
78   PRO, CO 263/21, 2 Jan. 1790.
79   A useful discussion of the role of a cleared and controlled landscape in creating a European 'colonial identity' appears in J. P. Greene. Changing identity in the British Caribbean: Barbados as a case-study. In N. Canny and A. Pagden, eds. *Colonial identity in the Atlantic world.* Princeton, N.J., 1987. pp. 213–67.
80   Second paragraph of the Act as proclaimed on 2 April 1791.
81   M. Kidston, J. Trevin, K. Rodney, A. Glasgow and N. Weekes. *Recent studies of the King's Hill Forest reserve.* ch. 10 this volume.
82   In April, 1991 Cyril Shallow, a farmer and banana grower living adjacent to the forest at Stubbs village, demonstrated to me the way in which the indigenous American

yam is sustainably harvested in the forest, and the way in which small amounts of surplus and fallen timber are gathered for local use. The access allowed to continue such practices has almost certainly contributed to the survival of the forest for so long within the boundaries of 1791.

83 Archives of the Royal Society of Arts, John Adam Street, London SW1: Index of eighteenth-century sponsored candidates for membership. Bannatyne is spelt 'Banntine' in the Society records.

84 Guilding. *Botanic garden*, p. 7.

85 Priestley. Observations on different kinds of air. *Philosophical Transactions of the Royal Society*, 62 (1772). 147–264. *Experiments and observations*, London, 1774; and On the noxious quality of the effluvia of putrid marshes. *Philosophical Transactions of the Royal Society*, 64 (1774). p. 91.

86 A. Anderson. An ascent of Morne Garou, a mountain in the island of St. Vincent, with a description of the volcano at its summit. *Philosophical Transactions of the Royal Society*, 75 (1785). 16–36.

87 Ibid.. p. 20.

88 Ibid., p. 30.

89 Benjamin Franklin. Meteorological imaginations and conjectures. *Transactions of the Manchester Philosophical Society*, 1784. pp. 373–7. This paper was written at Passy, France, in May, 1784.

90 Most significant of these was the American yam *(Dioscorea sativa and D. alata)*, still a vital part of the diet of the population living adjacent to Kings Hill (informant: Cyril Shallow, Stubbs village, Kings Hill).

91 Anderson. *Geography and history of St. Vincent*. (M5, Linnaean Society), transcription ed. R. A. and E. S. Howard, Harvard College. p. 5.

92 Ibid., p. 10.

93 Ibid., p. 36.

94 Ibid., p. 11.

95 Ibid., p. 18.

96 *Bignonia leucoxylon.*

97 Anderson. *Geography*. (Richard Howard transcription). pp. 37–9.

98 Long. *History of Jamaica*. III. pp. i–viii.

99 See Chapter 8 for details of Priestley's influence on Edward Balfour.

100 Relevant studies on the social ideologies of Priestley and his associates are S. Schaffer. Measuring virtue: Eudiometry, enlightenment and pneumatic medicine. In A. Cunningham and R. French, eds., *The medical enlightenment of the eighteenth century*. Cambridge, 1990; C. J. Lawrence. Priestley in Tahiti. In C. J. Lawrence and R. Anderson, eds. *Science, medicine and dissent: Joseph Priestley 1733–1804*. London, 1987. pp. 1–10.

101 L. J. Jordanova. Earth science and environmental medicine: The synthesis of the late Enlightenment. In L. J. Jordanova and Roy Porter, eds. *Images of the earth*. BSHS Monographs, 1, Chalfont St. Giles, 1978. pp. 119–46; S. Schaffer. Natural philosophy and public spectacle in the eighteenth century. *History of Science*, 21 (1983). 1–43.

102 Long. *History of Jamaica*. III. p. v.

103 Sir John Pringle's discourse, quoted in Long. *History of Jamaica*. III. p. vi. The discourse was made on his presentation of the Royal Society's Copley medal to Priestley in 1773.

104 Long. *History of Jamaica*. III. p. vii.

105 Anderson. *Geography*. p. 97.

106 Anderson. *Ascent of Morne Garou*. pp. 25, 27.

9 Mountain, Bush and Garden: The Historical Context of Environmental Conflict on St. Vincent

Adrian Fraser

This chapter aims to demonstrate a direct lineage between the eighteenth-century architects of environmental institutions and those who seek, today, to maintain the centrality of environmental issues on our developmental agenda. This chapter provides an historical context within which the issues surrounding the Kings Hill Forest Reserve and Botanic Gardens can be placed and understood. The sheer size of the mountain chain running from north to south through the centre of the island, the scale and slope of the forest, and the struggle over remaining land for cultivation have each limited the peoples' room to manoeuvre.

The Country Environmental Profile of St.Vincent and the Grenadines issued in the early 1990s has also identified problems which are of modern origin and associated with the drive toward tourism, sand mining consequent upon the increase in the establishment of modern concrete buildings and the expanded use of agro-chemicals as the country tries to keep up with the increasing competition for agricultural exports. This is seen especially in the efforts to meet the demands of a liberalized global market of the banana industry. Other problems are of long standing and are frequently mentioned in the historical literature, among these being soil degradation and deforestation, and related issues of squatting on Crown land, the use of forest resources for timber or construction, charcoal burning and intensive mono-crop cultivation.

The context, broadly speaking, is one of a colonial setting, with St.Vincent and the Grenadines being part of the periphery, servicing the colonial mother, first within a mercantilist production system and later industrialism and the spread of industrial capitalism, while the country remained a source of primary agricultural produce plus food for its people. It was all played out within the plantation as a unit for the organization of agricultural production, generating its own style of colonial politics and social relations. If there is one underlying and dominant theme that overlays this context, it relates to the question of land and the interplay between plantation and peasant production. This is not surprising since in a small country agricultural land represents the major economic and environmental resource – the resource of bush and garden. Because so much of St. Vincent is mountainous there has been competition for this scarce resource and I acknowledge that I am addressing conditions more on the big island of St. Vincent than on the Grenadine islands.

The first casualties in this struggle for land were the indigenous people whose partial exploitation of the land was considered something of a crime. These eighteenth-century newcomers were committed to intensive cultivation. As Sir William Young recognized it, 'A general appropriation of the country for so partial use and benefit, was not deemed consistent with the common law of nations, with the general interest of the colony, or with the rights of the British crown.'[1] The agenda was clear. The rationale was laid for the expulsion of the Caribs whose claim to ownership of the country and settlement on the best lands for planting sugar could not be tolerated at a time when this land was so much in demand. St.Vincent and the Grenadines became part of the British Empire in 1763 and sugar began to be seriously planted shortly after, although complete British possession and transformation of the economy and society did not really come until 1797, the year most of the Carib population was exiled from the country. John Davy referred to the 'exertions made' and the 'capital expended' in the period after the expulsion of the Caribs.[2] Botanist Alexander Anderson noted, 'Immediate cultivation took place, and in a few years the forests disappeared as far as the Carib boundary and many large, beautiful sugar estates have arisen.'[3]

The establishment of the Botanic Garden followed shortly under British control, prompted by a call in the Transactions of the Society of Arts for such an institution in the West Indies, geared for the propagation of medical and commercial plants and the housing of nurseries of valuable plants from distant lands. It took the interest of General Robert Melville, Governor of the Windward Islands, to translate this call into action.[4] The Kings Hill Forest Reserve was anchored by legislation in 1791. It was among the earliest pieces of environmental legislations in this part of the world. It was, according to E. D. M Hooper, 'originally reserved for rains by the Commissioners for the sale of lands in 1774.' Its legislative enactment was 'for the protection of the wood on a circular hill on the windward side of the parish near the sea coast'.[5]

This relationship between the preservation of forests and rain was in the consciousness of many at that time. Alexander Anderson was high in praise of the advantages that accrued to St.Vincent because of its chain of mountains covered with their native wood: 'Its atmosphere is more cool and moist than any other of its extent and produces frequent rains and showers in the dry season but seldom experiences a long run of dry weather at any time.'[6] He argued that the extermination of the native trees and woods in Barbados and Antigua ought to have been a warning to St.Vincent, for as he states, 'Nor is there any reasonable doubt that trees have a very considerable effect in attracting rain upon the certainty of which no crop depends so much as that of the sugar cane.'[7]

The topography of the country influenced the establishment of estates on the coastal areas, the interior being dominated by a mountain chain stretching from north to south. Communication was difficult inland and thus the land there remained vested in the Crown as Crown Lands. St.Vincent's late entry into sugar cultivation because of the long resistance of the Caribs to European colonization, in comparison to adjacent islands, might have influenced the extent to which planters allowed slaves the use of provision grounds for their own cultivation. Forbidden earlier, this was a way of allowing them to produce a part of their own subsistence and so reduce costs for the estates. Gertrude Carmichael, on her arrival in St.Vincent in 1820, was struck by slaves going to the market with produce held on baskets or wooden trays on their heads from their own gardens, their 'provision grounds'.[8] In fact, Vincentian slaves had access to three kinds of land for their cultivation. The kitchen garden was a small piece of land, usually behind their houses. There they planted provision and vegetables or fruit for their daily use. Provision grounds were back lands, marginal estate lands on the edges of estates. Most of the produce for their own use and for sale in the markets was cultivated there. In the period after Emancipation, these sometimes extended for about two acres.[9] Slaves also had access to 'yam pieces', about 40 square feet. These were among the best estate lands, about to be brought into cultivation by the estates. The slaves and ex-slaves had access, even though for a short period of time, to some of the best lands, while the estates benefited in having 'a clean and ameliorated surface to plant first crop canes'.[10] Some of the provision ground lands were actually Crown lands on to which some estate owners had extended their boundaries. So encroachment and squatting were early-established practices, benefiting both the large and small farmer.

Emancipation brought its own problems and placed an even higher priority on lands. Planters worried about surrendering their control over labour, tried not to sell lands in small lots and introduced other measures to limit the opportunities off the estates for the ex-slaves. The period, particularly after the 1846 Sugar Duties Act, demanded a reorganization of estates and adoption of new techniques of cultivation and organization. The extent of absenteeism meant that the planters who could make the decisions that were desperately needed were not available. Moreover receipt of the 1831 hurricane loan and periods of depression in the industry placed planters in debt. Some estates needed to be put in the hands of people with resources to cultivate and reorganize them. This was to some extent secured by the West Indian Encumbered Estates Act through which Alexander Porter acquired a significant number of the estates and became the dominant planter. Despite this, however, the abandonment and under-use of farmland became a vexed environmental problem, as shown by Hymie Rubenstein in this book.

As the nineteenth century progressed, and the sugar industry weakened, more appeals for land were made by the ex-slave population. The large planters still controlled the cultivable areas on the coast and the country's topography became a serious impediment to get to Crown lands which were mountainous, steep and located in inaccessible areas in the interior. Demands began to be made upon the authorities to have Crown lands available. As the economic situation deteriorated and with it the social and political climate, even some Lieutenant Governors supported this plea. But a Crown Lands Survey was a prerequisite for making such lands available. The last one was that of Byre in 1776 and it was hopelessly out of date. The planters, on the other hand, refused to vote money for a survey, fearing the possibility of the sale of Crown lands in small lots. Besides, as previously pointed out, many of them were major squatters, themselves having pushed their own estates beyond the Crown Boundary Line, and even on occasions rented some of their 'Crown Land' to labourers.

Despite the inaccessibility of Crown lands and the difficulty of getting produce to the markets, some ex-slaves also began to squat on Crown lands. Valid concerns began to be raised about deforestation and soil erosion, helping to strengthen planters attention to the emerging options for the ex-slave population. In his 1886 report, E. D. M Hooper made reference to constant charcoal burning which had destroyed much wood in sections of the Leeward side of the island. In commenting on Kings Hill, he noted that 'it was now placed in the hands of surrounding estate owners, and a heavy fine of 60 pounds was to be levied on anyone cutting or removing any timber from it. At the present time it is under wood, but the supervision is neglected, while from the appearance of its boundary, I should conclude encroachment has been permitted'. He was quite skeptical of the maintenance of the present up-keep of Kings Hill at the public expense. As Hooper states, 'Admittedly, it is for the immediate benefit of the adjoining estate, and if its being kept under wood is instrumental in bringing rain to its neighbourhood, I cannot conceive that the beneficial climatic effect resulting therefrom is more than local. It may be, and probably is, to the benefit of adjoining estates that Kings Hill should remain under wood, but it can scarcely be for the public to pay for its protection.'[11] As the chapter here by Kidston, et al. shows, Kings Hill forest was indeed diminished by encroachment, but less than Hooper feared.

The abolition of elected representation and the introduction of Crown Colony government, followed by the 1882 Royal Commission's recommendations, prompted the Crown Lands Survey and the ultimate sale and lease of these lands. An Ordinance establishing a Crown Lands and Survey Department was passed on July 10, 1891. Regulations were made for the sale of crown lands in small lots of not less than five acres. A system of renting out these lands was introduced in 1901. The overwhelming emphasis was now placed on renting because of the need to protect forest reserves. In fact, it appears that by the 1940s Crown lands were no longer sold, and were only rented or leased.

The Crown Lands Scheme was not satisfactory since the land was inaccessible and not very good for productive purposes. But at the same time there were cultivable coastal lands not being used. The economic situation continued to deteriorate so that the West India Royal Commission of 1897, which was set up to investigate conditions in the West Indian colonies, had to single out the situation in St. Vincent and call for the urgent implementation of land settlement. The 1898 hurricane dealt a deathblow to sugar and forced implementation of a Peasant Land Settlement Scheme. This was further pushed by the volcanic eruption of 1902 that forced government to find land for persons displaced from areas near to the foothills of the volcano. This was when the new role of the Botanic Garden changed, in order to regenerate agriculture as Robert Anderson's Chapter 1 in this book has established.

As part of an effort at agricultural diversification and resuscitation and the introduction of appropriate environmental practices, a Department of Agriculture was started in 1898. Agricultural Instructors assisted allottees of the land settlement plots with technical advice, and the supply of plants propagated at the Botanic Garden. In fact, titles to the land were withheld until allottees completed the payment for their lands, and during that time the regulations compelled them to carry out the instructions of the Agricultural Instructors. Among these too were instructions regarding the planting of trees to serve as windbreaks and to act as anti-erosion measures. But when land titles were given, supervision was withdrawn and land use regulations stopped, allottees resorted to their old practices. After the initial 1899 Land Settlement Scheme there was what can best be described as a marking of time since Government was still committed to estate production, to a system controlled by white planters.[12]

The Crown Lands and Peasant Land Settlement Scheme never met the expanding demand for land since official thinking centred around the viability of estates. The Land Settlement Scheme was extended when circumstances forced the hands of government. Following the initial scheme of 1899, there were few extensions up to 1912 and in 1932. But then the 1935 riots that helped to transform the political scene and brought new faces into the Legislative Council changed the dynamics of these schemes. The Working Men's Association formed by George McIntosh, which through its Labour Party dominated the Legislature, kept the issue of land settlement on the national agenda. In August, 1940, for example, the four elected members raised four different motions urging the provision of further land for land settlement. The motions were put together as one and passed.[13] Newspapers featured editorials and letters making calls for the extension of land settlement.[14]

Other developments had already taken place, including the Report of the 1939 West Indian Royal Commission that gave further ammunition to those pushing for land settlement. Earlier, C.Y. Shephard of the Imperial College of Tropical Agriculture, reporting on Agricultural Credit Societies in St. Vincent in 1931, strongly recommended continuing land settlement.[15] The Colonial Development and Welfare Programme provided needed funds for land settlement, and a land settlement policy was adopted in 1943. An ordinance was later passed creating a body to regulate and control land settlement and development.[16] The emphasis was put on leasehold rather than freehold tenure, leases to be granted for twenty-five years with the right to renew for another twenty-five years at the end of every ten years.[17] The Land Settlement Board was established in 1946 to oversee land settlement, and prepared a Land Settlement policy that was adopted by the Legislature. A new thrust toward land settlement therefore emerged.

The Land Settlement and Development Board in 1946 presented an Agricultural Policy Paper which was adopted by the Legislative Council. Again, it emphasized measures of conservation. It suggested that because of topographical and soil conditions, agricultural production be confined to certain areas and the remainder reserved and put under forest for protective purposes.[18]

Soil erosion continued to constitute a problem, particularly on the 'steep sloping lands of the peasants'.[19] Crown lands agreements spelt out measures related to soil conservation. Moreover, allottees on Crown lands were compensated for measures taken to protect the soil, establish soil erosion barriers, install contour trench systems, gully and water control measures, wind breaks and trees of economic value for erosion control.[20]

By 1951 rental arrangements included strict conditions governing husbandry and soil conservation procedures. By that year too the Crown was estimated to have owned some 36,000 to 40,000 acres in the interior, approximately 45 per cent of the total land area. Most of this land was kept as forest reserves with rules to prevent cultivation, cutting of trees, coal burning and entry of livestock, 'except when sections of that land might be rented'. In such cases of rental, Crown land regulations about the leasing of those lands would then apply.[21]

Indeed, an earlier proclamation of 1912 had reserved all Crown lands above 1,000 feet elevation, but this was observed more in the breach than practice. A Charcoal Ordinance (Cap. 98 of 1926 – No. 5 of 1906) had prescribed penalties for the unlawful burning of charcoal on lands of another. Crown Lands Ordinance (Cap. 77 of 1926 – No. 3 of 1906) prescribed penalties too 'for damaging boundary marks, squatting, illicit felling and being found in possession of timber or carrying axes and tools on Crown lands, assaulting officers and making charcoal'. A Crown Lands Forest (Declaration) Order of 1948 had set aside forest reserves in the Soufrière area, Mesopotamia and Colonarie.[22] However, in these areas too substantial encroachment began, and violation of such ordinances was common.

The Agricultural Policy adopted by the Legislative Council in 1946 was generally critical of prevailing practices, noting, 'Agriculture has been conducted in the past without concerted planning for the good of the land. The systems of agriculture practised in many parts of the island have led to soil deterioration and the loss of soil fertility, conditions which will have an adverse effect on agricultural production.' It then called for what it referred to as a balanced association between the people and the land 'in which the land should not be allowed to deteriorate by exploitation, abuse or neglect but should increase in fertility and productivity as a result of the activities and practices of the people'.[23] It was of the view that agricultural policy should be directed towards conservation of the soil for future and current use.[24]

There continued to be a repetition of some of the concerns that had been voiced over the years since measures to address them were never really observed. As early as 1866 E. D. M. Hooper had drawn attention to the severe effect of the illegal felling of trees and squatting on Crown lands. He had recommended the reservation for conservation purposes of forests on the Main Ridge. A 1944 Report on Forestry by the Conservator of Forests in Trinidad and Tobago had made reference to a 1936 report by A. Wimbush of the Indian Forest Service who recommended the reservation, demarcation and protection of existing forests on Crown lands. It noted, too, that forests on private lands were almost entirely ruined by indiscriminate shifting cultivation.[25]

Plantation dominance began to weaken in the early twentieth century. They had to accommodate themselves to external economic forces over which they had little control while plantations were, internally, locked in a battle, first with the ex-slaves and then an agro-proletariat, peasants and would-be peasants. All environmental resources were used within that struggle and all environmental issues were put on the agenda, often concealing deeper motives for retaining political and economic control. Failure to provide adequate lands to meet the growing demand by ex-slaves left little alternative to many of them but to squat on land not adequate for cultivation. Moreover they resorted to practices not in harmony with good environmental conservation. The poor, in their efforts to survive, often carry out activities that threaten their own environment.

The 1935 anti-government riots marked a turning point in St. Vincent. As part of a series of Caribbean-wide disturbances, they forced the British government to take note and reset its agenda. The establishment of a Royal Commission represented Government's response. Its report provided a serious indictment of colonial rule and stimulated a new political, social and economic agenda. The Agricultural Policy of 1946 that highlighted conservation issues, was to a large extent, influenced by that Commission's report.

While earlier attention was drawn to increasing pressure on the land from the rapid growth of a population almost entirely dependent on the soil, it later manifested itself through the growth of housing stock, and unplanned accommodation to the demands of the tourist industry. In recent times, the demands for housing itself began to impact on beaches through sand mining for concrete and road making and cutting trees for timber.

The rapid exploitation of the land was William Young's agenda as he argued in 1795 for the removal of the Caribs, and continued with a thrust toward development that had for long failed to consider the negative impact on the environment. It is only in very recent times that environmental issues have been put higher on this developmental agenda because of serious questions about the traditional approach to development. Efforts to focus on a more harmonious relationship between humans and the environment which came out of the 1972 Stockholm Conference on the Human Environment had been clearly indicated earlier in the 1946 Agricultural Policy.[26] The 1992 West Indian Commission recommended taking the West Indian Colonies into the twenty-first century, and was struck by major threats to their preservation despite the presence of legislation dating as far back as the 1940s in many countries. Interestingly, in St. Vincent and the Grenadines, such legislation and issues surrounding them were on the public agenda since the eighteenth century, just as a number of chapters in this book, including Richard Grove's, have clearly shown.

In some respects, the 1991 conference that gave birth to this publication was also an occasion to highlight the need for continuing environmental education and to keep environmental matters on the national agenda, in an era, described by the former Prime Minister of St.Vincent and the Grenadines as the 'Decade of the Environment'. The historical literature of this country is replete with concerns and issues related to the forest in the context of a long struggle between planters and peasants, between those owning large acreages of land and those seeking to own land. To some extent, this continues to be a story of gardens in the bush.

Notes

1   *An account of the Black Caribs of the Island of St. Vincent.* Compiled from the papers of Sir William Young, first published in 1795, Cass and Co. Ltd. pp. 21–22

2   John Davy. *The West Indies Before and Since Slave Emancipation.* London, 1971. pp. 166–167.

3   Alexander Anderson. *Geography and History of St. Vincent, West Indies.* Edition transcribed by Richard and Elizabeth Howard, and republished in 1982.

4   Lansdown Guilding. *An Account of the Botanic Garden of the Island of St.Vincent.* Glasgow, Griffin & Co, 1825.

5   *Report Upon Forests of St. Vincent.* Indian Forest Dept., London, 1886. Reprinted in *The Sentinel* newspaper, St. Vincent, April 8, 1888.

6   Anderson. p. 34.

7   Ibid., p. 37.

8   Adrian Fraser. *Peasants and Agricultural Labourers in St. Vincent and the Grenadines, 1899–1951.* Ph.D thesis. University of Western Ontario, 1987. p. 156.

9   W. K Marshall, ed. *The Colthurst 'Journal.* KTO Ltd., 1977. p. 170–1.

10   Ibid., p. 171.

11   Hooper. 1886.

12   Fraser. 1987. p. 111

13   *The Times.* Kingstown, August 17, 1940.

14   For example, *The Investigator*, February 8, 1936; *The Times*, September 10, 1938.

15   *S.V.A Agriculture Department Annual Report, 1938.* Appendix 2; Fraser, 1987. p. 111.

16   Minutes of the Legislative Council, June 28, 1945.

17   Fraser. 1987. p. 125.

18   Bernard Gibbs. *A Plan of Development for the Colony of St.Vincent.* Adopted by the St.Vincent Development Company, 1947. p. 250.

19   Gibbs. p. 250.

20   Gibbs. Appendix 2.

21   Government of the United Kingdom. *An Economic Survey of the Colonial Territories, 1951.* Vol .iv. The American and West Indian Territories, St. Vincent. p. 26.

22   Ibid.

23   Gibbs. p. 250.

24   Ibid., p. 254.

25   Gibbs, Appendix M, p.295

26   *The West Indian Commission Report, Barbados.* 1992. p. 217.

10 Recent Studies of the Kings Hill Forest Reserve on St. Vincent

Michael Kidston, Jorge O. Trevin, Kenneth P. Rodney, Amos Glasgow and Nigel Weekes

This chapter is a combination of two kinds of history: The first, of the physical boundaries of Kings Hill over a two-hundred-year period, and second, a history of environmental change from 1945 to 1990. These two histories suggest that despite great pressure (no less pressure than on nearby Crown forests), the Kings Hill forest has endured rather well. Its endurance is probably a result of the legislation created to protect the reserve plus the public's respect for Kings Hill. These two factors together have resulted in success, in terms of environmental value and preservation. In the first part of the chapter we emphasize the surveyor's history of the Hill, and in the second we document the actual changes in vegetation in this subtropical moist forest after 1945.[1]

A surveyor's perspective on the Kings Hill history

A study of the surveys of Kings Hill Reserve reveals one aspect of the history of this important ecological area: namely, challenges to its borders and the general endurance of the Reserve's original boundaries. The original Kings Hill legislation, passed by the Assembly on February 9, 1791, and given Royal Assent by Governor Seton on April 1, 1791, directed that William Urquhart and/or Alexander Ramsey should survey the boundaries of Kings Hill within three months of the publication of the Act.[2] Attached to copies of the Kings Hill legislation in the St. Vincent Court Registry is a plan of the survey, signed by W. Urquhart and dated June 5, 1791. It shows the "King's Road" passing through the Southerly portion of the Reserve in identical location and configuration as the Windward Highway is found today. The area of the Reserve in 1791 was determined to 22 hectares (54 acres).

The next survey plan of Kings Hill (Plan G216 in the present Survey Department filing system) was done in October of 1808, by Joseph Billinghurst, Crown Colony Surveyor. Mr. Billinghurst had discovered two small parcels of land, registered in the patent office, that had been granted to Michael Stubbs in 1774 but which had been inadvertently included within the 1791 Kings Hill boundaries. Plan G216 shows the location of these parcels, identifies some clearing and crops along the Northerly and Westerly boundaries of the Reserve, and also shows Carapan Road near the Northerly part of Kings Hill, and cutting through a small portion of it.

According to a note on plan G219, Mr. Billinghurst visited Kings Hill in March, 1812, along with Dr. Young and James D. Questell, acting as a Committee of the House of Assembly. They inspected the lands previously granted to Michael Stubbs, as well as some areas along the Northerly boundary that had been cleared. They proposed to relinquish claim to one of the two alienated parcels, and to exchange approximately 0.53 hectares (1.3 acres) of cleared land on the North boundary for the second parcel of Mr. Stubbs' property – a parcel which lay at the Easterly point of the Reserve and was still wooded. Mr. Billinghurst surveyed the boundary adjustments in June, 1815, with the Reserve now containing about 21 hectares (52 acres) [Plan G219]. Clearly the intent was to replenish Kings Hill with wooded land, twenty-one years after it was established.

In 1837, Lieutenant Governor Tyler appropriated 0.47 hectares (1.15 acres) of Kings Hill Reserve, adjoining the highway on the South boundary, for a Parish School to be established by the Church of England. Mr. Billinghurst surveyed this land on January 12, 1837, (Plan G1/84). A thorough search of the Court Registry records from 1809 through 1868 reveals no deed or mention of transfer of land from Kings Hill to the church. No school or access road exists, so the status of this school remains uncertain. Perhaps the idea of diminishing the forest this way was not acceptable to others, even if it pleased the Lieutenant Governor and the Church of England. No school was built.

In October of 1846, Mr. J. T. Foxl, Crown Colony Surveyor, prepared a survey on instruction from Sir John Campbell, Lieutenant Governor, showing encroachments made onto Kings Hill Reserve by adjoining estates (Plan G218). Mr. Foxl found Cubaimarou Estate to have cleared 1.2 hectares (3 acres) in the North and East portions of the Reserve and planted them in cane, Guinea grass and pasture; Diamond Estate had 1.4 hectares (3.5 acres) – including the planned school site – planted in cane and provisions. Perhaps someone was watching out for Kings Hill, and their alarm about encroachment reached the Lieutenant Governor's office.

The record is silent on the state's response to these encroachments, and indeed the next documented survey is nearly 66 years later. Plan G35 is a resurvey of Kings Hill done in 1912. Strangely, a copy of this plan is filed under plan G66 and has a note appended to it by Peter Casuth, Crown Colony Surveyor. In this note, Mr. Casuth states that he had resurveyed the

Reserve in April 1866, and found it to contain 52.8 acres, plus the 1.2-acre school site, making, in all, 54 acres (22 hectares). No copy of Mr. Casuth's 1866 survey plan has been found (the note will have been traced onto plan G35 from his earlier records).

The 1912 resurvey was the last complete resurvey of Kings Hill until the 1990s. The resurvey was done in June, 1912 by Mr. J. Smith, Crown Surveyor (Plan G35). He does not show the school site survey at all, but has shown a strip of land approximately 17 metres (55 feet) wide along the North boundary of the Reserve, containing 0.56 hectares (1.4 acres), as being apparently removed from the Reserve. No reason is given for deleting this area from Kings Hill – occupation and perhaps a monetary inducement by the encroaching parties has been suggested. In any case, several subsequent subdivisions of adjoining lands have used and accepted the 1912 boundaries as erected to define Kings Hill. Similarly the small portion of Kings Hill lying South of the Windward highway, containing approximately 0.08 hectares (0.2 acres), has recently been included in several subdivisions of Diamond Estate land. The effect of these disputed areas that originally belonged to the Reserve is minimal.

In 1991 the St. Vincent Forestry Division resurveyed the Kings Hill Reserve following the boundaries established by plan G35 in 1912. Nine of the thirteen corners marked with concrete pillars were still in place; two more corners had remains of old monuments, one monument was missing; and the thirteenth corner was shown as marked by an old Immortelle tree in 1912 – no sign of this tree was found. The Forest Division reestablished the missing and disturbed corners. There had been very little encroachment by adjoining land users onto the Reserve; on the Northerly boundary a narrow strip of clearing had taken place many years ago, but was covered in bush and small trees. Along much of the Easterly and Southerly boundaries, a bank caused by erosion at the juncture of the natural forest and the cultivated land followed the boundary.

Forest change on Kings Hill from a forester's perspective

Just before the Kings Hill boundaries were resurveyed in 1990, the Forestry Division also made an inventory of 0.405 hectares (1 acre) at the top of the Kings Hill Forest Reserve, the purpose of which was to repeat the methodology and location of a pioneering study carried out forty-five years earlier by J. S. Beard, and thus assess environmental change on Kings Hill. When J. S. Beard carried out this landmark study on the natural vegetation of the Windward and Leeward islands, between 1942 and 1949, he found that there were no longer undamaged examples of original seasonal forests.[3] However, he selected 0.405 hectare (1 acre) on the top of Kings Hill to describe the structure of what he named a semi-evergreen seasonal forest. Beard then commented, 'As there is a well-developed canopy and there are many large mature trees it may be that present structure does not differ much from the original.'[4] Beard worked in the Windward Islands from May, 1945 to April 1946. Growth in seasonal forests is reduced during a dry season that generally lasts, in these islands, from January to May. For all practical purposes, it is assumed that Beard studied Kings Hill in 1945. Forty-five years later, in October, 1990, the St. Vincent Forestry Division repeated the study in a manner that attempted to maximize the validity of direct comparisons with the first inventory. The reserve occupies 21.2 hectares (53 acres) on a 220 metre-high exposed hill on the windward or east side of St. Vincent, about 700 metres from the coast and surrounded by agriculture and pastures. Strong constant winds off the sea shape and slightly bend the exposed trees. A soil profile was taken on a side of the hill during a countrywide soil survey.[5] The soil is a dark brown loam of friable consistence, with abundant organic matter, changing toward a dark brown sandy clay loam at 30 centimetre depth and a yellowish red sandy clay loam at 45 centimetre depth. Parent material is pebbly agglomerate.

Average annual precipitation in the area is 1739 millimetres as registered in nearby hamlet called Rivulet for the period 1971–1989, and mean annual temperature is around 26.7°C. This last value corresponds to Kingstown, some six kilometres away from the reserve on the south coast of the island.[6] No meteorological station collects temperature data in the Kings Hill area, but using temperature and latitude values, the mean annual biotemperature was estimated, as suggested by Holdridge, to be 23.8°C.[7] Thus, the reserve falls into the Subtropical Moist Forest Ecological Life Zone.[8] In the Caribbean, this ecological zone generally allows high yields for a wide variety of land use systems, such as intensive food production on the flats, forage production on the moderate slopes, and tree crops on steep slopes.[9] For this reason, human activity is an ever-present characteristic on the landscape of this ecological zone.

Methodology

Beard laid out and described a one acre quadrat section 'at the very top of the hill', roughly a 80 metre by 50-metre rectangle.[10] Beard measured all the trees larger than one foot diameter in his plot, and tallied them into classes. He also made observations on the vegetation found on the plot and the slopes outside the quadrat section. There is no evidence that Beard measured individual tree heights, although he made general statements on canopy heights. The 1990 study utilized the same minimum diameter in the main plot, but the trees were not grouped into diameter classes for inventory purposes. Every tree was computed individually. All trees of five centimetres minimum diameter were measured, numbered and marked with aluminium tags.

In order to know the forest on the rest of the reserve better, two strips of continuous plots, one windward and one leeward, were inventoried in 1990, following the recently developed standard procedure for forest inventory in St. Vincent. Several tree heights were measured both in the main and hillside plots. Diameters of two figs (*Ficus citrifolia*) with high buttresses were measured 30 centimetres above the end of the buttress. The 1990 study attempted to obtain more measured data than those collected in 1945, while at the same time making direct comparisons possible. The 1945 and 1990 one-acre plots are unlikely to coincide in their exact location; nevertheless they certainly overlap and are identical in size. Comparative studies considering certain community parameters, like number of species, should not overlook sample size and location area, in order to avoid sampling biases.[11] While it is understood today that such large plots are not the most efficient way to obtain forest information, it was decided that making specific values comparable was more important than sampling efficiency.

Comparing the 1945 and 1990 studies

The top of the hill is today covered by a forest whose dominant, upper layer has as most common species: mastwood (*Mastichodendrum foetidissimum*), penny piece (*Pouteria multiflora*), and locust (*Hymenaea courbaril*). They are the emergent trees, with heights reaching more than 22 metres, and up to 26 metres in the case of one locust. This discontinuous upper layer forms a closed canopy in combination with a contiguous horizon of lower trees whose crowns develop at 14 to 18 metres. They are mainly: loblolly (*Gunpira fragrans*), gumbo limbo (*Bursera simaruba*), pods doux (*Inga fagifolia*), ironwood (*Chrysophyllum argenteum*), fig (*Ficus citrifolia*), sweetwood (*Lauraceae*), bitter ash (*Picrasma antillana*), and young trees of boardwood (*Simarouba amara*). Grigri palms (*Aiphanes erosa*) are found immediately under this second layer, reaching 11 to 14 metres in height. The shrub layer, containing shrubs and small trees under eight metres high, principally includes: bois agouti (*Guarea glabra*), black plum (*Guarea guidonia*), wild coffee (*Faramea occidentalis*), and small individuals of penny piece, sweetwood, ironwood and loblolly.

Ground vegetation consists of: *Odontonema nitidum*, large amounts of pods doux seedlings, a 'bamboo grass' (all of them also found by Beard) and seedlings of trees and shrub species, notably wild coffee, penny piece and locust (*Hymenae courhanie*).[12]

The largest diameter measured in 1990 is 106.8 centimetres for a locust tree. Beard registered the largest diameter in the 82.4 centimetre class, also for a locust tree. This shows a significant difference in maximum diameter for both plots, and also suggests that both measurements may correspond to the same tree. Likewise, maximum tree height in the 1990 plot is 26 metres, measured on the same locust tree. Beard, who did not register individual heights, quotes in his work 21.3 metres (70 feet) as maximum canopy height at Kings Hill. There is a reduction in the number of species for trees above minimum diameter. Twenty-one species were recorded in 1945 and nineteen species in 1990. Only single trees of new species were recorded in the plot in 1990, and two fairly well represented species of the 1945 plot were absent in 1990. They are wild coffee (which was, however, observed in the shrub layer and recorded in the subplots) and *Brosimum alicastrum*.[13]

For the hillside plots outside the one-acre quadrat, the results were significantly different on the windward and leeward sides.[14] On the leeward side, the taller trees are locusts (*Hymenae courhani*) and boardwoods with 17 to 18 metre heights. Forest composition is similar to that of the top, and this is common to all the layers, including ground vegetation. Shoemaker's bark (*Byrsonima coriacea*) and wild orange (*Swartzia simplex*) are found in the understory together with wild coffee and pods doux. On the third 50 metre-long plot, and bordering on private land, the forest continues. Here, boardwood, gumbo limbo and loblolly share the high canopy, and some Cliricidia trees indicate that cultivated land is close.

On the windward side, the trees are lower. Broken tops and small disturbances are more frequent, and at more than 50 metres from the top the emergent trees are not higher than 14 metres. Grigri palms are frequent and share the upper discontinuous layer with gumbo limbo, mastwood, bois agouti, pods doux, and locust. Tree heights are even lower toward the east and the bottom of the hill.

Beard did not make a detailed description of the forest at the sides of the hill, and did not discriminate windward and leeward sides in his brief account. However, at least two differences can be established between the 1945 and 1990 descriptions. One of them is the current absence of white cedar (*Tabebuia pallida*) on the slopes, a pioneer species that was part of the closed forest in 1945. The other is the generally absent 'large down or open patches' observed by Beard, with one exception – a clearing found down on the windward slope suggesting illegal agriculture in the reserve several years ago. The old opening is now covered by shrubs (*Piper sp.*), bamboo grass and young individuals of various trees. Human intervention on the reserve seems to be less today than what it was in 1945. In addition to the mentioned clearing, indications of human activity within the reserve boundaries are very little and limited to sporadic holes left on the hillside by people digging for wild yams, the suggestions of harvesting of small poles, and slight evidence of occasional recreational use of the top of Kings Hill.

These results permit a significant conclusion. At least two major inferences may be drawn. The first is that larger and probably more frequent preceding disturbances were closer in time to the 1945 study than to the 1990. The second inference is that the forest at the top of the hill has evolved from a building phase in 1945 to a current mature phase. Human intervention on the reserve seems to be less today than what it was in 1945.

Beard mentioned patches and disturbances on the sides of the hill at a degree that fortunately is not found today on Kings Hill. Also, in the description of the 'more or less undisturbed-looking' top of the reserve, he stated that the irregularly spaced dominant trees tended to occur in groups. Those groups are not apparent today. This means that gaps larger than those normally caused by single dead trees falling had a more direct effect on stand structure and composition in 1945. Beard seems to have found in 1945 a forest with an 'intermediate disturbance'[15] regime, in regard to both frequency and size of gaps formed. The disturbances were not so large or frequent as to allow a relative abundance of trees of colonizing species. But their size and frequency were enough to keep succession at a middle point in several patches of the forest. With disturbances becoming smaller and more sporadic after 1945, the small gaps were filled by shade-tolerant tree species.

This hypothesis of forest change in Kings Hill is corroborated by the results of the old and new studies. Particularly relevant for this interpretation are the direct observations of the level of forest disturbances in both cases, the reduction in the number of species of tallied trees, the changes undergone in species frequency, and dominancy, and the current abundance in the understory of tree species of the main canopy.

The disturbances observed during the two studies were already discussed. The reduction in number of species of tallied trees from 21 to 19 species is consistent with the higher diversity expected at the earlier intermediate stage in succession.[16] The changes in species frequency and dominance are significant. Today, the four most numerous species are climax species with one or more characteristics of typical primary species such as shade tolerance and large, less copious seed. In 1945, the two most frequent species were grigri and bois agouti. Today, both of them are more frequent on the windward slope of the reserve. Grigri is the most abundant species in this area marked by windthrow disturbances. Finally, the abundance of offspring of the dominant trees in the understory is consistent with a primary forest where gaps are small and infrequent. Small gaps and microsites that may be associated to them favour the growth of pre-existing shade-tolerant seedlings.[17]

Future changes in the forest at the top of the hill are difficult to anticipate due to the complexities of gap-phase dynamics. However, the forest is expected to continue evolving toward lower species diversity as long as disturbances continue being both small and infrequent. Species unable to establish themselves in heavy shade or small light gaps will go locally extinct in this scenario. This is unlikely to continue indefinitely, though. Hurricanes or windstorms will produce larger gaps sometime in the future. Also, the size of some individual trees that reach old age might produce larger gaps even in cases of single tree falls. The question at that time will be: to what extent will forest regeneration and further diversity be influenced by the small size and decreasing isolation of the reserve?

Afterword

The boundaries of Kings Hill and complexity of its forest remained relatively undisturbed in 2001. However on the area surrounding Kings Hill, the quiet landscape is being transformed.[18] Since 1998 houses and small farming estates have been developed in the wooded areas below the Hill, separated from the reserve only by the Windward Highway. Attendant environmental problems have emerged, including quarrying, removal of sand, and new problems such as how to dispose of solid waste in the area. In face of these new pressures can the Kings Hill forest be protected in the future, and how?

We suggested at the beginning of this chapter that the Kings Hill forest has endured not only because of legislation and enforcement, but because people have voluntarily observed the law. This popular compliance could be a result of growing environmental awareness – thanks to the efforts of community groups in the area, like JEMS. The Forestry Department seems to agree that the protection of the forest – and the broader issue of the island's environmental management – can be achieved through environmental education in schools, and alliance-building with interest groups in the St. Vincent community. Young people are currently taught about the effects of deforestation and the benefits of integrated forest development, but there is more to be done to extend government communication with special interest groups to develop effective strategies for safeguarding St. Vincent's forests and watersheds. The Forestry Division has thus embarked on a project to do just this kind of alliance-building over the next six years – resulting in an "environmental management" working document for St. Vincent. The project will include a resurvey of the Kings Hill forest, using the 1990 and 1945 methodology. It appears that Kings Hill forest growth and change is to play an important role for a long time to come.

In conclusion, the Kings Hill forest has evolved and matured. This has been possible because, as the resurvey has shown, there has been very little encroachment by adjoining land uses onto the Reserve. After 45 years of relatively undisturbed growth, the Kings Hill forest increased in height, base area per tree and diametre range. It decreased in species richness and trees per unit area, and generally evolved from a building phase to a current mature phase. Located in the Subtropical Moist Forest Life Zone of the life zone system, one of the most intensively used life zones of the world, lies a precious fairly undisturbed tract of forested land. In 2035, forty-five years from 1990, what will a restudy show? We hope this future study is done.

Notes

1 Both these studies were undertaken as part of the Forestry Project of St. Vincent and the Grenadines, 1988–92, and funded by the Canadian International Development Agency. The authors all participated in that project.

2 Government of St. Vincent, 2 Apr. 1791. Kings Hill Enclosure Ordinance. 1926 Rev. Ed. in K. H. C. Alleyne (Ed.). *The Laws of St. Vincent*, Vol IV. Government Printer, Kingstown, St. Vincent, 1970. pp. 2393–6.

3 J. S. Beard. The natural vegetation of the Windward and Leeward Islands. In *Oxford Forestry Memoir* 21, 1949. This is the same John Beard who worked in Dominica as described by Honychurch's Chapter 2.

4 Ibid. For a more complete account of Beard and 1990 the forest survey see: Jorge O. Trevin et al. Forest change in a subtropical moist forest of St. Vincent, West Indies: the King's Hill Forest Reserve, 1945–1990. *Commonwealth Forestry Review*. vol. 72(3). 1993.

5 J. Watson, J. Spector and T. Jones. *Soil and land use surveys, no. 3*: St. Vincent. Imperial College of Tropical. Agriculture, Regional Research Centre, University of the West Indies, St. Augustine, Trinidad, 1958.

6 R. A. Birdsey, P. L. Weaver and C. F. Nicholls. The forest resources of St. Vincent, West Indies. In *USDA Forest Service Research Paper* S0–229, Southern Forest Experiment Station, New Orleans, Louisiana, 1986.

7 L. R. Holdridge. *Ecología basada en zonas de vida*. Instituto Interamericano de Ciencias Agrícolas, San José, Costa Rica, 1979.

8 More complete site-specific temperature information would help to define whether the reserve is close to or on a tropical transition of that zone. St. Vincent lies within the hurricane belt and averages one hurricane every 25 years. Severe storms or hurricanes struck the island in 1780, 1830, 1886, 1898, 1921, 1967 and 1980.

9 J. J. Ewell, and J. L. Whitmore. The ecological life zones of Puerto Rico and the U.S.

Virgin Islands. *USDA Forest Service Research Paper* ITF–18, Institute of Tropical Forestry, Rio Piedras, Puerto Rico, 1973.

10   Unfortunately, this plot was not marked nor tied. The study team established and inventoried, in October, 1990, a plot of identical dimensions. It was not difficult to ensure a significant, yet unquantifiable, overlap with the original plot, given the topography of the hill. The flat top of the reserve is a narrow strip oriented east-west, roughly some one hundred metres long and twenty metres wide. This flat top gently decreases in altitude toward the west (six percent slope). The main axis of the 1990 study plot runs east-west on the top of the hill. The northern slope of the plot falls 32 percent on the east side and 35 percent on the west side. The southern slope falls 76 percent on the east side and 32 percent on the west side of the plot. Thus, approximately one third of the plot area is relatively flat, the rest is steep or moderately steep terrain. The new plot was tied to Trigonometric Station 379 VS, a concrete monument located at 25.90 metres on a 257° 22' bearing from the middle point of the plot's west side. It is planned to mark the four corners of the plot permanently.

11   R. E. Ricklefs. *Ecology*. Chiron Press, Portland, Oregon. 1976.

12   The 1990 one acre plot at the top of the hill contained 122 trees larger than the 9.7 centimetre minimum diameter at breast height. This represents 301 trees per hectare. Basal area per hectare is 27.7 metres and average quadratic diameter is 34.2 centimetres. By comparing the 1945 and 1990 plots, the 1990 plot registers 0.7 percent more basal area per hectare, and substantially more basal area per tree (24.6 percent) and mean quadratic diameter (11.8 percent). On the other hand, it shows a 19.2 percent reduction in the number of trees. All values refer to trees larger than 9.7 centimetres dbh.

13   'I highly respect Beard but I always had doubts about his mentioning of that species in Kings Hill. I never found that tree in SVG. I cannot say conclusively that this tree does not exist today in the island, in fact I have the vague idea that Amos Glasgow pointed to me "that is a *Brosimum alicastrum* tree" during a walk on Colonarie, and that he did it in that way, using the Latin name. The forest inventory made by Ken Rodney and the Division never found that species, which I know exists in Mexico and Cuba. The fact is that I do not know whether that species exists today in SVG, and in any case its local name is unknown or has been lost. In conclusion, it would not make sense to write a local name from outside St. Vincent, given the high number of local names for the Caribbean species and their close relationship with the local places and islands.' [Jorge Trevin]

14   For a brief taxonomy, see: Jorge Trevin et al. Forest change in a subtropical moist forest of St. Vincent, West Indies: the King's Hill Forest Reserve, 1945–1990. *Commonwealth Forestry Review*. vol. 72(3). 1993. The four 0.01 hectare subplots showed that approximately 625 additional trees per hectare may be found in the 5 to 9.7 centimetres dbh category. This is around twice the number of trees larger than 9.7 centimetres dbh. Thus, the total number of trees larger than five centimeters is estimated to be around nine hundred per hectare at the top of the hill. Most of the small trees inventoried in the subplots were species found in the higher layers: penny piece, sweetwood, ironwood and loblolly. Four species absent in the upper layers were tallied in the subplots: wild coffee, trumpet tree (*Cecropia peltata*), mahoe (*Daphnosis americana*) and bastard fiddlewood (*Vitex divaricata*). For each of these last three species, however, only one specimen was tallied.

15   J. H. Connell. Diversity in tropical rain forests and coral reefs. *Science 199*, 1302–10. 1978.
     J. H. Connell. Tropical rain forests and coral reefs as open non-equilibrium systems.

In Anderson, R. M., Turner, B. D. And Taylor, L. R. (Eds.), *Population Dynamics*. Blackwell Scientific Publications, Oxford, 1979. pp. 141–63.

16 J. H. Connell. Tropical rain forests and coral reefs as open non-equilibrium systems. In Anderson, R. M., Turner, B. D. And Taylor, L. R. (Eds.), *Population Dynamics*. Blackwell Scientific Publications, Oxford, 1979. pp. 141–63.

17 T. C. Whitmore. Tropical rain forest dynamics and its implications for management. In Gomez-Pompa, A., Whitmore, T. C. and Hadley, M. (Eds.), *Rain forest regeneration and management*, Man and the Biosphere Series Vol. 6, UNESCO, Paris, 67–89. 1991.

18 The Afterword to this chapter is based on conversations with Nigel Weekes, when he was Chief of the Forestry Division, Saint Vincent & the Grenadines, in April, 2001. [Editors].

11 'Bush', 'Garden' and 'Mountain' on the Leeward Coast of St. Vincent and the Grenadines, 1719–1995

Hymie Rubenstein

The most important environmental resources in St. Vincent and the Grenadines have always been what rural folk call 'bush' and 'garden'. Both terms have a variety of overlapping meanings. 'Bush' sometimes refers to remote and/or high altitude Crown lands still in their pristine or near-pristine state of vegetation. The term is also used to describe privately owned holdings located in easily accessible areas, which have reverted to wilderness because of years of neglect. 'Garden' is sometimes used as a verb (as in 'He does garden that piece of land') and sometimes as a noun. When used as a noun, it usually refers to a plot of land that is currently under intensive or extensive cultivation regardless of its locale or whether it is situated on publicly or privately held land. Less often, a garden refers to the entire piece of land that is owned or operated by an individual regardless of whether it contains any standing crops or not (as in 'She na go to she garden for years'). Accordingly, a garden may be a small patch of cultivated land situated on Crown lands far removed from the bulk of gardens located near villages or other concentrated sites of human habitation. Conversely, a long uncultivated piece of privately owned land situated just outside the boundaries of a village may be 'in high bush' due to the overseas residence of its owner but still sometimes referred to as a garden.

In the long, narrow coastal valleys of the Western (or Leeward) side of the mainland of St. Vincent island, bush and garden are mediated by a third term, 'mountain'. Mountain is implicitly contrasted with 'village', the face-to-face compact settlements ranging in size from a few hundred to a few thousand people where most leeward people live, and its flat, low elevation environs. Since most, but not all leeward villages are seaside communities, mountain generally refers to the increasingly hilly and rugged regions situated inland from the many coastal communities that dot the Western side of St. Vincent. Since 'mountain' is a place rather than a type of land use or form of ownership, mountain lands may be either in bush or in garden and they may be either privately or publicly held. Still, given that so much arable land held by smallholders (peasant cultivators owning or working under five acres of land) on the leeward coast is 'in the mountain', the three terms are often used interchangeably as in 'He gone a bush/garden/mountain to plant some peas.'

My aim is to examine the shifting historical and complex contemporary interface between bush, garden and mountain on the leeward coast of St. Vincent from the first permanent European settlement in 1719 to my last ethnographic field trip to the island in 1995. Because the unfolding of historical events and socio-economic processes even in the lone domain of the use of land resources in such a small island like St. Vincent are exceedingly diverse and complex, especially when a time span of almost 300 years is being considered, the focus of this paper is on a single locale, Leeward Valley (a pseudonym), on the south-central leeward coast. Since the limited amount and fragile nature of agricultural land in the valley renders its sustainable use problematic, particular attention is paid to its curious underuse – by the presence of so much coastal and mountain land 'in high bush' – over the past few decades by the inhabitants of Leeward Village (also a pseudonym), the large seaside community of 2,300 people at the foot of the valley.

The people of Leeward Village are at the centre of the complex nature and use of garden, bush and mountain land. Despite considerable adversity, they have always exhibited an ability to prevail, if not prosper. Adversity has come in many forms. The country has had more than its share of devastating natural disasters – volcanic eruptions, hurricanes and droughts.[1] Social and economic constraints have included forced bondage under slavery, the oppression of ill-paid estate labour, the exploitation of colonialism, and the marginalization of Third World poverty. The use of land resources has been a crucial 'mode of resistance' to these natural and human forces, part of the creative attempt to shape a new way of life in the face of considerable hardship.[2]

Thus the underuse of potentially arable land should not be interpreted to devalue the importance of land in general or the work ethic of the people in particular. As elsewhere on the leeward coast, bush/garden/ mountain are critically important to the lives of many Leeward Villagers, including those who not presently engaged in agrarian effort. The land is a place to hunt and gather wild produce; a locale for either intensive or extensive plantation and peasant cultivation to satisfy home, community, national, regional, and international needs; the site of a variety of valued fruit trees; a place to temporarily escape the noise and congestion of face-to-face village confinement; an outlet for capital investment, sometimes even land speculation; and a means to acquire the prestige and semi-economic security of owning a piece of real property.

Even in periods of diminished or declining use, garden and bush land have involved the cultivation of many crops and the culling of a multiplicity of forest products having home use and cash-sale value. The main plantation and/or peasant cash crops have been coffee, tobacco, spices, sugar cane, cacao, cotton, arrowroot, bananas, coconuts, starchy tubers, dozens of leafy vegetables, and marijuana. Many of these have also formed an important part of the diet of many peasant households. The mountain has also yielded other important resources: firewood for cooking; hardwoods for house and furniture construction; and wild plants for medicinal purposes.

Despite the importance of bush/garden/mountain, there is a curious environmental contradiction in Leeward Valley, a contradiction that is mimicked in many parts of the Caribbean. On the one hand, garden land is limited in amount and fragile in nature, features that render its sustainable use problematic. On the other, much of the privately held garden land is in 'high bush' and is used only to harvest tree fruits or to pasture cattle, sheep and goats.

This contradiction is best seen as the unfolding of events and processes in both the valley and the larger island-society during several identifiable historical periods: (a) French yeoman cultivation, 1719–1763; (b) large-scale plantation cultivation and slave gardening, 1764–1838; (c) estate economic deterioration and the rise of semi-peasant farming, 1839–1905; (d) declining estate cultivation and mature small-farming, 1906–1959; (e) the end of the estates and the decline of peasant gardening, 1960–1995; and (f) marijuana farming, 1971–1995.

French yeoman cultivation, 1719–1763

St. Vincent received its first European settlers in 1719 when a small group of French small holders from nearby Martinique began working lands on the leeward coast of the main island purchased or leased from the native Carib inhabitants.[3] Leeward Valley may have been among the first of the areas settled by these cultivators. Situated between lateral spurs of hills branching off from the island's north-south mountain range and bisected by a swift but narrow, rock-strewn stream, Leeward Valley contains nearly 4,000 acres, counting hilltop and immediately adjacent regions as well as the primary and secondary forested Crown lands located high on the mountain sides. Only 30 to 40 percent of this area is suitable for intensive cultivation. From a broad, flat foot and placid black sand Leeward Bay, the valley extends backward and upward an increasingly rugged three miles. These local physical features – level valley floor, protected bay, freshwater stream – are also shared by many other leeward locales and account for their European settlement and the use of their agrarian resources.[4]

Though agricultural production was limited – most French cultivators owned only a handful of slaves and only a few farms exceeded 100 acres in size – the cocoa, tobacco, coffee, and other food items and spices grown for the overseas French market supported about 100 of what Mintz has called 'early yeomen'.[5]

Large-scale plantation cultivation and slave gardening, 1764–1838

After English settlers began occupying the valley following the signing of the Treaty of Paris in 1763, which transferred St. Vincent and the Grenadines (hereafter referred to by its local acronym SVG when this label applies to the entire nation state rather than to the main island of St. Vincent) to Britain, some three-quarters of the French small farmers voluntarily left or were forced off the island. The twenty-five or so who remained where obliged to either buy back their holdings or rent land from the new British colonists or the Crown. The twenty-nine holdings into which the valley was divided by 1776 totaled 1,209 acres, for an average size of 40 acres, and were held by seven owners, nineteen renters, and an unknown number of 'poor settlers'.[6]

The period between British occupation of the valley and Emancipation in 1838 was marked by the consolidation of most of the small holdings into a few large ones, the continuing forcing out of the French, and the conversion from mixed farming to monocrop sugarcane cultivation. Small farming was incompatible with commercial sugar production and by 1827 the consolidation of smaller holdings had long been completed. The valley now contained only four distinct plantations totaling 1,175 acres.[7]

The economic prosperity that prompted this consolidation was short-lived and SVG's brief flirt with real plantation prosperity lasted a mere 30 to 40 years. The rapid expansion in Vincentian sugar production during the last third of the eighteenth century began to give way to stable outputs and declining profits during the first third of the nineteenth. Overproduction of British West Indian sugar, combined with competition from cheaper sources in the region, produced both a glut in the English market and a growing metropolitan unwillingness to maintain the artificial colonial tariff and trade preferences that had been put in place during the early days of the industry.[8]

The 740-acre Leeward Valey Estate, always the largest plantation in the valley, is a good illustration of the resultant process of plantation indebtedness. Though located on flat lands in the valley, ideally situated for intensive sugar cane cultivation, the estate gradually began accumulating liabilities during the last part of the eighteenth and early part of nineteenth century. By 1813 its absentee owner was obliged to mortgage the estate, its slaves, and all its sugar output to a London merchant company as security for payment of the debt.[9]

Field slaves formed the bulk of the island population during the plantation slavery era. On Leeward Valley Estate in 1780, this included most of its 137 slaves. Unlike places like nearby Barbados where subsistence cultivation was discouraged because nearly all lands were suitable for highly-profitable sugar cane cultivation, the large pockets of steeply sloped but arable secondary lands in St. Vincent allowed the slaves to reduce plantation expenses by supplying nearly all their own foodstuffs. With seeds and plants provided by the plantation they grew produce in small gardens behind their houses in the slave quarters and in larger 'provision-grounds' on distant mountain lands ill suited for commercial sugar cultivation. The house gardens contained a variety of subsistence and cash crops, most of which are still grown by peasants today: watermelons, beans, peas, cabbages, turnips, carrots, tomatoes, pumpkins, christophenes, cucumbers, various herbs and spices, and such starchy tubers as cassava, tannias and arrowroot.[10] The more distant mountain gardens contained the main subsistence crops, plantains and bananas, as well as yams, eddoes, tannias and maize. Again, all of these crops are still grown today in much the same way by the direct descendants of these slaves. Some vegetables were cultivated by the slaves only for sale at the market, and if there were a surplus, even food staples might be sold there, another practice that still continues.

Slaves also raised stock – chickens, ducks, pigs and goats – for home use and market sale and many even sold fish caught in the streams that passed through their estates. Those living on plantations close to the capital, Kingstown, sold animal feed, wood and European vegetables to its residents. Though the slave codes prohibited it, some slaves made and sold charcoal; others gained access to cash by hiring themselves out to 'head people' – senior slaves – on their own or neighbouring estates; and some also worked as agricultural labourers for other whites during their free time and were paid in cash or in kind. The processing and sale of agricultural crops was an additional source of cash revenue for many slaves. These included farine, a kiln dried oatmeal made from cassava, laundry starch, also made from cassava, and arrowroot starch. Again, all of these activities are still visible today among Leeward Village peasants.[11]

Surplus garden produce, processed food, meat and fish were sold in special slave markets held in Kingstown every Sunday. The disposal of produce took the form of market exchange and barter, the latter involving the swapping of slave goods for '...bread, salt pork, salt beef, mackerel, corned fish, cakes, or other nice things'.[12] Although cash sale has totally replaced barter, once more, this retail trade continues today in the weekday and Saturday markets in the capital.

While the attempt by planters to minimize their costs of production by obliging the slaves to be as self-sufficient as possible placed an additional burden on them, the various extra-plantation activities that they carried out – the unsupervised cultivation of crops, the processing of foodstuffs, the market sale or barter of fruits and vegetables, the rearing of stock, etc. – also pre-adapted them to become a semi-independent peasantry following Emancipation.

This pre-adaptation was also fostered by the four-year apprentice-ship period that preceded full Emancipation in 1838 because the new 'semi-slaves' retained their houses, home and mountain gardens, and continued to grow crops and rear domesticated animals for subsistence use and market sale.[13] It is the skills developed during slavery and apprenticeship that still sustain the small farmers of Leeward Village.

Economic deterioration of big estates and the rise of semi-peasant farming, 1839–1905

A failure to modernize manufacturing techniques, increasing competition from cheaper cane grown elsewhere in the region, steadily declining sugar prices throughout the 1800s, the removal of British tariff protection, and the production of less expensive European beet sugar must have dis-tressed Leeward Valley estates in the same way that it afflicted Vincentian plantations generally during the second half of the nineteenth century.[14] As the sugar industry was slowly dying, a new crop, arrowroot, was beginning to take its place, and there are the remains of several old pro-cessing factories scattered throughout the Leeward Valley. A herbaceous perennial yielding a high quality starch, arrowroot was actually grown and manually processed by Vincentian estate slaves for local domestic sale from at least the early part of the nineteenth century.[15]

The arrowroot boom was no long-term panacea for Leeward Valley estate's economic woes. Owner absenteeism and indebtedness continued and the estate was auctioned in 1849 to another London mer-chant house. It was resold in 1885 to a local Vincentian planter, the first island resident to own it in more than a century.[16] Despite its debts, the estate had steadily increased in size since 1829 because of the ongoing purchase of small adjacent holdings and the illegal *ad hoc* appropriation of Crown lands on upper hillside slopes, and totaled 850 acres when acquired in 1885. After the death of the owner, the estate was auctioned to two Vincentian planters in 1901.

Though Leeward Valley and adjoining estates were chronically in debt and repeatedly sold during the second two-thirds of the nine-teenth century, so tenaciously did the planter class hold onto its prop-erties, regardless of their financial viability, that few valley ex-slaves were able to become freeholders during the first six decades of the post-Emancipation period. By 1899, the valley was divided into only twelve holdings. The smallest eight of these totaled less than 150 acres, or 8.2 per cent of valley acreage: one was 4.5 acres, one was five acres, another was 13 acres, three were 20 acres, one was 25 acres, and one was 40 acres.[17] Moreover, four of these holdings, the 40-acre and the three 20-acre farms, had only been acquired in 1896 when their owner – an individual of mixed racial descent – bequeathed her 100-acre estate to a nephew, a god-daughter, a bookkeeper, and a fourth individual.[18]

The two Vincentian planters who had bought the estate in 1901 promptly resold it to the Crown the next year to provide agricultural land and house-spots for refugees dispossessed by a devastating eruption of the Soufrière volcano in the northern part of the island two months earlier. A block of 450 acres at the remote upper end of the estate was set aside for the emigrants and established valley residents interested in purchasing land of their own. The remaining 400 acres – prime agricultural land on the sloping seaward part of the estate – were sold to an island planter who had spent many years working in the United States and whose father's estate had been destroyed by the 1902 eruption.

In distinction with plantations, there is little data available on the productive activities of Leeward Valley residents. Small peasant farmers for most of this period, and the bulk of the adult population, combined peasant cultivation on patches of estate-owned and Crown mountain land not suitable for large-scale commercial cultivation with wage-labour on the plantations to eke out a precarious living, a material way of life that differed little from slavery. Estate wages were very low, freehold land was nearly impossible to acquire, and alternate sources of work were scarce. For this reason, many Leeward Valley residents migrated to nearby islands like Trinidad in search of higher levels of living and better working conditions.

The catastrophic Soufrière eruption in 1902 challenged plantation hegemony by altering land holding patterns and setting in motion a process that continues today. The cataclysm resulted in the resettlement of several hundred people in Leeward Village. Each family displaced from their North Leeward communities was granted a piece of garden land ranging in size from one-half to just over three acres depending on household size and whether any land had been owned in the ravaged area. In addition, many refugees and native-born villagers bought or were granted extra holdings after the first distribution had been completed. In all, 145 holdings were portioned out between 1902 and 1907.[19] These lands were located in two mountain regions: various blocks towards the head of the valley and a large swathe on top of the long, flat ridge overlooking the southern part of the valley. Far from access roads and sources of water, many of these parcels were steeply graded, poorly drained, or stony. They represented portions of the valley's largest estate that had always been agriculturally peripheral or were never cultivated save as provision grounds for estate workers during and after slavery.

Most people who acquired these plots could not support themselves solely by cultivating them. At most, they continued as semi-peasants, obliged to combine daily or recurrent estate labour with work on their small mountain holdings. Even though their peasant agrarian activities – which also included rearing pigs, chickens, sheep and goats, and manufacturing and selling charcoal – often involved no more than a few hours of work a few days of the week, they should not be discounted. Not only did such efforts supply fruits and vegetables for home use on a regular or seasonal basis, they also supplemented low estate wages through the sale of agricultural surpluses and domesticated animals. In this way the garden in the bush constituted the heart of the household economy.

Declining estate cultivation and mature small farming, 1906–1959

Crops grown on Leeward Valley estates during the early years of the twentieth century were nearly identical to those grown during the latter part of the nineteenth. On Leeward Valley Estate, still the largest property in the valley, despite its reduction to 400 acres, sugar cane continued to be the most important export crop, followed by arrowroot and cotton, the latter introduced in 1902. By 1930, arrowroot and cotton had switched places. Sugar cane was still predominant in both acreage and earnings until 1943 when its cultivation on the main estate stopped due to its unprofitability. Cotton and arrowroot were the primary plantation crops from then until the mid-1950s when they were surpassed by bananas, a crop first introduced in 1954.

This movement from crop to crop reflected the declining fortunes of all Leeward Valley plantations. By the late 1930s, Leeward Valley Estate began to experience financial and other problems from which it never recovered. Plagued by a combination of poor markets and low prices for its produce, difficulties in securing cheap labour during periods of high migration from Leeward Village (to Kingstown, SVG's capital, and to other Caribbean islands), and indifferent management after the owner's death in the late 1940s, the family heirs responded by continuing the practice, begun by their fathers during the 1930s, of selling off estate lands to peasant cultivators. Peasant plots averaged five acres during the early years of this period. Nearly 90 per cent were below this mean and one-third was between one and two acres in size. Most post-Soufrière explosion era purchases of estate lands were made by valley residents through earnings from recurrent or extended wage-labour migration to various Caribbean and circum-Caribbean destinations, a movement that began during the early post-Emancipation period but which picked up dramatically from the 1920s.[20] If these land purchases are lumped together with the earlier post-Soufrière eruption land grants and other purchases made between 1902 and 1907, the result was a dramatic increase in the number of valley freehold parcels to about 300 by 1955, nearly a 30-fold increase since 1899. Like its counterparts throughout the country, Leeward Valley had become a stronghold of mountain peasant cultivation.

Except for sugar cane, which requires an extensive land base, valley farmers grew many of the same cash crops as the estates. Cotton and arrowroot were still being cultivated by valley peasants long after they were abandoned on Leeward Valley Estate, further testimony to their resilience in the face of acute adversity. Starchy roots and tubers – sweet potatoes, yams, tannias, dasheens, eddoes and manioc – have always been grown for both home consumption and market sale by smallholders, regardless of external market conditions. Other fruits and vegetables such as maize, pigeon peas, beans, tomatoes, cabbage, bananas, plantain, cacao, onions, peppers, peanuts and cucumbers have also been regularly planted by many small-farmers. All pieces of land except the smallest have always contained one or more breadfruit, mango, or coconut trees. Except for holdings over three acres, at least half the tubers and tree crops were used for subsistence. Of the surplus root crops, other vegetables, and tree crops, most were sold in the village or in the Kingstown market by the women of the household.

As elsewhere in the island, valley peasant cultivation has always been unmechanized and the main tools have been simple iron hoes, machetes and forks. Unlike the slavery era when men and women were obliged to work together on identical field tasks, peasant cultivation has always been based on a partial division of labour according to sex. Men do most of the land clearing and other preparation for planting such as digging long furrows in the soil, and women do most of the weeding. The sowing of seeds, the planting of cuttings and tuber sections, the manuring of the growing crops, the harvesting of produce are performed by both sexes. Both sexes were not always available in every house for work in the garden; in some cases women alone were heads of the household, and in some of those cases might get help from mature sons.[21]

Dying estates and the decline of peasant gardening, 1960–1995

The approximately ten-year export pre-eminence of bananas, from the mid-1950s to the mid-1960s, was the shortest of any valley cash crop.

On Leeward Valley Estate, reduced to 295 acres by 1971 because of ongoing sales of agricultural plots and house spots of varying size to resident peasant farmers and overseas wage-labour migrants, banana cultivation ended after the destruction of an entire planting by high winds. Arrowroot was abandoned a couple of years later. The entire estate was planted in coconuts in 1969. Most of the trees were struck by disease and coconuts were never a source of estate revenue.

Despite the slow and steady death of the estates as agrarian enterprises, their disproportionate place in the valley land tenure system continued. Even in 1971 the four largest properties still accounted for fully 39 per cent of all valley acreage. The sale of estate lands, especially the continued division of Leeward Valley Estate into one-acre lots and small house spots, continued from the 1970s through the 1990s. Today, the estate has been reduced to less than 100 acres and most of its flat seaside portions are covered with new dwellings built by returning overseas migrants. Leeward Village is more like Leeward Town and former gardens and bush have become covered with concrete.

Small farming, like estate cultivation, in Leeward Valley always has been constrained by severe social, economic and natural forces. So unmanageable have some of these forces been that the result has long been the gross underuse or outright abandonment of arable land. Bush has replaced garden in many parts of the valley. In 1971 the 1,463 acres of valley and neighbouring lands controlled by villagers were divided into 418 separate plots over 0.1 acres held under several forms of freehold, leasehold, and other tenure arrangements. Data based on ethnographic research are available for 222 of these plots totaling 1,074 acres. Of these 222 plots, 137, or 62 per cent, received no annual cultivation during the 1970–71 crop year. In fact, many of them were in 'high bush' barely distinguishable from the natural vegetation on remote Crown lands. The remaining 85 plots totaled 756 acres and contained 108 acres of non-arboreal cultivation. In total, only 10 per cent of the 1,074 acres in the 222 holding sample were being farmed.

The factors accounting for the under-cultivation of valley lands during the late 1960s and early 1970s are complex. Demographic factors included the overseas residence of many landowners and former agricultural labourers; imbalances in the adult sex ratio adversely affecting the traditional division of labour; and an aged land-owning population. Ecological factors involved the distant location of holdings; a steep and rugged topography; soil infertility and erosion; a stony land surface; small holding size making cultivation uneconomical; and a lack of agricultural experience among many landowners. Economic factors included low wages for agricultural labour; insufficient funds for planting; the disappearance of markets for traditional crops and unreliable markets for others; low crop prices; competing wage-labour or self-employment activities; the theft of agricultural crops; and alternate land uses (investment, real estate speculation and animal husbandry). Social factors involved a decrease in labour exchange arrangements and friction between employers and labourers. Finally, ideological factors included an aversion towards agricultural labour, especially among young people.

By 1988, potential valley agrarian acreage had declined to 1,440 acres because of the sub-division and sale of larger holdings, including parts of Leeward Valley Estate, into building sites under 0.1 acres in size. The overall valley acreage was divided into 382 separate plots over 0.1 acres held under several tenure arrangements. Of these 382 plots, 163, or 43 per cent, contained no continuing cultivation. Of the remaining 219 plots, data is available for 204 of them together making up 627 acres of land surface. Of these 627 acres, 202 acres, or 32 per cent, were covered in farm produce. Taking uncultivated and cultivated plots together, only 14 per cent of the 1,408 acres for which there is data were covered in farm produce in the 1987–88 crop year.

Compared to the 1970–71 crop year, there was a substantial increase – from 38 per cent to 57 per cent – in the number of plots of land containing any cultivation. Though there were far fewer idle pieces of land in the valley, the intensity of cultivation – the proportion of the 1,408 acres that was covered in standing crops – was only 14 per cent, hardly a radical increase from the 10 per cent intensity of cultivation observed in the 1970–71 crop year. Once again, much potential garden land was abandoned or near abandoned 'high bush'. Of those who regularly visited their own holdings (or surreptitiously visited other people's holdings), many did so only to cull mature tree fruits or graze one or two cattle, sheep, or goats.

Ganja farming in Leeward Valley, 1971–1995

Despite what appears to be a stable undercultivation of arable land, the Leeward Valley agrarian situation has fundamentally changed over the past 20 years. Although this change has not produced a dramatic increase in traditional cultivation, the transformation has been important nevertheless because it suggests important linkages and priorities in the factors affecting the underuse of valley farmland, on the one hand, and the dynamic and changing relation between garden, bush and mountain, on the other. The alteration has been founded on the production of an illegal crop: marijuana.[22]

In 1970, 30 per cent of the valley adult working population was employed in farming or agricultural wage-labour. In 1988, 25 per cent of the population was thus engaged. Though this suggests a decreased interest in working land as a principal vocation, proportionately more young men are occupied in farming today than in the last few decades. In 1970, 13 per cent of farmers or farm labourers were less than 30 years old; in 1987, this figure was nearly 29 per cent. An important reason for this demographic transformation was the emergence in the mid-1970s of ganja as a new cultigen. On the one hand, marijuana (*Cannabis sativa*) is simply the latest in the long series of valley crops. Like most other plants, it is grown both for home consumption and commercial sale. On the other hand, unlike all other plants that have been met by either government support or indifference, marijuana is an outlawed substance in SVG, involvement with which brings forth severe juridical sanctions. Concomitantly, its planting has been associated with much internecine conflict and crop theft, many police raids and ganja seizures, several imprisonments, and numerous costly fines. But for many poor young village men and youths such deterrents have not been enough to dissuade them from growing marijuana. Confronted with few money-making alternatives and tempted by the potential for very high returns, these individuals willingly have decided to risk imprisonment, personal injury and the destruction or theft of their crops by engaging in the commercial production of ganja. In short, the presence of marijuana, together with a lack of economic alternatives, has encouraged a movement 'back to the land' by dozens of young village males.

Introduced to the valley some time after 1971, ganja has been grown in all locales, on all types of land, under a variety of tenure and labour arrangements, and for different motives.[23] During early years of marijuana cultivation, some teenaged boys were even bold enough to cultivate a few plants in home-based indoor and/or outdoor gardens, in much the same way that many villagers have a small herb or vegetable garden beside their house, a practice that goes back to the days of slavery. These young men were able to do so without much fear of apprehension because the police only slowly became aware of ganja's introduction and spread in SVG from about the mid-1970s.

But most ganja growing has occurred outside of village boundaries on both private and public lands. From Leeward Valley Estate lands bordering the village perimeter to the most remote and barely accessible virgin forest mountain lands, from flat bottom areas near the sea to the highlands jutting out from the island's central mountain range, from owned to rented to Crown lands the ubiquity of marijuana cultivation is testimony to both its hardiness as a plant and to the perseverance and determination of those who grow it. Ganja has been cultivated by single growers, by pairs of farmers, and by teams of up to seven members. Some people grow only marijuana with the intention of marketing the bulk of their crop; others cultivate just a few ganja plants mainly for their own use or to supplement other subsistence and cash crops; still others grow a few subsistence crops while they wait to harvest their main crop of marijuana. A few people who grow little or no marijuana of their own purchase small portions for resale to others.

The first marijuana grower in the community was a middle-aged farmer who obtained some ganja seeds in 1973 from a recurrent labour migrant who had just returned from a season of sugar cane in central Florida. He planted these seeds on his rented piece of distant mountain land.[24] Word of the farmer's marijuana growing efforts was reported to a government agricultural officer who instructed the farmer to destroy the nearly mature plants. Though the farmer complied with this directive, one of his sons and two of his nephews were able to obtain some of the plants' seeds. Second and third generation seeds quickly spread from one grower to another.

At first, most growers raised a handful of plants, mainly for personal use and occasional sale, on concealed scrub portions of their own property or on immediately abutting Crown lands. As the police began to crack down from the late 1970s, as the theft of mature crops became more common, and as more and more people became interested in the market cultivation of the plant, large gardens of an acre or more began to be planted on higher up the mountain. Today, nearly all marijuana cultivation occurs on these remote Crown mountain lands.

Nearly all ganja growers are males. Of the 143 villagers who have at some time tried their hand at marijuana planting, only eight, or less than six per cent, are female. Most of the remaining 135 males are between their late teens and mid-thirties. These 135 males represent over one-quarter of the adult male village labour force and nearly one-half of village male farmers. These are dramatic features of marijuana growing because one-third of village farmers are women and most of those who cultivate only traditional crops are men and women over 35 years of age.

These 135 present and former ganja farmers generally relate differently to garden, bush and mountain than do those who grow only traditional crops. Legal crops are cultivated in readily visible gardens close to access roads; ganja is planted in concealed areas far off the beaten track. Ordinary crops are planted in gardens as close to home as possible to reduce travel time and distance; marijuana is planted as far from the village as possible to reduce the possibility of accidental discovery. Legal crops are cultivated via the traditional sexual division of labour; growing ganja is almost exclusively a male activity. Ordinary farmers visit their plots on a regular basis, returning home after a day's work; ganja farmers 'live with the herb' during the last month or two of cultivation, sleeping in crudely built shacks high in the mountain to protect their precious crop from human predation.

Because they spend much more time there than do traditional farmers, many ganja farmers contrast the mountain to the village, using Rastafarian terminology to refer to the latter as 'concrete'. Accordingly, the village is a place of false Western commercial values and chronic interpersonal conflict to these ganja farmers. The mountain is the place of nature in the raw and of 'peace, love, and harmony'.

Analysis

There is much irony in the underuse of arable land in Leeward Valley, in the transformation from garden to bush of coastal and mountain lands between the last three decades of the eighteenth century and the first five decades of the twentieth century. This is because the overexploitation and ecological degradation of cultivable land and other environmental resources rather than their underuse is the main worry in an era so concerned with sustainable development. SVG is not a West Indian anomaly in this regard. The 'quiet crisis' of agrarian stagnation is widespread in the entire Commonwealth Caribbean and most of its countries are marked by much underused and idle farm land even when agriculture is the mainstay of the economy.[25] This is regrettable because the intensification of agricultural production has long been identified as the primary ingredient in raising the self-reliance of many of the Caribbean islands.[26] In his annual statement for 1980, the President of the Caribbean Development Bank pointed out that:

> For several decades now we in the Caribbean have been talking about our deficient food production and the need to become more self-sufficient in food. It is also well known that we can increase local food production without reducing the volume of traditional agricultural export crops, since both land and labour are available to do both things. One does not have to look far to see that not much has been achieved in this much discussed goal. ...[27]

In fact, the farming situation in SVG has deteriorated between the early 1960s and early 1970s with land devoted to agriculture decreasing by nearly 20 per cent. For a country where most exports are agricultural products, two-thirds of the labour force employed in agriculture, and so much land idle or underused, SVG is surprisingly dependent on imported food.[28] Even the three staples of the diet – wheat and flour products, rice and sugar – are brought to the island, along with most or all locally consumed dairy produce, poultry, grains and cereals.

Under-cultivation is a problem in both the plantation and peasant sectors. Of the 39,475 acres of farmland, only 26,000, or 66 per cent, are suitable for crops and pasture. Of this 26,000 acres, 6,300, or 24 per cent, are idle or underutilized, a situation the World Bank called '… a luxury the country can ill afford'. Much of this acreage has reverted to secondary forest – to extreme mountain bush – another irony in an era so preoccupied with 'saving the forest'. Yet the SVG Development Plan 1986–1988 statement implies another paradox: 'Land is very scarce for both agriculture and non-agricultural use. The demand for suitable land for housing, agriculture and industry significantly exceeds the supply. Given this situation, the efficient use of land is vitally important.'[29] This is paralleled in a Caribbean Conservation Association/Island Resources Foundation 'environmental profile' of SVG:

> One of the most serious threats to sustainable economic growth in the Caribbean is the increasing degradation of the region's natural ecosystems and a concurrent deterioration in the quality of life for Caribbean people. The task of reversing this unfortunate trend requires better knowledge and under-standing of the region's unique environmental problems and the development of appropriate technologies and public poli-cies to lessen and even prevent negative impacts on our frag-ile resource base. The irony of underused and idle lands is no laughing matter in a society where working the soil is the sin-gle most important occupation and farmland the single most important environmental resource. As with soil erosion, such lands 'reduce the amount of land available for growing food, decrease yields and increase the cost of food production'.[30]

Leeward Valley mimics the whole island in regard to all of these issues, including the apparent contradiction between scarce and idle lands. Nearly every landless villager wants some land to plant a garden, build a house, invest overseas earnings, or gain the prestige and economic security of owing a piece of permanent property. But most villagers own no land at all, nor are their prospects for acquiring any property very good given the high price of real estate. Yet the agricultural stagnation characteristic of the large valley estates also marks peasant holdings. Most were either idle or underused in the late 1960s and early 1970s even though with 30 per cent of the Leeward Village adult working population employed in commercial and peasant farming agriculture has always been the single most important valley economic activity.

Overproduction, competition from cheaper sources of supply, the removal of tariff protection, a failure to modernize manufacturing tech-niques, owner absenteeism, poor or disappearing markets, low prices, difficulties in securing cheap labour, and indifferent management have already been mentioned as affecting national and local productivity within the plantation sector. To these may be added the multiplicity of factors affecting peasant production.

The cultivation of ganja in Leeward Village teaches two important lessons about these factors: (1) that some of them are much more important than others, and (2) that the nation's agrarian decline is neither inevitable nor irreversible. These are important considerations because SVG's prospects for sustained economic well-being, albeit at levels far below First World standards, lie in primary agricultural production rather than tourist development or industrialization. This is because there are no important natural resources except for the land itself and because the country's few white sandy beaches – the Caribbean's main tourist attraction – are confined to the ecologically fragile and limited 17-square mile Grenadines, the chain of tiny islands that stretch from the main island to neighbouring Grenada to the south. As for other commercial development, with high wage levels by Third World global standards and with no natural mineral resources of value to the First World, SVG has attracted few overseas industries looking for cheap materials or labour.

Though it would be difficult to envision the long-term viability of an economy based on the production of an illegal substance, the growing of marijuana nevertheless provides important clues about the prioritization of factors affecting legal agricultural production. Crop theft has so frustrated many ganja growers that they have given up planting marijuana. Praedial larceny is often mentioned by community members as a reason for not cultivating traditional crops or restricting cultivation only to certain areas, and the ganja experience suggests that this factor may be more important than is usually thought in agrarian research. Praedial larceny originally meant livestock theft in the Caribbean, but now it refers to ganja theft, though the cultivation itself is not legal. Conversely, with ganja often grown on very distant holdings or barely accessible mountain lands, far from access roads and sources of water, comes the suggestion that these factors may be exaggerated when given as explanations of under-cultivation. So may demographic factors such as the number of potential farmers in a community and the adult sex ratio. The importance of owning the land that is being worked, the size of holdings, and previous agricultural experience may also be less important than is sometimes thought. But what ganja cultivation most clearly shows is that the fundamental factors influencing cultivation are prices and markets. Indeed, together with the desire for marijuana consumption, these features are so fundamental that they have encouraged cultivation among individuals who would not otherwise have engaged in any agrarian activity.

The average sale price of ganja – $EC 300 per cured pound in the 1990s – is some sixty times the peak seasonal price of its nearest licit rivals. At least three new houses, two motor vehicles, a motor boat, and a motorcycle have been acquired from profits from the sale of ganja in this area. Several growers have purchased expensive stereo systems as well. A few men in their early twenties have several thousand dollars in bank savings, an unheard of amount for poor people of that age without overseas migration.

Ganja growing may also have affected community vocational preferences. Based on research conducted on the island during the early seventies, Hourihan suggested that there was '... a widespread aversion towards agricultural work among Vincentian youths ...'[31] and that white-collar work was preferred to any kind of manual labour. In a questionnaire on educational and occupational choice administered in 1970 (before the cultivation of ganja) to nearly 200 children in the Leeward Village primary school, I found that not one student cited agriculture as a desirable activity.[32] Conversely, when asked to name the worst village occupation for men and women, agriculture was ranked second to cleaning streets and repairing roads. But it was not agriculture as such that was impugned. Rather, it was the actual field labour that was seen as arduous, unremunerative and demeaning, and agricultural workers were occasionally referred to by the old slave pejorative, 'field niggers'. In other words, given the physical demands, low status and poor economic return from hoe and cutlass work, whether based on estate employment or independent small-scale farming, most younger people tried to avoid it if they could and accepted nearly any economic alternative that was available. In an almost identical questionnaire administered in the same village school in 1988, the results were somewhat different. While farming was not viewed as a particularly desirable activity, several children did choose it as an ideal job for a man. Conversely, only a few students saw farming as an unsuitable activity, but only for women, and several other jobs were given lower standing. If this reflects a real change in vocational values, I suspect that marijuana production is one of the reasons why. With alternative wage-labour and self-employed economic choices in such short supply and with high potential earnings from ganja, many young men have turned to the land for their livelihood.

Some of this land, especially in more remote or steeply sloped mountain regions, has not been worked for decades or more. Much virgin forestland that has never been farmed is being cultivated as well. While the farming of such lands may have adverse environmental effects, many of those doing so would be unemployed or underemployed except for the alternative of ganja cultivation.[33] This is because without the incentive of marijuana growing young village males would hardly take up farming by choice since the intense efforts and low rewards of small-scale own-account cultivation are well known to them. In short, formerly idle hands are working formerly idle lands.

Ganja cultivation also encourages the cultivation of other crops. 'You can't eat the herb' so that once the decision to begin or expand ganja growing is made other crops are often planted to feed the farmer and his family during the lengthy periods between marijuana sales. Surpluses from this other cultivation are sold or given away, an important consideration in a country where food imports are so high.

But the cultivation of marijuana is illegal and it is therefore difficult to be sanguine about its long-term agrarian effects. Like the other major cash crops in the valley – tobacco, sugar cane, arrowroot, cotton, and bananas – the role of marijuana may be short lived. The United States Drug Enforcement Agency has described SVG '...as the major drug problem in the Organization of Eastern Caribbean States...' and concluded that '...St. Vincent is second only to Jamaica in marijuana production'. The government of SVG has responded to American pressure to combat ganja production by supporting several U.S.-organized helicopter operations in the main ganja growing areas in the densely forested northern part of the island that have resulted in the destruction of millions of marijuana plants and the seizure of hundreds of pounds of cured ganja. As in other countries, including one of the world's largest marijuana producers, the United States itself, such sanctions have been marginally effective at most. Even if it were possible to control production in a country with such a mountainous terrain, so much unsupervised Crown land, and such chronic poverty, ganja's enduring legacy may be that is has fostered a reduction in the stigma attached to leaving the village for the mountain to transform bush to garden. This is a vital consideration in a society whose long-term economic viability can only be assured through agrarian effort.

Notes

1 Bonham C. Richardson. Catastrophes and Change in St. Vincent. *National Geographic Research* 5(1), 1989. pp. 111–125.
2 Sidney W. Mintz. *Caribbean Transformations*. Chicago: Aldine, 1974. pp. 131–145.
3 Thomas Coke. *A History of the West Indies, Containing the Natural, Civil and Ecclesiastical History of Each Island*. Liverpool. 1808. p. 181.
   Charles Shepard. *An Historical Account of the Island of St. Vincent*. London: Ridgway and Sons, 1831. pp. 23–25.
4 Hymie Rubenstein. The Utilization of Arable Land in an Eastern Caribbean Valley. *Canadian Journal of Sociology*, 1(2), 1975. p. 84.
5 Sidney W. Mintz. *Caribbean Transformations*. Chicago: Aldine, 1974. pp. 146–156.
   Charles Shepard. *An Historical Account of the Island of St. Vincent*. London: Ridgway and Sons, 1831. pp. lix–lxvii.
6 Charles Shepard. *An Historical Account of the Island of St. Vincent*. London: Ridgway and Sons, 1831. pp. lix–lxvi.

7   Ibid.
8   Eric Williams. *From Columbus to Castro: The History of the Caribbean, 1492–1969.* London: Andre Deutsch, 1970. pp. 280–290.
    David Lowenthal. *West Indian Societies.* London: Oxford University Press, 1972. pp. 54–55.
9   Hymie Rubenstein. *Coping With Poverty: Adaptive Strategies in a Caribbean Village.* Boulder: Westview Press, 1987. pp. 88–89.
10 A. C. Carmichael. *Domestic Manners and Social Conditions of the White, Coloured, and Negro Population of the West Indies.* 2 volumes. London: Whittaker, Treacher, 1833. pp. 136–137, 162–178.
11 Ibid. pp. 165–166, 177–179, 196, 283, 165–166.
12 Ibid. p. 176.
13 John B. Colthurst. *The Colthurst Journal: Journal of a Special Magistrate in the Islands of Barbados and St. Vincent, July 1835 – September 1838.* Millwood, New York: KTO Press, 1977. pp. 170–171.
14 Sir Alan C. Burns. *History of the British West Indies.* London: Allen and Unwin, 1954. pp. 658–662.
    Eric Williams. *Capitalism and Slavery.* London: Andre Deutsch, 1964. pp. 361–390.
15 Op. cit. A. C. Carmichael. pp. 177–178.
16 Hymie Rubenstein. *Coping With Poverty: Adaptive Strategies in a Caribbean Village.* Boulder: Westview Press, 1987. p. 89.
17 St. Vincent. *Saint Vincent Government Gazette.* Kingstown, St. Vincent: Government Printing Office, 1899.
18 Ibid. p. 91.
19 Ibid. p. 92.
20 Ibid.
21 See also the observations on gender and gardens in Lennox Honychurch's chapter on Dominica.
22 Hymie Rubenstein. Ganja as a Peasant Resource in St. Vincent: A Preliminary Analysis. In *Small Farming and Peasant Resources in the Caribbean.* John S. Brierley and Hymie Rubenstein, eds. 1987. pp. 119–133.
    Manitoba Geographical Studies 10. Department of Geography, University of Manitoba, Winnipeg, Canada, 1988.
    Hymie Rubenstein.. Mirror for the Other: Marijuana, Multivocality, and the Media in an Eastern Caribbean Country. *Anthropologica* 37(2). 1995: pp. 173–206.
    Hymie Rubenstein. Coping With Cannabis in a Caribbean Country: From Problem Formulation to Going Public. *New West Indian Guide* 72(3&4). 1998a: pp. 205–232.
    Hymie Rubenstein. You Na Want Stop. *Anthropology Newsletter* (39)8. November, 1998b: pp. 60, 58.
    Hymie Rubenstein. Ganja and Globalization: A Caribbean Case-Study. *Global Development Studies* 2(1&2). 2000a: pp. 223–250.
    Hymie Rubenstein. Reefer Madness Caribbean Style. *Journal of Drug Issues* 30(3). 2000b: pp. 465–497.
23 Hymie Rubenstein. Ganja as a Peasant Resource in St. Vincent: A Preliminary Analysis. In *Small Farming and Peasant Resources in the Caribbean.* John S. Brierley and Hymie Rubenstein, eds. 1988. pp. 119–133.
    Manitoba Geographical Studies 10. Department of Geography, University of Manitoba, Winnipeg, Canada. 1988.
24 Ibid.
25 John P. Augelli. Land Use in Guadeloupe. *Geographical Review* 52(3). 1962. p. 438.
    W. Andrew Axline. *Agricultural Policy and Collective Self-Reliance in the Caribbean.* Boulder: Westview Press, 1986.

John S. Brierley. Idle Lands and Idle Hands in Grenada, West Indies. *Rural Systems* 11(4). 1984.

John S. Brierley. Idle Land in Grenada: A Review of Its Causes and the PRG's Approach to Reducing the Problem. *Canadian Geographer* 29(4). 1985.

Center for Economic and social Studies of the Third World. *Small Farmers in the Caribbean and Latin America*. United Nations Educational, Scientific and Cultural Organization, 1984.

Herman J. Finkel. Patterns of Land Tenure in the Leeward and Windward Islands and their Relevance to the Problems of Agricultural Development in the West Indies. In *Peoples and Cultures of the Caribbean*. Michael M. Horowitz, ed. Garden city, New York: Natural History Press, 1971. p. 298.

Frank Long. The Food Crisis in the Caribbean. *Third World Quarterly* 4(4). 1982. p. 752.

Carleen O'Loughlin. *Economic and Political Change in the Leeward and Windward Islands*. New Haven: Yale University Press, 1968. pp. 100–104.

Stuart B. Philpott. *West Indian Migration: The Montserrat Case*. London: Athlone Press, 1973.

26 Economic Commission for Latin America. *Strategies for Third World Countries During the Third Development Decade*. Port of Spain, Trinidad, 1980.

Center for Economic and Social Studies of the Third World. *Small Farmers in the Caribbean and Latin America*. United Nations Educational, Scientific and Cultural Organization, 1984.

West Indian Royal Commission Report. London: HMSO CMD 6607. 1938–1939.

27 Caribbean Development Bank. *Statement by the President 1971–80*. Bridgetown, Barbados, 1980.

28 Gary Brana-Shute and Rosemary Brana-Shute. *The Unemployed of the Eastern Caribbean: Attitudes and Aspirations*. Washington: United States International Development Agency, 1980.

St. Clair Leacock. Social and Cultural Factors in Production by Small Farmers in St. Vincent and the Grenadines of Arrowroot and Sweet Potatoes and their Marketing. In *Small Farmers in the Caribbean and Latin America*. Center for Economic and Social Studies of the Third World. United Nations Educational, Scientific and Cultural Association, 1984. pp. 167–185.

St. Vincent and the Grenadines. *St. Vincent and the Grenadines Development Plan, 1986–1988*. Kingstown, St. Vincent and the Grenadines: Central Planning Division, Ministry of Finance and Planning. 1986, p. 29.

St. Vincent and the Grenadines. *Digest of Statistics for the Year 1990, Number 40*. Kingstown, St. Vincent and the Grenadines: Statistical Unit, Central Planning Division, 1992.

29 St. Vincent and the Grenadines. *St. Vincent and the Grenadines Development Plan, 1986–1988*. Kingstown, St. Vincent and the Grenadines: Central Planning Division, Ministry of Finance and Planning, 1986. p. 32.

30 Caribbean Conservation Association/Island Resources Foundation. St. Vincent and the Grenadines Country Environmental Profile. Barbados, 1991. p. i.

31 John J. Hourihan. Youth Employment: Stubbs. In *Windward Road: Contributions to the Anthropology of St. Vincent*. Thomas M. Fraser, Jr., ed. Amherst, Massachusetts: Department of Anthropology, University of Massachusetts, 1973. pp. 29–34.

32 Op. cit. pp. 133–136.

33 Caribbean Conservation Association/Island Resources Foundation. *St. Vincent and the Grenadines Country Environmental Profile*. Barbados, 1991. pp. 39–45, 71–72.

Appendix

An Account of the Botanic Garden in the Island of St. Vincent from its First Establishment to the Present Time (1825)

Rev. Lansdown Guilding

AN ACCOUNT

OF THE

BOTANIC GARDEN

IN THE

ISLAND OF ST. VINCENT,

FROM ITS FIRST ESTABLISHMENT TO THE PRESENT TIME;

BY THE

REV. LANSDOWN GUILDING, B.A.

FELLOW OF THE LINNÆAN SOCIETY OF LONDON, AND MEMBER OF THE GEOLOGICAL
AND WERNERIAN SOCIETIES OF EDINBURGH.

GLASGOW:

PUBLISHED BY RICHARD GRIFFIN & COMPANY:

PRINTED BY ANDREW AND JOHN M. DUNCAN,

PRINTERS TO THE UNIVERSITY.

1825.

REPRINTED FOR THE ARNOLD ARBORETUM
BY THE MURRAY PRINTING COMPANY,
FORGE VILLAGE, MASSACHUSETTS
1964

House of the Superintendent.

Glasgow. Printed for R. Griffin & Co.

Lith J. Watson Glasgow

Lith Rev.d L. Gielstrup 2. 1 1844

TO

W. J. HOOKER, LL.D. F.R.A. & L.S.,

&c. &c.

REGIUS PROFESSOR OF BOTANY IN THE UNIVERSITY OF GLASGOW,

THIS SHORT ACCOUNT,

OF THE

BOTANIC GARDEN OF ST. VINCENT,

IS DEDICATED,

AS A TOKEN OF ESTEEM,

BY HIS VERY FAITHFUL FRIEND

LANSDOWN GUILDING.

AN ACCOUNT

BOTANIC GARDEN

OF THE

ISLAND OF ST. VINCENT.

THIS GARDEN seems to owe its origin to certain advertisements in the *Transactions of the Society of Arts*, for 1762, and the four following years, offering rewards to any one who should cultivate a spot in the WEST INDIES, in which plants, useful in medicine, and profitable as articles of commerce, might be propagated: and where nurseries of the valuable productions of Asia, and other distant parts, might be formed for the benefit of his Majesty's colonies.

General Melville, who was then Chief Governor of the ceded islands, while he resided in St. Vincent, with a laudable and patriotic zeal, resolved to commence the task; and in 1765, gave, and cleared at his own expense, twenty acres of land in the most favourable situation he could find, about half a mile distant, in a northerly direction from Kingstown, and abundantly supplied with water. To this, in 1766, another portion of ground was added. Thus commenced the establishment which this excellent man employed himself in improving, till his return to Europe; when, no longer able to inspect its progress, he continued, by his interest and exertions in England, to obtain for it every encouragement it could require, and to his latest days, when weighed down by age and infirmities, he did not cease to show the lively interest he took in its welfare.

B

Del. Revd L. Guilding B.A. 1824.

J. Watson Lith. Glasgow.

VIEW OF THE BOTANIC GARDEN ST VINCENT.

Taken from the Superintendent's House.

Dr. George Young, Surgeon to the Forces, the principal medical officer stationed in the island, was first intrusted with the charge of the ground, which he held for many years. In 1774, the Doctor made a report of his progress to the Society of Arts, which they were pleased to reward with a present of fifty guineas. In the troubled times which succeeded, the Garden was much neglected and injured, but was again restored in 1785, and somewhat increased, by Alexander Anderson, Esq. Surgeon, who was shortly afterwards appointed its Superintendent.

At this period the Institution was taken under the protection of Government, who supported it with great liberality till it was presented to the Colony in 1822. In 1792 it was increased, but it suffered in some degree during our contest with the French and Caribs. Mr. Anderson with great pains collected all the most remarkable of the native plants, and in his excursions to other islands, obtained many curious species. In his travels over our own mountains, in 1784, he discovered the crater of Morne Soufriére, which probably exceeds in magnitude and beauty that of any other volcano in the world: an account of this regular and noble basin,

"which seems to lead into a lower world,"

was published by the *Royal Society*, in their *Transactions* for the year 1785.

About 1787, the *Clove*,* and several varieties of *Cinnamon*,* * were introduced

* *Caryophyllus aromaticus.*   * * *Laurus Cinnamomum.*   The introduction of these inestimable plants, together with some particulars respecting them, is thus related by Dr. Anderson, in letters addressed to the Society of Arts in 1797 and 1800, and published by that body in the 16th and 20th volumes of their Transactions:

"CARYOPHYLLUS AROMATICUS.—*Clove*.

"The first plant of *Clove* was received from Martinico, at the same time as the Cinnamon. As it is a very tender plant while young, it was frequently lost when three or four feet high, and sup-

from the French islands, to which they had been brought by their ships from Asia. The *Clove*, shortly after this period, was cultivated zealously in Dominique. In Jamaica the *Cinnamon* was planted on a large scale in many parts of that extensive colony.

posed out of danger, but was fortunately preserved by layers, one of which at present is six feet high and healthy. This, with ten other young plants, are all the garden as yet possesses.

" The leaves are strong of the Clove, and retain their flavour after drying. For culinary purposes they are a substitute.

" At what age or size the plant produces seeds, as yet I am ignorant.—*December* 24, 1797."

And again in 1800, Dr. Anderson writes from St. Vincent:

" The *Clove* is an elegant little tree: *that* in the garden now bearing, is about eight feet in height, and the stem, near the ground, is about two inches in diameter. That so small a tree should bear fruit, I ascribe to its being raised from a layer. The nature of the plant is not yet well known in the West Indies. All the information I have heretofore received as to the culture of it has for the most part been imparted from ignorance, or from ill intentions; and consequently has led me into errors on that subject, by which I have often lost the original individual: but I have always been so fortunate as to preserve an offspring or layers from it.

" From the difficulty of preserving the plants, it naturally occurred to me that I had adopted a soil not congenial to them, as I find that all other East India plants thrive luxuriantly in the garden; and I am by no means ignorant, that all plants, although originally from a barren soil, always prosper best in a rich one, when transplanted from their natural situation. I therefore tried them in the best earth I could select, adding thereto plenty of manure; at the same time, I also planted others of the same age and size in various other soils without manure. The consequence has been, that those in the manured ground are thriving luxuriantly, of which that now bearing is one; while the others have failed, or are so sickly, that they never will arrive at maturity.

" Since this I have fortunately met with the *Herbarium Amboinense* of Rumphius, and find that he corroborates my idea respecting the nature of the soil.

" It is a plant that loves the shelter of other trees to windward of it, but not so as to overshade it, as Rumphius observes. When fully exposed to the wind, it does not answer so well; but rich land, or manure in bad land, is what agrees best with it.

Books of great value, which had any reference to the plants likely to be cultivated, were now sent out by his Majesty, who was pleased to patronise the garden, and felt much concern for its prosperity. Mr. Anderson, in 1791, sailed to Guiana in search of valuable plants, where his zeal was amply rewarded. He

" It is propagated by laying down the young branches in boxes, or in the ground, if they can be brought in contact with it. If the earth is kept moist, they will root in six months.

" I suspect that the best mode in rearing it from seeds, is to put these in the earth where the plants are to remain ; and if planted in the manner of a thicket, or from eight to ten feet apart, they will prosper better than when farther separated or scattered. This I find to be the case with most individualsof the same species.

" I have ventured to send an account of the fructification, as the parts appeared to me. There is probably more than one species, as Rumphius's figures of it differ.

Caryophyllus aromaticus.

" *Perianthium* quadripartitum ; laciniæ ovatæ, concavæ, persistentes.

Petala quatuor ovata, sessilia, conniventia, clausa, caduca.

Nectarium tetragonum, integerrimum, concavum, apicem germinis cingens.

Filamenta numerosa, subulata, in basi calycis inserta ; *antheræ* ovatæ, erectæ, biloculares.

Germen inferum, clavatum—*Stylus* subulatus, filamentis brevior. *Stigma* obtusum. *Drupa* ovato-turbinata, calyce incrassato coronata.

Nux oblonga, glabra, unilocularis."

" The specimens of the spice which I have also sent, are dried by various modes, some according to the directions of Rumphius; and by some of the processes they are rendered larger than by others. Whether that may be the only advantage gained, or which is the best mode of curing it, rests with the Society to determine. It is to be observed, that every part of the plant, in an eminent degree, possesses the same property, as to taste. All these specimens are gathered in the same stage, viz. when the flower bud appears entirely red, which is when the Corolla begins to rise, previously to its falling off. This happens at sun-set. The morning of the same day is the proper time to collect them for drying. There is something very singular as to the formation of the flowers. In September, 1799, clusters of them were so far formed, that I looked for their expansion every day; none of them however opened till the March following, a period of six months. I began to imagine that, from the smallness of the plant, it had not sufficient vigour to bring them to maturity. However, I was agreeably disappointed : scarcely more than two

now received from one of the Universities of Scotland the degree of M. D., and was elected a fellow of the Royal Society of Edinburgh. Pleased with his incessant attention and useful labours for the benefit of the public, the Society of Arts presented him with their silver medal, elected him a corresponding member (1798),

flowers, and frequently only one, expands in the same day. To have the spice therefore in perfection it is requisite to go over them every morning, collecting those that have the appearance of opening in the evening.

" The leaves are a good substitute for the fruit, in culinary purposes."

" LAURUS CINNAMOMUM—*Cinnamon ;* Three kinds.

" One of them has been common in the French islands for many years, and was introduced into the garden, near thirty years ago, by Dr. Young. It is the *Laurus Cinnamomum* of Jacquin, which he found in the woods of Martinico, and conjectures to be the same as the Ceylon Cinnamon. Although in some parts it has a resemblance to the true Cinnamon, yet on the whole it seems essentially different.

" The leaves have the strongest affinity, and the chief part of its property seems concentrated in them. They smell and taste strongly of Cinnamon, and, for culinary purposes, are a good substitute.

" The bark of those branches of the same size and age as those from which the finest Cinnamon is obtained, possesses nothing but a rough astringent taste ; that from the oldtrunk, which is very thick, is sometimes strong of the spice. The thin membrane next to the wood is pleasant, but difficult to separate from the thick brittle bark.

" Whether or not this is the *Cassia lignea*, or the true Ceylon Cinnamon degenerated through neglect, I cannot determine; be that as it will, it is no occidental plant, as it has no affinity with, or habit of, the American species. It undoubtedly has been introduced from the East into these Islands. Jacquin might naturally take it for an indigenous plant, not adverting to its propagation by birds. Birds are fond of the seeds, and may readily disseminate them in the woods ; and indeed we know that they have been instrumental in rendering many foreign plants common in these islands.

" From three small trees found in the garden in 1785, one hundred trees are at present producing seeds. It is something singular that it can only be increased by seeds, whereas the other two kinds grow as readily by layers and by cuttings as by seeds.

" It is an erect handsome tree, from fifteen to twenty feet high, with compact erect branches, and thrives in any soil or situation.

C

BOTANIC GARDEN,
from the bottom of the Central Walk.

Drn. Revd. L. Guilding F.L.S. 1824.

Lith. J. Watson, Glasgow.

and gave him many other tokens of their approbation, while they published from time to time the communications made to them on the progress of his labours.

Every exertion was made, as well by private individuals, as by the authorities in England, to render his Majesty's Botanic Garden of St. Vincent the source from

" The leaves are of an oval-spear shape, with three longitudinal ribs united above the base (triplinervia) ; the under side of a yellow colour.

" The other two kinds were introduced from the East Indies by the French, in 1785 and 1786. A plant of each was sent to the garden in 1787. The first was from Martinico, by a gentleman, then a correspondent and fellow-labourer, for the true Ceylon Cinnamon. It was four inches high, and prospered remarkably well; so much so, that at present there are thirty young trees, producing seeds, with nurseries of several hundred young ones, exclusive of those already sent to the different islands. It grows erect as the former ; the branches are shorter and more compact, forming the shape of a cone.

" The leaves are oval, with three longitudinal ribs; sometimes five are united at the base : the under side is of a sea-green colour.

" It readily grows from cuttings and layers, as it also does from seeds. Upon the branches of three or four years old, the bark is very fine. It seems best when the sap is in greatest plenty, or rising, and is then easily peeled off : at other times it strongly adheres to the wood. During the operation, the juice squeezed out is whitish, and rather insipid. It acquires strength in drying; but whether it is best dried in the sun or the shade, I cannot determine. Specimens, done in both ways, accompany this paper. The leaves are hot and biting, and taste much of the Clove, but little of the Cinnamon.

" The third sort was also a small plant, sent to the garden for the true Cinnamon, by a gentleman of St. Lucia, in return for plants transmitted him from the garden. He obtained it from the captain of a frigate, from the Isle de France bound to St. Domingo, with a cargo of valuable plants, but which had put in there for refreshments. The leaves of this kind are broad, of an oval oblong shape, with five distinct ribs united at the base ; the under side a yellow green : they smell and taste as those of the former kind. Its bark seems to be the best of the three ; and its habit, or mode of growth, differs very much from the former two. It rarely grows above eight feet high, if left to nature, but divides, near the ground, into very long slender branches, spreading horizontally; the lower ones are procumbent, but they may be trained up straight. The branches, however, are always much longer, more slender, and with fewer secondary ones than the others. It has the appearance of another species."

which valuable plants might be spread over the adjacent islands. Trials were made to introduce plantations of *Cactus Coccinellifer* and to propagate the *Cochineal Insect.**
Many valuable seeds from Asia were sent here by the Board of Trade : at a subsequent period others were forwarded by the Board of Agriculture. A considerable number were procured from correspondents in North America, almost all of which are now flourishing and dispersed over our colonies.

The Superintendent's salary was first fixed by Government at 7s. 6d. a day. It was afterwards increased to 10s., and at a subsequent period to £1, which, with rations, enabled him to live in comfort and respectability. No proper dwelling had been provided till 1798-9, when Sir George Young, Bart., a warm and zealous friend to this establishment, procured an order that a comfortable and convenient house should be erected ; in 1804 and 1808 it underwent some trifling repairs, but is now in a most ruinous condition from neglect. So rapid is the destruction of buildings within the tropics from the effects of heavy rains, and the attacks of the *Termites.*

So great was the interest taken in this Garden, which promised to be a source of much profit to the colonies, and of commerce to the mother country, that his Majesty was pleased, in 1790, to send a ship to the South Seas† to procure for it the bread-fruit *(Artocarpus incisa)* and every other valuable tree that could be obtained.

* *Coccus Cacti.* Our insect, though covered with a thick floccus, is without doubt a mere variety of the true *Coccus Cacti*, but clothed with a down, which its introduction into a moist and rainy climate has rendered necessary, and which the animal can produce at pleasure.

† Amidst the many public and beneficial acts which emanated from the breast of our patriot king, and which contributed so essentially to the lustre of his crown and the happiness of his subjects, that which was to put us in possession of so many useful plants was perhaps one of the most important.

The lamentable termination of this first voyage is known to every one. When the vessel was about to return, loaded with its harvest, the sailors of the Bounty mutinied, and overcoming Captain Bligh, with those who remained faithful to their duty, set them adrift on the ocean in a long boat, with a very scanty supply of provisions. Happily, after indescribable hardships, they reached the coast of New Holland, from thence they proceeded to Timor and Batavia ; and at the latter place obtained a passage to England. Among the other fruits (says Captain Bligh) lost by the mutiny, were a thousand plants of the Bread-fruit. A few seeds of little value were all they could rescue from their savage crew.*

Not discouraged by the fate of the first, the King determined to fit out a second ship of discovery, and shortly afterwards Captain Bligh set sail in the Providence. If, among the more important cares of his empire and his generous exertions in the cause of science and humanity, there was any one object more pregnant with benevolence than another, it was that which, while it increased the comforts and means of subsistence, multiplied, at the same time, the happiness and numbers of mankind. It was that of extending and communicating the bounties of nature from one end of the world to the other. It was that of transplanting and conveying, for mutual accommodation, the most valuable productions of distant regions, and thus by a reciprocity of benefits, enlarging the general interests and enjoyments of the human

---

* The mutineers of the Bounty took possession of a small island, without a river or harbour, in the South Pacific Ocean, now called Pitcairn island, west long. 133° 20′ 45″, and south lat. 25° 22′, where they founded a colony : their retreat was discovered by an American vessel in 1808. The history of the mutiny and of Admiral Bligh's second expedition, has been given in the 4th volume of the Edinburgh Encyclopædia, p. 445. See also Quarterly Review, vol. 13, and the Edinburgh Philosophical Journal, vol. 3. p. 380.

race.* With what affection then should we reverence the memory of a Sovereign†
to whose paternal solicitude for the welfare of his remote subjects it is owing that so
many of the richest stores of the vegetable kingdom, transplanted from the happy
islands, the delicious groves of the Southern hemisphere, now flourish in our climes,
and are become denizens of our soil. Although some unaccountable indifference
has prevented these valuable acquisitions, obtained by the munificence of our King,
from being appreciated as they deserved,—should our common enemy who has now
fallen (in those gigantic strides which mocked all human calculation), have reached
the shores of Hindostan and rendered the islands of Asia subservient to his will,
these treasures would then have obtained their due estimation ; we should have
wondered at our own negligence, and lamented that the benefaction of our Royal
master had not been better improved. A strict attention to the cultivation of those
valuable exotics would not only render us independent of foreign succours, but
might in time furnish new incitements to industry, fresh improvements in the arts,
new subjects for our commerce.

In December, 1792, Captain Bligh touched at St. Helena on his return, and in
January, 1793, attended by Captain Portlock of the assistant brig, landed the best
portion of his valuable cargo, about 530 plants, on the shores of St. Vin-

---

* The *Bread fruit* is now known from Spanish Guiana to the kingdom of New Granada :
Thus (as Humboldt relates the curious fact,) the western coasts of America, bathed by the Pa-
cific Ocean, receive from the English settlements in the West Indies, a production of the
Friendly Islands.

† Independent of the virtues of the king, whose first cares were the glory of the nation, the
stability of the laws, and the security of the people, where is merit that he did not encourage ?
where is genius that he did not foster? where is the public good he was not assiduous to promote?

cent.* The young trees which were as vigorous as if they had only travelled from our mountains, instead of having crossed a wide and troubled ocean, were instantly planted out, and after a proper interval distributed among the colonies. Having performed this duty, Captain Bligh proceeded to Jamaica where another portion

* On the cultivation and the uses of Otaheite Bread Fruit, Dr. Anderson has the following remarks in the 16th volume of the Transactions of the Society of Arts, p.328 :

" In June, 1793, of the original plants fifty were reserved in the garden, to yield future supplies for the different islands; of those a few were two feet high, or half an inch in diameter in the stem; most of them from six inches to a foot in height. In October, 1794, some began to produce fruit; in March following all of them. At present most of the trees are about thirty feet high; the stem, two feet from the ground, from three to three and a half feet in circumference.

" The fruit comes out in succession the greater part of the year; from November till March fewer than at any other time. But as there are six varieties of the tree and fruit in the garden, some kinds are loaded, whilst there is scarcely any fruit on the others; so that some one of them is always in fruit. The number one tree produces is very great, often in clusters of five or six, bending the lower branches to the ground. According to the different varieties, the fruit is of various shapes and sizes, in weight from four to ten pounds, some smooth skinned, others rough or tuberculated. Taken from the tree before maturity, the juice is of the colour and consistence of milk, and in taste something similar. It issues for more than ten minutes in a continued stream, and thickens into a glutinous or adhesive substance.

" The fruit is in the greatest perfection about a week before it begins to ripen: at that period it is easily known, from the skin changing to a brownish cast, and from small granulations of the juice. When ripe it is soft and yellow, in smell and taste like a very ripe melon: in that state, hogs, dogs, and poultry, are fond of it. For Bread, the best mode of dressing it, is baking it entire in an oven as bread. When properly prepared, laying aside all prejudices, and with a little custom, it is equal to, if not better than any kind of bread, as it is lighter and very easy of digestion. Boiled like yams, it is very good, and by many preferred to being baked. Negroes either eat it in that condition, or cut it in half and roast it in the ashes. It may be sliced in the same way as bread, and toasted on a gridiron. For a pudding scarcely any thing equals it. After baking or boiling, formed into a mass like dough, and then baked as biscuit, it is nearly the same as biscuit and will keep as long.

" From the first appearance of the fruit (when of the size of an egg), it is three months before they are full, or fit for eating. Having no formation of seeds, the tree produces its progeny by

was delivered, and with the remainder (destined for his Majesty's gardens at Kew) set sail for Europe. The total number of plants delivered amounted to 1,217 ; besides, there were 700 reserved for Kew. In 1794 the bread-fruit began to bear.

In 1798, a catalogue was made of all the plants within the bounds, conveniently arranged ; and another was published by the Society of Arts in the 25th volume of their transactions.*

In 1803, 10 acres were taken from the adjoining crown lands, commonly called the Barrack land, and added to the garden.

suckers from its roots, at the time it begins to yield its fruit; and a numerous young family arises at the distance of from three to thirty feet from the parent stem. For two years past several hundreds of them have been transported to the different islands. Independent of its utility, the tree is one of the handsomest, and for ornament would be anxiously sought after in any country. It is hardy, a tough wood, and resists the severest gusts of wind.

" Besides the Otaheitan, Captain Bligh brought from Timor some plants of the East India Bread-fruit, two of which he left in the garden. Although the fruit is esculent, yet it is far inferior to the other, and a bad substitute. It is ill-shaped, and of a soft pulpy substance ; it has no seeds, but propagates itself as the former does.

" The seed-bearing kind, in its external habit, is hardly to be discriminated from the true, yet in fruit it differs very much from it, containing no esculent substance; but its seeds, in number from forty to eighty, and sometimes one hundred, are in appearance like chesnuts. When roasted or boiled, they are preferred, by many people, to bread-fruit. Negroes are very fond of them.

" The fruit is nearly of the size of the bread-fruit, and is covered with prickles like a hedge-hog. As the seeds readily vegetate, Nature has no occasion for pushing up plants from the roots, as in the bread-fruit. Previous to the arrival of the Providence, a young plant of it was sent to the garden from Martinico for the true bread-fruit. It grows as fast, and gives fruit as soon, but rises to a larger and stronger tree. In the French islands it is known by the name of *Chataignier de Malabar*."

* As the communications published in this volume of the Transactions of the Society of Arts appear to be the last that were made by Dr. Anderson, we shall insert them verbatim in the APPENDIX B: and this we do the more willingly, because the list of plants above alluded to will give some idea of the extent of the services rendered to the garden during Dr. Anderson's superintendence.

Mr. Lochead, who afterwards succeeded Dr. Anderson, had obtained from Cayenne several *Nutmegs** and other plants which he had nursed in Trinidad with the
greatest care. These in 1809 were introduced by Captain Dix of his Majesty's sloop
Cygnet, who readily undertook the charge of them by permission of Admiral

* Dr. Anderson, however, had the honour of introducing the Nutmeg into St. Vincents, as
appears from his two letters inserted in the 21st and 22d volumes of the Transactions of the
Society of Arts : both of which, as they show the great zeal which this excellent man evinced in
furthering the objects of the Institution, are here inserted.

" From Trinidad I took the liberty of addressing a few lines to you, mentioning my being
there on a botanical excursion ; and, having omitted to inform the Society, previous to my departure, of my good fortune in obtaining two Nutmeg plants from Cayenne, I now do so. I
had the pleasure, on my arrival at this place, of receiving your letter of May, informing me of the
intended honour of a medal for me from the Society. Of this honour I am fully sensible; and
the Society may rest assured that my constant endeavours will be to merit it, and by every
means in my power to forward their intentions. For the information of the Society, I enclose a
list of some useful articles introduced into the garden since I had the honour of addressing them
on the subject of the most valuable plants in it.

" As the true Nutmeg has long been a great desideratum, after being well informed it was at
Cayenne, I lost no time, after the cessation of hostilities, in endeavouring to obtain it. A good
opportunity soon offered, by a gentleman from this island going there, on his own private business, who has always been anxious to serve me. Under his care I sent some boxes, with such
plants as I conceived were not there, and desired him to deliver them as from this garden. This
commission he fully executed, and in return brought me two fine young nutmeg plants, and several of the true black pepper, with some others, as I have specified, from Cayenne, in the
enclosed list. These were accompanied with a very polite letter from the Governor, Victor
Hugues, and a list of several East India plants of which he is in want, and which, unluckily,
the garden does not yet possess.

" I mentioned to you, I think, from Trinidad, that Governor Picton was anxious to establish
a garden there on a large plan. Whether that can be accomplished or not, is beyond my sphere of
knowledge. The situation is well adapted for such an institution, not only for investigating the
many useful and curious plants of that colony, but also for introducing those of South America.

" Through Governor Picton's friendship and assistance, I was enabled to bring a great num-

Cochrane, who then commanded on the station. These trees have borne well for many years, and considerable nurseries are established both here and in Trinidad. Even our young plants of both sexes have this year produced their flowers in great abundance.

ber of boxes filled with living plants to the garden. Many of them were rare and curious, and several of them useful. He attached the Government schooner to my command for two weeks, along the Gulf of Paria.

" The natural site of this garden being on a declivity, with scarcely any level surface, most of the soil is washed off, and it is with difficulty that young plants, particularly seedlings, can now be reared in it. Many of the oldest trees are dying; but adjoining to it, is what is commonly called the Barrack-land, in the possession of Government. A part of this, and that the most adjacent, is very level, and consequently would be a valuable acquisition to the garden. The Governor says it will be added to it. I am, with great regard, &c.

ALEXANDER ANDERSON.

Botanic Garden, St. Vincent, July 28, 1802.

" List of useful plants introduced into his Majesty's Botanical Garden in the Island of St. Vincent, from the 24th December, 1801 to the 24th June, 1802:

	FROM
Aucuba japonica, ...	England.
Calamus Rapha (Palm)	Cayenne.
Camellia japonica, ...	England.
Couma guianensis, Aublet (fruit), ...	Cayenne.
Gomuter (East India Palm), . . .	Board of Agriculture.
Mimosa Catechu (Terra Japonica), . . .	Sir J. Banks.
Myristica officinalis, or true Nutmeg Tree, (Two young plants flourishing.)	Cayenne.
Parapou Palm (fruit.esculent), ...	——
Paravoa tomentosa (Dimorpha tomentosa) Aublet . .	——
Phaseolus Mungo, ...	Dominica.
Phormium tenax (New Zealand flax-plant,) . . .	England.
Piper nigrum, verum (six plants), ...	Cayenne.
—— Cubeba, ...	Trinidad.

F.

Worn out with toil, the venerable Anderson began to decline, and in July, 1811, resigned the garden to his estimable friend and fellow-labourer William Lochead, Esq. M. W. S. Edinburgh. In 1812 this gentleman was confirmed in office, but shortly afterwards suspended by the Governor. In October, 1813, he was restored to his charge by an order from the authorities in England.

					FROM
Pistacia Terebinthus,	.	.	.	.	England.
Robinia Nicon, Aublet,	.	.	.	.	Cayenne.
Symphonia globulifera,	.	.	.	.	Trinidad.

ALEX. ANDERSON, Superintendant."

" SIR,

" I am honoured with yours of the 5th of July last. My long silence was owing to my absence from the garden, to which I returned from Trinidad in the end of June.

" I have the pleasure of informing you, that the wished-for addition of land to the garden has been obtained, and a valuable addition it is; the whole being a good soil, and in a great part level; at least, so much so, that, with the precautions I have taken, it cannot be injured by the torrents of rain, which have totally destroyed the old garden. The new part I reserve for the more valuable plants, as I proceed to procure them. For this enlargement, the garden is much indebted to the exertions of the Society of Arts, and those of General Melville.

" The two Nutmeg trees are thriving luxuriantly; my sincere wish is, that they may be male and female. I think it rather strange, that plants of them, as well as of other useful productions of the East, have not been before now sent to these Colonies. Except the two Nutmeg plants here, I believe there is not another individual in any of the British Islands on this side of the Atlantic. To the French we are indebted for all the most valuable of the East India plants we at present possess.

" On this side the water, Lord Seaforth is the only man at present who is using any exertion for the introduction of new and useful productions, or for the promotion of science: for these objects he spares no expense or labour. He sent a gentleman to Cayenne, in hopes to procure some of its valuable plants, but in vain; for Victor Hugues was not so generous to him as to me; all the liberty he got, was permission to pick indigenous plants. Lord Seaforth intends to

On the 8th of September, 1811, the virtuous Anderson was numbered with the dead. To this industrious and respectable botanist the garden owes its prosperity. Since his death it has in some degree declined. The greater part of his useful life was diligently employed, not only in the scientific examination and cultivation of the stores committed to his care, but also in enriching the establishment with every thing either useful or curious, that lay within the reach of his indefatigable researches. In pursuit of those objects which constitute the favourable study of the botanist, his active labours, his intense assiduity, could only be equalled by that urbanity and alacrity so conspicuous in his constant endeavours to oblige ; and that zeal and pleasure which he always evinced in rendering the good intentions of his Majesty as beneficial as possible to the colonists at large. The following verses were written by a friend who had followed him to the grave :—

make application to the King, to be allowed to send a ship to the East Indies, with the sole intention to bring plants and seeds directly to this garden. I hope he will succeed.

" If it is in my power to forward any thing from hence, that may be acceptable to the Society, I shall regard myself honoured in their commands. Any plants or seeds from England, which you can furnish, that are likely to prove useful in food, commerce, medicine, or economy, will be a great acquisition to this garden. Merely as a sample for the Society, I have transmitted you a few seeds of different plants; also a little Terra Japonica, or inspissated juice of *Mimosa Catechu.* If the Society think it will prove a substitute for the Eastern, or if the article is of value at present, pray inform me, as I can make any quantity of it, having plenty of the trees. The only process I used was, to boil pieces of the wood and bark together in a common earthen pot ; therefore it may perhaps not be equal in taste and colour to that of the East Indies.

" Some Tea Trees, Pepper and Mulberry, which I have planted in the new ground, are thriving remarkably well, as is the Manna Ash. The Mulberry I fancy to be of little value: If it is, let me know, that I may increase it. I am ever, &c.

ALEX. ANDERSON."

Botanical Garden, St. Vincent, Nov. 18, 1803.

Ye lonely shades and melancholy bowers,
    In conscious woe your tearful dew-drops shed,
Fade every green, and droop unseen ye flowers,
    Instinctive droop—for Anderson is dead !

He to whose charge creative Nature gave
    Her varied treasures of exotic bloom :
He rests extended in the barren grave—
    He lies for ever in the hollow tomb !

E'en now the dirge,—the song of death, pervades
    Your desert walks, and loads the sobbing breeze,
Saddens the echoes of your twilight glades,
    And breathes its spirit thro' the murm'ring trees !

Congenial solitude sits brooding round ;
    Nor smiles the garden, now, to meet the morn ;
But weeds and withered foliage strew the ground,
    While chokes the Spice beneath the noxious thorn.

Each widow'd plant in sensitive decay,
    And seeming sorrow, to the earth reclines,
Throws from its stalk the sick'ning buds away,
    Or to the sun with fainted petal pines.

No more the ground-dove, cooing from the brake,
    Nor wren familiar with her matin song,
Nor hum of opening day, his sleep shall wake,
    The sleep of death !—how dread—how deep—how long !

Then vain ye scenes forlorn—ye seek in vain
    Your fond, your peaceful tenant's wish'd return—
Though dies the blossom to revive again,
    No embryon hope revives the silent urn !

But not to dark oblivion art thou gone,
    Or unlamented pass'd, bless'd shade, away—
For faithful mem'ry graves thy church-yard stone,
    And pious friendship guards thy sacred clay !

5

And here, as oft the child of Nature strays,
    (And thou wert Nature's child and guardian too,)
The sad remembrance of more pleasing days,
    To fancy's eye thy image shall renew.—

" Here"—shall he say, as o'er some favourite spot,
    Where even now thy footsteps print the sand,
Awhile he stoops—and tears his cheeks shall blot,
    And bathe the flow'ret planted by thy hand—

" Here" (shall he say) " his wonted path he took,
    Ere yet the sunbeam kindled on the wave,
Peace in his heart, and mercy in his look,
    To lead the labours of the willing slave :—

" For he to all, the father and the friend,
    Ne'er bade the sorrowing captive kiss the rod,
But still his life conforming to his end,
    Their thoughts* with his exalted to their God.

" There where their arms those clust'ring bread-fruits spread,
    And spicy Palms their graceful columns rear,
E'en now methinks before I see him tread,
    Or mid the shrubs his voice instructive hear.

" Or where yon Mango canopies so wide,
    With boughs impervious to the mid-day heat,
There on that bank, the brawling brook beside,
    In letter'd ease, he took his noontide seat.

" And when descending down the western hill,
    The shadowy evening drew her dewy close,
There in the porch, like sainted hermit still,
    He sought and found contentment with repose !"

---

* This truly good man and excellent Christian was not only the kindest master, but the moral and religious preceptor of his negroes.

F

But now he's gone!—life's fitful dream is o'er,—
O ! frail and light illusion, swiftly fled!—
Mourn then ye shades—ye rocks his fate deplore,
Weep Nature, weep—for Anderson is dead !

Mr. Lochead did not long remain in the enjoyment of his situation ; on the 22d of March, 1815, he joined his much lamented predecessor. His remains were deposited under one of the trees of the garden, a little above his dwelling-house, and covered by a neat and simple tablet. His widow, assisted by Mr. Billinghurst, was allowed to remain with the usual salary for nearly a year and a half, and the duties were performed by Mr. Herbert, an ingenious man, well qualified for the task.

It now became necessary that a successor should be appointed. Through the interest of Sir Joseph Banks, Mr. George Caley, and his assistant Mr. M'Cray, were sent to take charge of the establishment, and arrived on the first of August, 1816. The former gentleman had spent many years of his life in the forests of Australasia, and had brought home an abundant harvest from a field in which Brown, and other celebrated travellers, had already gleaned. His animals were purchased by the Linnæan Society, and are placed in the museum of that learned body. It is to be regretted that his services in the West Indies have not been equally valuable. His residence at the garden had been made distressing from beginning to end, by continued and malicious trespasses, the violent assaults of strangers, and the encroachments of the neighbouring planters. Though much credit is due to him for the stern and inflexible honesty with which he defended the rights of the garden, it is yet much to be wished that a more liberal indulgence had been given to those who wished to visit this enchanting spot.

In 1821, the Government, wearied probably by the constant complaints that had been made, determined on giving up the garden, which for so many years had been maintained at a great expense to the mother country, exceeding even of late the yearly sum of £700 Sterling. This step did not fail to cause great surprise. The Nutmeg and other valuable spices had arrived at maturity ; the Cloves were producing annually a million of seed : and the garden, which had hitherto been comparatively of little use, was about to realize the hopes that had been entertained by its Royal Patron. Had a small guard from the neighbouring garrison done duty near the house, which might have been ordered without difficulty, the Superintendent might have been protected in the discharge of his duties, and the grounds have flourished as in the days of Anderson.

The custody of the garden was resigned by Mr. Caley, December 24th, 1822, who returned to England in the month of May. The great seal was attached to the grant on the day the garden was given up by the Superintendent, and Mr. Herbert, with a small party of labourers, was appointed by the Governor to cultivate the land. The disappointment felt at its abandonment by the crown, has been fortunately dispelled by the choice of the colonial Superintendent, under whose eye the establishment is in a very prosperous condition. Every facility is afforded by this obliging man for satisfying the curiosity of visitors, and seeds and plants are distributed on a proper application to the Governor.

The extent of the garden, which is of irregular figure, as will be seen by the diagram, TAB. II, does not exceed 39½ acres. The three drawings which accompany these notes, will give a tolerable idea of this interesting place.

The higher and hilly parts are a dense forest of useful *Woods*, *Fruits*, and *Palms*, the bottom is the only part which has the least resemblance to the formal arrangement of an European garden.   Here Nature is unconfined, and this beautiful wilderness is without doubt the most charming residence of Flora in all her domains.   A noble avenue, interrupted only by a single towering *palm (Areca Catechu)* runs from the house to the bottom, giving a view of the bay, the town, and a group of smaller islands within the government.   A narrow walk leads the stranger round the bounds of this tropical nursery, and at the bottom affords a sight of the bold blue outline of the noble mountain which terminates the landscape.

Dr. Anderson having already published a list of the plants, I shall only notice a few of the most remarkable, not in order to give even the outline of a Flora, but to enable the botanic reader to form an idea of the physiognomy of the grounds, and the aspect of the vegetation.

The higher division, crowded with trees of larger growth, is perhaps most calculated to interest the European visitor.   If he derives any pleasure from the beauties of picturesque scenery, on entering the silence of this solitude, he will be scarcely able to define what most excites his admiration, the individual beauty and contrast of forms, or that eternal spring and luxuriance of vegetable life which reigns around. Nature here appears prodigal of organic matter.   The ground seems overloaded with plants which have barely room enough for their developement.   The trunks of the older trees are every where covered with a thick drapery of Ferns,* Mosses,† and

---

* *Polypodium phyllitidis.   P. crassifolium.   P. lycopodioides.   P. pendulum.   P. aureum,* &c. *Tænitis graminifolia.   Acrostichum sorbifolium.   A. crinitum,* &c. *Hemionitis lanceolata. Lomaria scandens.   Aspidium exaltatum.   A. articulatum.   Grammitis serrulata.   Vittaria lineata.   Bernhardia dichotoma.   Trichomanes muscoides.   T. reptans,* &c. &c.

† *Calymperes rigidum et Guildingii (Hook.)   Hookeria albicans.   Neckera filicina.   Orthotrichum cirrosum, Pterogonium fulgens,* &c. &c.

Orchideous plants,* which diffuse into the air the richest odours, and almost conceal from sight the noble plant that upholds them. Their growth is favoured by the great moisture of the air ; and these pretty parasites, sheltered from the direct rays of the sun, are seen ascending on every side even the larger branches. So great is the variety of vegetable beauties which sometimes decorate a single trunk, that a considerable space in an European garden would be required to contain them. Several rivulets of the purest water urge their meandering course through the brushwood : various plants of humbler growth,† which love humidity, display their beautiful verdure on their edges, and are sheltered by the wide-spreading arms of the Mango, (*Mangifera indica*), Mahogany (*Sweitenia Mahogani*), Teak (*Tectona grandis*), *Mimosæ* (*M. Lebbek, nilotica, Catechu, &c*), and other woods remarkable for their stateliness, and clothed in wild and magnificent pomp. The vegetation every where displays that vigorous aspect and brightness of colour so characteristic of the tropics. Here and there, as if for contrast, huge masses of trap, blackened by the action of the atmosphere, and decayed *Tremellæ*, present themselves : those blocks which in colder climates would be doomed to eternal barrenness, or at most would only nourish the pale and sickly Lichen, here give support to creeping plants of every form and colour, which cover with yellow, green, and crimson, the sides of the sable rock. In their crevices the succulent species are daily renewed, and pre-pare a soil for larger tenants ; from their summits the old man's beard, the *Rhipsalis (R. cassutha Hook.)* and similar weeds, which seem to draw their nourishment from

* *Epidendrum speciosum, umbellatum, lineare, cochleatum, nutans, ciliare, uniflorum ; Ornithidium coccineum,* with many other *Orchideæ.* United with these appear innumerable plants of the smaller *Piperaceæ,* and the *Tillandsiæ,* which often colonize every limb.

† Various species of *Pothos, Arum, Solanum, Melastomaceæ, Costus,* and independent *Piperaceæ.*

G

the air, hang pendant, floating like tattered drapery at the pleasure of the winds. At a distance is seen the *Trumpet tree* (of *Browne*), whose leaves seem made of silver plates, as the blast reverses them in the beams of the mid-day sun. In a solitary spot rises a wild fig tree,* one of the gigantic productions of the torrid zone. Nature in her playful moments had decked this scene for her amusement, and some retiring thoughtful scholar on the massive ribs which, like the buttresses of a tower, support the base, has painted, in large white characters, the names of his favourite Muses. All the beauties which Nature has lavished on the equinoctial regions are here displayed in their fairest and most majestic forms. Above the rocky summit of the hill the arborescent ferns (*Cyathea aspera?* *arborea*, *&c.*), the principal ornaments of our scenery appear at intervals, *Convolvuli* and other creepers have climbed their high stems and suspended their painted garlands. The fruits† of our

---

* The huge limbs of this *Ficus*, covered with perpetual verdure, throw down often from the height of 80 or 90 feet a colony of suckers of every possible size, from that of packthread to the vast cable of a ship, without any visible increase in their diameter, and without a joint: these reaching the ground become other trees, but still remain united,—happy symbol of the strength which proceeds from union. At other times the suckers, blown about by the winds, are entangled round the trunk or some neighbouring rock, which they surround with a net-work of the firmest texture, as if the hand of man had been employed. This species or one nearly allied to it (*an T. religiosa ?*) has obtained great celebrity in India from the most remote antiquity, where it grows to an enormous size. The Gentoos repaired under it to adore the Supreme Being; the Brahmins to conciliate disputes, and settle their code of laws. They often built Pagodas among its branches. Here it is the favourite shelter of the solitary *Ramier* (*Columba caribæa*) which feeds upon the berries.

† *Carica Papaya. Prunus noyeau. Terminalia Catappa. Achras sapota. Coccoloba vinifera** Laurus Persea, Mammea americana. Psidium polycarpon, &c. &c.

This tree is a good example of the power with which the vessels of vegetables perform their office, when planted in the neighbourhood of our roughest coasts. In whatever direction the leaves may point, the upper inert polished surface receives

country scattered around within our reach, and the wide green leaves of the *Musa* (*M. paradisaica*, and *sapientum*) and *Heliconiæ* (*H. caribæa*, *Bihai*) planted beneath, serve to contain them for our refreshment, and to convey water from the neighbouring spring. On every side innumerable *Palms* of various genera,* whose leaves curl like plumes, shoot up majestically their bare and even columns above the wood. The portion below the house of the Superintendent has been devoted to the reception of the spices, the medicinal, and other more useful plants,† which are placed in situations most favourable to their growth, rather than with a view to scientific order. In the same group are seen the precious *Nutmeg* (*Myristica officinalis*) exposing in the centre of its bursting drape, the seed surrounded by the crimson mace : the *Cassia* (*C. fistula*) with its pendent pods of curious length : the magnificent *Lagerstræmia* (*L. Reginæ*), displaying one extended sheet of lovely blossoms : the *Lecythis* (*L. bracteata*), with its sweet and painted blossoms, scattering its fetid fruit, so much resembling the fatal shell, that one might suppose a company of artillery had bivouacked in its shade. The *Calabash* (*Crescentia Cayete*) with its large green pericarp, so useful in the poor man's hut, and the screw pine (*Pan-*

* *Areca Catechu, A. oleracea, A. montana. Cocos nucifera. Caryota urens. Phœnix dactylifera*, &c. &c.

† *Copaifera officinalis. Geoffræa inermis. Sapindus Saponaria. Bignonia leucoxylon. Cedrela odorata. Hernandia Sonora. Hymænea courbaril. Plumeria rubra, alba. Poinciana pulcherrima. Averhoa Bilimbi. Bixa orellana. Canella alba. Cinchona caribæa. Dracæna Draco. Fraxinus Ornus. Gossypium arboreum, religiosum. Guaiacum officinale. Hæmatoxylon campechianum. Myrtus Pimento. Quassia amara, simarouba, excelsa. Ricinus communis. Abrus precatorius. Allamanda cathartica. Guilandina Bonduc. Jatropha Curcas, gossypifolia. Hura crepitans. Bombax Ceiba. Guilandina Moringa*, &c.

and retains a considerable quantity of the saline particles of the spray ; while the under surface is kept free from crystals by the constant action of the pores.

danus adoratissimus), with its fruit carved in rude and curious workmanship, and its
ribbed stem supported on a bundle of faggots.   Assembled together are the various
fruits* transplanted from the islands of Asia and other distant lands, or the nations
of the Antilles, attracting, by their nectared flowers, the gaudy humming birds.
You behold the *bread fruit* (*Artocarpus incisa*) of the Friendly Islands, the most
precious gift of Pomona, and the *Jack* of India (*A. integrifolia*) bearing its pon-
derous fruit of the weight of 60 or 70 lbs. on the trunk and arms,—huge deformities
for the lap of Flora.   Here too a stunted *Cork tree* (*Quercus Suber*), and a small
European oak (*Q. robur*), sadly contrast their sickly forms with the proud offspring
of the tropics.   The *Vanilla* (*Epidendrum Vanilla*) with its long suckers, the *Black
pepper* (*Piper nigrum*) of Asia, hang suspended on the boughs ; the gaudy blossoms
of the *Passiflora* and the long tubes of the *Solandra* (*S. grandiflora*) appear amidst
the wood, mingling their blossoms with those of the neighbouring trees in wild con-
fusion : while, at intervals, the *Agave* (*A. vivipara*) throws up its princely column
of fructification from a host of spears.   Innumerable *Cacti*† and *Euphorbiæ* covered
with fruits or flowers, differing in the articulations of their stems, the number of their
ribs, and the disposition of their spiculæ, give variety to the scene.   At every step,
plants‡ remarkable for their beauty or fragrance ornament your path.   But I should

* *Morus tinctoria.   Theobroma Cacao.   Achras dissecta.   Aleurites triloba.   Anacardium*
occidentale.   Annona muricata, reticulata, squamosa.   Averrhoa Carambola.   Carolinea insignis.
Chrysobalanus Icaco.   Cicca disticha.   Citrus decumanum, &c. *Dialium guineense.   Jambolifera*
pedunculata.   Inocarpus edulis.   Malpighia glabra, urens.   Mangifera indica.   Punica granatum.
Spondias Mombin, myrobalanus, dulcis, &c.

† *Cactus coccinellifer, melocactus, triangularis,* &c.   *Euphorbia dichotoma, antiquorum,* &c.

‡ *Laurus Camphora.   Hibiscus tiliaceus, Rosa sinensis, mutabilis,* &c. *Cassia floribunda.   Crota-*
laria arborea, incanescens, &c.   The crimson *Erythrinæ.   Tournefortia glabra.   Justicia picta,*

tire the reader by continuing to enumerate the vegetable wonders of this paradise. In proper beds prepared for them we meet with the useful herbaceous species or the vegetables with which our tables are supplied.* By the side of every rivulet rise large clusters of the *Bamboo (Bambusa arundinacea)*, without a doubt the most generally useful of our plants. Nothing can exceed the beauty of this arborescent gramen, which rises to the height of 60 or 80 feet, waving its light and graceful foliage at every breath of the winds. The *Cycas (C. revoluta)*, and several kindred plants, so valuable for their nutritious fecula, are scattered about, attaining their greatest height in spots where nothing is allowed to impede their free development.

St. Vincent's, December 14th, 1824.

coccinea. Salvia coccinea. Tabernæmontana citrifolia. Myrtus fragrans, buxifolia. Nerium Oleander. Iris martinicensis. Pancratium caribæum, &c. Mimosa pudica, &c. &c.

* *Amomum exscapum, Zingiber. Curcuma longa. Arachis hypogæa. Maranta globulifera, arundinacea. Arum esculentum, sagittifolium. Convolvulus Batatas, esculentus. Jalapa Turpethum. Cytisus Cajan. Dioscorea sativa, alata. Dolichos pruriens, unguiculatus, &c. Hibiscus esculentus, Sabdariffa. Jatropha Manhihot. Solanum Melongena, lycopersicon. Jechium edule. Dorstenia contrayerva.*

APPENDIX B.

(REFERRED TO AT P. 15.)

Copy of two letters addressed by Dr. Anderson to the Secretary of the Society of Arts, relative to plants cultivated in the Royal Botanic Garden of St. Vincent's.

"'Sir,

" From my long silence you will conceive me either neglectful or ungrateful to the Society; but this is not the case. The reason is, I had nothing of consequence to mention relative to the Garden, and it would be trespassing on your time, and interfering with matters of consequence by troubling you with trifles.

" I am grieved to inform you that I have lost one of my Nutmeg trees; unfortunately the other, which prospers luxuriantly, turns out to be a male plant, consequently worth nothing. I blame myself, in some measure, for this loss, by taking too much care of it, and not letting Nature take her own way. Unluckily the war precludes any correspondence with Cayenne, or I would have replaced it from thence. The same cause has cut off all supplies from other parts. Through the medium of a gentleman who was here last year from Cuba, I expected to have had, before now, some of the productions of Mexico and adjacent parts of the continent, particularly Myroxylon, or Balsam of Peru; however, if I do not procure it through that channel, I have found out another from whence I have hopes.

" The Gomertur Palm, which produces the material for cordage in the East Indies, is thriving here surprisingly, and, I think, might be rendered a valuable production to these islands. The mode of its producing the fibrous web, and the guard or protection surrounding, clearly points out that Nature intended it for the use of man; one tree produces an astonishing quantity. I think the fibres from the plants in this garden are stronger than the specimens I have seen from the East Indies. A small piece of the web, with its protector, I now transmit you. I have great reason to think that but few plants have been raised by the planters in the different islands, from the large quantities of seeds I have dispersed amongst them. The fact is, that no attention, except by a few individuals, is paid to any other plant but the sugar cane, and no other is in estimation with them.

"The *Bread-fruit* although one of the most valuable productions yet sent them, is neglected and despised, unless by a few persons. They say that negroes do not like it, and will not eat it, if they can get any thing else; but this is not really the case, as I know, and can declare from experience, that the very reverse is the fact, when once they are a little accustomed to it. The fact is, that the planters hate giving it a place on their estates, as they regard it as an intruder on their cane land, and they dislike any other object but canes. As to futurity, they think nothing of what may be the wants of themselves or negroes three or four years hence. Even their most valuable mill-timber, than which nothing is more daily wanted by them, they are constantly destroying instead of preserving. They import it at an exorbitant rate, and the importation is precarious. With proper economy and management, there are few necessaries for themselves or negroes, but which might be raised on their own estates, instead of importing them from America, unless it be lumber, and probably, even that might be procured, in time, in the back, cool, and mountainous situations. I am trying what may be done from the pine tribes. I am happy that many are now paying some attention to the Cinnamon, as the demands on me for the plants are frequent, which I impute to the specimens of it which I have shown.

"The *Black peppers* have not yet produced increase; but I have them in plenty, and am trying them in various situations, and can easily multiply them by cuttings; unluckily I can procure no information as to their culture in the East Indies, or of the soil or situation in which they thrive best.

"I send you some more *Cloves*, the last year's produce of two small trees. Next year I expect a produce from several others. You will also find inclosed a lump of gum resin from *Cocholu odorata*. As it issues in large quantities from wounds in the bark, it might be procured in plenty from Trinidad, if found useful. Trees of it, of enormous size, are abundant there. Other specimens of *terra japonica* would have been sent with some other articles, if all my attention had not been engrossed by the late addition to the garden: the same cause has prevented me from making excursions to other islands for larger supplies of plants. I remain, with most sincere regard,

" Sir,

" Your obliged and obedient servant,

" ALEXANDER ANDERSON.

" *St. Vincent's, June* 9, 1806.
" To C. Taylor, M. D. Sec."

" Sir,

" Since your last letter to me, very little matter interesting to the Society has occurred, and few acquisitions made to the garden subservient to medicine or commerce. War interrupts correspondence in Natural History as much as speculations in commerce.

" For 18 months past I have had expectations of some useful plants from Mexico, and other Spanish colonies in that quarter, by the way of Cuba ; but from thence the transportation must be circuitous by North America, and, after that, subjected to loss and interruption before they can reach St. Vincent. I have therefore given up all hopes whilst the war continues.

" As the Society may be desirous to know the present state of the garden, I have transmitted a catalogue of the variety of plants it contained on the 24th September last. There are many more from different quarters received without names, or those that are known by the aborigines, and I cannot arrange them until they flower. I am, with great respect,

" Sir,

" Your most obedient Servant,

" ALEXANDER ANDERSON.

" *Botanic Garden, St. Vincent, Nov.* 1, 1806.

" To C. Taylor, M. D. Sec."

CATALOGUE OF PLANTS

IN HIS MAJESTY'S BOTANICAL GARDEN IN THE ISLAND OF ST. VINCENT,
SEPTEMBER 24, 1806.

COMMERCIAL AND MEDICINAL.

Acorus Calamus.
Acer saccharinum.
Aloe perfoliata.
Amomum Zingiber.
Asclepias asthmatica.
Aristolochia odoratissima.
———— trilobata.
———— anguicida.
Arnica montana.

Bixa Orellana.
Cactus cochenilifer.
Canella alba.
Caryophyllus aromaticus.
Cassia Senna.
—— glauca.
—— Fistula.
—— javanica.
Cinchona cymosa.

Cinchona caribæa.
Convolvulus jalapa.
———— Turpethum.
Copaifera officinalis.
Coriandrum officinale.
———— testiculatum.
Curcuma longa.
Cycas revoluta.
Dorstenia Contrayerva.

I

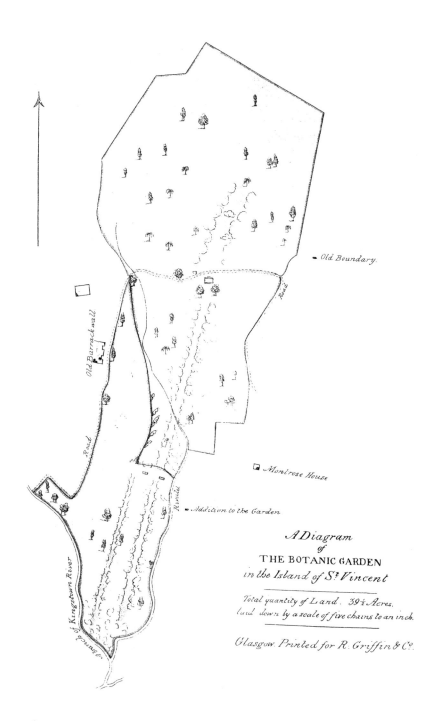

Old Boundary.

Old Barrack wall

Road

Road

Kingstown River

Branch of

River

Montrose House

Addition to the Garden

A Diagram
of
THE BOTANIC GARDEN
in the Island of St Vincent

Total quantity of Land. 39¼ Acres.
laid down by a scale of five chains to an inch.

Glasgow. Printed for R. Griffin & Co.

Dracæna Draco.
Epidendrum Vanilla.
Fraxinus rotundifolia.
——— Ornus.
Gossypium arboreum.
——— hirsutum.
——— religiosum.
Guaiacum officinale.
——— sanctum.
Hæmatoxylon campechianum.
Kæmpferia Galanga.
Laurus Cinnamomum.
——— Cassia.
——— Camphora.
——— Sassafras.
Mimosa nilotica.
——— Senegal.
——— Catechu.
Morus tinctoria.
Myristica officinalis.
Myrtus Pimenta.
Olea europæa.
Pedalium Murex.
Piper nigrum.
——— longum.
——— Cubeba.
——— Betle.
Quassia amara.
——— Simaruba.
——— excelsa.
Quercus Suber.
Rheum compactum.
Ricinus communis.
Saccharum officianum.
——— rubrum.

Sesamum indicum.
——— orientale.
Smilax Sarsaparilla.
Thea viridis.
—— Bohea.
Theobroma Cacao.

ESCULENTS.

Alpinia globulifera.
——— (Maranta ?)
Amaranthus viridis.
——— caudatus.
——— melancholicus.
Arachis hypogea.
Areca oleracea.
—— alpina.
Artocarpus incisa, Otaheite.
——— E. Indies.
——— seminifer.
Arum esculentum.
—— sagittifolium.
Canna indica, floribus maculatis.
Cleome pentaphylla.
Cocos aculeatus.
Convolvulus Batatas.
——— esculentus.
Cucurbita Pepo.
——— verrucosa.
Cytisus Cajan.
Dioscorea sativa.
——— alata.
——— bulbifera.

Dioscorea quinquiloba.
Dolichos unguiculatus.
——— uncinatus.
——— purpureus.
——— tuberosus.
Glycine subterranea.
Helianthus tuberosus.
Hibiscus esculentus.
——— Sabdariffa
Holcus saccharatus.
——— Sorgum.
Jatropha Manihot.
Musa paradisaica, Otaheite.
Myrosma tuberosa.
Oryza sativa.
Paripou Palm.
Phaseolus lunatus.
——— maximus.
——— glaber.
Pistacia Terebinthus.
Ravenala edulis.
Solanum Melongena.
——— lycopersicon.
Sicyos edulis.
Tacca pinnatifolia.
Zizania palustris.

MEDICINAL.

Abrus precatorius.
Allamanda cathartica.
Amomum sylvestre.
——— racemosum.
Amyris ambrosiaca.

Andropogon Schœnanthus.

————— insulare.

Argemone Mexicana.

Asclepias-curassavica.

————— gigantea.

Ballota suaveolens.

Begonia obliqua.

Bignonia alliacea.

————— opthalmica.

————— capreolata.

Bocconia frutescens.

Bombax Ceiba.

Capsicum baccatum.

————— frutescens.

Cassia occidentalis.

——— bicapsularis.

——— Tora.

——— herpetica.

Chenopodium anthelminti-
cum.

————— multifidum.

Clinopodium rugosum.

Chiococca racemosa.

Cissampelos Pareira.

Cissus cordifolius.

Clusia alba.

——— flava.

Commelina communis.

Convolvulus brasiliensis.

Conyza lobata.

Costus spicatus.

Croton flavens.

————— argenteum.

Dolichos pruriens.

Eryngium fœtidum.

Eupatorium nervosum.

Euphorbia thymifolia.

Galega officinalis.

Gardenia Genipa.

Geoffræa inermis.

Guilandina Bonduc.

Heleconia Bihai.

Heliotropium indicum.

Hura crepitans.

Jatropha Curcas.

————— multifida.

————— gossypifolia.

Ilex vomitoria.

Iris martinicensis.

Justicia pectoralis.

————— procumbens.

Lantana involucrata.

Lobelia siphilitica.

————— assurgens.

Melissa officinalis.

Mimosa pudica.

Momordica Charantia.

Nepeta pectinata.

Nerium antidysentericum.

Ocymum americanum.

Pancratium caribæum.

Parthenium Hysterophoros.

Passiflora Murucuja.

————— lutea.

Paullinia pinnata.

Petiveria alliacea.

Phytolacca icosandra.

Picramnia Antidesma.

Piper Amalago.

——— reticulatum.

Piper decumanum.

——— obtusifolium.

——— pellucidum.

Plumbago scandens.

Plumeria rubra.

————— alba.

Poinciana pulcherrima.

Rauwolfia nitida.

Rosmarinus officinalis.

Ruellia tuberosa.

Ruta graveolens.

Scoparia dulcis.

Securidaca scandens.

Sisyrinchium latifolium.

Smilax China.

————— laurifolia.

Solanum triste.

————— racemosum.

Spigelia anthelmintica.

Spilanthus salivaria.

————— urens.

Tournefortia volubilis.

Triumfetta Bartramia.

————— lappula.

Vandellia diffusa.

Verbena jamaicensis.

Waltheria americana.

IN ECONOMY.

Agave americana.

——— vivipara.

——— cubensis.

Alpinia altissima.

Amyris elemifera.
———— balsamifera.
Andropogon bicornis.
Arundo Donax.
Bignonia paniculata.
Boerhavia diffusa.
Bromelia picta.
Capraria biflora.
Caripa guianensis.
Carthamus tinctorius.
Cecropia peltata.
Ceratonia Siliqua.
Cordia dichotoma.
Crescentia Cujete.
Cucurbita lagenaria.
Daphne occidentalis.
Erythrina corolladendrum.
———— excelsa.
Elais guineensis.
Ficus tinctoria.
Galega toxicaria.
Gleditsia triacanthos.
Gomutu, E. India Palm.
Gouania scandens.
Guilandina Moringa.
Hibiscus tiliaceus.
Hippomane biglandulosa.
Isatis tinctoria.
Maranta arundinacea.
Mimosa unguis Cati.
———— tortuosa.
———— eburnea.
———— Ceratonia.
———— tamarindifolia.
———— Intsia.

Momordica operculata.
Morus papyrifera.
Myristica americana.
Ochroma lagopus.
Oxalis frutescens.
Pandanus odoratissimus.
Parkinsonia aculeata.
Phaseolus Mungo.
Phormium tenax.
Piscidia erythrina.
Pisonia aculeata.
Poinciana coriaria (Cæsal-
pinia).
Prunus noyeau.
Pterocarpus Draco.
Rhizophora Mangle.
Sapindus saponaria.
Sida indica.
———— alnifolia.
Theobroma Guazuma.
Trixia toxicaria.
Vitex trifolia.
Volkameria aculeata.
Zanthoxylon clava Herculis.
———————— tinctorium.

VALUABLE WOODS.

Adelia arborea.
Amerimnon album.
Arundo Bambos.
———— spinosa.
Avicennia tomentosa.
Bactris clavata.
Bignonia leucoxylon.

Bignonia pentaphylla.
———— serratifolia.
———— monophylla.
Bucida Buceras.
Bumelia nigra.
———— latifolia.
———— excelsa.
———— tomentosa.
Cæsalpinia cristata.
Calophyllum Calaba.
———————— acuminatum.
Cedrela odorata.
Chrysophyllum glabrum.
Citharexylon cinereum.
———————— quadrangulare.
Coccoloba pubescens.
Cordia Geraschanthus.
Coumarouna odorata.
Cupressus disticha.
Diospyrus Ebenum ?
Hernandia sonora.
———————— ovigera.
Hippomane mancinella.
Himenæa Courbaril.
Juglans alba.
Juniperus bermudiana.
———————— virginiana.
Laugeria excelsa.
Laurus paniculata.
———— borbonia.
———— salicifolia.
———— caribæa.
———— nigra.
Mimosa peregrina.
———— lebbeck.

Mimosa odoratissima.

———— arborea.

———— grandis.

Myrodia turbinata.

———— patens.

Myrtus latifolia.

———— crassifolia.

Parivoa grandiflora.

Pinus sylvestris.

Piratinera guianensis.

Polypodium arboreum.

Possira simplex.

———— cauliflora.

Petrocarya exsucca.

Quercus Robur.

———— rubra.

———— alba.

———— nigra.

———— Phellos.

———— sempervirens.

Robinia pseudacacia.

———— violacea.

Sophora arborea.

Sterculia fœtida.

———— platanifolia.

———— Ivira.

———— hirsuta.

Swietenia Mahagoni.

Tectona grandis.

Tetraptera aceroides.

Theobroma caribæa.

Trichilia arborea.

Vitex divaricata.

Vouapi Simiri.

FRUITS.

Achras Sapota.

———— mammosa.

———— argentea.

Adansonia digitata.

Aleurites triloba.

Anacardium occidentale.

Annona muricata.

———— reticulata.

———— tuberculata.

———— Cherymolia.

Artocarpus integrifolius.

Averrhoa Bilimbi.

———— Carambola.

Bagassa guianensis.

Blakea cauliflora.

———— racemosa.

Bromelia Pinguin.

———— Karatas.

Cactus melocactus.

———— grandiflorus.

———— triangularis.

———— Pereskia.

Carica Papaya, Africa.

Carolinea Princeps.

Chrysobalanus Icaco.

———— microcarpa.

Chrysophyllum Cainito.

Cicca disticha.

Citrus Aurantium.

—— Decumanum.

—— medica.

—— myrtoides.

Coccoloba uvifera.

Coccoloba barbadensis.

Cookia grossularioides.

Cocos nucifera.

Curna guianensis.

Cratæva capparoides.

Dialium guineense.

Diospyros Lotus.

Duroia eriophila.

———— glabra.

Eugenia malaccensis.

———— Jambos.

———— floribunda.

———— uniflora.

———— tainitensis.

Ficus Carica.

—— benghalensis.

—— trigona.

Jambolifera pedunculata.

Inocarpus edulis.

Juglans sativa.

Laurus Persea.

Macoubea guianensis.

Malpighia glabra.

———— lucida.

———— urens.

Mammea americana.

Melicocca bijuga.

———— dioica.

Mimosa fagifolia.

———— Inga.

———— farinosa.

Mangifera indica.

Mouriri lucida.

Musa sapientum, rubra. Otaheite.

K

Omphalea diandra.

Parinari montana.

Passiflora laurifolia.

———— quadrangularis.

———— maliformis.

———— fœtida.

Pekea tuberculata.

—— trifolia.

Phœnix dactylifera.

Psidium maliforme.

———— guianense.

———— aromaticum.

———— polycarpon.

Punica Granatum.

Rhamnus Jujuba.

Saouari glabra.

Sorbus domestica.

Spondias Mombin.

———— Myrobalanus.

———— dulcis.

Tamarindus indica.

Terminalia Catalpa.

Ximenia americana.

EXOTICS, CURIOUS
OR ORNAMENTAL.

Abroma augusta.

Acrostichum rhizophyllum.

Agave soboliflora.

Ægiphila martinicensis.

———— Manabea.

———— scandens.

Adelia acidoton.

Adenanthera pavonina.

Æschynomene grandiflora.

———————— Sesban.

———————— indica.

———————— aculeata.

———————— sensitiva.

Aletris hyacinthoides.

Alophyllus racemosus.

Alpinia grandifolia.

———— dichotoma.

———— capitata.

———— maculata.

———— polystachia.

———— hirsuta.

Althæa racemosa.

Alstrœmeria Salsilla.

Amaryllis belladonna.

———————— formosissima.

———————— longifolia.

———————— humilis.

———————— sarniensis.

———————— vittata.

———————— aurea.

———————— Atamasco.

Amerimnon latifolium.

———————— flexuosum.

———————— volubile.

Amomum Mioga.

Amorpha fruticosa.

Andromeda paniculata.

Anethum graveolens.

———————— Sowa.

Anguria heterophylla.

———————— glandulosa.

Anisophyllum pinnatum.

Anthemis Chia.

Aucuba japonica.

Annona asiatica.

———— palustris.

———— exsucca.

Apalatoa spicata.

———— aptera.

Apeiba Tibourbou.

Aralia capitata.

—— heterophylla.

Ardisia clusiæfolia.

———— punctata.

———— pulchella.

———— parasitica.

Areca Catechu.

Aristolochia glandulosa.

Arctotis tristis.

Arethusa lucida.

———— picta.

———— pusilla.

Arum arboreum.

—— seguinum.

—— maximum.

—— fœtidum.

—— lingulatum.

—— hederaceum.

—— bicolor.

—— repandum.

—— hastatum.

Asclepias viminalis.

———————— repanda.

Asphodelus fistulosus.

Asplenium soboliferum.

Aster divaricatus.

—— dumosus.

Aster vernus.
Athanasia annua.
Atragene austriaca.
Atropa arborescens.
———— physaloides.
Azalea rosea.
Bactris minor.
———— sagittata.
———— gracilis.
Bannisteria laurifolia.
———— chrysophylla.
———— nitida.
———— latifolia.
———— dichotoma.
———— cordifolia.
———— villosa.
———— mutica.
———— purpurea.
Basella alba.
———— rubra.
Bauhinia divaricata.
———— variegata.
———— tomentosa.
———— aculeata.
Begonia glabra.
———— hirsuta.
Bellis maritima.
Berteria guianensis.
Besleria melittifolia.
———— lutea.
———— serrulata.
———— cristata.
———— trinervia.
———— corymbosa.
———— pulchella

Betula Alnus.
Bignonia Catalpa.
———— æquinoctialis.
———— pubescens.
———— crucigera.
———— echinata.
———— glandulosa.
———— argentea.
———— stipulacea.
———— ramiflora.
———— inflata.
———— punctata.
———— tubulosa.
———— fluviatilis.
———— stans.
———— incisa.
———— radicans.
———— indica.
———— filicifolia.
Blakea trinervia.
Blechnum heptaphyllum.
Bombax carolineoides.
Bontia daphnoides.
Bromelia polystachia.
Brownea speciosa.
Bryonia laciniosa.
Buttneria aculeata.
———— latifolia.
Cacalia coccinea.
Cactus phyllanthus.
——— tetragonus.
——— heptagonus.
——— peruvianus.
——— pendulus.
Cæsalpinia Sappan.

Canna glauca.
Casearia ramiflora.
———— nitida.
———— crenata.
———— undulata
Calamus raphia.
Calinea dioica.
Calycanthus florida.
Camellia japonica.
Cananga laurifolia.
Capparis cynophallophora.
———— tortuosa.
———— Breynia.
———— frondosa.
———— jamaicensis.
Cardiospermum fruticosum.
Caryota urens.
Cassia viminea.
——— bacillaris.
——— Sophora.
——— glauca. East Indies.
——— planisiliqua.
——— bracteata.
——— floribunda.
——— chamæcrista.
——— pentagona.
——— mollis.
——— grandis.
Casine Maurocenia.
Canarina equisetifolia.
———— torulosa.
Ceanothus africanus.
Celosia cristata.
———— paniculata.
———— castrensis.

Celosia carnosa.

Celtis Lima.

Centaurea crupina.

Cephaelis muscosa.

———— tomentosa.

Cerbera Thevetia.

Cerinthe minor.

———— maculata.

Cestrum diurnum.

———— vespertinum.

———— laurifolium.

Chelone barbata.

Chimarrhis cymosa.

Chiococca bahamensis.

Chionanthus caribæa.

Chomelia spinosa.

Chrysanthemum indicum.

————— tricolor.

Chrysophyllum argenteum.

Cipura paludosa.

Cissus trifoliatus.

Cleome viscosa.

———— spinosa.

Clematis florida.

Clitoria ternatea.

———— erecta.

———— arborea.

Clinopodium graveolens.

————— procumbens.

————— repens.

Clerodendron infortunatum,
flor. plenis.

Clusia rosea.

——— multiflora.

Coccocypsilum violaceum.

Coffeaoccidentalis

Combretum laxum.

———— decandrum.

Columnea scandens.

Colutea frutescens.

Comocladia ilicifolia.

Conceveiba guianensis.

Conocarpus erecta.

————— racemosa.

Convolvulus speciosus.

————— maximus.

————— malabaricus.

————— maculatus

————— bicolor.

————— flavus.

————— parviflorus.

————— quinquefolius.

————— pentaphyllus.

————— heptaphyllus.

————— dissectus.

————— repens.

————— martinicensis.

Conyza arborescens.

———— trinervia.

———— alata.

Corchorus fruticosus.

———— olitorius.

———— capsularis.

Cordia macrophylla.

——— Sebestena.

——— juglandifolia.

——— virgata.

Coreopsis reptans.

———— chrysantha.

Cornus florida.

Cornutia pyramidata.

Coronilla scandens.

Corypha frondosa.

Costus arabicus.

——— speciosus.

——— malaccensis.

Couratari guianensis.

Cratæva capparoides.

Crescentia cucurbitina.

Crinum americanum.

———— asiaticum.

———— zeylanicum.

Crotalaria arborea.

————— laburnifolia.

————— verrucosa.

————— retusa.

————— incanescens.

————— chinensis.

————— procumbens.

————— lateriflora.

————— alata.

Croton aromaticum.

——— fœtens.

——— punctatum.

——— gossypifolium.

——— pallens.

——— polygamum.

——— trilobum.

Cupania americana.

——— macrophylla.

Curatella americana.

Cynanchum maritimum.

————— hirtum.

————— suberosum.

————— latifolium.

Cytisus tomentosus.

Dalbergia procumbens.

———— caudata.

Daphne cneorum.

——— collina.

Datura fastuosa.

——— Tatula.

Dianella cœrulea.

Digitalis obscura.

Dipsacus lacinatus.

Dioscorea vivipara.

———— filiformis.

———— guianensis.

———— rajanoides.

Diospyros tetrasperma.

———— inconstans.

Dodonæa viscosa.

———— triquetra.

Dolichos Lablab.

——— lignosus.

——— roseus.

——— spicatus.

——— acinaciformis.

——— grandiflorus.

Dodecas surinamensis.

Dorstenia cordifolia.

Dracæna ferrea.

Dracontium pertusum.

———— palmæfolium.

———— scandens.

Echites undulata.

——— umbellata.

——— nutans.

——— biflora.

Ekebergia capensis.

Elais americana.

Elaphrum laurifolium.

———— trifolium.

Embothrium adiantifolium.

Epidendrum vanilloides.

———— altissimum.

———— carthaginense.

———— coccineum.

———— speciosum.

———— umbellatum.

———— ramosum.

———— elongatum.

———— satyrioides.

———— lineare.

———— cochleatum.

———— cucullatum.

———— spatulatum.

———— nocturnum.

———— ciliare.

———— corymbosum.

———— proliferum.

———— nutans.

———— difforme.

———— uniflorum.

———— multiflorum.

Eranthemum semperflorens.

Ehretia tinifolia.

——— Bourreria.

——— exsucca.

Euphorbia tithymaloides.

——— cotinifolia.

——— lathyrus.

——— dichotoma.

——— glauca.

——— antiquorum.

Euphorbia neriifolia.

Erithalis fruticosa.

——— alpina.

Erythrina crista galli.

———— carnea.

Erythroxylon havanense.

———— distichum.

Ethulia sparganophora.

——— bidentis.

Eucomis punctata.

Eupatorium Dalea.

———— corymbosum.

———— scandens.

———— secundum.

Eugenia barbadensis.

——— ramiflora.

——— glauca.

——— baruensis.

Exacum guianense.

Fagara myrtoides.

Fraxinus crispa.

———— lentiscifolia.

Ficus retusa.

——— religiosa.

——— indica.

——— americana.

——— laurifolia.

——— virens.

——— racemosa.

——— pertusa.

——— rigida.

——— hirsuta.

——— glauca.

Fuchsia coccinea.

Galega carribæa.

L

Galega purpurea.

———— virginiana.

———— dichotoma.

———— hirsuta.

Gardenia florida, flor. simp.

———— ————flor. plenis.

———— Thunbergia.

———— crinita.

———— armata.

———— Randa.

———— aculeata.

———— dumetorum.

———— longiflora.

———— microphylla.

Gentiana Coutoubea.

Gesneria tomentosa.

———— coccinea.

Glycine caribæa.

———— picta.

———— rubicunda.

———— bimaculata.

Gomphia nitida.

Grewia pilosa.

Guettarda speciosa.

———— scabra.

———— lucida.

———— salicifolia.

———— macrophylla.

Gustavia augusta.

Gypsophila perfoliata.

Hamelia coccinea.

———— chrysantha.

———— corymbosa.

Hedyosmum articulatum.

Hedysarum latifolium.

Hedysarum gangeticum.

———— Vespertilionis.

———— gyrans.

———— bupleurifolium.

———— linifolium.

———— lagopodioides.

———— glomeratum.

———— altissimum.

———— triquetrum.

Helicteres Isora.

———— baruensis.

Heliconia marantifolia.

———— psittacorum.

———— flexuosa.

———— hirsuta.

———— glauca (caribæa.)

Heliotropium gnaphalioides.

———— fruticosum.

Hemerocallis flava.

———— alba.

Hemionitis palmata.

Hibiscus rosa sinensis, flor.

———— simplicibus.

———— flor. plenis.

———— mutabilis, flor. plen.

———— gangeticus.

———— rugosus.

———— diversifolius.

———— vesicarius.

———— Trionum.

———— Abelmoschus.

———— vitifolius.

———— ficulneus.

———— radiatus.

———— Manihot.

Hibiscus cannabinus.

———— heterophyllus.

———— hispidulus.

———— turbinatus.

———— Spinifex.

Hillia parasitica.

Hirtella americana.

———— paniculata.

Hippocratea scandens.

Hoffmannia pedunculata.

Hydrolea spinosa.

Hypericum monogynum.

———— barbatum.

———— latifolium.

———— guianense.

Jacquinia armillaris.

Jasminum officinale.

———— Sambac, flor. plenis.

———— simplicifolium.

———— azoricum.

Jatropha urens.

———— procumbens.

Indigofera hirsuta.

Ipomæa repanda.

———— carnea.

———— bona nox.

———— filiformis.

———— coccinea.

———— speciosa.

———— umbellata.

———— tuberosa.

———— macrophylla.

———— grandiflora.

———— Quamoclit, flor. coc-

cineis.

APPENDIX.

APPENDIX.

Ipomœa Quamoclit, flor. albis.
Iris chinensis.
— versicolor.
— virginiana.
Itea Cyrilla.
Justicia nitida.
—— picta.
—— coccinea.
—— speciosa.
—— pulcherrima.
—— carthaginensis.
—— paniculata (secunda.)
—— umbellata.
—— spinosa.
Ixia chinensis.
Ixora coccinea.
— alba.
— secunda.
Kæmpferia coronaria.
Kitaibelia vitifolia.
Kœlreuteria paniculata.
Lagerstrœmia flos reginæ.
Lantana radula.
—— Camara.
—— aculeata.
—— bullata.
—— annua.
Latania. Palm.
Laurus nobilis.
—— indica.
—— fulgens.
—— verticillata.
—— ecalyculata.
Lavenia decumbens.
Lawsonia inermis.

Lawsonia spinosa.
Lecythis bracteata.
Ligusticum levisticum.
Leonurus Marrubiastrum.
———— tataricus.
Lignotis elliptica.
Ligustrum vulgare.
Limodorum Tankervilliæ.
———— altum.
———— palmæfolium.
———— corniculatum.
———— spathaceum.
———— parasiticum.
Linum narbonense.
———— strictum.
Lisianthus glaber.
———— chelonoides.
Limonia triphylla.
———— mauritanica.
Liquidambar styraciflua.
Liparia pinnata.
Lobelia surinamensis.
—— racemosa.
Lycium japonicum, flor. plenis.
Lygeum Spartum.
Macrocnemum coccineum.
Magnolia cœrulea.
Malachra radiata.
Malanea sarmentosa.
Malpighia nitida.
———— Mourila.
———— crassifolia.
———— coriacea.
———— coccigera.
Malvaviscus populneus.

Mammea littoralis.
———— verrucosa.
Manettia coccinea.
———— alba.
Maranta sylvestris.
Marcgravia umbellata.
Marila racemosa.
— speciosa.
Medicago scutellata.
———— orbiculata.
———— aculeata.
———— hispida.
———— coronata.
Melaleuca linarifolia.
———— obliqua.
Melastoma acinodendron.
———— holosericea.
———— quadrangularis.
———— hirta.
———— lanata.
———— decussata.
———— spatulata.
———— biflora.
———— umbellata.
———— elegans.
———— Tamonea.
———— agrestis.
———— argentea.
———— spicata.
———— fragilis.
———— ciliata.
———— triphylla.
———— grandifolia.
Melia Azederach.
Melvillia speciosa.

Menispermum carolinianum.

Microtea debilis.

Mimosa latifolia.

———— jugata.

———— tergemina.

———— purpurea.

———— plena.

———— virgata.

———— vespertina.

———— latisiliqua.

———— angustifolia.

———— decurrens.

———— glauca.

———— conglomerata.

———— Entada.

———— scandens.

———— palustris.

———— longifolia.

———— casta.

———— sensitiva.

———— argentea.

———— bahamensis.

———— quadrivalvis.

———— asperata.

———— eglandulata.

———— from Botany Bay.

————   do.

————   do.

————   do.

Metrosideros lanceolata.

Menyanthes indica.

Mirabilis jalapa; alba, flava,

———— —— purpurea.

———— longiflora.

Moquilea guianensis.

Monnieria trifolia.

Moræa iridioides.

Morus hybrida.

—— rubra.

—— tatarica.

Mullera moniliformis.

Muntingia Calabura.

Myginda rhacoma.

———— latifolia.

———— myrtoides.

———— retusa.

———— lineata.

Myrobalanus fertilis.

Myrospermum elegans.

Myrsine africana.

———— retusa.

Myrtus communis, latifol. et

————   angustif.

———— fragrans.

———— virgultosa.

———— disticha.

———— crenulata.

———— buxifolia.

———— obtusifolia.

———— cerasina.

———— Ugni.

———— lucida.

———— ramiflora.

———— paniculata.

Nerium oleander, rubrum et

———— ———— alb.

Nigella sativa.

———— damascena.

Ocymum gratissimum.

———— album.

Ocymum tenuiflorum.

———— thyrsiflorum.

Olea fragrans.

Onopordum illyricum.

Œnothera grandiflora.

———————purpurea.

Ophioglossum scandens.

Origanum majoranoides.

Oxalis frutescens.

Panax Morotoni.

—— attenuata.

Pancratium amboinense.

Parivoa tomentosa.

Paullinia asiatica.

———— glauca.

———— punctata.

———— capsularis.

———— Vespertilionis.

———— multiflora.

———— biflora.

———— cœrulea.

———— serrata.

Pelargonium capitatum.

———————— grossularioides.

———————— zonale.

Pentapetes phœnicea.

Petræa volubilis.

———— erecta.

Pittosporum lanceolatum.

Petrocarya rigida.

Phaseolus Caracalla.

———————— vexillatus.

———————— lathyroides.

———————— aconitifolius.

Phœnix farinifera.

Phyllanthus racemosa.

———— Conami.

———— longifolia.

———— mimosoides.

———— glauca.

Plumeria obtusa.

——— pudica.

Piper geniculatum.

—— verrucosum.

—— aduncum.

—— peltatum.

—— argenteum.

—— Malamiri.

—— verticillatum.

—— acuminatum.

—— trinervium.

Pistia Stratiotes.

Pitcairnia angustifolia.

———— racemosa, flava et coccinea.

Platylobium hieracifolium.

Plumbago rosea.

Plukenetia volubilis.

Pisonia inermis.

——— coccinea.

Podalyria latifolia.

Populus nigra.

Poterium Sanguisorba.

Pothos acaulis.

——— odorata.

——— lanceolata.

——— cordifolia.

——— crassinervia.

——— palmata.

Portulaca triangularis.

Portulaca pilosa.

——— uniflora.

——— paniculata.

Posoqueria longiflora.

Prockia Crucis.

Pterocarpus Ecastaphyllum.

———— lunatus.

Prinos glaber.

Prunus pensylvanica.

——— virginiana.

Psoralea corylifolia.

Psychotria repens.

——— herbacea.

——— parasitica.

——— argentea.

——— citrifolia.

——— crocea.

——— laurifolia.

——— glabrata.

——— nervosa.

——— macrophylla.

Pultenœa stipularis.

Pyrus Pollveria.

Rauwolfia scandens.

Rhamnus theezans.

——— trinervis.

——— gynandra.

Rhexia hypericoides.

——— hirsuta.

——— bicolor.

——— geniculata.

——— glomerata.

——— palustris.

Rhododendron ponticum.

Rhus toxicodendron.

Rhus lucidum.

austrole.

Rivina octandra.

Robinia Nicou.

——— candida

———littoralis.

Rondeletia americana.

———— arborea.

Rolandra argentea.

Rosa semperflorens.

Rubus fruticosus.

Rudbeckia triloba.

———— caribæa.

Ruellia ciliaris.

Rumex aureus.

——— dentatus.

——— vesicarius.

Ryania speciosa.

Sagittaria sagittifolia.

Sagus? Palm.

Salix babylonica.

Salvia coccinea.

—— pseudococcinea.

—— dominica.

—— nilotica.

—— hispanica.

—— viridis.

—— Æthiopis.

—— latifolia.

Samyda serrulata.

—— crenulata.

Sambucus Ebulus.

Sapindus auriculata.

Saponaria vaccaria.

Satyrium elatum.

M

Satyrium spirale.

Saururus cernuus.

Schousbœa speciosa.

———— oppositifolia.

Schradera clusioides.

Sebæa aspera.

Serratulaanthelmintia.

Sida periplocifolia.

——— atrosanguinea.

——— cristata.

——— secunda.

——— multiflora.

——— cistoides.

Sideroxylon dioicum.

Sideroxyloides ferreum.

Silene rubella.

——— viridiflora.

Siphonanthus indica.

Sloanea dentata.

Solanum laurifolium.

———— verbascifolium.

———— bombense.

———— glanduliferum.

———— diphyllum.

———— pulchellum.

———— paniculatum.

———— hirtum.

———— fuscatum.

———— triphyllum.

———— mammosum, 5 dac-
tylon.

———— sessilifolium.

———— obscurum.

———— bahamense.

———— polygamum.

Solanum flexuosum.

———— scandens.

Solandra grandiflora.

Sophora occidentalis.

——— tetraptera.

Soramia denticulata.

Spermacoce stricta.

Spiræa salicifolia.

——— opulifolia.

Staphylea sambucina.

Stœbe arborea.

Styrax glabrum.

——— fragrans.

Susiana maritima.

Symphoria globulifera.

Symphytum officinale.

Tabernæmontana citrifolia.

———————— echinata.

Taligalea campestris.

Tamarix gallica.

Tamonea heterophylla.

Terminalia benzoin.

———————— trinitensis.

Thrinax parviflora.

——— acaulis.

Thuja occidentalis.

——— orientalis.

Tillandsia utricularis.

———————— lingulata.

———————— paniculata.

———————— monostachya.

———————— polystachya.

———————— racemosa.

———————— flexuosa.

———————— coccinea.

Tournefortia glabra.

———————— hirsutissima.

———————— cymosa.

———————— maculata.

Tradescantia cristata.

———————— umbellata.

———————— erecta.

———————— bicolor.

———————— ciliata.

Tribulus cistoides.

Trichilia barbata.

Trichosanthes anguina.

Trifolium officinale.

Triopteris citrifolia.

———————— volubilis.

———————— acuminata.

Trixia aspera.

——— erosa.

Turnera ulmifolia.

———————— pulchella.

Urtica baccifera.

——— altissima.

Urena typhalœa.

Valeriana dentata.

Vandellia erecta.

Verbascum Boerhavii.

———————— Blattaria.

Varronia lineata.

———————— curassavica.

———————— bullata.

———————— annua.

Vinea guianensis.

Viola Hybanthus.

——— ornata.

Veronica filiformis.

Vitex capitata.
—— guianensis.
Uniola paniculata.
Volkameria mollis.
Vouapa bifolia.
—— pinnata.
Utricularia alpina.
Uvaria longifolia.

Wedelia frutescens.
Weinmannia pinnata.
Xeranthemum lucidum.
Ximenesia encelioides.
Xylophyllum latifolium.
Xiphidium album.
Xyris indica.
Yucca gloriosa.

Zamia integrifolia.
Zanthoxylon clava Herculis.
———— ramiflorum.

Kinkina, St. Domingo, Angostura Bark.

THE END.

GLASGOW:
ANDREW & JOHN M. DUNCAN,
Printers to the University.

Index

Numbers in **bold** indicate illustrations